NO WAY OUT

THE IRISH IN WARTIME FRANCE

1939–1945

ISADORE RYAN

MERCIER PRESS
IRISH PUBLISHER – IRISH STORY

For Sophie and Killian

MERCIER PRESS

Cork

www.mercierpress.ie

© Isadore Ryan, 2017

ISBN: 978 1 78117 487 6

10 9 8 7 6 5 4 3 2 1

A CIP record for this title is available from the British Library

Printed and bound in the EU.

CONTENTS

LIST OF ABBREVIATIONS

BAVCC   Bureau des archives des victimes des conflits contemporains

BEF   British Expeditionary Force

BOAC   British Overseas Airways Corporation

DEA   Department of External Affairs

DFA   Department of Foreign Affairs

EPI   Expert Publicité Internationale

FF   French Francs

IRA   Irish Republican Army

LVF   Légion des Volontaires Français

NAK   National Archives, Kew, London

NAI   National Archives of Ireland, Dublin

NCO   Non-Commissioned Officer

POW   Prisoner of War

RAF   Royal Air Force

SHD   Service historique de la Défense

SSAE   Service Social d'Aide aux Emigrants

STO   Service du Travail Obligatoire

YMCA   Young Men's Christian Association

ACKNOWLEDGEMENTS

I would like to thank the following people in particular for their help in preparing this book:

Brendan O'Kelly, Connecticut, and Kina Avebury, London, for priceless information provided on their uncle Count Gerald O'Kelly de Gallagh.

Lyulph Lubbock for lending me the diary that Count O'Kelly kept during his youthful business trip to the Far East before the First World War.

Henry O'Byrne, Château de Saint Géry, for background information on Mary O'Byrne, Count O'Kelly's mother.

Fr Terence McLoughlin, Galway, for his reminiscences of Count O'Kelly in Lisbon; and Denise Hanrahan at the Irish Embassy in Lisbon.

Éamon Kerney, Dublin, for sharing information on his father, Leopold Kerney, and other Irish diplomats.

David Sweeney, Huntingdon, United Kingdom, for details on his uncle Patrick Sweeney; and Kieran Ginty in Ballycroy, County Mayo, for help in tracking down information on the same individual.

Jonathan Owen, New Zealand, for information on his aunt Florence Dassonville (née Owen).

Gordon Revington and Breda Joy in County Kerry for detailed information on Janie McCarthy.

John Clancy (deceased), Dublin, for his help in retracing the life of his relation Fr Kenneth Monaghan; Alan Randall, Carmarthen, Wales, Menevia Diocesan Archivist, for further extensive information on Fr Monaghan, as well as the other Passionist priests in Paris during the war; and David Blake, Museum of Army Chaplaincy, Hampshire.

Ann Lawson, United Kingdom, and Felix Rice, Castleblaney,

County Monaghan, for their help in retracing the life of family member Stephen Rice.

Jean O'Hara, Ballybrack, for material supplied on John Confrey and other *Luimneach* crew members.

Paul Shaw, archivist for the Poor Servants of the Mother of God order, for ferreting out plenty of long-buried material relating to the Irish convent in rue Murillo in 1939–1945.

Kevin Brownlow in London and Cari Beauchamp in Los Angeles for their help in gathering background material on Michael Farmer; and Patrick Vignaud in the departmental archives in Tulle for tracking down the record of court proceedings against him.

John Morgan, trustee of the Escape Lines Memorial Society in Dublin, for information on Mary Elmes and other Irish people in France during the Occupation.

Michael Moores LeBlanc, Canada, for supplying extensive information on escaped Allied airmen and their helpers in France.

Verena Neusüs at International Tracing Services in Bad Arolsen, Germany, for her help in supplying information on Irish political detainees in Germany.

Enno Stephan, Varel-Obenstrohe, Germany, for his help on the activities of Abwehr agent Oskar Pfaus in Paris.

Sylvie van der Elst, Brussels, for digging up administrative details on Agnes Flanagan.

Tricia Welsch, Bowdoin College, Brunswick, Maine.

INTRODUCTION

In February 1941 the Irish Legation to the État français, set up in Vichy following France's defeat by Germany in June 1940, sent a cable to the Department of External Affairs (DEA) in Dublin stating that 'the number of Irish citizens and those of Irish birth now requesting passports who are or soon will be destitute is about 300 (not including religious)'.[1] If one includes the religious, those not in danger of falling into destitution and those who did not request an Irish passport (James Joyce being the most famous example), then it seems reasonable to suggest that the number of Irish or quasi-Irish people in France at this time was somewhat higher than 300. The DEA estimated that there were between 700 and 800 Irish people still in France in November 1941, but another estimate from the same year put the number of Irish in occupied France alone at 2,000.[2] Along with priests and nuns, a high proportion of these people were governesses to well-to-do French families. One also finds 'men of letters' such as Samuel Beckett, a number of men and women working in the horse industry around Paris, students and teachers, as well as people involved in a variety of other professions, many of whom had already been in France for years. This book will relate the wartime experiences of some of these people – from well-known figures, including James Joyce and Samuel Beckett, to the misadventures of more obscure individuals such as Stephen Rice and Una Whyte.

Some of those in France at this time had chosen to be there. On 3 September 1939 Samuel Beckett rushed back to Paris from Dublin and tried to join the French army, famously justifying this rash decision by stating that he 'preferred France in war to Ireland in peace'.[3] In 1945 the bold Una Whyte, an eccentric art student from County Leitrim, wrote to Irish consular officials working hard for her release from a cold and hungry winter spent in a French prison: 'I hope repatriation is not the condition of my release.'[4]

But more typically, many Irish wisely decided to leave France in 1939–1940. Those still in the country when the Germans overran it grew ever more anxious to leave, as living conditions progressively deteriorated. James Joyce had arrived in Paris from Trieste in 1920 with no serious plans to stay for more than a few days, but ended up staying there for over nineteen years because, as he said to Arthur Power, it was 'a very convenient city'. But the war forced Joyce from Paris, first to a small village in the centre of France and then eventually to Switzerland where his wife, Nora, told Seán Lester, last secretary of the League of Nations, that she had been trying for the previous two or three years to convince her husband to return to Ireland.[5] However, escape from occupied France proved well-nigh impossible for most people.

In short, Beckett aside, it would no doubt be an exaggeration to say that the Irish actually 'preferred' wartime France to neutral Ireland. Most Irish still in France when the Germans conquered the country in June 1940 were probably there more by chance or by necessity than by choice, having, for one reason or another, failed to organise their departure in time. A small number of Irish managed to return to Ireland during the Occupation, having had to face a wall of bureaucracy to obtain the various entrance and exit visas needed to get to Lisbon, and then having to stump up large sums of money to secure a place on a British Overseas Airways Corporation (BOAC) flight to the United Kingdom or on one of the Irish merchant ships plying their trade between Iberia and Ireland.

The Irish community that remained in France was replenished at intervals by others who invariably wished they were somewhere else. These included, most notably, shipwrecked seamen and shot-down airmen on the run. At the outbreak of war, France's Irish community was also augmented by a few individuals interned by the Third Republic under measures that bore a resemblance to the *loi des suspects* that sent people to prison without trial during the French Revolution.

Coming from virtually the only English-speaking country not to declare war against Germany, Irish men and women had a unique status in occupied France that heightened Vichy French and German suspicions about them. Many Irish people in France did not have an Irish passport; some, like James Joyce, did not want one and clung to their British identity instead, at least initially. The Irish in occupied France thus found themselves caught up in two internment drives launched by the Germans in the early part of the Occupation. The first, in the autumn of 1940, resulted in several dozen Irishmen being interned, mostly in the camp set up in a military barracks in Saint-Denis, just outside Paris. A second wave of internments at the end of 1940 focused on those who had been left behind in the first round-up – women (including members of religious orders) and old men. Irish people were initially placed with other English speakers in an old, unheated military fort in Besançon in eastern France. While many were quickly released, some were then transferred to a more comfortable camp in the spa town of Vittel.

Whether detained or not, one common thread unifying the Irish in France during the war was penury. Ireland's diplomats in Vichy were reduced to living on ration cards, but for many others it was much worse. Examples of people who did not suffer from lack of financial resources are hard to come by. Before America joined the war at the end of 1941, Irish people in France with British passports could count on food and money that the British authorities were able to channel through American charities. But those with Irish passports – and after Pearl Harbour even those with British passports – were excluded from this lifeline and were dependent on help from Ireland, which the authorities were slow to organise and always keen to restrict to a bare minimum.

Matters were not helped by the strict capital controls the Irish authorities exercised. After much hesitation, a system was put in place in the course of 1941 to allow families in Ireland to send money to their hard-pressed relatives in France. But the maximum that could be sent each month was £15 per adult. This monthly allowance was raised by 50 per cent in the spring of 1944 – but in the meantime high inflation for a steadily falling supply of basic necessities, combined with a lack of work, meant that many Irish, like their French neighbours, fell below the breadline.

The installation in 1940 of the Demarcation Line made communication between German-occupied northern France and the southern rump, which was left unoccupied until November 1942, extremely difficult. During the military debacle of May–June 1940 that led to France's defeat, Irish people joined the exodus of fearful French who headed south, away from the advancing Germans. Many found themselves in southern France when an armistice was signed in June 1940. These people lived a perilous existence, unable to return to their jobs and homes without special authorisations (even though, ironically enough, intra-French communication became easier after the Germans marched into the *zone libre* in November 1942).

The Irish were lucky to have the benefit of the services of 'special plenipotentiary' Count Gerald O'Kelly de Gallagh, who bravely side-stepped German and Vichy French instructions for all diplomatic staff to be based in Vichy. This colourful, unjustly forgotten Irishman managed to combine outstanding service on behalf of the Irish community in France with somewhat less avowable business dealings during the war. For the first year of the Occupation, O'Kelly ran consular services out of the premises of his wine company, Vendôme Wines, on the Place Vendôme in the centre of Paris. Combined with the Legation staff in Vichy, O'Kelly and some of his business friends were able to provide a measure of relief to Irish people and ensure that most of them were quickly released from internment – sometimes through the liberal distribution of locally printed Irish passports.

The Irish in France – or at least in Paris – also had other places to turn. Of special importance was St Joseph's church, run by Irish Passionists, on the avenue Hoche in the 8th arrondissement. Before the outbreak of war, the church had been a meeting place for the cohorts of governesses that Ireland supplied to upper-class French families; during the war, Irish people who knocked on the presbytery door could reliably depend on a bed for the night or a bite to eat. St Joseph's church also helped downed Allied airmen as they tried to escape France, earning thanks from the American War Department after the conflict. Another rallying point was the convent on the rue Murillo, not far from St Joseph's, staffed by Irish nuns from the Poor Servants of the Mother of God order. Before the war, the nuns in rue Murillo ran a hostel for Irish and British girls in the French capital who were studying or working as governesses. The nuns continued this activity throughout the Occupation – although few of the convent's lay residents were able to pay for the spartan fare on offer. Even in 1946 lodgers and nuns alike were still pleading for parcels from the Irish Red Cross.

The vast majority of the Irish stuck in France in 1940 were apolitical, and simply intent on survival in increasingly difficult circumstances (when not looking for ways to get out of France via Lisbon). As was the case with most of the native population, the Irish in France hunkered down and had little energy left over to become actively involved politically for one side or the other. But, as always, politics had an unfortunate tendency to catch up with individuals. Just as the Service du Travail Obligatoire (STO) scheme that coerced young Frenchmen to work in German factories proved an outstanding recruiter for the Maquis (those legions of young Frenchmen who lived in complete autarchy in the wilderness, occasionally turning into Resistance fighting units), so the appearance of shot-down Allied airmen in their midst pushed Irish people to become involved in their exfiltration from France.

Irish involvement in Resistance activities went further. Samuel Beckett collated and translated Resistance reports for transmission to London, and Janie McCarthy sent reports to London right from the start of the Occupation. Dubliner Robert Vernon was a radio operator for a Resistance movement in the south of France, and the British occasionally sent agents of Irish origin into occupied France, including Special Operations Executive agents Mary Herbert, Patricia O'Sullivan and William Cunningham. But things should be kept in proportion: just as the actual contribution of the French Resistance to the Anglo-American liberation of France in 1944 is debatable, the involvement of France's Irish community in the struggle against Nazism made little difference to the outcome of the war.

A number of Irish whom the Germans attempted to use against the Allied cause made brief appearances in Paris (Frank Ryan, Desmond Nolan, Joseph Lenihan), but the only two known French residents who were troubled in any serious way by French justice after the Liberation were Michael Farmer and Denis Corr. The former's tendency to consort with the Gestapo earned him a few months of detention, while shopkeeper Corr and his wife became noted for their collaborationist tendencies in the southern town of Biarritz. But the sum of these individuals' contributions to the German war effort can confidently be estimated at virtually nil.

Overall, one discerns a sliding scale of involvement in the conflict among the Irish residents of France, whether on one side or the other. At one end, examples of fully committed members of the armed Resistance – those involved in blowing up troop trains or placing bombs, acts often carried out by the communists – are hard to come by. The Irish were far more prominent in what has been termed 'civil resistance', which involved helping Allied airmen, publishing and distributing propaganda tracts, and sending messages to London. No Irish person seems to have tilted to the other extreme of the sliding scale by becoming involved in the Milice (the paramilitary force set up by the Vichy government to combat the Resistance) or in Gestapo outfits that systemically practised torture of their victims. Nor are there many clear-cut cases of the Irish acting as *Vertrauensmänner* (V-men or moles) for the occupiers.[6]

Perhaps the most intriguing destinies were lived by those Irish people in France who do not fit easily into the categories of *résistant*, of *collabo* or even of apolitical immigrant just trying to survive. They could best be described as interlopers, in the wrong place at the wrong time. They were in France by chance and unable to get out, except sometimes in a cattle truck heading towards concentration camps in Germany and further east. A couple of Irishmen even washed up on French shores and spent almost the entire period of the Occupation roaming around Paris penniless and homeless, without any possibility of getting back to Ireland, dependent on handouts from charities and from the Irish Legation in Vichy.

There were efforts to help Irish citizens – as exemplified by Count O'Kelly's deeds in Paris – but means were limited and communication inside France, let alone with Ireland, was difficult. The Legation's ability (and sometimes willingness) to deal with the Irish who did not have Irish passports was even more restricted. It did help by issuing passports to people it felt could legitimately claim one, hence helping some individuals to extract themselves from detention and others to avoid it altogether. But while Irish passports were granted quite quickly to a few people whose claims to one were tenuous (Susan Hilton, Desmond Nolan, Florence Owen), others with more legitimate claims but who did not meet the Legation's favour often had to wait a bit longer.

The cautious approach of Irish officialdom is most evident in the treatment of Jews. Attention was given to the idea of granting Irish entry visas to about 200 Jewish families who had been placed in the internment camp in Vittel. But after much shuffling of paper between Dublin, Vichy and Berlin, German refusal to strike a deal with the Irish meant that nothing came of the scheme, or of one to charter a ship to bring Jewish children to Palestine. Moreover, both these projects originated with Jewish groups in London; as Professor Dermot Keogh has pointed out, the Irish authorities did not act proactively to save Jews in occupied France.[7] Irish honour was upheld by the voluntary aid provided by people such as Mary Elmes, who worked for a Quaker organisation and was honoured as a 'righteous among nations' by Israel after the war; by the Irish Red Cross, which set up a field hospital in Normandy in 1945; and by the Irish nursing sisters who worked in various French hospitals during the war years.

To conclude, the experiences of the Irish in France between 1939 and 1945 varied considerably. But all suffered from the breakdown in communications with the home country and, to different degrees, from the scarcity of basic necessities and a lack of financial resources. Older people and people in poor health suffered the most, while the younger generation muddled through. Indeed, while the bravery of some individuals deserves to be saluted, what is perhaps most remarkable is just how resourceful the Irish in France were when in truly dire straits. This is their story.

1

TROUBLE AT THE LEGATION

The Irish Legation moved into its new premises at rue de Ville-just (now rue Paul Valéry) in the posh 16th arrondissement of Paris in early 1931, having been housed briefly at 7 rue Georges-Ville, just around the corner. Bar a hiatus from 1940 to 1944, the Legation was to remain there until 1954, when the new Irish embassy transferred to its current location at rue Rude, a short distance from the Arc de Triomphe.

The first of Ireland's plenipotentiaries to occupy rue de Villejust was Count Gerald O'Kelly de Gallagh et de Tycooly, a member of the so-called 'Clongowes Mafia' who occupied many diplomatic positions in the early years of the Irish Free State. But the count, who played a central role in the fate of the Parisian Irish during the German Occupation, quickly found himself out of favour when the new government of Éamon de Valera came to power in 1932. He was forced into early retirement in 1935, aged forty-five, having spent much of his adult career serving Ireland.[1]

In many respects, O'Kelly was a remarkable man, described as *'brillant et subtil, agréable causeur et spirituel'* (brilliant and tactful, a delightful conversationalist and witty) by a distant French relative.[2] Born into a family of Catholic landowners in Gurtragh, north County Tipperary in 1890, he went to school at Clongowes Wood and then studied at the Royal University.[3] His title was the legacy of an ancestor who had served the Habsburg Empire during the reign of Empress Maria Theresa in the eighteenth century.[4] His father was John Appleyard O'Kelly, whose family had arrived in Gurtragh in 1830, and his mother, Mary O'Byrne, also had illustrious Wild Geese ancestors and was born and grew up in a manor house near Toulouse in south-west France.

Unlike three of his brothers, O'Kelly did not serve a stint as a fur and wood trader in Canada. 'I think,' wrote his brother Donal many years later, 'it must have been because nature had endowed him from birth with a built-in radar set which gave him advance warning when the slightest threat of physical work appeared on the screen.'[5] Instead, he travelled via Canada to Japan, where he tried to sell advertising, with various degrees of success, to businesses in Yokohama and other Far Eastern cities on behalf of *Kelly's Directory*.

O'Kelly was still working for *Kelly's Directory* in London when he, like his brothers Joseph and Ambrose, joined the British army on the outbreak of war in 1914. He served in the Army Service Corps, rising to the rank of lieutenant, although he only spent eight months in all in France. Since the Army Service Corps was responsible for logistics, it is unlikely he was ever in the front line, but he was sent back to England from France suffering from 'neurasthenia' (shell shock) in May 1918 (he may have been caught out by the massive German offensives of spring 1918 that penetrated deep into Allied lines).

O'Kelly was still convalescing in Gurtragh when he was demobbed in 1919 – at which stage he told the army he was interested in entering the diplomatic service.[6] History was kind to his ambitions, for in July 1919 he was appointed Irish representative in Switzerland by the First Dáil and was employed in disseminating propaganda for Irish independence at the first League of Nations in Geneva, before being sent in 1921 to Brussels, first as diplomatic agent and then as trade agent to Belgium. While he spent most of the 1920s in Belgium, O'Kelly played an important part in Ireland's lobbying for a temporary seat at the League of Nations council in 1930. Thanks to his mother, O'Kelly spoke fluent French and at various stages of his life published quite brilliant translations of Omar Khayyám's *The Rubáiyát* and Rudyard Kipling's poetry into French.[7] Given such a background, the count was a natural choice as Ireland's first fully accredited minister plenipotentiary to France in late 1929.

Yet, less than six years later O'Kelly was unceremoniously removed from his position as 'envoy extraordinary and minister plenipotentiary' at the age of forty-five.[8] Theories for this sudden halt to O'Kelly's sixteen-year diplomatic career abound. As well as being a wine connoisseur, the count was a snob, hobnobbing with minor nobility around Europe, conscious of his illustrious antecedents, and his reputation as a *bon viveur* may not have been to the liking of some of his austere superiors. Perhaps there were personal factors involved too, as he had antagonised Joseph Walshe, secretary of the DEA back in Dublin. Although a fellow graduate of Clongowes, and despite the fact that both men had served Sinn Féin on continental Europe before the Anglo-Irish Treaty, Walshe allegedly did not appreciate the quality of the reports O'Kelly was sending back to Dublin and the latter 'did not deliver the diplomatic results demanded by Dublin'.[9]

The Irish authorities may not have appreciated O'Kelly's presence at some official events organised by the British embassy in honour of British royalty either. Yet he had proved himself to be punctilious about defending Ireland's standing as a nation throughout his diplomatic career, whether in France, Switzerland or Belgium. For example, invited as representative of the Irish Free State to an international athletics meeting in Brussels in 1926, he was aghast to see the Union Jack raised and hear 'God Save the King' ring out just as the Irish team entered the stadium. He was quick to point out the mistake to the embarrassed Belgian officials, who found the Irish tricolour to hoist. But as the army band did not know the tune of 'Amhrán na bhFiann', and as O'Kelly was, according to himself, unable to hum it, the Irish athletes marched around the sports venue to the tune of the Norwegian national anthem instead.[10]

O'Kelly had benefited from a conscious decision by Ireland's first Minister for External Affairs, George Gavan Duffy, to staff Ireland's foreign missions as far as possible with the cosmopolitan scions of upper- and middle-class families, who would have the necessary social credentials to crack diplomatic Europe's elitist social circles. He fitted the bill perfectly. But as an appointee of the previous pro-Treaty regime, O'Kelly was an obvious target when Fianna Fáil – which came to power in 1932 – started to look to reward its supporters with suitable postings. His dry wit may also have worked against him. On a visit to Paris shortly after his election in 1932, Taoiseach Éamon de Valera – who also acted as Minister for External Affairs – is said to have been appalled when, in answer to a query from him about what the French thought of the Irish, O'Kelly replied, 'They do not even notice we are there.' De Valera's misgivings can only have been heightened after a dinner with O'Kelly and his wife, Marjorie Stuart, when the latter remarked, 'I didn't know you were in prison.' More simply, it could well be that, as part of a normal rotation of diplomatic personnel, O'Kelly was recalled to a posting in Dublin, which he refused. Whatever happened, he was discharged from the role of minister plenipotentiary by government decision with effect from 30 June 1935 – although with a tidy lump sum and a relatively generous pension. He was also given the largely honorific title of 'minister plenipotentiary special counsellor', which he retained throughout the war years.

After he had left the diplomatic service, O'Kelly turned to the wine trade as a means of earning a living, setting up a business in London in 1936. The company was registered in Paris in 1938 with capital of FF300,000 and the express aim of 'organising the placement of wines and liquors abroad, especially in the UK'. He chose a very prestigious business address, 8 place Vendôme in the 1st arrondissement, from where Vendôme Wines started trading on 1 July 1938. A Frenchman with long experience of the wine trade, Maurice Prévost, was appointed sales director and manager/administrator.

After a short interlude, O'Kelly was replaced as minister plenipotentiary in Paris by the former chief Sinn Féin organiser in London, Art Ó Briain, who was much older than O'Kelly and in poor health but had more solid pro-de Valera credentials. (Gavan Duffy had tried to oust the anti-Treaty Ó Briain as Ireland's representative in London in April 1922.)[11] There was no love lost between Ó Briain and O'Kelly, as can be gleaned from a letter that the former wrote, shortly after his appointment, to Leopold Kerney, Ireland's plenipotentiary in Madrid. 'The funniest thing about O'Kelly is that ... the department have apparently consented to make him a consultant to the Paris Legation. This is really a good joke, and you would hardly think that the dept. would act so stupidly ... I have had nothing but trouble as an inheritance from that same O'Kelly, both in the Legation and the Chancery. I am finally getting rid of all the servants he left.'[12] In another communication to Kerney, Ó Briain mentioned that O'Kelly had been pensioned off. 'I am told he was offered a job in the stationery office which he would not accept,' Ó Briain wrote with obvious glee. 'I hear he has gone down to Spain, so you may see him. Despite all the petty trouble he gave you, he will not hesitate to approach, if he thinks he can get something from you.'[13]

Ó Briain retired in 1938 and was replaced by Seán Murphy as minister plenipotentiary to France, with Con Cremin serving as first secretary.[14] Murphy and Cremin were more conventional career civil servants than O'Kelly, but they too had gone to school at Clongowes Wood.[15] Having studied law for a time at the Sorbonne, Murphy had acted as secretary to the Sinn Féin delegation to the Paris peace conference in 1919 and served as trade and general agent for the Irish Free State in Paris in 1923, working out of an address in the 16th arrondissement.

Together, Murphy, Cremin and, in an unofficial capacity, O'Kelly tried to look after the needs of the Irish community in Paris, and France in general, during the years 1939–1945. These needs were vast and continued to grow as the war ground on and civilian suffering increased.

2

ALL QUIET ON THE WESTERN FRONT

James Joyce moved into an apartment at 34 rue des Vignes in the 16th arrondissement in Paris in April 1939 – the last but one of twenty-one addresses in his family's nineteen years in Paris. While other foreign residents might have thought of leaving Paris as the Hitlerian menace grew in the late 1930s, the Joyces were anchored to Paris by their daughter, Lucia, whose mental health problems had led to her admittance to a closed institution in 1936. But Joyce was not in Paris when France and Great Britain declared war on Nazi Germany on 3 September 1939. The previous month, he and his wife, Nora, had left Paris for a seaside holiday at Etretat in Normandy, where his grandson, Stephen, was at summer camp. After a brief stay in Etretat, Joyce travelled to Switzerland to look into the possibility of transferring Lucia and the rest of his family there in the event of war. He came back briefly to Paris in late August to check up on Lucia, who was a patient at the clinic of Dr Achille Delmas in Ivry-sur-Seine, in the southern suburbs. He found out that Dr Delmas had made arrangements to transfer his patients to the French Atlantic coast as war clouds loomed ever larger. Joyce travelled to La Baule, near Nantes, on 28 August to await Lucia's arrival in the vicinity. While there, he met an Irish-American friend from Paris, Dr Daniel Patrick O'Brien of the Rockefeller Foundation.[1] James and Nora Joyce were staying at the Hôtel Christophe in La Baule, when Britain and France declared war on Germany on 3 September, and they were still there when Lucia arrived at the Clinique des Charmettes in Pornichet, close to La Baule, eight days later. She was soon suffering repeated mental crises and found the occasional air-raid alarm particularly disturbing.

Joyce's other child, Giorgio (father of Stephen), also had issues. By 1939 Giorgio's relationship with his wealthy Jewish-American wife, Helen Fleischmann-Kastor, was increasingly tormented, as she suffered from chronic schizophrenia. Helen had been sent to a clinic in Montreux, Switzerland, in April 1939, but by the outbreak of war she was back in Paris. She travelled to Etretat to retrieve Stephen from summer camp and then moved with him and Giorgio into a farmhouse in Beynes, to the west of Paris. Helen's behaviour became increasingly erratic and was not helped when she bumped into Giorgio and the rich art patron Peggy Guggenheim dining together in a Paris restaurant. Helen's distress quickly convinced Giorgio, who had his own problems with alcohol, to take it upon himself to remove Stephen from her custody. When Giorgio and his entourage turned up at the farm in Beynes, Helen started to throw rocks at them, but Giorgio managed to retrieve Stephen and brought him to live briefly with Alex Ponisovsky, who had been James Joyce's Russian teacher and had been the focus of Lucia's attentions a few years earlier.

At this time, early September 1939, James and Nora Joyce were still on the Atlantic coast, but in mid-October, once they were satisfied that Lucia had been comfortably installed at the Clinique des Charmettes, the Joyces travelled back to Paris to support Giorgio. James swore he would return to La Baule to look after Lucia once he had sorted out his affairs in the French capital, but he never saw her again.

Along with Giorgio and Stephen, James and Nora moved back briefly to the apartment in the rue des Vignes. But it soon proved impossible to stay there – the apartment building's heating system had been turned off just as the weather was turning bitterly cold. The Joyces, therefore, booked into the Hôtel Lutetia on the boulevard Raspail in the 6th arrondissement, where they remained until December. Meanwhile, Helen was brought to a *maison de santé* in Suresnes, in the comfortable western suburbs of Paris, where she remained until May 1940 when her brother got her out of Europe via Genoa. Helen spent the remainder of the war in a sanatorium in Connecticut.

The rift between Giorgio and Helen contaminated James Joyce's friendship with his literary factotum, Paul Léon (brother-in-law of Alex Ponisovsky), who took a more nuanced view of the rights and wrongs of the two parties. There was a temporary cooling of relations between the two men, culminating in a demand from Joyce that Léon should return all his papers, including publishing contracts. But this rift lasted only a short time before Joyce patched it up. Low on funds, Joyce needed Léon, whom he knew could be depended upon to obtain money from a variety of sources and to sort out his tax arrears.

***

Like Joyce, the other most famous Parisian Irishman, Samuel Beckett, was absent from Paris on 3 September 1939. On that day Beckett was on holiday at a rented house in Greystones, County Wicklow. But, earnest Francophile that he was, Beckett decided to return right away to his flat at 6 rue des Favorites in the 15th arrondissement. Taking the mail boat from Dún Laoghaire to Holyhead, he travelled by train to London and then to Newhaven and embarked on the ferry for Dieppe, arriving back in Paris on 4 September, where he tried to enlist in the French army.

An indication of how relatively serene the mood was in Paris in the opening weeks of the war can be gleaned from a letter that Beckett wrote in late September 1939 to George and Gwynedd Reavey in London, stating that he 'ran into Peggy Guggenheim at the Dôme with a brand new car & drinking Pernod'.[2] He re-started his awkward relationship with the American heiress and art lover and was with her one night in a friend's house when

Guggenheim fell down the stairs, dislocating her knee. According to Guggenheim, Beckett 'just stood by quite helplessly in his usual paralysed state'.[3] But nothing much seemed to happen otherwise as the cold winter weather set in. By early December Beckett's status had still not been sorted out. He had applied for an Irish passport in September 1939, but it had not come through, and he had received a mere acknowledgement letter in response to his offer to serve in the French army. He wrote to the Reaveys in London that he was 'heated and hot watered' and rarely went out.[4]

Assuming the role of *homme à tout faire* (general factotum) in place of Paul Léon, Beckett saw James Joyce frequently during the latter's final weeks in Paris. During this time, Joyce spent and drank heavily and took Beckett back to collect some things from the flat in the rue des Vignes, where the Joyces had left all their possessions when they decamped to the Hôtel Lutetia. On one occasion Joyce sat down and played at the piano he had left behind in the flat: he sang loudly for half an hour, with shaking voice and hands. 'What is the use of this war?' he is said to have asked Beckett on the same occasion.[5]

Furniture designer and architect Eileen Grey was also absent from Paris at the outbreak of war. Thanks to her moneyed family, Grey, originally from Enniscorthy in County Wexford, had been able to buy an apartment at 21 rue de Bonaparte in the 6th arrondissement in 1907, which she owned up to her death in 1976. But fame and fortune had allowed Grey to buy and build other properties as well, most famously a Modern Movement-style house called E–1027 at Roquebrune-Cap-Martin, between Monaco and Menton on the Mediterranean coast. In 1934 she built another house, called Villa Tempe a Païa, on the route de Castellar in Menton, within a couple of kilometres of the Italian border. Grey was there when war broke out in September 1939 and was still there in June 1940 when the Italians declared war on France and occupied the region.

In contrast to Joyce, Beckett and Gray, Fr Vincent Travers, administrator of the Irish College in rue des Irlandais in the 5th arrondissement, was in Paris on 3 September 1939. Around seventy Irish clerical students had lived and studied at the Irish College at any one time, but in an account he wrote after the war, Fr Travers (who was born in Gurteen, County Sligo in 1900 and died in Dublin in 1987) remembered how, just days before the declaration of war, he helped the last two residents apart from himself – nuns from the Sisters of St Joseph of Annecy who ran the Irish College's 'domestic affairs' – to board a train for the ferry back to England.

The Winter War broke out between the Soviet Union and Finland in November 1939, but little or nothing happened on the Western Front between September 1939 and May 1940 (the period known as the Phoney War). This period proved largely uneventful, bar the odd air-raid scare and the installation of some fire-fighting equipment by air-raid wardens in one of the college halls. Fr Travers had prepared a shelter in the Irish College cellar: 'one of the finest shelters in Paris … Nothing save a direct hit could damage it', according to the priest. Even though the cellar wasn't an officially designated shelter, 'a few of the neighbours came to it and, truth to tell, I wasn't sorry to have their company'.[6] He was even able to cross over to Ireland in December 1939 for a few weeks, coming back to Paris in early 1940 to find a series of burst pipes. Otherwise, right up to the unleashing of the Blitzkrieg against the Low Countries on 10 May, 'things went on quietly, though uneasily. There was no scarcity of anything. The cafés, theatres and cinemas were crowded. The blackout was lessened considerably and people had ceased to carry gas-masks.'[7]

Another Irish Parisian, Margaret Kelly, better known as 'Bluebell', was also present in Paris on the day war was declared, having given birth to her first child in July. After her own birth in the Rotunda Hospital in Dublin in 1910, Margaret had been quickly given up for adoption by her parents to a dressmaker named Mary Murphy, who made ends meet by doing some house cleaning. Murphy moved to Liverpool some time after the Easter Rising in 1916, taking Bluebell (a nickname given to Margaret by a Dublin doctor) with her. Bluebell was contracted by Scottish dance-company manager Alfred Jackson to dance in Berlin in the late 1920s. But in the summer of 1930, and again in 1931, Jackson asked her to go as a holiday replacement to the Folies Bergère in Paris. While there, Bluebell accepted a job not far away at the Casino de Paris in the rue de Clichy, but she soon left and returned to the Folies Bergère as 'captain' of her own dance group, the Bluebell Girls.

In March 1939, at Trinité church in the 9th arrondissement, Bluebell, already pregnant, married a stateless Jew of Romanian origin called Marcel Leibovici, who led the house orchestra at the Folies Bergère and was the Bluebells' 'astute financial advisor'.[8] The couple lived close by, at 83 rue Blanche, overlooking another institution of Paris night-life, the Moulin Rouge. Upon the outbreak of war in September 1939, Bluebell disbanded her dance troupe, but she decided to stay in Paris because of her husband, who did not relish having to move across the English Channel, especially in view of his murky citizenship. Events were to prove this a tragically wrong decision. As the Phoney War dragged on after Christmas 1939 and into early 1940, the Folies Bergère contacted Bluebell with a view to putting on a new show, but the theatre director apparently informed her that he would prefer if she did not come to the theatre, for fear of incurring the wrath of the Germans for employing the wife of a stateless Jew, should they ever get to Paris. Bluebell did not forget this weasel-like attitude in the following years.

As the Phoney War continued almost without incident, some people became complacent. Many Irish Parisians were entitled to an Irish passport but would have had to surrender their British passport to obtain one. Given the calm of the opening months of conflict and the superior resources at the disposal of France and Britain in the war against Germany, changing passports did not seem urgent, and might even be counterproductive. What was the value of holding the passport of a small, insecure, neutral country, with little by way of an international presence, when set beside a document issued by the world's greatest empire? Irishwoman Maria Bergin wrote from Briançon in the French Alps at the beginning of March 1940 to reject an offer of an Irish passport, for she had 'decided that a British passport would be more useful to me under current circumstances. Eire's neutrality might make difficulties with Allied officials and as I do not intend to return to Eire I'm afraid Irish passport is not the most useful of two.'[9] We do not know if Bergin was to regret her choice.

The most famous non-recipient of an Irish passport was James Joyce. Throughout the 1930s Joyce rejected any notion of giving up his British passport – perhaps because of a residual grudge against his homeland, or for the more prosaic reason that he did not wish to jeopardise welfare payments he received or might expect to receive from London.[10] When the Legation suggested in the last months of his life that it could help him more if he registered as an Irish citizen, Joyce, in Richard Ellmann's words, 'refused to accept in wartime something he did not desire in peacetime'.[11] But it is perhaps not the least of the paradoxes surrounding Joyce that his own unwillingness to take out an Irish passport did not stop him seeking one for his son and daughter.

A very astute Mr Mulcahy, writing from Brussels just before Christmas 1939, had a different attitude to James Joyce. In Brussels, the British embassy had told Mulcahy he was eligible for a British passport, but he had decided it would be better to have his expired Irish passport renewed. 'Owing to the very uncertain times we are living in and as we are never sure that we may be invaded here by the Germans, for this reason I would prefer an Irish Free State passport as our country is neutral and the Germans would have no authority to take me prisoner,'Mulcahy wrote to the Legation in Paris.[12] Veteran newspaperman William Weldon O'Mahony ('a freelance Paris correspondent for various British newspapers specialising in wireless, motoring, beekeeping and popular science') was also granted a full five-year passport in late 1939.[13]

Sligo native John McMorrow, writing from Bournay in the south-eastern suburbs of Paris, was also convinced that he would be better off with an Irish passport. He was, he explained to the Legation in a letter of October 1939, 'a citizen of Eire travelling in France on a British passport, so I want to get it exchanged for an Irish one'. McMorrow had been a waiter at the Savoy in London and had come to France the previous July to study French because, he explained, 'to get a good job as a waiter any place you need French'. He had found work in a hotel in Cannes on the Côte d'Azur, but it had closed down upon the outbreak of war in September, and McMorrow had ended up staying with an American gentleman at the Château de Boussy-Saint-Antoine beside Bournay. McMorrow was a bit anxious because the French police had told him that 'if I don't get it changed I may be lifted anytime for the British Army on account of my passport'.[14]

Another long-time member of the Irish community who gave up her British passport in return for an Irish one was Janie McCarthy. McCarthy, who was born in Killarney in 1885, had left Ireland to become an au pair with a French family in Brittany in 1910. She later studied for a degree in French and English at the Sorbonne and thereafter began to teach English, first in the Breton town of Vannes and then in Paris. Her obituary in *The Irish Times* in 1965 stated that 'she had as pupils many sons and daughters of royalty from as far away as Indochina'.[15] McCarthy (whose file in the Service historique de la Défense confusingly suggests she was a man) was to become a determined resister right from the start of the German Occupation (a record few native French would have been able to emulate), working for a series of Resistance networks between 1940 and 1944. McCarthy's Irish passport quite possibly saved her from internment in Besançon or Vittel, where many British-passport holders ended up in 1940. But later in the Occupation, given her deep implication in French Resistance activities, McCarthy's passport would probably not have spared her the fate that befell many of her French associates in the Resistance – deportation to Ravensbrück, the concentration camp for female political prisoners in Germany.

As a number of Paris Irish pondered over passports in the early months of the war, at least one man was clear where his loyalties lay. Writing from Castle Forbes in County Longford, Bernard Forbes, the eighth Earl of Granard and a former member of the Seanad, informed Lord Halifax, the British Foreign Secretary, that he would be 'delighted' to place his house at 73 rue de Varenne in the exclusive 7th arrondissement at the disposal of the British government. The house, Granard explained, was a big one, 'about the size of the British Embassy, and during the last War my father-in-law lent it to General Pershing where the General Headquarters of the American Expeditionary Force in Paris were established'.[16] However, the British found they had no use for the premises (which, in fact, originally belonged to Granard's rich American wife, Beatrice Mills, who had inherited the *hôtel particulier* from her father).[17]

Meanwhile, the Joyces decided the best thing for their grandson, Stephen (now without his mother), was to send him to Saint-Gérand-le-Puy, near Vichy, where their American friend Maria Jolas had relocated her bilingual school. In December 1939 Nora, James and Giorgio decided to join Stephen in Saint-Gérand-le-Puy, taking up Jolas' invitation to spend Christmas together. So, on 23 December, Samuel Beckett put the Joyces on an evening train from Paris. Except for a suitcase of clothes and toiletries, they left everything they owned at their flat at the rue des Vignes as James Joyce said goodbye to the French capital for what would be the last time. Just a few months later, the Hôtel Lutetia, where he had been staying since October, was requisitioned by the Abwehr, the German military intelligence service, and from late 1944 to mid-1945 the Lutetia served as a sorting centre for deportees repatriated from Germany.

Even in the confines of a remote village in central France, James Joyce did not give up his propensity to change address – the Joyces changed abode four times in Saint-Gérand-le-Puy and its environs in the time they stayed there. He discovered that the dreariness of rural life at the dead of winter did not suit him, and the precarious health of both himself and Nora (suffering from arthritis) did not help. Nevertheless, bar a two-month stay in Vichy, the nearest town, Saint-Gérand-le-Puy was their home for the best part of a year.

Giorgio, equally bored with village life, left for Paris shortly after the New Year and seems thereafter to have led a dissolute existence. Initially, he moved back to the Lutetia, where he resumed an affair with Peggy Guggenheim and tried to convince her to move in with him. But Guggenheim was wary of Joyce, writing that she 'certainly did not want to get so much involved with him'[18] (although the fact that Giorgio was officially married to Helen Fleischmann-Kastor did not cause her any qualms). Maria Jolas wrote to her husband in America that 'Giorgio's life is now shrouded in mystery, he gives no news of himself, lets weeks go by without writing, and, even when he was here, gave literally no inkling as to the life he is living in Paris.'[19] As late as April 1940, even Giorgio's father did not know where his son was in Paris or what he was up to, for Giorgio had 'retreated to a life beyond the horizon of anyone the Joyces regarded as a friend', in the words of Carol Loeb Shloss.[20]

3

DETENTION AND DESTITUTION

In a lightning campaign that began with an attack on the Low Countries on 10 May 1940, the Germans smashed through successive French defence lines, bypassing the famous Maginot Line. Within a few weeks, the French had lost their war and the British Expeditionary Force (BEF) had to be evacuated from Dunkirk and other Channel ports. Paris was declared an open city on 11 June and the Germans marched into the French capital three days later.[1]

As the Germans approached, the small Irish community in Paris had to decide what to do. Those who held Irish passports could expect that some level of protection would derive from them being citizens of a neutral state. But many others who had not bothered to change their British passports for Irish ones could expect a rougher ride if they did not get out of the French capital before it fell.

Then there were Ireland's two top diplomatic representatives, Con Cremin and Seán Murphy. On 10 June, having already destroyed reams of confidential Legation papers some days before, Murphy consulted the US ambassador, Bill Bullitt, 'a good friend of Ireland', on whether to evacuate Paris or not.[2] In the end, Murphy decided that the Legation had no choice but to follow the contingency plans that the French government had drawn up for the diplomatic corps in the event of an emergency. Ahead of the long journey he knew he would have to make, Murphy had repairs carried out on the embassy's Packard by a mechanic from County Down called Daniel McAllister, who had been resident in Paris since 1915 and who was recommended by Count O'Kelly de Gallagh.[3] Cremin and Murphy loaded up their cars

early on the morning of 11 June and, along with freshly arrived
Legation secretary Ina Foley, set off to follow the French government, whose initial intention was to establish itself in Tours. They
left with Fr Travers, who had finally decided it would be best to
try to get away, even though it was now almost too late.

On 18 June 1940, a week after they had fled Paris, four days
after the city had fallen and four days before France signed an
armistice with Germany, Seán Murphy wrote a long letter to
the DEA from Ascain, a small village in the extreme south-west
corner of France, close to Biarritz and right next to the Spanish
border.[4] Murphy described how, after its departure from the
French capital, the Legation had finally halted in this village, far
from their first officially designated assembly area near Tours. The
letter is worth quoting at length because of the insight it gives into
the sheer chaos and panic that overwhelmed French officialdom in
the weeks following the German assault on France in May 1940:

> Shortly after the outbreak of war in September last, I received a letter
> from the French Protocol to the effect that among other possibilities
> considered by the military authorities was that on the departure from
> Paris of the President of the Republic 'a residence would be placed
> at the disposal of the Heads of Mission so that they might be able
> to continue to fulfil their functions with the aid of reduced staff ...'
>
> I heard nothing further about the matter until with the turn
> taken by the war in Belgium and northern France, I thought it better
> to ascertain the exact arrangements contemplated, in the event of
> moving, both for accommodating the Legation and in providing
> transport for the staff and luggage. I first approached the Nuncio, as
> Dean of the Corps. He was under the impression that a special train
> would be provided for the transport of luggage and of members of the
> Corps other than Head of Missions who, he believed, were expected to
> reach their future quarters in their own cars. He advised me, however,
> to address myself to the Protocol for all details. I, therefore, had an

interview with the Chef de Protocole. From him I ascertained the name and situation of the Château in the Tours region allotted to us. Beyond that, he could furnish me with no particulars and suggested that the best thing for me to do would be to go and see the place. It was already clear, however, that there would be no special train and that the various missions would have to make their own arrangements for transport of staff and luggage. On the 29th May I went to visit the Château du Grand Boucher, Ballan Miré, Tours, where we were supposed to go ...[5] The Château proved to be a three-storey house standing in its own grounds with a courtyard, a garage and over the garage four small rooms ... When we saw it the proprietor with a companion was living in it although he was absent at Paris that day. If the house were completely empty, it would have been possible, in case of necessity, to use it for the Legation ... It was clearly, however, quite out of the question to install a Legation in the building unless the proprietor were to leave it. When I got back to Paris, I informed the Chef de Protocole of the actual state of affairs and gave him my views as to the possibility of it being used by our Legation. As he was not able to give me any information as to whether the owner would stay on, as I understood that the government had not in fact requisitioned it and as it seemed abundantly clear that the proprietor had deliberately altered the house so as to prevent a Legation being installed in it, I decided that it would be rash to rely on it as a possible residence and that by far the wiser course would be to assume that we would have to make our own arrangements both in regard to our accommodation as well as in regard to our transport. The question of transport did not present any real difficulty as my car was capable of carrying all of the staff and the Secretary's car could carry such official luggage as we would require to bring with us. Events moved too rapidly, however, for us to be able to make arrangements in regard to accommodation.

Having to leave Paris to follow the government became more and more a likelihood as time went on. All through the week ending on the 9th June it seemed inevitable we would have to take that step. It was known on the other hand, because of the government's decision ... not to leave Paris except at the last possible moment, that one should be prepared to leave at very short notice ... Among other questions which were considered was that of leaving a member of the staff to look after the Legation and, in the event of no member of the staff remaining, of leaving a concierge at the Legation ... I felt that there was no point in any member of the staff remaining both because of the relatively unimportant nature of our interests in Paris and because no member of the staff had any *locus standi* vis-à-vis the French (or German) authorities ... As for leaving a concierge on the ground, ... I could not feel sure that the presence of a concierge, no matter how reliable, might not lead to some abuse ... I, therefore, paid off the concierge on the 10th June and, in accordance with the terms on which he was engaged in 1931, gave him a month's salary in lieu of notice. Before leaving Paris on the morning of the 11th I saw to it that all outside entrances to the Legation and Chancery were locked ...

On the morning of Monday 10th June we received a note from the Protocol advising us that ... the government 'saw no objection to our moving into the provinces' ... I therefore made all arrangements for leaving early on the following morning ... That evening I called on the American ambassador to ascertain what course he proposed to follow and whether he had any information as to what the missions of other neutral states were doing. He informed me that he was aware that all or practically all the Heads of Mission in Paris had either already left on the 10th or proposed to leave by the 11th. As far as he himself was concerned, he intended to remain in Paris because of the tradition in the American Service that the diplomatic representative in Paris remain there whatever should happen. Apparently this course of action was followed in 1870 and in 1914 ...

I knew that Father Travers, rector of the Irish College in Paris, was anxious to leave the city in the event of the French government deciding to evacuate the capital. It was his intention in such an event to get to the House of his Order (Vincentian) at Rennes. As soon as our decision to leave had been taken, I communicated with him and offered, if he so desired, to take him with us to Tours where another House of the Order existed. He accepted this offer. On the following morning, therefore, we all assembled at the Legation, i.e. the Secretary, Mr O'Byrne, Mme Froc, Miss Foley and Father Travers. We left the Legation for Tours at 8 a.m. An unusual and very dirty fog lay over Paris that morning whereas the weather up to then for a fortnight previously had been extremely fine with complete absence of cloud. This fog would appear to have been that which the official communiqué of the evening of the 11th alleged had been artificially created by the Germans with the object of crossing the Seine at various points west of Paris, the nearest of which was about 40 miles away. We understood that the roads leading out of Paris towards the south were likely to be heavily encumbered with traffic on account of the huge voluntary exodus of the civil population which was taking place. We, however, chose the direct road to Tours which runs through Versailles, Chartres, Châteaudun, Vendôme and Château Renault. The total distance from Paris to Tours by this route is 235 kilometres … In normal circumstances, the journey would be performed in less than 3 and a half hours. As soon, however, as we had got to Garches, which is about two and a half miles out, we ran into a heavy line of traffic running in the same direction. The result was that it took us over an hour to reach Versailles, a distance generally covered in about 20 minutes. We reached Epernon, which is c. 40 miles from Paris, at about 11 a.m. At this point, we, with the rest of the line of cars, were obliged by the military authorities to leave the main road for Chartres. Until we got as far as Gallardon, a distance from Epernon of 15 miles, our progress was relatively rapid. To cover the distance from Gallardon to Sours, however, (about 10 miles) it took us about three hours. This was by far the most unpleasant part of the journey as we were advancing by stages only from 10 to 50 yards at a time and the day had become exceedingly hot. We reached Sours at about 2.30 p.m. On arriving here I decided to see the military authority to insist that, as we were on an official journey, we should be allowed to take the main road. This was conceded and we therefore went to Chartres (about 5 miles away) at a normal pace and from there by the main route to Châteaudun (about 27 miles), which we reached about 3.30 p.m. All the hotels and restaurants at Châteaudun were overflowing and short of food but we finally succeeded in getting something to eat. We left for Vendôme (25 miles away) by the main road, at about 4.30 p.m. On this stretch we did not encounter anything like the same volume of refugee traffic as on the whole journey as far as Sours. From Vendôme to Château Renault, a distance of over 15 miles, progress was relatively good for most of the way. We had a puncture, however, some distance before Château Renault and immediately afterwards ran into a traffic block which it took us almost three quarters of an hour to clear. From Château Renault we took the reserved main road to Tours (20 miles away). It rained rather heavily on this stretch. We ultimately arrived at Tours towards 9 p.m.

I thought it best on arrival at Tours … to call to see the Prefect and ascertain from him the exact position in regard to the Château allotted to us. He informed me at once that this chateau was no longer available as the owner had installed a large number of relatives. I gathered from him that the experience in regard to our chateau was not an isolated one and that the Nuncio and a few ambassadors who had arrived the previous evening had had to spend the night in chairs in his house. He said that there was no room whatever available at Tours but asked his chef de cabinet to see what he could do for us. The latter went to great pains in the matter and ultimately succeeded in securing for us more or less by means of requisition, a total of three rooms in the Hôtel de l'Univers, regarded as the best hotel in the town. We left the Prefecture for the hotel at about 9.30. Just as we left the anti-aircraft defences set up a strong barrage which continued more or less without interruption until towards 11 p.m. As the sky was overcast, it was impossible to see who was being fired at but the flames of the bursting shells were clearly visible. When we reached the hotel we found the place in a state of considerable chaos. I eventually succeeded in getting, in addition to the three rooms obtained for us by the Prefecture, another one for my chauffeur and his wife who had accompanied him from Paris. We had, therefore, a total of four rooms for eight people as Father Travers found it impossible to locate the House of his order that night ... The hotel management, however, told us that it was no longer possible to serve dinner on account of the 'alerte'. They advised me to try a restaurant further down the street. We did so but were informed that 'not an egg remained'. We had, therefore, nothing to eat that night.

It was quite evident that Tours was in a complete state of chaos which was only likely to grow in subsequent days with the increasing influx of refugees on their way through to the south and of government officials coming to be installed in the region. My experience had also convinced me that it would be quite useless to expect any assistance whatever in the matter of obtaining accommodation from the Protocol. At the same time so long as we were in a position to be in contact with the government, there seemed no strong reason why we should be in very close proximity to them. I, therefore, decided to proceed towards the south in the hope of obtaining accommodation, intending to go, if necessary, as far as Bordeaux. Poitiers, which represented our first stop and where we had lunch ... was completely full, both with refugees and the administration of the Belgian government. Angoulême, the next stage of the journey ... was likewise completely full and there was nothing whatever to be had in the hotels. We, therefore, continued to Bordeaux which we reached on the evening of the 12th at about 8 p.m. I, at once, called at the Prefecture as offering our best hope of obtaining accommodation in Bordeaux if, as I thought would be the case, the hotels were full. I was unable to see the Prefect but had an interview with the Secretary General who, by coincidence, happened to be the nephew of the [Irish] Legation architect ... He undertook to do what he could the following day to get us suitable accommodation. As regards accommodation that night ... he finally succeeded in securing for us a total of three rooms, one in the Hotel Continental and the others in the Terminus ... The following morning, I called as arranged, at the Prefecture to have an interview with Mr Ziwes.[6] I was, however, unable to do so as he was in conference all morning. The explanation of the conference was that the government had the previous night decided to move to Bordeaux. Mr Ziwes ... told me that their arrangements had been completely upset by the sudden decision of the Government and intimated that there was little hope of any kind of suitable accommodation being placed at our disposal at least in the immediate future. This was my own judgment from the crowds which I could see in Bordeaux and from the developments which had taken place in the matter of hotel accommodation. Our hotel had that day been requisitioned for the Government and it was only by reason of the fact that our room was already regarded as requisitioned by the Prefecture for us that we were able to remain in it. Practically all other clients of the hotel were ordered to leave it in the course of the day. It has since been stated that by that date Bordeaux contained a population of three times as great as its normal population (about 250,000). As before leaving Paris the possibility of our having to go even further south had not been excluded, I had asked the Special Counsellor [Count O'Kelly de Gallagh] who was leaving Paris for Ascain to look into the prospects of our obtaining accommodation in that region. It seemed unlikely that I could make any useful contact with the Foreign Office on the next day, Friday the 14th. I, therefore, paid a visit to Ascain which is about 120 miles south of Bordeaux. I found that Count O'Kelly had, in fact, been able to secure accommodation in Ascain itself for the whole party in the event of our requiring it and that he had also succeeded in finding rooms which could serve as an office. I, therefore, decided to move the whole party down to Ascain. I returned to Bordeaux the same evening and we left for Ascain at 3 p.m. on the following day (Saturday 15 June). I had spent the morning in Bordeaux in an effort to get in touch with the Ministry of Foreign Affairs but, though I ascertained where they were supposed to be, it proved impossible to find any member of the Ministry either there or elsewhere.

There are in all at least about 25 heads of missions in the Biarritz, St Jean, Ascain area. In addition there is at Biarritz a considerable number of members of the staffs of other missions. From what I have since gathered from some of my colleagues it seems that my decision to push on in the first instance from Tours and in the second instance from Bordeaux was a wise one. Their experience in regard to the accommodation allotted to them at Tours was similar to mine and some of them have informed me that accommodation which was alleged to have been assigned to them near Bordeaux after the government decided to move there was not available.

In his post-war account of his solitary five-year vigil at the Irish College, Fr Travers gave his own version of the dash from Paris with Cremin and Murphy on 11 June.[7] It was, the Sligo man wrote, a beautiful sunny morning, but for a strange thick fog that descended on the city and that turned out to be a burning fuel dump. Before leaving the Irish College, Fr Travers had posted an official notice provided by the Legation on the main door of the college stating 'that the building was Irish property and therefore not to be molested'. The Irish cars soon were caught up in an endless stream of refugees heading south, away from the advancing Germans. The going was very slow as far as Chartres, where Murphy asked for permission to use the road reserved for military use. Along this road, Fr Travers was able to witness the disintegration of the French army at first hand. 'Occasionally,' he wrote, 'we came upon disorganised-looking groups of French soldiers building roadblocks, but everything seemed to be in great disorder. Innumerable French officers seemed to be transporting their families out of the danger zone. Indeed, I heard that not a few of them requisitioned cars for that purpose.'

Thirteen hours after leaving Paris, they reached the city of Tours, a mere 240 kilometres from the centre of the French capital. Fr Travers' idea was to catch a train from Tours to St Malo and to look for a ship to carry him to England. It was not to be. Having said goodbye to the Legation staff, who continued south-west to Bordeaux to catch up with the French government, Travers, perhaps naïvely, went to obtain a military visa for his passport so he could leave France. Instead, Travers had to cope with bureaucratic delays and Luftwaffe bombardments in Tours that ensured he missed any chance of getting on a train to the Atlantic coast and a possible passage back to England. Over a series of days, Travers went daily from his makeshift lodgings at an orphanage run by nuns to the station in Tours in the hope that train services had been restored. But each time such hope was dashed, for by this stage the French railway system was in chaos.

The Irish priest witnessed the blowing up of the main bridge across the Loire in Tours by the French on 18 June and found himself 'uncomfortably close' to French positions that were shelled by the Germans. He also witnessed a German air raid on Tours on 20 June, the incendiary bombs causing a huge fire that blazed out of control and destroyed part of the city centre. On 21 June, a day before France signed an armistice with Germany, Tours fell to the Germans. After the crash and roar of cannons and bombs over the previous two days, Travers remembered that a 'great silence' descended after the city fell. He said mass at the orphanage chapel that same day and, after an early breakfast, went out to find Germans in the streets. According to the Irishman, 'they didn't seem to be the barbarians the French expected. On the whole they conducted themselves modestly as victors, and with great propriety towards the inhabitants.' And so the Occupation began.

Fr Travers, conscious he would never make it back to either England or Ireland, waited in the orphanage in Tours for well over a month, during which time he developed a serious stomach complaint that he ascribed to the water. Finally, on 26 July, he hitched a lift back to Paris in a van with a group of nuns. The journey was slow, and once the party had to purchase petrol from the Germans.

Fr Travers eventually made it back to the Irish College, which he found just the way he had left it over six weeks before and with the air-warden people still using one of the college halls to store equipment. Apart from a janitor, Travers spent the next four years alone in the college, fending off with equal determination both hunger and attempts by various organisations to requisition the building. During all that time, Travers maintained that he received only one or two letters from Ireland.

Ten days after his detailed 18 June report to the DEA about the Legation's evacuation from Paris, Seán Murphy sent two further reports to Dublin from Ascain: one detailing again the circumstances of the Legation's meanders across France, the other focusing on geopolitical developments. Murphy had no original insights to offer into the reasons why the French had decided to seek an armistice on 22 June, and pointed simply to 'public pronouncements' to explain why the French had, controversially, decided not to move the seat of government to French North Africa and continue the fight from there. The main argument against such a course of action, Murphy wrote, was that it 'would have involved abandoning the French of the Metropole, a course which the Government was not disposed to take'.[8]

The collapse of the Third Republic led to its replacement on 10 July by a new regime called the État français, with the eighty-eight-year-old 'hero of Verdun', Marshal Philippe Pétain, as its chief of state.

By the first days of July, Murphy and the rest of the Legation had moved back from the extreme south-west towards the centre of France, to a village called La Bourboule near Clermont-Ferrand, from where he wrote his next long report. Murphy explained that the various diplomatic corps had followed the French government, which had been obliged to leave Bordeaux after the Germans occupied it. By 3 July Murphy had received word that the French government had decided to pitch its tent in Vichy, to the north of Clermont-Ferrand. The next day, 4 July, Murphy, Cremin and Count O'Kelly, with the rest of the Legation staff, headed north from Ascain, stopping again in Bordeaux in an unsuccessful search for petrol. They pressed on to Limoges, where the German military authorities accorded them 100 litres – just enough for the convoy of three cars to get to Vichy, where they arrived sixteen hours after leaving Ascain. But tired and hungry as the diplomats were, they could find no accommodation for the night in Vichy until Murphy bumped into the secretary-general of the French foreign ministry, Charles Roux, who found them three rooms at the Hôtel du Parc. Since the same hotel was earmarked to house Pétain and part of the new government of the État français the following morning, the Irish had to pack their bags again. Accommodation had been reserved for them in La Bourboule, over 100 kilometres away, from where Murphy wrote his missive to Dublin. But within a few days, the new government had found its bearings, and accommodation was found for the Irish Legation back in Vichy, this time at the Hôtel des Lilas.

***

A couple of days before the fall of Paris on 14 June, Bluebell, along with her husband and baby, had joined the mass exodus fleeing southwards before the advancing Germans. They, like the Irish Legation, headed for Bordeaux, where they had friends and from where they hoped to catch a ship to England. But the clogged roads meant that it took Bluebell five days to reach the outskirts of Bordeaux, only to be prevented by gendarmes from entering the city proper, where the stream of refugees had become unmanageable.

Having managed to rent a house in a village near the city for a couple of months, Bluebell and her Jewish husband concluded that there was no longer any possibility of getting to England. With their funds running low, and fearful of what might have become of their apartment, they returned to Paris in the autumn of 1940. They found their apartment on the rue Blanche untouched and the city returning to a semblance of normality, although an 11 p.m. curfew was in force. But things were not normal for Marcel Leibovici. As a foreign Jew he was required to register with the German authorities – something he wisely refused to do.[9] Leibovici also had to deal with the government in Vichy. The newly installed regime of Philippe Pétain actually protested against German interference in the 'Jewish question' and promulgated its own statute on Jews in October 1940. The statute excluded Jews from many professions and from the public service, and it allowed the French police to intern stateless Jews and those of foreign origin. Leibovici was a perfect target. Fearful of being picked up in the street, he stayed indoors as much as possible, making some money from composing music under a pseudonym. Bluebell arranged the occasional dance show in small theatres, but her actions were soon limited when she discovered she was pregnant with her second child.

Samuel Beckett had seemed undecided about what to do if the Germans seized Paris. On Monday 10 June he wrote to a friend to say that he was free for a game of billiards on the following Friday afternoon, but only 'on condition that we stay in Paris. Suzanne seems to want to leave. Not me. Where would we go and with what?'[10] But by 12 June, a day after Paris had been declared an open city, Beckett had allowed himself to be convinced to leave by his girlfriend, Suzanne Deschevaux-Dumesnil. Bringing just as much as they could carry, they made it onto one of the last trains to leave the Gare de Lyon before the Germans arrived, joining the exodus of Bluebell and other Irish Parisians from the city. By the evening of 12 June they had arrived in Vichy, where they booked into the hotel where James Joyce was staying.

In April 1940 James and Nora Joyce had moved from Saint-Gérand-le-Puy to the Hôtel Beaujolais in Vichy, where they had heard that their old friend Valéry Larbaud was staying (Larbaud had graciously lent his apartment to the homeless Joyce family in Paris during the summer of 1921). But the Joyces and Beckett were turfed out of the Hôtel Beaujolais in mid-June as the new French government requisitioned accommodation. Missing the arrival of the Legation in Vichy by just a few days, the Joyces were forced to move back to Saint-Gérand-le-Puy. Beckett and Suzanne, armed with money that Larbaud gave them in return for an Irish cheque, walked out of Vichy and then climbed onto a train that took them as far as Toulouse. However, without adequate papers it was impossible to stay there, so they went first to Cahors and then to Arcachon, a seaside resort near Bordeaux, which they reached on 24 June 1940. There, they looked up their friend Mary Reynolds, an American artist, and her more famous lover, fellow artist and inveterate chess player Marcel Duchamp.

With the money that Valéry Larbaud had given him, Beckett was able to rent a seaside house, the Villa St Georges. Although the Germans had reached Arcachon on 25 June, the day after Beckett and Suzanne had arrived in the town, the couple stayed there for the remainder of the summer of 1940, with Beckett and Duchamp spending much of the time playing chess. In early September the two couples decided to travel back to Paris, with

Beckett and Suzanne returning to their studio apartment in rue des Favorites in the 15th arrondissement. While Beckett had been holed up in Arcachon, some effort had been made to locate him. He had managed to send a postcard to his friend George Reavey, who was working at the British Institute in Madrid. In turn, Reavey had contacted the Irish Legation in Madrid, which naturally contacted the DEA in Dublin. Then, on 9 August, the Legation in Vichy received a wire from the DEA in Dublin with the words 'Please wire position of Samuel Beckett'. Once back in Paris, and having been informed that the Irish authorities were looking for him, Beckett called on special plenipotentiary Count O'Kelly, who was back in the city as well. Beckett asked O'Kelly to contact his brother Frank, who was living in the garret he had lived in himself at 6 Clare Street in Dublin. Frank was to arrange for Beckett's monthly allowance of £20 (the product of income from property he had inherited from his father) to be sent to him via the DEA and the Legation.[11] In the weeks following his return, Beckett managed to obtain the Irish passport he had applied for months earlier and to persuade O'Kelly to supply him with the following letter, dated 28 November 1940:

> I, the undersigned, Minister Plenipotentiary and Special Counsellor at the Irish Legation, certify that Monsieur Samuel Beckett, an Irish citizen, 6 rue des Favorites, Paris (15ème) exercises the profession of writer. His writings, of which one notably is on Marcel Proust, have been published in London since the year 1931.[12]

Meanwhile, having been evicted from the hotel he was staying in with Nora in Vichy in June 1940, James Joyce found himself back in the forlorn little village of Saint-Gérand-le-Puy. He and Nora passed their remaining six months in the village between the Hôtel du Commerce and their last French abode, the Maison Ponthenier, a dank little house hidden in a side street. Shortly after the fall of Paris and their departure from Vichy, they were joined in Saint-Gérand-le-Puy by Paul Léon and their son, Giorgio, who quickly became known in the locality 'for his fondness for cognac and for the local girls'.[13]

With France divided between a *zone libre* (free zone) in the south administered by the regime of Philippe Pétain, and a northern part occupied by the Germans, Joyce found it impossible to maintain contact with his sick daughter, Lucia, who was still in Pornichet on the Atlantic coast. By late 1940 a year's worth of bills that still had to be paid for Lucia's hospitalisation added further to Joyce's anxieties, for the writer's financial lifelines from British and American publishers, including the funds he used to receive from Harriet Weaver in London, had been disrupted. In retaliation for a British decision to freeze all German assets in the United Kingdom, Germany blocked the accounts of British citizens living in France. However, Joyce was still able to receive a subsidy from the British government via the US authorities in Vichy, which also helped channel money from Helen Joyce's parents in New York, the Kastors, designated for their grandson, Stephen. With the United States still neutral at this stage of the war, Joyce also decided to try to channel royalties due to him from Random House in New York via the US embassy in France, which was then to forward the fees due for Lucia's hospitalisation. However, aside from Lucia's clinic fees, the rent on the apartment in rue des Vignes in Paris, where he had left most of his papers, was not being paid.

Joyce's need to find a way to meet his financial commitments and to ensure that his possessions in Paris were put into safe-keeping meant that Paul Léon was pressed into service once again. Like Giorgio Joyce, Léon had fled Paris for Saint-Gérand-le-Puy with his wife just ahead of the Germans' arrival and had spent the summer of 1940 correcting drafts of *Finnegans Wake*. At the beginning of September, he decided to go back to Paris, where his wife, Lucie Noël, had already returned to her job as a journalist at the *New York Herald Tribune*. Joyce asked Léon to get into his apartment in the rue des Vignes, by any means, to retrieve his papers. Between his return to Paris and early 1941, Léon made various trips to Joyce's abode to rescue what he could of Joyce's possessions before they were seized by bailiffs in lieu of rent. Léon managed to acquire a number of papers and other items by bribing the concierge and explaining to her that he was only picking up some of his own things that he had left behind. Twice he employed a handyman with a pushcart to transport Joyce's possessions from rue des Vignes to his own home at rue Casimir-Périer in the 7th arrondissement, somehow avoiding arousing the suspicions of the Germans or the French police.

Some of Joyce's papers also ended up in Irish hands. In a hand-scribbled note of a conversation he had with Count O'Kelly on 22 January 1941, Con Cremin wrote that 'Léon has handed over to Count O'Kelly 19 sealed envelopes to be given to the National Gallery [*sic*] and containing correspondence stretching over the past 10 years.' In fact, Léon handed over a trunk with nineteen envelopes with the proviso that, in the case of his and Joyce's death, the material should go to the National Library of Ireland after the war and remain sealed for fifty years after Joyce's death.[14] When the trunk was opened in 1991, it was found to contain an early draft of *Finnegans Wake* as well as 'items such as postcards and theatre programmes and letters between Joyce and family members and friends during his final years in Paris'.[15] More of Joyce's papers (bar one suitcase) were sent to a lawyer, Maître Charles Gervais, where they remained until 1949, when Joyce's widow, Nora, and Giorgio retrieved them and put them up for sale.

Back in Saint-Gérand-le-Puy, James Joyce tried repeatedly to have Lucia sent to a clinic in Switzerland, where he and Nora planned to join her. While he might not have been interested in holding an Irish passport, the urgency of the moment meant he was not going to forego the benefits Irish citizenship might confer on his sick daughter. Joyce thus wrote a series of feverish letters to the Legation in Vichy, in green ink, asking for its assistance in Lucia's case and expressing his willingness to take up a Legation offer of Irish passports for both her and Giorgio (but not for himself).

Writing from the Hôtel des Lilas in Vichy at the end of August, the Legation drew up a letter of recommendation in English and German, which, it was hoped, would help speed Lucia Joyce's way from the French Atlantic coast to Switzerland. 'Lucia Joyce, single, born Trieste 26th July 1907, undergoing medical treatment for Cyclothymie for past eight years at Clinique Dr Achille Delmas, 25, rue de la Mairie, Ivry-sur-Seine, now Les Charmettes, Pornichet, Loire Inférieure. To be moved, accompanied by male and female nurse, to Burg Hölzli, Irnanstalt, Zurich,' read the letter.[16] It had been written by Seán Murphy, based on an 'informal talk' that he had had with a member of the German embassy during his trip to Paris a few days earlier. But the Germans soon hardened their stance on foreigners travelling in France. On 26 November 1940 Murphy wrote to Joyce in Saint-Gérand-le-Puy to express his 'surprise and disappointment' at a letter received from the German embassy, via Count O'Kelly, stating that it would be impossible to allow Lucia to travel to Switzerland. This was in spite of the assurances he had received in August, when Murphy had been given to understand that 'Lucia's journey would not give rise to any difficulty in spite of her holding a British passport'.[17] It now turned out that Lucia's British passport did cause problems (as a letter of 4 November from the German embassy implied).[18]

On 1 December 1940 Joyce wrote again to Murphy from Saint-Gérand-le-Puy. His writing, still in green ink, was close to illegible. Finding the German attitude 'exasperating', Joyce wrote that Giorgio was going shortly to nearby Vichy 'with various suggestions concerning my daughter's case'.[19] Murphy was ever willing to help, even though the Joyces were British subjects, going so far as writing a note to Seán Lester, acting secretary-general to the ill-fated League of Nations in Geneva, to inform him that Joyce was coming his way and to ask him to provide as much help as he could in getting Lucia out of France. Finally, in mid-December 1940, James, Nora and Giorgio Joyce received news that they had been granted a visa to Switzerland. On 14 December 1940 they crossed the Swiss border and three days later reached Zurich – where they had already sat out the First World War. By contrast, Lucia didn't make it out of occupied France for the duration of the war.

***

While a number of Paris Irish quit the French capital ahead of the Germans' arrival and found it difficult to move back to the city thereafter, at least one well-known Irishman went against the flow. Frank Ryan was a prominent leftist republican, a member of the Irish Republican Army (IRA) and a former editor of *An Phoblacht*. He led the 'Connolly Column', a contingent of Irishmen who fought on the republican side during the Spanish Civil War, before being captured at the end of March 1938. On the night of 15–16 July 1940, in somewhat murky circumstances, he was released by General Franco from prison in Burgos in northern Spain into the hands of agents of the Abwehr (German military intelligence), who valued Ryan's IRA connections. Before being transferred to Germany (where he died of tuberculosis in June 1944), Ryan was driven by Kurt Haller, section leader of Abwehr (II) Amt I West, responsible for espionage operations in Britain and Ireland, from the Spanish border to Paris, where he was to stay for a couple of weeks as a guest of German military intelligence.

Ryan arrived in the French capital on 17 July. He was brought first to the Hôtel Lutetia on the boulevard Raspail, where the

Joyce family had been living a few months before but where the Abwehr had since set up its Paris headquarters. There exists a photo of Ryan from that time stretched out on the grass in a Paris park, perhaps the nearby Jardin du Luxembourg, reading the international press.[20] On the day after his arrival the Abwehr brought Ryan for dinner to La Tour d'Argent, overlooking the Seine, at the time considered one of the finest restaurants in Paris. According to Haller, after the deprivations he had known in Spain in the previous four years, Ryan was 'completely flabbergasted by the whole thing and thought he was dreaming!'[21] Haller also said after the war that Ryan did not spend his entire Paris stay in the Lutetia, but instead 'was accommodated in a country house requisitioned by the Brandenburgers [an elite Wehrmacht unit]'.[22] This is a reference to the Château de la Celle in La Celle Saint Cloud in the western suburbs of Paris, where the Brandenburgers set up a training camp during the summer of 1940.

On 20 July Helmut Clissmann, an Abwehr operative who had lived in Ireland before the war and had been instrumental in Ryan's release, met the Irishman in Paris. But initial German attempts to convince Ryan to embark on a sabotage mission to England came to naught. On 4 August Ryan and Clissmann left Paris together for Berlin, where Ryan met his ideological foe, Seán Russell, who had been head of the IRA's army council before the war. Overcoming their pre-war political differences, Russell and Ryan set off for Ireland in a U-boat from Wilhelmshaven on 8 August, but a landing on the coast of County Galway a few days later was called off after Russell died (apparently from a burst gastric ulcer). The U-boat headed back to Lorient, from where Ryan made his way to Berlin, possibly via Paris. According to Ryan's MI5 file, he was in France again in early 1941, with Breton nationalist leader Guy Vissault de Coëtlogon affirming that he met Ryan in Rennes in February/March 1941.[23] The file mentions also that Ryan met another Breton leader, Olivier

Mordrelle, head of the Breton National Party, in Rennes in December 1940 (Ryan had previously met Mordrelle in Paris in 1937). However, Kurt Haller doubted that any of these meetings ever took place.[24]

De Coëtlogon deserves a brief mention in his own right because of his close links with Irish republicans and his efforts to gather intelligence on Ireland on behalf of the Germans. In 1943 de Coëtlogon worked briefly for Section VI of the SS's Sicherheitsdienst at 11 boulevard Flandrin in the 16th arrondissement, an area of the city where the Nazis based a large part of their security and espionage efforts. Before being given the task of recruiting a sabotage group, de Coëtlogon's duties in Section VI consisted of filing reports from agents in Ireland and newspaper articles of interest. In September 1944 de Coëtlogon was captured by the Americans in Brittany and handed over to the British for interrogation. The Breton told MI5 that the material he received from agents in Ireland 'consisted of such matters as attitude of the people to the American occupation of Ulster, and the activities of the Dáil; anything, in fact, that would prove to the German people that the Propaganda Ministry was completely "au fait" with everything happening in Ireland'.[25] The French executed de Coëtlogon in the spring of 1945.

Abwehr files contain references to one other Irish guest of German military intelligence during 1940. Among the people Abwehr officer Johann Rauh met in Paris towards the end of 1940 was a certain 'Dewett', the cover name for 'an Irishman approximately 1.75m tall, robust, blond, blue eyes, oval face and with a light complexion. He was approximately 35 years old.'[26] The man in question was Joseph Lenihan, born in 1906 in Ennistymon, County Clare and a relation of the Fianna Fáil political dynasty. Lenihan was somewhat disreputable, telling British interrogators that 'he had been involved in an IRA gun-running enterprise as the producer of forged frontier passes, and had served a nine-month sentence on discovery of his enterprise'.[27] After a failed attempt to sail to England from Jersey (where he was working on the potato harvest at the time of the German invasion), he had been enlisted by the Abwehr to train as a wireless-telegraphy operator during the summer of 1940. Lenihan underwent training in The Hague as well as in Paris, where 'he met many Abwehr officers and NCOs from the notorious Hôtel Lutetia and enjoyed the confidence of them all'.[28] While being paid a relatively modest monthly salary of FF1,000, Lenihan attended a six-week course in espionage techniques and meteorology at a German military intelligence training centre at 22 avenue de Versailles in the 16th arrondissement in preparation for a parachute drop into England.[29] During his stay in Paris, Lenihan was locked up in prison, having become involved in a brawl in the bar of the Normandy Hôtel in rue Saint Honoré, close to the Louvre. In his account to British interrogators, Lenihan said that he had been overheard by some German soldiers speaking English, leading one officer to accuse him of being a spy and another to point a pistol at him. 'The insult and menace were too much for Lenihan,' wrote the British report. 'He slapped them down and himself into gaol. His friends at the Lutetia secured his release on the following day.'[30]

An attempt to parachute Lenihan into Ireland in January 1941 was aborted, when the aircraft's heater broke down and Lenihan suffered frostbite, earning him a three-month stay at the Hôpital Beaujon (now called the Hôpital Foch) in Suresnes, outside Paris. Finally, on 17 July 1941, Lenihan was dropped over Summerhill in County Meath. But instead of broadcasting weather forecasts back to occupied Europe, the first aim of his mission, he hid his radio transmitter in a hedge and made his way to Dublin. From there he took a train to Athlone, where he spent some time with friends and family before crossing the border into Northern Ireland to give himself up to the British authorities. British attempts to use Lenihan against his former employers were not wholly successful. According to one of his MI5 handlers, he became very restless and was caught 'joining the crew of a fishing boat leaving Fleetwood … to fish off Donegal'.[31] Lenihan's file states, with no hint of irony, that after he had told the British all he knew, 'he left Ham Common [an MI5 interrogation centre] with a clear conscience, probably to continue in his homeland the legitimate struggle against the British oppressor'.[32]

***

The early weeks of the Occupation turned out to be eventful ones for St Joseph's church on the avenue Hoche in the posh 8th arrondissement of Paris. St Joseph's was an important rallying point for the Irish community and largely run by Irish priests from the Passionist order. Perhaps the most colourful character officiating there at the time was Fr Kenneth Monaghan, who had been appointed to St Joseph's in 1938. Called Michael in civilian life, Monaghan (who was born in Drumcliffe, County Sligo in 1893 and died in Wales in 1969) had already lived a packed life by the time he arrived in Paris. He had served as a commissioned officer in the Rifle Brigade on the Western Front in the First World War. Captured in 1917, he spent the rest of the war in a prisoner-of-war camp in Germany. In the year of his capture, Monaghan's nineteen-year-old brother James was killed when the ship he was serving on was sunk. After his liberation in November 1918, Monaghan joined the British force sent to Archangel to help the White Army fighting against the Bolsheviks, but there too he was captured. He made it back to England as part of a prisoner-of-war exchange and, after a short time working in a bank, decided to enter the priesthood, where he took the name Fr Kenneth.

Monaghan was appointed chaplain in the BEF during the calamitous military campaign of May–June 1940. In June 1940 he seems to have made it with the dregs of the BEF as far as Bordeaux, where he was taken prisoner. Although Seán Murphy intervened, pointing out that Monaghan was Irish by birth and that the Legation was prepared to grant him an Irish passport, he was forced to concede in those early days of the Occupation that 'the Germans ... do not regard us as having any *locus standi* vis à vis them and anything they may do is an act of grace'.[33] Yet, perhaps on foot of the Legation's efforts, Fr Monaghan was released and made his way back to St Joseph's in Paris in the late autumn of 1940.

Along with Fr Monaghan, other Passionists at St Joseph's in 1940 included the community's superior, Fr Cornelius O'Grady (born Ballaghaderreen, County Roscommon, 1890; died London, 1961), and Fr Alphonsus O'Farrell (born Loughrea, County Galway, 1888; died London, 1958). While Fr O'Farrell would, according to his obituary, 'scarcely ever speak about those years', Fr O'Grady was made of sterner stuff.[34] Having previously officiated in Dublin and London, he had been sent to the French capital in the late 1930s and was appointed superior of St Joseph's in 1939. Fr O'Grady, who remained at St Joseph's until 1950, was a highly popular figure. According to his obituary, he 'handled the Germans with tact and courtesy and was rescued from several awkward predicaments by his ready wit', while his 'fluent, though not exactly classical, French was a constant source of amusement' for his French entourage.[35] The obituary further asserts that the war years saw O'Grady 'at his best' and that, at a time of strict rationing, he could sometimes be seen 'tramping across Paris and climbing steep stairs to take a few eggs or a little butter to a poor Irish or English governess'. These sentiments are echoed by Con Cremin, first secretary at the Legation, who mentioned in one of his reports to Dublin that Fr O'Grady was doing a lot to alleviate the financial distress of the Irish colony in Paris.

St Joseph's survived the aggressive anti-clericalism of the French government in the early 1900s. During this troubled time for French Catholicism, the Passionists managed to have the church placed under the official protection of the British government, which meant that it was not expropriated by the French state and that, unlike other congregations, the Passionists were not forced to leave France. But in 1940 the official protection provided by the British government meant that the church aroused German interest. Even leaving aside the British protection that St Joseph's enjoyed, the Germans had every reason to be suspicious of the priests who officiated there, as Fr Monaghan and Fr O'Grady were both British-passport holders.

Fr Monaghan's role during the war remains murky. After the war, the US authorities recognised that the priests at St Joseph's had helped Allied escapees during the Occupation and, according to some accounts, Fr Monaghan even served as a liaison officer between the British secret services and the French Resistance.[36] Certainly, he seems to have used his status and origins to get away with activities that would have been impossible for almost any other English speaker in Paris at the time.

In August 1940 the large drop in his congregation (and in money from the collection box) was making Fr O'Grady anxious, as was the fate of Fr Monaghan, who had not yet been released by the Germans. An impromptu visit from the German authorities constituted a further worry. Motivated by the perception that St Joseph's was an English church, the Germans sealed a number of rooms in the presbytery with the intention of examining their contents in the coming days. But things took a turn for the better for St Joseph's when the chaplain-general of the Wehrmacht, who was residing in a hotel opposite the church and who came on several occasions to say mass there, intervened to have the seals broken.

The staff of Irish Passionists (including Fr Monaghan) would soldier on throughout the Occupation, during which time St Joseph's became the main focus point for the Irish community in Paris.

***

In early July 1940 a semblance of organisation began to emerge in newly defeated France with the establishment of the État français, run out of Vichy and supported by various right-wing and far-right supporters of Philippe Pétain. Ahead of the convening of the French parliament on 9 July to declare Pétain head of the État français, officials endeavoured to find accommodation in the spa town for foreign diplomatic missions. This involved requisitioning the town's numerous hotels, with the Irish Legation briefly assigned to cramped quarters in the small Hôtel des Lilas on avenue Victoria.

Before taking up residence in the new seat of government in Vichy, Seán Murphy sent a long message to Dublin from La Bourboule on 8 July. This thoughtful report, which attempted to give an insight into the mood of the French people and its leaders right after France's surrender, begins with some carefully chosen words: 'The result of the war seems to be accepted without active discontent.' Although Murphy conveyed the view of most of the French press that 'France may become a great power in a very short time', he thought that there was 'a distinct possibility of the French Government and public cherishing illusions as to France's future', and asserted that, 'There is no doubt that France's defeat is in a large measure due to the rot which seems to have pervaded all French life for years past.' And with the experience of his flight from Paris still fresh in his mind, Murphy told Dublin that in France 'the public administration must have been one of the most inefficient in the world, as far as getting work done was concerned. The war only brought into relief the defects of the system.'[37]

Murphy then turned to mundane matters, describing the

complete breakdown of French civilian administration, including the French foreign ministry, in June 1940. Recalling the problems he had had finding accommodation in Bordeaux, he was of the opinion that the delegations of Allied nations were treated far better than the Irish Legation. Indeed, whether in the case of the supposed fall-back premises for the Legation in Tours, or in the gallivanting across central France in the aftermath of the French defeat, the French government seemed to have little regard for Ireland's diplomatic representatives.

Yet Murphy managed to meet top Vichy officials quickly. He met Charles Roux, secretary-general of the Foreign Office, on 15 July 1940, twelve days after the British attacked the French fleet at Mers-el-Kébir. (Since the French ships had been disarmed under the terms of the armistice with Germany, the French had had no way to defend themselves. The French lamented the deaths of 1,300 men that day against the deaths of two British airmen.) Murphy also met Admiral François Darlan, who was to rise to become *de facto* prime minister of the Vichy regime for a time, before being progressively sidelined in 1942 (and assassinated in Algiers in December of that year). When Murphy met him in the summer of 1940, Darlan was still head of the French navy and Minister of the Marine. Over lunch with Murphy on 27 August, the admiral, still smarting from the British attack at Mers-el-Kébir the previous month, opined that Winston Churchill was an 'irascible drunkard' and that 'British admiralty tactics had not changed for the past 100 years'.[38]

Dublin showed great interest in the new regime being established in Vichy. Some in Ireland wanted to curry favour with the regime, in the belief 'that Britain has lost the war and at very most could only achieve a stalemate which might leave her part of her Empire, but it is recognised everywhere that she has no hope of regaining her influence in Europe', according to a note to Vichy from Joseph Walshe in Dublin. Walshe went on to write that 'the sympathy of whole country is with Pétain … It is felt here that our destiny henceforth will be cast with that of continental Catholic nations. At this present stage, it is to be expected that France should have internal difficulties. The results of Front Popular regime which destroyed France cannot disappear overnight.'[39]

The disruption caused by invasion and defeat meant that shortages were already the order of the day. According to the oil tycoon Nubar Gulbenkian – who visited his father, Calouste, in Vichy in late summer 1940 – responsibility for distributing the monthly petrol ration the Vichy government allotted to foreign diplomats was given to the doyen of the diplomatic corps, the papal nuncio.[40] But in reality, the task fell to a young priest and to Con Cremin. Indeed, Cremin, his equivalent at the Argentinian embassy and a representative of the apostolic nunciature formed a committee that met each morning in the Hôtel du Parc, seat of the Vichy government, with a view to centralising fuel requests from the various diplomatic missions and forwarding them to the authorities.

Meanwhile, it was decided (apparently without much consultation with Dublin) that the best man to look after Irish affairs in the occupied zone was Count Gerald O'Kelly de Gallagh. By the end of July, thanks to his ambiguous status as 'minister plenipotentiary, special counsellor to the Legation' (plus a liberal use of bluster, which he had raised to an art form over the years), O'Kelly managed to get back to Paris – a feat that Ireland's top representative, Seán Murphy, was unable to replicate. In early August Murphy informed Dublin that foreign diplomats were forbidden from crossing the Demarcation Line that the Germans had just established between occupied France and the *zone libre*. Murphy had been unaware of this ban when he had set out for Paris on 3 August with the Lithuanian ambassador and the papal nuncio, Valerio Valeri. The diplomats got as far as Moulins, less than sixty kilometres north of Vichy, when German officials told them that special authorisation was needed if they were to cross the nearby Demarcation Line. After a fruitless wait for this authorisation to come through by telephone, Murphy turned back towards Vichy.

As soon as he had returned to Paris, the ever-capable O'Kelly set about trying to convince the Germans to grant permission for his two colleagues from the Legation (Murphy and Con Cremin) to travel to Paris to check up on the Irish community left behind there and on the state of the Legation's premises in rue de Villejust. Relatively quickly, O'Kelly managed to organise a permit for Murphy and Cremin to spend five days in Paris, from Saturday 17 August to Thursday 22 August 1940. Travelling by car from Vichy, Murphy told Dublin that 'there is little sign along the road of extensive havoc wrought by the war. Apart from some partially broken bridges and rather extensive damage … to the aerodrome at Orly, about six miles south of Paris, I noticed nothing in particular.' Murphy and Cremin were stopped at a number of checkpoints, but they got through the last one, some thirty kilometres before Paris, 'with little delay'.[41]

According to a message sent to Dublin on his return to Vichy, when he arrived in the French capital Murphy went straight to the Legation premises at rue de Villejust, where he found everything intact, including the Irish tricolour he had left flying in front of the building on 11 June. The day after their arrival, Cremin and Murphy called on Fr Travers, who was back in Paris, as well as Fr O'Grady at St Joseph's and Fr Francis Griffin from County Clare, a member of the Holy Ghost order (who was still in Paris in the early 1950s). Murphy also visited a certain 'Sister Olivia and community'. The plenipotentiary brought Fr O'Grady and Fr O'Farrell from St Joseph's, Fr Travers from the Irish College and Monsignor Bartoli, secretary to the apostolic nunciature, to lunch on 19 August, along with O'Kelly and Cremin.

In his 27 August report to the DEA in Dublin, Murphy

judged that the most striking feature about Paris during his visit
there was 'by far its relative emptiness'. Murphy quoted an official
estimate that at the beginning of July 1940 the population of the
city had dropped to just over one million from a total pre-war
population of close to three million (by way of comparison, the
modern-day population of Paris is about 2.2 million). Apart from
the Champs Elysées, wrote Murphy, 'the streets on the whole …
had a very empty air'.[42]

Somehow, between seeing people at the Legation, Murphy
managed to squeeze in a visit to the Irish College on rue des
Irlandais on 20 August. Bar Fr Travers, the college was deserted
at this stage. Unlike St Joseph's, it had not been visited by the
German authorities since their takeover of the city on 14 June. But,
by sheer coincidence, while Murphy was talking to Fr Travers at
the college after lunch, a German officer accompanied by soldiers
and a French civilian came to inspect the premises with a view to
installing some of his men there. The Frenchman tried to impress
on the German officer that the college was British property. But
Murphy and Fr Travers countered that the Irish College was the
property of the Irish bishops, who used it to lodge ecclesiastical
students 'at present on holiday', and that Ireland was not at war
with Germany. Fr Travers thought that the German 'got tired of
the argument' and 'went away under the impression that we were
expecting students back in September'.[43] Murphy then gave Fr
Travers a signed document in Irish, French and German to post
on the door stating that the college was Irish property.

There were no subsequent attempts by the Germans to requisition the college during the war. But various French organisations sought to get their hands on it, especially as the destruction wrought by bombardments and the lack of any new building
activity meant that France in general and Paris in particular faced
an acute housing crisis during the war. The Irish bishops did give
permission to a French seminary to use the premises, but be-

cause of what Fr Travers termed 'various difficulties', the permission was never availed of. However, local air-raid wardens did store equipment there, while Fr Travers allowed the authorities to use some of the college rooms to store emergency food supplies. 'Apart from the fact that it was for a humanitarian purpose,' wrote Fr Travers, 'it also ensured that the place was not sought for less desirable purposes.'[44]

Within days of seeing off the half-hearted attempt to requisition the Irish College, Fr Travers received a visit from another German officer, but this time from one who came in a personal capacity. The officer, Franz Born, told the priest that he had spent fifteen years as an 'organist and professor of music in Carlow'. Born, who had taught music at St Mary's, a seminary school in Knockbeg, County Laois, not far from Carlow, was organist at Carlow Cathedral and is described in an article entitled 'Knockbeg in the Nineteen Thirties' as 'a splendid upstanding German … who spoke as if he had never left his native Prussia. He had a gentle face, but no capacity to communicate love of his subject.'[45] According to Fr Travers, 'he was a very nice fellow. He told me that he had a bet with a fellow officer of six bottles of champagne that the Germans would be in London in three weeks. He was bubbling over with optimism.' Born was enthusiastic about Hitler and couldn't understand why the Irish disliked him. But while he supported the regime (he had become a Nazi Party member in 1937), 'he did not like the Nazi methods; for instance, in the way they influenced and controlled his own children'.[46]

Born was in charge of prisoner interrogation for the Wehrmacht, a task that should have given him some insight into the war. Yet, over several conversations with the man, Fr Travers concluded that 'on a number of important things in the course of the war his knowledge was lacking'. Travers saw the German before he set off to partake in the Russian campaign in the second half of 1941 and again after he had spent a winter there. But when

Travers saw Born next in the course of 1942, 'he was a changed man physically. Though still confident of the outcome of the war, he did not minimise the hardships the Germans themselves had to bear.' Travers saw Born one last time, six months before D-Day in 1944, by which stage the latter was convinced that Germany would lose the war. Born, according to Fr Travers, died of a heart attack before Germany's unconditional surrender in May 1945.

***

On his return to Paris at the end of July 1940, O'Kelly began to receive visits from numerous Irish people left in Paris 'who were anxious to obtain Irish papers so as to avoid difficulties with the German authorities'.[47] These people were all informed to turn up at the embassy on rue de Villejust on 19 and 20 August, during Murphy and Cremin's visit. An advertisement was to be placed in *Le Petit Parisien* to this effect (although an archival search suggests no such notice appeared). Murphy and Cremin also tried to convince the Passionists at St Joseph's to use their influence to persuade the Paris Irish to take out Irish passports.

Murphy broached the issue of passports in a telegram he sent to Dublin on 23 August, a day after he arrived back in Vichy. In the telegram, Murphy covered much the same ground as in another message to Dublin four days later, but provided more detail on the Paris Irish he had met. He said he found the Paris Irish to be worried, but holding up. 'The majority of them though born in Ireland hold British passports and are now very anxious to obtain Irish passports,' he wrote. The telegram continues:

> Although they are not likely to be interned they have to report daily. I took applications for passports and registration and promised to issue passports valid for one year renewable gratis when registration affected. The majority are living on small savings and will soon be destitute. In most cases relatives in Ireland will not be able to assist

them: others have no relatives there. Stock of passports exhausted. I consequently propose to have document printed here which will state that it is exchangeable for normal national passport as soon as circumstances permit.[48]

With travel for Irish diplomats between Vichy and Paris difficult, a certain amount of latitude was given to O'Kelly as Ireland's 'special counsellor' to verify candidates for these locally printed one-year passports.[49]

In spite of the concerns about losing access to funds sent from Britain via American organisations still in Paris, the number of applicants for Irish passports steadily grew. On 8 January 1941, for example, O'Kelly informed the Legation in Vichy that he was sending down 100 applications for passports. (Some of these were for nuns who did not wish to pay for the documents on the grounds of poverty – but Murphy was deaf to their pleas.)[50] Anybody considered apt for registration in the eyes of the Legation, after producing an appropriate document such as a birth certificate, was granted a one-year passport until registration formalities and background checks had been completed. But these temporary passports could be renewed for a further year when the registration process had been completed. A 'guarantor' was generally needed to vouch for the *bona fides* of the applicant – a role that, in some cases, O'Kelly seems to have assumed himself.

The system of guarantors was ineffective in preventing abuse, for there are several instances of one-year passports being granted on very dubious grounds. By contrast, there are also cases of individuals who could legitimately lay claim to an Irish passport having great difficulty in obtaining one because of stalling by Legation officials. Some people who applied for Irish passports were rejected either due to the lack of Irish parentage or, in the case of women, because they had surrendered their original passports upon marriage to take the nationality of their husbands. The question of passports was a constant cause of disagreement throughout the war.

There can be little doubt that O'Kelly was anxious to help as many people as he could in the early months of the Occupation, when internment of British nationals was the order of the day. But his dispensing of temporary one-year passports raised eyebrows among the German authorities as much as among the DEA back in Dublin. Indeed, the practice of granting one-year documents to people who had simply 'applied for registration' was an extraordinarily liberal way to distribute valuable neutral-country passports. The lack of stock of Irish passports 'of the normal kind' meant that O'Kelly distributed a large number of the 'special form of passport' of local design. A stop was put to the practice by the DEA in March 1941, after which only full passports were issued to properly registered citizens.

Many of the new applicants for Irish passports had lived frugal lives before the war, but their financial difficulties increased significantly as the Occupation curtailed normal economic activity and links to financial lifelines back home were cut. The Irish authorities were acutely aware of these problems, but only slowly put in place mechanisms to help. To start, in the autumn of 1940, the DEA decided it needed a list of names and addresses of Irish passport holders who were stuck in France and might need special assistance for the duration of hostilities. This led the Legation in Vichy to approach Fr O'Grady in St Joseph's to gather the names of Parisian Irish in need. Fr O'Grady himself had a British passport that had expired. He was entitled to an Irish one but turned down the offer, at least for the time being, 'as the fact of his holding a British passport enables him to get funds … from the American embassy (as representing British interests), whereas this recourse would be closed to him if he held an Irish passport'.[51] However, within a few months, following a brief internment by the German authorities, Fr O'Grady had changed his mind, duly completing a Declaration of Nationality towards the end of 1940.

Gathering the names of Parisian Irish in need proved no simple matter. A letter from Fr O'Grady dated 7 October 1940 seems to contradict Murphy's contention that the majority of the Parisian Irish were 'very anxious' to obtain Irish passports. 'For some reason, which I am quite unable to explain, I got the idea that you wanted the names of nationals who were without means of subsistence,' wrote Fr O'Grady to the Legation:

> That, in itself, was simple enough, but when those concerned understood that I was sending the names to you and through you to the authorities at home there was a regular howl of disapproval. Under no circumstances would they consent to have their names made public even though starvation was the alternative. It mattered not at all that there would be no publicity. Their pride, which we can all understand, even if we do not approve, would not consent.[52]

In any case, claimed Fr O'Grady, the Irish were not too badly off:

> Strictly speaking, there are very few around Paris who are without means of subsistence for the reason that most of them have British passports and are receiving help through the American Embassy Red Cross Fund. It is only those who have Irish passports who are denied this assistance and of those there are few without some means of living.

Yet, while Fr O'Grady estimated there were only 'perhaps ten or twelve who are on the rocks', he was of the opinion that all the Paris Irish, whether they held British or Irish passports, 'are amply living on the margin line'. The allowance from the Red Cross was, he said, 'scarcely sufficient' to cover their modest needs and did not cover their rents. Consequently, wrote Fr O'Grady, 'many of them, while able to procure food, are terribly behind on the payment of their rooms. In a few of the worst cases, I have succeeded in getting an increase for them. In all, there are from fifty to sixty that we know of and occasionally a new one turns up.' Worried as Fr O'Grady was about the situation of the Irish in Paris in October 1940, one other matter concerned him greatly: 'What will happen if America comes into the war?'[53]

The autumn of 1940 saw the first appearance of Una Whyte on the radar screen of the Legation, when she applied for a new passport. Whyte, who was living at 23 rue de Naples in the 8th arrondissement at that time, reported that a couple of months earlier her passport had been stolen from her bicycle, which she had parked at the entrance of the Académie Colarossi, the prestigious art academy in Montparnasse where she had been enrolled in drawing classes since the beginning of 1939. Whyte had travelled back to Paris in January 1940 for a new term at the Académie Colarossi after a Christmas spent at home. As her decision to return to Paris in the midst of the Phoney War and subsequent events would indicate, Whyte (born in Cashel, County Tipperary, in 1916, but brought up by a land-owning family in the townland of Greenaun near Dromahair, County Leitrim) was a rather whimsical, headstrong young lady. In recounting her visit to the Legation premises, O'Kelly, in September 1940, said he found her 'genuine but original. I took her for a boy when she came in' and noted, 'she is a queer dour creature but I think her yarn is true'.[54]

***

By the autumn of 1940 Irish people in France were facing detention as well as destitution. Those who carried British passports or whose status as Irish citizens was in some doubt could be detained by the Germans as enemy aliens. The French police made ample use of increasingly xenophobic legislation that had been introduced in the late 1930s in reaction to an influx of refugees from eastern Europe and from the Spanish Civil War. Thus, a 12 November 1938 decree allowed for the internment of foreign 'undesirables' in special centres. A year later, on 18 November 1939, a further decree was passed that extended the threat of internment to 'individuals dangerous for national defence and public safety'. Such measures gave the police latitude to lock up any foreigner they considered a menace to public order or national security, not only foreigners who had actually committed a crime. Legislation even allowed the police to incarcerate any foreigner found without an identity card or a proper residence permit.

Adam Lang, a Dubliner, was to find out just how stringent French legislation had become. In a rapid succession of letters that betrayed his desperation, Lang wrote to the Legation in Vichy from the internment camp at Argelès-sur-Mer in French Catalonia, close to the Spanish border. This camp had been set up by the French to house an influx of refugees after the final defeat of republican forces in the Spanish Civil War at the beginning of 1939. But Lang found himself at Argelès because he had tried to get into Spain, not out of it. His file card mentions he had been picked up and arrested on 8 August 1940 at Le Boulou, a railhead in the Pyrenees close to the Spanish border and just twenty kilometres from Argelès.[55]

Lang sent his first letter to the Legation shortly after his arrival at the Argelès camp. Cogently, and in a very neat hand, Lang explained that the French police had picked him up because he had no passport:[56]

My identity I cannot prove, for all my papers were aboard my ship *River Clyde* when I left her in Le Havre on 29 May, because when I left the ship, without leave, to celebrate winning 1,000 francs at cards, I became involved in a fight with the 2nd engineer and I hit him in the face with a bottle, so rather than face imprisonment I left for Rouen. It was being evacuated so I went to Evreux, then circled Paris to the South and stayed in an evacuated house until the Armistice. I then entered Paris to find the Legation closed.[57]

After a fruitless detour to the American embassy, and with his money gone, Lang decided to make for Spain and had gotten as far as Le Boulou, less than ten kilometres from the border. Although the French police in Paris had apparently issued him with some sort of transit document, he was detained and brought to Argelès. All that Lang wanted from the Legation was a passport for, he said, 'I shall be only too pleased to say good-bye to this place.'[58]

He explained that he had been born in Dublin on 4 November 1901 and that his parents (both born in Dublin, he claimed) had been living at 9 High Street in Balbriggan at the foundation of the Irish Free State. Well versed in the conditions he needed to meet to obtain an Irish passport, Lang admitted that his 'periods in Ireland have been brief [between] leaves from ships, and jobs in Scotland and London'.[59] He had been around two years in Ireland in total since the creation of the Irish Free State in 1922, having worked in Britain since the age of nineteen. He had also worked as a gardener at Hyde Park in London for over two years but claimed he had been sacked in 1938 because of his Irish origins. He had worked on a small steamer called the *Dinard Castle* until April 1940, when he joined the crew of the *River Clyde*.

In a letter dated 11 September 1940, the Legation in Vichy gave a cautious response to Lang's request for papers. The Legation would, said the letter, be prepared to issue him a passport if he could satisfy the Legation that 'if in possession of a travel document you would have a reasonable prospect of returning to Ireland'.[60]

Considering that the wheels of officialdom were moving too

slowly, Lang kept bombarding the Legation with missives in his neat handwriting. On 17 September he replied from the camp infirmary to the Legation's letter, explaining that he had been in contact with the American Friends Society (the Quakers) in nearby Perpignan about getting back home. If he obtained a passport from the Legation plus a visa for Spain, he had no doubt he could make it to Ireland, where he was engaged to be married. Four days later, on 21 September, he wrote again, after he had once again been in contact with the Quakers. The latter had told Lang that there were ships leaving from Lisbon for England. Lang would need money from the Legation to get to Lisbon, but he promised he would refund all sums granted, suggesting he could go back to work immediately on the trawlers that operated out of the Isle of Bute, where he had worked before the war.

On 24 September Lang wrote again, this time to explain that he had been unable to find any money to pay for passport photographs. By now, he was dependent on his Spanish co-detainees for succour. 'This is pretty hard on them,' Lang wrote, 'for they have so little themselves.'[61] Informed of Lang's plight, the Legation sent him the money for passport photographs. But then, in a letter to the Legation on 11 October, Lang recognised that an Irish passport in itself would not be enough to get him out of France. He would need Spanish and Portuguese visas as well – not forgetting money for transportation.

Almost a month later, Lang was still in Argelès. He wrote to the Legation on 5 November to express his disappointment that he had had no word since he had sent the required passport photos to Vichy. Finally, on 30 November, Seán Murphy replied to Lang's plans. He could issue a passport only upon payment of a fee (FF111). Murphy would have been prepared to make an exception, but he confirmed Lang's fears that a passport would not be enough to help him get through Spain. Without all the necessary visas and without financial means, it was highly likely that Lang would be imprisoned in Spain, Murphy wrote. Even supposing Lang managed to travel through Spain, it was unlikely the Portuguese would grant Lang an entry visa to Portugal unless he had booked his passage from Lisbon in advance. The best course of action that Murphy could see was for Lang to arrange with friends and relatives in Ireland to contact the DEA in Dublin and have them make the necessary travel arrangements. That is all we hear of Adam Lang in the archives. By late 1940 a number of nationalities were being repatriated from Argelès camp, and by the end of 1941 it was closed as a place of internment. Lang was probably fortunate to have jumped ship in Le Havre, for HM trawler *River Clyde* was blown up by a mine on 4 August 1940.[62]

Lang was not the only Irish sailor to suffer internment. On 4 September 1940 the *Luimneach*, an unescorted Irish steamer belonging to the Limerick Steam Ship Company that plied the route between Drogheda and Huelva in south-western Spain, was sunk by U-46 in the Bay of Biscay. One man died in the attack, but the rest of the crew escaped in two lifeboats. One of the lifeboats was picked up by a Spanish trawler and brought to Spain, while the other, containing five Irish passport holders, three British passport holders and one Belgian, was rescued by a French fishing boat and brought to western France.

In an account he wrote for RTÉ after the war, a crewman from the *Luimneach*, sixty-five-year-old Dubliner John Edward Confrey (a veteran mariner, who had served on the battle cruiser *Princess Royal* during the Battle of Jutland in 1916), described how he was landed at Port-Louis, at the entrance to the port of Lorient, on the night of 8 September 1940, and then was brought into Lorient itself. The Irishmen were interrogated in Lorient and 'marched about from place to place as hostages' until they were placed, on 9 September, in the stables of a French cavalry barracks 'without anything in it only some dirty loose straw and a few dirty army rugs or blankets'. The crewmen were given some coffee substitute 'without sugar or milk and a couple of loaves which we could not cut with a knife' and he was 'almost frozen to death with the cold'. The following day the *Luimneach* survivors were brought to Vannes, a town east of Lorient, where they were given 'some warm pea soup', and then to the village of Saint-Avé, where the nine men were placed in an internment camp, a place that Confrey described as 'reeking with sickness, no medical attention or drugs. People falling dead, bad food, bad accommodation, large wooden huts about 30 in each hut.' Conditions were so bad there that after a couple of weeks two trainloads of internees were taken to a different camp at a place he called Montréal (actually Montreuil-Bellay in the Loire valley, which was used as an internment camp for foreigners early in the war before being used to detain itinerants and gypsies). Food was bad in this camp, which housed a large number of Jews and was rife with 'sickness and death' according to Confrey. Finally, at the end of October, a trainload of internees, including the men from the *Luimneach*, was taken to the Grande Caserne, a French military barracks in Saint-Denis, just outside Paris ('about as far from Paris as Bray from Dublin', in the words of John Confrey), which the Germans had transformed into an internment camp.

Conditions in Saint-Denis were much better for the crewmen and for the 1,700 or so other internees that Confrey estimated were being held there. There were plenty of British and Irish doctors and the Red Cross was able to bring in supplies. Count O'Kelly was able to call upon the FF10,000 given to him by John Francis Keane – a businessman friend of his and an ex-internee at Saint-Denis – to buy bread and cigarettes for the shipwrecked sailors (as well as for other Irish detainees), while Janie McCarthy paid regular visits to the internees. Even better, the five *Luimneach* crewmen from the Irish Free State were 'liberated as prisoners at large in Paris' according to Confrey, while O'Kelly arranged for them to be repatriated.

But it was not until the end of January 1941 that these men were sent home to Ireland via Lisbon. It took them five days to travel by train from Paris to Lisbon, including two days when officials who deemed their travel documents were out of date held them up at the Spanish border. They finally left Lisbon for Ireland by boat on 23 February. But of the five that set out from Portugal, only four arrived back in Ireland almost two months later, on 16 April, after a long stay-over in England. Ordinary seaman John Moran from Scattery Island in the Shannon estuary did not make it because, according to Confrey, he 'lost his mind on board of [*sic*] ship coming home and had to be put under restraint for the safety of himself and others as well'. He was sent to an asylum in Scotland. Once back in Ireland, Confrey himself joined another ship, the *Irish Beech*, which plied the waters between Ireland and England from 1941 to the end of the war, in between expeditions to Newfoundland.[63]

The Germans did not release two other members of the *Luimneach* crew (Nazareno Batello from Malta, and E. Richards from Bristol) because they held British passports. The *Luimneach*'s chief officer, John McKelvey from Belfast, also had a British passport, but after his detention at Saint-Denis with the other crew members, he was neither sent to a prisoner-of-war camp nor repatriated. Instead, because of his advanced age (he was sixty-six in 1940), McKelvey was left to fend for himself in Paris for the next four years. During his forced sojourn there, McKelvey seems to have relied on help from various social services and the occasional Red Cross package. In March 1942 a telegram from the Legation to Dublin described McKelvey as being in 'good health' and living at the Hôtel de Nantes at 7 rue Denis Poisson in the 17th arrondissement.[64]

Because it was written in the heat of the moment, a carefully typed letter from the pugnacious Arnold Kerney is one of the best accounts of the circumstances in which many Irish people were rounded up and interned in Saint-Denis. Kerney (brother of the Irish ambassador to Madrid, Leopold Kerney) was married to an Englishwoman and working as an accountant for American Express when war broke out. He was picked up by the Germans at his home in Louveciennes in the wealthy western suburbs of Paris at 10.30 a.m. on Tuesday 8 October 1940. A few days after being released on 17 October, an obviously vexed Kerney wrote the following account of his brief misadventure to the Legation:

> I presented my Irish passport but they refused to accept this as a reason for not arresting me. The soldier speaking English said he was only taking me to Versailles to have my papers verified so I expected to be immediately brought before a superior officer there and be immediately liberated. This was not done. I was brought to the German Police Depot in the Versailles region on the road to Vaucresson and kept in a room without any food or drink till 7.00 p.m. when on our making signs of hunger to sentry, we were supplied with a plate of soup and some bread. At 8.00 p.m. we were marched up to the officer in charge at the main entrance and placed in an autocar. While we were taking our seats, I broke rank and spoke to the officer in charge in company with a fellow prisoner, Mr O'Driscoll, another Irishman. We presented our Irish passports and explained our case, that as neutrals we were not liable to arrest, seeing that in our country German citizens are free, in spite of tremendous pressure by the Churchill government to force us to fight for England.
>
> He paid no attention to this explanation, which was carefully put to him by an English-speaking officer.
>
> We were then sent out to Fresnes. There we were not admitted, so were driven in to Paris and after various peregrinations were lined up before the Rue du Cherche Midi prison. There again they would not take us in, so [we] were driven to Versailles prison, where also admittance was refused, and were then taken back to our original arrest station.

It was then about 12.00 midnight and there we hung about for an hour when we were again put in the autocar and driven back to Versailles prison and admitted.

There the officials explained that all the cells were occupied by five civilian prisoners, all hardened prisoners, not fit to associate with us, and as no accommodation was to be had, we were forced to sleep on the bare stone floor, no blankets or bedding being supplied. As I had come away without any overcoat or anything in the way of covering, and am 53 years old, I suffered considerably during the night and still have twinges in my loins.

Wednesday, Oct. 9th:

We were taken to the Grande Caserne, St Denis (Seine) and there interned with the English prisoners in spite of our protests to every German officer we came across in the course of our examination.

Thursday, Oct. 10th:

Not permitted to approach any German officer or communicate with anyone outside.

Friday, Oct. 11th:

In walking through the ground floor corridor, I was accosted by an officer who told me he was the Colonel in charge of the Camp. I at once saluted him by removing my hat and had a very friendly talk with this gentleman who speaks English fluently, and like every other German officer I came into contact with, was courteous and polite.

However he refused to take any action when I told him that as an Irish citizen, I should be immediately liberated; saying I must put a demand in writing to the committee of Englishmen dealing with the internal affairs of the camp. This committee is composed of prisoners chosen among themselves. I at once explained that as an Irishman I objected strongly to being forced to apply to any English organisation in my discussion with the German military authorities and pointed out that the English do not care a damn how many Irishmen are imprisoned, being very angry with us for not joining in their war and helping to fight their battles.

The worthy colonel did not seem to understand this point of view and walked away.

Saturday, Oct. 12th:

I wrote to my wife but was forced to hand this to the English Committee (letter not delivered on Oct. 18th). Still not allowed outside communications.

Sunday, Oct. 13th:

Mr O'Driscoll's daughter looking for her father came to this caserne and insisted on seeing one of the officers. This gentleman understood our position at once and sent for O'Driscoll who then told him I was also there.

Monday, Oct. 14th:

The above mentioned officer sent for O'Driscoll and myself and had a cordial conversation to the effect that he had put our case before the higher authorities. Two parcels arrived from my wife who probably found all prisoners were here, but was not allowed to see me, nor was I allowed to see her.

Tuesday, Oct. 15th:

We are still in prison, surrounded by Englishmen. I have not yet seen my wife or anyone from outside, no visits being permitted to me.

Wednesday, Oct. 16th:

At 5.30 p.m. brought to the Officer who had a German in civil [*sic*] dress with him. I was very cordially received and told I was free and would get an official certificate ensuring me from further mistakes of this sort.

I thanked them, told a few of my experiences for which they expressed surprise and in view of the lateness of the hour and the necessity of packing up, getting across Paris and catching a train on the reduced St Lazare service, decided to stop overnight in the Camp and leave after breakfast on the Thursday morning.

Thursday, Oct. 17th, 9.00 a.m.:

The above mentioned officer handed me my pass which is so worded as to guarantee me against further blunders by the authorities and told me I was free.

I thanked him, but pointed out that as they had brought me from my home they should logically convey me back there, seeing they had confessed to having made a mistake. I was informed this could not be done, so I got home as best I could by my own means.[65]

Brief as his confinement was, Kerney stated that he had been so incensed by the experience that he demanded FF200 in relation to his 'illegal arrest and detention by the German military authorities'. The FF200, he wrote, was to cover 'out of pocket expenses incurred by my wife who had to make four separate journeys to Paris, take her meals there, trace my whereabouts, go to St Denis, have her meals in Paris'. The amount was also 'for my extra expenses providing my transport back from St

Denis and three separate journeys to Paris in reference to this affair, necessitating meals in Paris'. Kerney wrote that his claim 'obviously should be settled at once, and without prejudice to my further claim for illegal arrest and detention, and the various indignities suffered ... which I trust will be met in the same cordial and amicable spirit as has characterised all personal contacts with German officers'.[66]

After release Arnold Kerney was left unperturbed in Louveciennes for the rest of the Occupation, but his wife, Amy, who held a British passport, was sent to the internment camp in Besançon in December 1940. Throughout the Occupation, Kerney's brother Leopold sent him parcels of food and clothing via the consular bag to Vichy. From Vichy, the goods were ferried to Paris by Count O'Kelly.[67] On 26 August 1944, a day after Paris was officially liberated, the Germans exploded an ammunition barge on the Seine close to Kerney's house in Louveciennes. The house was badly damaged in the explosion, forcing Kerney to retreat to the home of an Irish friend in Brittany, where he spent the winter of 1944–1945.

The Kerney incident of October 1940 had some positive repercussions for Irish detainees in general. A few days after her husband had been taken away by the Germans, Mrs Kerney had called on O'Kelly in Paris and, in the latter's words in a letter to Vichy, 'made a big fuss about it and took the opportunity to raise again the whole question of the attitude of the military authorities to Irish citizens'. Throughout the autumn of 1940, the 'fuss' created around Arnold Kerney enabled O'Kelly to get a number of other Irishmen liberated from internment at Saint-Denis. These included Mr O'Driscoll, mentioned in Kerney's letter to the Legation, and three acquaintances of O'Kelly – businessmen John Francis Keane, shipping agent John Kirwan and retired journalist Joseph Barrett Brandreth. Furthermore O'Kelly stated that he was sure he would soon be able to spring four other Irishmen from Saint-Denis (John Pilkington, Victor Collins and two individuals called O'Dare and Brenan-Hyde). Another detainee, Fr Monaghan of St Joseph's, was not in Saint-Denis, but 'the order for his liberation had been issued', according to O'Kelly.[68]

Release from internment was not necessarily the end of vexations for the Irish. Ex-internees were expected to sign on at a designated police station or military outpost every day. Thus, Mr O'Dare wrote to the Legation in the autumn of 1942 to complain that since he had been released from detention in October 1940, he had had to turn up at the nearest police station at ten o'clock every morning to sign his name. 'If I was to start work my employer would look at me by asking him to leave for one hour everyday.'[69]

Some better-connected internees used their own levers of influence to gain release from detention. Francis O'Dea had been picked up by the Germans in late 1940 and interned in the military barracks at Saint-Denis because he held a British passport. But O'Dea was also a chartered accountant and a partner in the international audit firm Lybrand, Ross Brothers & Montgomery. Thus, unlike other detainees, he could call on support from highly articulate professional contacts. In early 1941 the Lybrand head office in New York prepared food parcels to be sent to O'Dea via the Red Cross and wrote to one of its client firms, the Switzerland-based chemical company Sandoz, to intercede with the Legation based on O'Dea's claims to Irish nationality 'by reason of his ancestry'. O'Dea, who was working in the Lybrand office on the boulevard des Italiens when the Germans arrived in June 1940, had been born in Glasgow of an Irish father (from County Clare). He had had a wide-ranging international career, having left Europe for the United States in 1929, but had returned to Europe in 1935 to take up a posting with Lybrand, first in Berlin and subsequently in Paris. Lybrand need not have worried too much about O'Dea, for even as the firm was writing to Sandoz and organising food parcels for him, O'Kelly had already decided to grant him a temporary Irish passport, which was enough to get him out of Saint-Denis. In October 1941, before he departed with his wife for the United States via Lisbon, Francis O'Dea left FF10,000 with the Legation for the relief of distressed Irish nationals in France – in recognition of the efforts undertaken by the Legation on his behalf.

***

Among the Paris Irish who directly felt the consequences of German Occupation early on was Limerick woman Frances Moran. On 19 October 1940 the German embassy informed the Irish Legation that a school called Clairbois in Petit-Clamart outside Paris (a suburb that became famous twenty years later as the site of an assassination attempt on President Charles de Gaulle) could not be vacated as it was needed for military purposes. This was bad news for fifty-two-year-old Moran, who had been living in France for thirty years, including eighteen in Paris, and who had for much of that time been running the Clairbois finishing school for the daughters of well-to-do families. Moran left Paris on 11 May 1940, a day after the Germans had launched their Blitzkrieg against France and the Low Countries, and headed south to safety. In November 1940 she was stuck in Lury-sur-Arnon, in the *zone libre*, but was anxious to get back to her school, in spite of the German refusal to vacate the premises. In March 1941 she wrote to the Legation to inform it that she had endeavoured to get through to Paris but had been turned back. Soon after this failure, however, she managed to cross the Demarcation Line at a point further west and went to live at an address in rue de Phalsbourg in the 17th arrondissement in Paris. But while her freshly issued Irish passport afforded her some protection against internment, the Germans were still using her old school as a *Solatenheim* (a recreation area for soldiers), thus depriving her of her old job and a regular income. In May 1941 Moran had no other choice but to give up her lease to the property in Clairbois and put all the school furniture into safekeeping. She herself was unsettled, and inquired to the Legation about the possibility of going to the United States. It appears that after this Moran did not contact the Legation again and it is not known what happened to her.

Daniel McAllister, the fifty-four-year-old mechanic from County Down who had repaired Seán Murphy's car in June 1940, also decided to flee his home (in Courbevoie in the inner suburbs of Paris) before the advancing Germans. In late 1940 he wrote to the Legation from an address in Lyon, looking for an Irish passport. He needed papers, he explained, to go back to the garage he ran in Neuilly in the western suburbs of Paris, 'as this inactivity is terrible for me, not forgetting the expense with all going out and nothing coming in'.[70] McAllister's daughter, Hélène, added in an enjoinder that one of her father's brothers was a commandant in the Irish army in Athlone and another was a member of An Garda Síochána in Cavan. All the McAllister family, she claimed, had 'suffered in their native Ulster because of their recognised patriotism for Ireland. It is really a strange and sad fate that he should now suffer for being considered as an Englishman!'[71] Despite their best efforts, it was to take the McAllisters two and a half years to get back home to Courbevoie.[72]

The Paris Irish encountered many other administrative problems in the early months of the Occupation because of Ireland's historical attachment to Great Britain. In October 1940 O'Kelly described how several Irish girls had complained to him that, even though they held Irish passports, their *cartes de travail* (work permits) described them as a *sujet britannique* 'and that consequently they were made report daily to the authorities as if they had been British'. Furthermore, he wrote, 'in some cases, even when the party concerned had never held anything but an Irish passport ... officials insisted on the description "sujet britannique"'.

The problem was quite acute in O'Kelly's eyes, as 'my office is besieged by perfectly sound Irish citizens described as "britannique" on their French papers and whose employers threaten to denounce them as such'.[73] O'Kelly easily won over the Germans, but convincing supercilious French police officials to remove or amend the mention of *sujet britannique* for Irish citizens proved more arduous. Eventually, after negotiations with the general secretary of Vichy's delegation in the occupied territories, Count Alain de Boissieu, instructions were issued to French police stations to make the necessary changes. O'Kelly then had a notice placed in the daily newspaper *Le Matin* on 17 November 1940 (he afterwards complained that the FF1,800 bill from the newspaper was 'exorbitant') to inform Irish passport holders that:

> The Legation of Ireland, in agreement with the relevant French authorities informs that as from today all Irish nationals holding a valid Irish passport or a provisional certificate of nationality issued by the Legation of Ireland in France may, upon presenting themselves to the foreigner service of their region have the erroneous mention 'British subject' that sometimes appears on their identity cards or work permits substituted by the mention 'citizen of Ireland'.

The status of people from Northern Ireland was more complicated. The case of Belfast man John McKelvey from the *Luimneach* – left behind in Paris while other survivors from the vessel were repatriated to Ireland – testifies to this complexity. O'Kelly's view was that 'whatever may be the judicial position from the point of view of the Constitution, I fear we cannot give passports to such persons without prejudicing our whole position with the German authorities.[74] The latter have told me that they will accept the Legation's word for the *bona fides* of any Irish citizen but that, of course, Northern Ireland must be considered as England.'[75] O'Kelly also found himself dealing with a number of people who were born in the United Kingdom, but who laid claim to assistance from the Irish Legation because one of their parents was born in what became the Irish Free State. The German authorities were reticent about releasing such individuals, claiming that 'an English man desirous of doing spy work in France might easily slip through the net by claiming Irish nationality'.[76] By way of compromise, the Germans proposed that they, in such cases, would contact the German Legation in Dublin to verify the veracity of individual claims to Irishness.

Distinguishing between 'British' and 'Irish' identity was difficult at the best of times, and there was much blurring of lines when it came to distributing passports in the early part of the Second World War. Perhaps O'Kelly and his colleagues in Vichy genuinely wanted to help people in distress. Or perhaps they were, as O'Kelly admitted, simply overworked (and consequently became somewhat careless). Whatever the case, temporary passports (valid for one year) were distributed liberally for a period.

The case of William Ernest O'Hea, born in London of an Irish father in 1897, illustrates how the system worked. O'Hea was required to produce his father's birth certificate to be registered on the 'register of nationals'. Obviously anxious to obtain Irish papers, O'Hea kept up a lively correspondence with the Legation throughout the summer of 1940 in an effort to speed things along. He even tried to track the homeless Legation in the mayhem of Bordeaux in July 1940. On 29 July 1940, from an address in Perpignan, he again wrote to the Legation, which at that time was provisionally installed in the Hôtel des Lilas in Vichy. O'Hea was told in August 1940 that the consent of the Minister of Justice would be needed before he could be entered on the register of Irish nationals kept by the Legation. However, in light of the difficulties of communication, the Legation was 'prepared to assume that this consent would be forthcoming and to issue you a passport valid for one year and capable of renewal, free of charge, for a further four years'.[77]

Once consent had been granted, people were entitled to a five-year passport. In other words, anybody with some proof that he had an Irish father (or even grandfather) had a reasonable hope of being granted a one-year Irish passport by signing the Declaration of Nationality. Even though O'Hea was unable to produce his father's birth certificate, he still received an Irish passport in September 1940 on the basis that his French identity card stated that his father had been born in Dublin – and he was able to include his French wife on the same Irish passport.

In October 1940, armed with his one-year Irish passport, O'Hea approached the French authorities to have the nationality on his French ID card changed from British to Irish. 'I know that Irish and British alike live freely in the unoccupied part of the country,' he wrote to the police prefect in Perpignan, 'but that could change and I might end up repeating the adventure that one of my Irish friends in Paris went through. He spent three months in Fresnes prison because he was considered English, after which he was released and presented with an apology, which was not enough to bring him back to health.'[78] Yet even though O'Hea was granted a full Irish passport upon expiry of the one-year version given to him in 1940, events were still to catch up with him in January 1943, as we shall see later.

O'Kelly's friend John Francis Keane was also granted a one-year Irish passport in October 1940 on the mere promise of producing his father's birth certificate.[79] His newly minted Irish passport seems to have been enough to get Keane out of the internment camp at Saint-Denis. One of Keane's friends was an Australian dental surgeon called Joseph Dawson Buckley, born in 1878. A widower who normally resided in Nice, he was briefly interned at Drancy (the same makeshift internment camp soon became notorious as the main transit point for Jews on their way to Auschwitz) in late 1940 and early 1941. While there, he was put in charge of the canteen but was 'frequently absent on buying expeditions'.[80] O'Kelly was happy to grant Buckley a temporary Irish passport based on the Irish birth of both his parents. Buckley's father was James O'Brien Buckley, born in County Cork in 1838, and his mother was Anne Roach, born in the same year in County Roscommon. The family had emigrated to Australia in 1860, where their son was born.

Equally lucky to obtain a passport was Graeme Fenton, a commercial manager who had been born in Belfast in 1886 but had left Ireland with his parents in 1898 and honestly stated he had no intention of returning. He, like so many others, was interned in the military barracks at Saint-Denis, where O'Kelly visited him on 22 October 1940. After their meeting, Fenton explained that his birth in Belfast was a pure accident. His mother, who was from County Donegal, came from 'a very old Irish family called Kelso-Reid'. She happened to be travelling in a horse-drawn brougham while heavily pregnant, but 'the horse bolted, and my premature birth was a result of that accident'. His father came from County Sligo but had been sent to Paris by Dunlop in 1896 ('it was my father who tested ... the first pneumatic tyre invented by Mr Dunlop'). Fenton was brought up in Fermoy, County Cork, until the age of twelve but then joined his parents in Paris and had never been back to Ireland since.

At least Fenton was honest about the reasons for seeking an Irish passport. 'As I have not resided in Ireland since 1898, I have had no occasion to apply for an Irish passport. Under the present circumstances, however, I am desirous of obtaining one.'[81]

Yet, for all O'Kelly's efforts, Fenton was to remain in Saint-Denis until June 1942, by which stage most other 'Irishmen' had been released. In addition, the Germans continued to consider him a British citizen, which meant, according to a letter from the Irish Legation in Vichy to its equivalent in Berlin, that 'he is not allowed to be out after sundown, he cannot do any journeys and he is obliged to sign daily the register of British citizens of his arrondissement'.[82] Nonetheless, Fenton survived the war and died at the British hospital in Levallois-Perret in June 1963.

The laxity in the delivery of Irish identity papers was noticed back in Dublin, so in spring 1941 Murphy passed on to O'Kelly a note from Dublin requesting that in cases:

> … where passports have been issued to persons who are not actual citizens, please explain at once to holders that i) passports were issued provisionally pending registration, ii) any relief we may decide to give will be confined to actual Irish citizens and iii) if desired, any passport fee paid will be refunded if they surrender passport immediately … As from today passports should not be issued to persons who are not full citizens under Irish law. In the cases of application for registration, passports are not to be issued until registration [is] completed.[83]

Before matters were tightened up, another beneficiary of this somewhat haphazard system was Desmond Patrick Nolan, a reprehensible individual who wrote from an address in Nice in the south of France to apply for an Irish passport in October 1939. In his application, Nolan neglected to mention that he was on the run from British justice because of a series of sex crimes. A year and a half after his application, a Special Branch report to MI5 revealed that Nolan, who was born in Plymouth of Irish parents in 1907, had been sent to a reformatory school when he was fourteen for 'indecently assaulting a girl of nine years'. Then he went to a borstal for three years in 1927 'for obtaining a railway ticket by false pretences (three other cases were taken into consideration)' and in 1933 was arrested (but acquitted) 'for having carnal knowledge of a girl aged 20, against her will'.[84] Finally, in 1939, Nolan – who had by then married three times – failed to appear at Bristol assizes to answer further charges of rape and indecent assault and was thought to have escaped to Portugal. A report from the Bristol police concluded that 'there is little doubt that the prisoner had a most captivating manner with females, that he is utterly immoral and that he has not the slightest scruple in resorting to force, if necessary, to obtain sexual intercourse with any woman or girl whom he succeeds in persuading to keep his company'.[85]

By October 1939 Nolan, his third wife and two children had got as far as Nice. Before the French defeat of June 1940, the British tried to have Nolan extradited from there back to the United Kingdom. But once the Vichy government broke off diplomatic relations with London in July 1940, following the Royal Navy's attack on the French fleet at Mers-el-Kébir, Nolan was safe from the risk of having to appear before a British court. French justice was another matter, for in October 1940 Nolan was arrested in Nice on embezzlement charges.

Such was the man to whom the Irish authorities decided to grant a one-year passport in November 1940 because of his father's birth in Dublin. In December 1940 Nolan, now under lock and key, wrote directly to Taoiseach Éamon de Valera in Dublin to request a direct passage to Ireland on the strength of his newly minted Irish passport. In the same month Nolan and his wife escaped from detention in Nice, leaving behind the youngest of their children, Ana Margarite, who was three months old, and bringing with them the older two, two-year-old Sheila Elizabeth and one-year-old Michael Patrick. Nolan and his wife then turned up in Lisbon as 'refugees from Nice', according to a 17 December letter from the British Consulate General in that city. Nolan lied to the consular authorities, telling them he and his wife had lost their British passports. He also told them that it was his intention to settle in Ireland, where his father lived, and said he wanted to organise for money he still had in an account in Paris to be sent there.

But Nolan created an 'unfavourable impression' at the consulate, which told the Foreign Office in London that he had been 'attempting to obtain private information about sailings, questioning British seamen in bars'.[86] He was bound to remain on the British intelligence service's radar, not least because in May 1940 one of his neighbours in Colindale, north London, told police that Nolan had said 'that his sympathies are with Germany' and he believed that Nolan was still a member of the Fascist Party.[87] Nonetheless, over the four months he stayed in Lisbon, Nolan received £90 in financial assistance from the British consular authorities because of guarantees from his father ('which subsequently proved to be worthless', according to a memo from the DEA to the Legation in Berlin in October 1942).[88]

**

As the Irish Legation was officially accredited to the Pétain government, the premises in rue de Villejust remained closed and Paris Irish in need of assistance were directed to a temporary chancery opened on the premises of O'Kelly's wine company at 8 place Vendôme instead. O'Kelly faced a number of problems of an administrative order in the first months of the Occupation, although postal connections became a little more structured from October 1940, when the German authorities organised a daily postal service between consular services remaining in Paris and the diplomatic corps in the *zone libre*. Official correspondence, as well as letters from individuals, could now be sent between occupied France and the *zone libre* but 'had to remain open and be written in German or French'. For a time thereafter, correspondence between the Legation in Vichy and O'Kelly in Paris was therefore conducted in French.

Yet communication difficulties remained. On 23 January 1941 Murphy informed Dublin that he could send letters that had come from Ireland to Vichy destined for Irish citizens on the other side of the Demarcation Line in occupied France only 'when I find a colleague going to Paris who is willing to run the risk of taking them over the line'. But such opportunities were rare 'owing to the increasing severity of the German authorities in this matter'. Otherwise, most matters relating to Irish citizens in occupied France had to be dealt with during telephone calls with O'Kelly. 'This system is not of course satisfactory,' wrote Murphy, 'but it was the only possible one.'[89]

By the autumn of 1940 O'Kelly had an enormous workload and requested an extra typist, 'as the work takes at the moment practically the whole time' of his secretary Louise Froc, who also had to issue 'explanatory certificates' to people who needed them.[90] Some of his work involved actively seeking out the Paris Irish at their abodes or checking up on the flats they'd left behind.

In early December 1940 Bluebell's British passport caught up with her. At six o'clock one morning Bluebell, by now several months pregnant, was awakened by the ringing of her doorbell. Two policemen had come with a summons for her to present herself at the nearest police station. She was to bring with her a small suitcase containing the barest essentials. From the police station, she was put in a city bus along with other women and brought to the Gare de l'Est. Almost 2,000 women with British passports recorded by the Germans as living in the Paris area were rounded up on that December day. The women were put in third-class train carriages, each presided over by female German guards. They remained locked in the immobile train in the Gare de l'Est for an entire day, without anything to eat or drink, before departing for an unknown destination.

Bluebell's party travelled through the night and well into the next day before it reached Besançon, a large town in the east of

France, not far from the Swiss border, where they were confined in the Vauban military barracks near the town centre.[91] The old, unheated Caserne Vauban, renamed Frontstalag 142 by the Germans, had been converted into a detention camp for civilians, both men and women, from enemy nations (which at this stage of the war meant citizens of Great Britain and her dominions). The pregnant Bluebell was put in a freezing dormitory with eighteen other women and given her first hot meal since leaving Paris.

Immediately he heard the news of her detention, Bluebell's husband, Marcel, who had been lying low to avoid being picked up himself, decided to break cover and go to see O'Kelly at the ad hoc Legation chancery on place Vendôme. The count wasn't in Paris when Marcel called, but the Legation secretary, Louise Froc, typed a memo for the Irish diplomat in which she stated that:

> … the husband of Mme Margaret Kelly came to the Chancery about his wife, an Irish citizen, who seems to have been sent away by train from the Gare de l'Est. I suggested he should try to contact you with papers that prove her Irish identity so that you can do what's needed for her. In the meantime, I'll get a provisional certificate of identity ready for her on the basis of the passport request forms that he left with me.[92]

O'Kelly quickly got on the case and managed to have Bluebell liberated from the Caserne Vauban on New Year's Eve 1940, along with three Sisters of Mercy.

By late 1940 Seán Murphy was reporting growing disquiet in France about the direction in which the country was heading. Meetings between Pétain, Pierre Laval, the effective kingpin of the Vichy regime, and Adolf Hitler at Montoire-sur-le-Loir in central France in October 1940 came as a 'complete surprise', wrote Murphy a month later. The policy of collaboration with the

Germans that Laval and Pétain intended to follow 'was received here by public with mixed feelings, and even more so in occupied territories'. Laval was 'universally unpopular and distrusted, and public are afraid he may lead [the] Marshal into an impasse from which he cannot retreat'.[93] Pétain, who was concerned that Laval's eagerness to take the initiative in dealings with the Germans might mean he himself was sidelined, used Laval's unpopularity to sack him in December 1940 and even have him arrested. But Laval was quickly released on the insistence of the German ambassador to France, Otto Abetz, who helped engineer his return to Vichy and his installation as *chef de gouvernement* in April 1942.

After 1940, Murphy's detailed reports on the political and economic situation in France became more infrequent, giving way to occasional, more succinct updates. The drying up of detailed political reports back to Dublin was due in large part to increasing disillusionment with the paucity of anything to report (indeed, Ireland's diplomatic representatives passed a lot of their time in Vichy playing golf and going to the local racecourse).[94] On 13 January 1941 Murphy wrote to the DEA in Dublin that he considered 'weekly telegraphic reports might often be sheer waste of money for lack of news. Will send reports whenever matters of interest to report.'[95]

Instead, Seán Murphy and Con Cremin were increasingly subsumed by the onerous task of running a diplomatic mission out of a couple of hotel rooms with hardly any resources, and with poor communications, while being subject to severe rationing. Plausibly, Murphy may also have felt his efforts were unappreciated by Dublin and may have felt unable to reconcile his views with those that Dublin would like him to take. Soon after arriving in Vichy, Murphy's quite sceptical take on the new Pétain regime was already in stark contrast with that of the secretary of the DEA, Joseph Walshe, who was much more favourably disposed towards

France's new strong man.[96] Walshe wrote a memorandum to Éamon de Valera on 21 June 1940 that began: 'Britain's defeat has been placed beyond all doubt. France has capitulated. The entire coastline from the Arctic to the Pyrenees is in the hands of the strongest power of the world ... Neither time nor gold can beat Germany.'[97] This might have been the case in the summer of 1940, but by early 1941 Murphy – whose ear was closer to the ground – felt compelled to write to Dublin that 'the great majority of the public feel that their only hope is in a German defeat, and they are inclined to sit and wait for that to happen'.[98]

4

ORGANISING HELP

On 7 January 1941 F. T. Cremins, *chargé d'affaires* at the Irish Legation in Berne, wrote to Seán Murphy to tell him that, as well as seeking assistance from the Irish authorities, James Joyce had contacted the American embassy in Berlin with a view to extracting his daughter, Lucia, from occupied France. In his reply on 13 January, Murphy detailed the efforts he had also undertaken for Lucia Joyce, including bringing her case up with the German authorities during his first visit to occupied Paris in August 1940. Murphy explained to Cremins that Lucia 'was in a position, if she so desired, to apply for and probably obtain Irish nationality' and that James Joyce was in fact interested to know whether 'it would be well to have his daughter obtain an Irish passport'. Murphy said that he'd told Joyce that 'she [Lucia] was perfectly entitled to claim citizenship by registration and that, if she should apply for registration, I would be prepared to issue her a passport valid for one year pending the decision of the Minister for Justice on her application'. Murphy thought – perhaps correctly – that, for the Germans, Lucia's application 'at this stage might only be regarded … as a ruse', given that she already held a British passport. But as long as Lucia held a British passport, the Legation could do little more for her. Murphy thus approved of Joyce's decision to contact the American foreign services, which had been in charge of British interests since the fall of France.[1]

Not knowing that James Joyce was dying (he died in a hospital in Zurich during the night of 12–13 January), Murphy also mentioned to Cremins that he was 'surprised to learn' that Joyce had approached the Legation in Berne on behalf of Lucia, 'especially as he does not seem to have informed you of what he knew of my efforts in this respect already'. Murphy seemed vexed, especially as he had repeatedly advised Joyce to apply for an Irish passport for his daughter during the summer of 1940. 'If he had decided on this course in the first instance, I have no doubt that she would have been allowed to undertake the journey to Switzerland long since. He, however, showed no inclination to follow it at the time.'[2]

Joyce's death in January 1941 brought all the somewhat convoluted efforts to extricate Lucia from occupied France to an end. According to Carol Loeb Shloss, neither Nora nor Giorgio Joyce were nearly as assiduous as her father on Lucia's behalf. But she was not entirely forgotten: the Joyces' long-time benefactor Harriet Weaver continued to send some money to pay for her clinic fees. All Giorgio could find to write to Maria Jolas on 17 February was 'I hope Dr Delmas has not put Lucia in the street as needless to say I cannot pay him nor can I communicate with him.'[3]

After his return to Paris in September 1940, Samuel Beckett kept a relatively low profile. Like other Parisians, he and Suzanne Deschevaux-Dumesnil fretted over declining food supplies and the absence of heating in their flat in the rue des Favorites. During this time he renewed his friendship with the newly demobilised Alfred Péron, whom he had first met at Trinity College, Dublin back in 1926. Péron helped Beckett with the translation of the Irishman's first novel, *Murphy*, while Beckett proceeded to work on his second novel, called *Watt*. In early June 1941 Beckett sent a curt telegram to his family in Dublin, via O'Kelly, that read: 'Monsieur Beckett est en excellente santé et ne manque de rien'.[4] At the beginning of August he wrote to Francis Stuart in Berlin, who commented: 'He seems to be living there even more cut off from Ireland and isolated than am I.'[5] Ensconced in his apartment at rue des Favorites, Beckett sent a further short, reassuring message to his family in Dublin in December 1941.

By this stage Beckett had joined the French Resistance. The introduction to Volume 2 of Beckett's letters mentions that he occasionally acted as a courier for André Salzman, whose speciality was finding money for clandestine anti-German publications.[6] But Beckett's name is most closely associated with a Resistance network called Gloria SMH, which was established by Jeanine Picabia, daughter of the well-known avant-garde painter Francis Picabia. Beckett was introduced to the network by Péron – although when is a matter of debate. His Resistance file at the Service historique de la Défense mentions that he was active from 1 September 1941 to 1 September 1942.[7] However, Beckett told British security officials after the war that 'he was introduced to the Gloria organisation in November 1941 by Alfred Péron'.[8]

Beckett became involved in collating, translating and synthesising reports received from various people working for the Gloria SMH network. Once he had typed up his reports, he brought them to a man he knew as Jimmy the Greek, who lived in avenue du Parc de Montsouris (now called avenue René Coty), about three kilometres from Beckett's apartment. There, the documents were micro-photographed before being smuggled out of France. Although the real, strategic value of Resistance intelligence gathering is debatable, Beckett undoubtedly ran huge risks.[9] But he survived undisturbed as part of a clandestine organisation that seems to have had some success in breaking down its activities into small, relatively watertight cells – to the extent that British intelligence officers after the war concluded: 'Although Beckett appears fairly intelligent and well educated, he knew very little about the organisation of SMH/Gloria.'[10]

In early 1941 Beckett's acquaintance and James Joyce's fixer, Paul Léon, was still trying to look after the property that the Joyces had left behind in Paris when they fled to Saint-Gérand-le-Puy. Léon asked Count O'Kelly to place seals on the Joyces' apartment on the rue des Vignes as a way of dissuading intruders.

Léon was really afraid that the landlord might seize the Joyces' property for non-payment of rent over several months. Count O'Kelly was instructed not to accede to Léon's request by the Legation in Vichy, 'as no member of the [Joyce] family holds an Irish passport'. Thus it was that, in May 1941, the owner of the rue des Vignes flat 'illegally auctioned off some of the Joyce's pictures and furnishings' at the Drouot auction house in the street of the same name in the 9th arrondissement.[11] All was not lost. Léon had already managed to cart off Joyce's papers before the bailiff's arrival, while his brother-in-law, Alex Ponisovsky, gave him FF20,000–25,000 to buy up what he could at the auction. With this money, Léon managed to buy all of Joyce's books that he considered worthwhile, except 'a copy of *Pomes Penyeach* with original lettrines by Lucia Joyce. A rue de Seine bookseller went up to five thousand francs and made it clear he was ready to go higher.'[12] Léon's wife, Lucie Noël, who found it 'most painful … to see the Joyce family belongings go under the hammer', bought back 'a whole trunkful of linen and odds and ends which I thought Mrs Joyce might want to keep'. Among other things, she got 'Joyce's tooled leather writing pad and his paper knife', which she managed to send to Nora Joyce in Zurich.[13]

Léon, a Russian Jew born Paul Léopoldovitch, was to pay for his unstinting efforts to rescue Joyce's affairs. Given the mounting prosecution of Jews, especially foreign Jews, it is little wonder that Samuel Beckett was dismayed to see Léon still openly walking around the city, when he ran into him in August 1941. Léon explained to Beckett that he had decided to delay his departure from Paris because his son, Alex, had to pass his baccalauréat exam the next day, 21 August 1941. On that same day, Léon was rounded up and sent to Drancy internment camp.

***

As Paris settled down under the Occupation, Count O'Kelly tried to deal with increasing distress among the city's Irish residents. Because of his nebulous status as 'minister plenipotentiary, special counsellor', the Irish could argue he was not formally covered by the insistence of the Pétain government that all diplomatic representatives be based in Vichy. Thus, initially at least, O'Kelly avoided the stifling atmosphere of provincial France in wartime. Yet some suspicions swirl around the circumstances of his emergence as *de facto* man-in-charge in Paris. Charles Bewley, formerly the Irish minister in Berlin, had, like O'Kelly, been turned out of the Irish diplomatic service in the 1930s. Unlike the count, however, there was no return to grace for Bewley, whose dismissal in 1939 was because of his increasingly overt Hitlerian sympathies. Once the Occupation began, the German authorities may have been happy to have somebody capable of representing Irish interests in the occupied zone. O'Kelly was an obvious choice, especially in light of the glowing recommendation he received from Bewley, still resident in Berlin.[14] This arrangement suited everybody. The Irish had somebody to look after their interests in Paris, the Germans had a pragmatic, experienced interlocutor, and O'Kelly re-found an ego-boosting role for himself in the diplomatic service that would likely have the welcome side-effect of serving and protecting his Paris-based wine business.

In 1938 O'Kelly had installed Vendôme Wines at 8 place Vendôme in the most exclusive part of the city. As he built up his business, O'Kelly's contacts with minor nobility throughout France and Europe, and his co-opting of a number of high-class shareholders, undoubtedly opened doors for him. Maurice Prévost, the general manager of the firm, was an early French air pioneer, well known in international aeronautic circles, who had gone into the champagne business in his native Reims after the First World War. He brought valuable connections in the Champagne region to Vendôme Wines, as well as a raft of potential customers among flying circles.

By the outbreak of war, O'Kelly had begun to build up a solid clientele, especially in the United Kingdom. Remarkably, while the French defeat of June 1940 severed Vendôme Wines' access to the British market, the company managed to survive as a going concern right throughout the Occupation, with Prévost managing the firm on a day-to-day basis, and as late as 1943 an advertisement for Vendôme Wines appeared in the Paris commercial directory, the *Didot-Bodin*. With many of the main German command posts in Paris situated in a small perimeter around the place Vendôme, most of Vendôme Wines' custom during the Occupation was, perhaps inevitably, German. The *Kommandatur* for Greater Paris, for example, was at the Hôtel Meurice on the rue de Rivoli, the offices of the Wehrmacht's chief of staff were on place de l'Opéra, and the Ritz Hotel, Hermann Göring's place of residence during his frequent sojourns in Paris, was at 15 place Vendôme, directly opposite Vendôme Wines.

Once installed in France, the Germans appointed *Verwalter* (administrators) to companies that had foreign capital. Hans Gechter from Hanover was appointed to Vendôme Wines, as the company had a number of shareholders who were enemy nationals, including the Earl of Granard; Anthony Cunard (a member of the famous shipping-magnate family and whose mother was an Irishwoman); Edith Howard of Ballina Park, County Wicklow; an English doctor, Francis Howard Humphries; and a Dutchman, Edward Leyba, a diplomatic representative for Paraguay in Paris.[15]

Vendôme Wines' capital increased to FF475,000 in late 1939 and then to FF1 million in September 1941, without any apparent consultation with the existing United Kingdom-based shareholders. The capital increase of 1941 had the welcome effect of cutting the share of Vendôme Wines held by enemy nationals like Cunard and Humphries from 35 per cent to around 10 per cent. To be able to do this legally, the status of the company was changed from that of a *société anonyme* (SA) to that of a *société à responsabilité limitée* (SARL), more suited to small companies and requiring a far lower share capital. Importantly, the number of partners legally required for an SARL is just two, compared with a minimum of seven for an SA. After the 1941 capital increase, O'Kelly's stake in the company went up from about 26 per cent to 44.5 per cent, with his wife, Marjorie, holding one share. London Irishman and Paris resident John Francis Keane also became an important shareholder. Keane, whom O'Kelly had managed to free from the internment camp in Saint-Denis in the autumn of 1940, had his own company, called Expert Publicité Internationale, on the rue de Châteaudun in the 9th arrondissement and fought a long-running battle with the Germans to convince them the company was not controlled by enemy interests. Thanks to his Irish passport, provided by O'Kelly to secure his liberation from Saint-Denis, Keane was able to invest in Vendôme Wines without too many questions being asked by the Germans.

Based on his reports, Hans Gechter appears to have taken his task to heart, while remaining relatively fair in his dealings with Vendôme Wines. In September 1941 he wrote a long report on the business for the German authorities. In it, he mentioned that 'Graf' O'Kelly was 'of Irish nationality and probably an enemy of England'. Gechter wrote that Vendôme Wines' customers were made up of 'connoisseurs from the upper reaches of the diplomatic world and high society' and claimed that 'Since the entry of German troops, about 75% of the company's business is with German customers, and most particularly with some high-ranking personalities, but not in large quantities.'[16]

Two documents, probably emanating from Vendôme Wines itself, give a similar picture of the extent of the company's dealings with the German occupiers (and possibly were the foundation of Gechter's report in September of that year). A few lines written on notepaper from the Hôtel Lancaster, possibly by Maurice Prévost, mention '*clientèle actuelle 75–80% allemande*' in reference to Vendôme Wines. More explosive still is the other document, which presents an elaborate list of the '*clients allemands de la Vendôme*'. The document is unsigned and undated but was probably drawn up by somebody at Vendôme Wines to demonstrate its *bona fides* and detract attention from the former prevalence of British shareholders in its capital structure. The first three clients mentioned on this list are Reichsmarschall Göring, Consul General Neuhausen and Marshal Milch. Hermann Göring needs no introduction. Franz Neuhausen was a close friend of Göring (they were both Luftwaffe men) and was appointed to look after economic affairs in Serbia after the Wehrmacht overran Yugoslavia in April 1941. He amassed a fortune between 1941 and 1944 but was arrested by the German authorities in August 1944 for alleged corruption and spent the end of the war in detention. Marshal Erhard Milch was in charge of the strategic development of the Luftwaffe. Before the war, he had been involved in the nascent airline industry in Germany and helped set up Deutscher Aero Lloyd. Vendôme Wines had many other customers from German flying circles; among other top clients mentioned in the list was the Aero Club von Deutschland, for example. Prévost's contacts in international aeronautic circles seem to have stood Vendôme Wines in good stead, as did its position on the place Vendôme, just across from the Luftwaffe's headquarters in the Ritz.

Hans Gechter, in his September 1941 report to his superiors, judged that Vendôme Wines was 'consistently undercapitalised', hence justifying the capital increase of that month, and the German opined that the disruption caused by the war made the firm's prospects highly uncertain. Gechter wrote that it was 'very difficult for the firm to replenish stocks given circumstances, and all the more so that prices have increased substantially and producers' stocks continue to dwindle'.[17] Vendôme Wines tried to get round its difficulties by turning more to Porto and sherry – which would explain a visit to Spain and Portugal made by Gechter in autumn 1943 on behalf of Vendôme Wines (perhaps accompanied by Prévost and/or O'Kelly) as well as on behalf of a number of other companies he 'represented'. In a report written before his departure, Gechter said he was undertaking the trip to Iberia 'to firm up relations with existing partners and to find new ones'.[18] His journey seems to have been paid for by the German military authorities, but Gechter incurred FF2,900 in incidental expenses that he charged back to Vendôme Wines. (Gechter undertook another commercial trip to Spain in March 1944, but this time Vendôme Wines did not feature among the companies he represented).

Gechter became more upbeat about Vendôme Wines later in the Occupation. In a note to the military authorities that he glued to Prévost's report for financial year 1943, the German *Verwalter* wrote that 'there was a not inconsiderable improvement in turn-over in the first nine months of 1943 … compared to the same period of 1942. The number of clients has also risen considerably, and export customers have increased substantially compared with 1940.'[19] Perhaps the business contacts that Vendôme Wines had established in Spain and Portugal were beginning to pay off? Although charges and taxes meant that Vendôme Wines made a net loss again in 1943, it actually made an operating profit of FF370,000 (about €81,000 in today's money, taking into account inflation) in that financial year.

One other member of the O'Kelly family tried to establish a commercial foothold in wartime France. O'Kelly's older brother, Ambrose, possessed the same wanderlust as the rest of the clan and had ended up in Romania as representative of the Marconi company before the war. There he married a member of the local nobility called Elena Filipescu. Ambrose wrote directly to Seán Murphy in Vichy from his home in Bucharest in January 1941 to ask him to forward letters to his mother (who had been stranded in her ancestral castle near Toulouse by the outbreak of the war) and to his brother Gerald, because letters sent by regular post did not arrive. In his letter, dated 29 January, Ambrose referred to the so-called Legionnaires' Rebellion, which saw members of a paramilitary force called the Iron Guard rise up against the country's recently installed leader, Ion Antonescu. The revolt led to a pogrom that killed over 100 Jews. Ambrose described the revolt as 'a dangerous moment and fraught with great anxiety' and compared it with the Easter Rising in Dublin in 1916, 'in spite of the fundamental difference that here the movement sprang from no patriotic inspiration as the creed of the Green-shirt rebels would have been better symbolised by red'.[20]

Although communications were difficult, Ambrose periodically tried to reach Gerald. In November 1941 he wrote directly to Ireland's 'special counsellor' in Paris to ask him to arrange a visa, 'as I have stated my reasons for wishing to go to Vichy to discuss my business in Ireland and Spain'.[21] What 'business' Ambrose had in mind is not clear, but it possibly involved trade in commodities between Romania and western Europe. So unappealing was the prospect of another winter without fuel that the Legation decided in 1942 to ask Ambrose to approach the Romanian foreign ministry to ask it to authorise the export of fifteen tonnes of petroleum. Other legations had received similar authorisations. According to correspondence from May 1942, the Legation was to look after payment and transport of the fuel once its export had been authorised.[22] A month later, the Legation had not received a reply from Ambrose, prompting his brother Gerald to send a follow-up telegram on 3 June. It turned out that Ambrose had written to the Legation on 9 May, but the letter had been lost. Fortunately, he had kept a copy, which laid out clearly the steps that needed to be taken to buy Romanian oil.[23] The issue rumbled on until October 1942, when Murphy wrote to the German Consul General in Vichy, Krug von Nidda, for permission to send a train-loaded oil tank to cross German territory to pick up the Legation's consignment of Romanian petroleum.[24]

Before then, in the autumn of 1940 and early 1941, while O'Kelly was trying to keep his wine business afloat and simultaneously coming to the aid of the Irish colony in Paris, some early forms of resistance to the German occupiers began to emerge. It was a coincidence that the first radio liaison between London and the French Resistance was established at 8 place Vendôme, the address where O'Kelly had his wine company and ran the Irish Legation's 'temporary chancery'. On the third floor (Vendôme Wines occupied the mezzanine) was La Maison des fils et petits fils de Maurice Duclos, a family firm of commodity brokers. Maurice Duclos himself had belonged to a secretive far-right group called La Cagoule before the war, but after the French defeat in June 1940 he quickly rallied to the cause of the Free French under General de Gaulle. Duclos was sent from London in early August 1940 with the task of establishing an information-gathering network in newly occupied France. This network, baptised Saint-Jacques (after Duclos's code name), quickly gathered new recruits and commenced its activities out of the premises of the family firm on place Vendôme in September 1940.

Saint-Jacques' mission largely overlapped that of MI6, which had begun to sow the seeds of a vast spy network called Mithridate that had started to gather information for London right from the moment of the June 1940 defeat. Among its early recruits was Janie McCarthy, an English teacher from Killarney. She may have been co-opted by Elisabeth Barbier, with whom she was to work closely in the Resistance over the following three years. It is unclear how McCarthy came to know Barbier, who was twenty-seven years younger. Perhaps the Irishwoman became acquainted with her through Barbier's mother, Camille Fouchet d'Estmaur, or perhaps Barbier was a pupil of McCarthy's. In any case, interrogated after her repatriation from the Ravensbrück concentration camp in 1945, Barbier mentioned that she, McCarthy and a Danish national of Russian origin called Natacha Boeg had begun to collate reports on enemy troop movements as early as September 1940. McCarthy specialised in collecting information on enemy rail traffic in northern France, travelling on one occasion as far as Hirson, close to the Belgian border, along with a former railway inspector called Paquin (who later belonged to a Resistance movement called Résistance-Fer).

One member of Saint-Jacques, Lucien Fleets, was exfiltrated to London and parachuted back into France in January 1941, along with a transmitter and a trained radio operator to send reports back to London. But the transmitter broke down and the Germans smashed the Saint-Jacques network during the summer of 1941. It also became steadily more difficult for Mithridate to transmit reports to London, with Barbier admitting after the war that 'a visit from the German police in 1941 had curbed her activities'.[25] However, Barbier, McCarthy and Boeg managed to avoid arrest and quickly thought of other ways to help the Allied cause.

***

While O'Kelly balanced the roles of diplomat and wine merchant to Hermann Göring, and while Janie McCarthy made her first (but by no means last) contribution to the French Resistance, other Irish Parisians became interlopers in a conflict in which Ireland was not officially taking part.

After his release from detention in the autumn of 1940, Fr

Kenneth Monaghan returned to St Joseph's on the avenue Hoche and became, together with his superior, Fr O'Grady, a go-to person for English speakers stranded in Paris – most especially Irish people, for whom St Joseph's was an important anchor point. Perhaps inevitably, Fr Monaghan became involved in efforts to help Allied soldiers and downed airmen to escape capture.

In a BBC documentary broadcast in 2005, Bill McGrath recalled how Fr Monaghan had helped him escape from occupied France in 1941.[26] McGrath, who was born in Clones, County Monaghan, on 25 July 1920 and brought up in County Fermanagh, had joined the Royal Air Force (RAF) on the outbreak of the war. In a disastrous bombing mission over Aalborg in Denmark in August 1940, McGrath's plane crashed and he was seriously injured. He was sent to a hospital in northern Germany, where he received specialist treatment for his badly injured arm, and thereafter to a prisoner-of-war camp. McGrath was so seriously injured that the Germans considered he was unlikely to fight again, making him a perfect candidate for a nascent prisoner-exchange scheme between Great Britain and Germany. McGrath was moved to a transit camp situated on the Bruyères racecourse in Rouen to the west of Paris in October 1941 in preparation for the prisoner swap. There he met another RAF prisoner, Oliver James, who had had part of his arm amputated. But James and McGrath soon got wind that the prisoner exchange scheme was being abandoned, so they decided to escape together.

Through McGrath's 2005 account and the account that Oliver James gave to British military intelligence in 1942, it is possible to reconstruct the two men's adventures.[27] On 21 November 1941, using a pair of pliers left behind by workmen, McGrath and James cut through the wire that separated the prisoner-of-war camp from the German officer quarters and clambered over the old racecourse grandstand. According to James's account, they made it through the Rouen suburbs as far the village of Les Essarts, less than twelve kilometres away. There they were advised to try to make it to Oissel, seven kilometres further east, and there catch a train to Paris. But they became lost on their way to Oissel and ended up back in Les Essarts. In desperation, they went to the nearest church, where they met the local parish priest who was conducting a catechism class for children. The priest took them in, fed them and gave them civilian clothing. On 24 November, three days after their escape, the RAF men finally made it to the train station at Oissel and bought tickets for the 5 p.m. train to Paris (a whip-round for escapees among the British officers at the POW camp in Rouen had ensured that McGrath and James had some money with them). According to James, the men paid well above the normal price for their tickets and, since the train was crowded, they had to stand in the corridor for the entire trip. But at least they arrived unnoticed at Saint-Lazare station on a dark Monday evening. They knew they would soon be arrested if they didn't find a place to stay indoors before curfew. So, with what little money they had, they paid a prostitute to put them up for the night.[28]

The following day, on the run in a strange city and not knowing what to do, James and McGrath went to see another priest. But they had less luck than in Normandy. The priest was a 'pale, flabby chap', according to McGrath, who 'shook like a jelly and told us to go away'. But at least the cleric did not betray them. They bought a guide to Paris in a nearby metro station and from that learned where the Anglican church was, in rue d'Aguesseau, close to the British embassy on the rue du Faubourg Saint-Honoré. But the church was closed and at its entrance was pinned a note explaining that it was under the protection of the American embassy. So McGrath and James decided to walk to the nearby embassy, passing on their way 'any amount of Germans' and even walking by Gestapo HQ, according to McGrath. They also happened upon the Red Cross's Prisoner of

War Service, housed in a large hall on a side street with a sign outside that read 'all help given to prisoners of war', according to the Irishman. The two men walked in and found an old woman knitting. She brought them into another room full of women, where the two escapees explained their predicament. A little while later a man was summoned who seemed somewhat less enthused by the two airmen's presence. He locked them in a room at the top of a staircase, telling them he would be back. With no means of escape, James and McGrath feared the man had left to fetch the police, or even the Germans.

Luckily for them, this did not happen. 'Amazingly enough, into this room came a monk,' McGrath remembered in the BBC documentary many years later. The 'monk' (in fact Fr Monaghan from St Joseph's) asked them a number of detailed questions to ascertain whether they were genuine escapees or German infiltrators.[29] McGrath was asked where he was from, where he had gone to school, who his schoolmaster had been, and whether he knew the name of a nearby monastery. Since McGrath (like Samuel Beckett) had been a pupil at Portora Royal School in Enniskillen, he knew the name of the Graan Monastery in the same town where Fr Monaghan had been a seminarian. Convinced that the two men were genuine escapees, Fr Monaghan organised for a photographer to come and take passport photos for various travel permits and false papers. He also arranged for the two men to meet a doctor who specialised in helping downed airmen. The doctor obtained tickets for a southbound train and told them to get off in Nevers, just before the Demarcation Line, where they were to meet a fellow doctor who would try to organise their onward journey. Fr Monaghan accompanied the two men to the station, giving them FF150 apiece.

McGrath and James stayed three weeks in Nevers in a succession of safe houses (including the home of the local police chief) before a boat smuggled them across the Loire river, which marked the border between occupied France and the *zone libre*.[30] They then found themselves taken on by the Pat O'Leary escape line (despite the name, founded and run by a Belgian), which brought them down to Marseille in December 1941. From Marseille, they moved west along the Mediterranean coast as far as Perpignan, close to the Spanish frontier. In Perpignan they booked into the Hôtel d'Angleterre, where a suspicious owner confronted the two foreigners. When they explained who they were, the hotelier put them in touch with a Spanish smuggler who agreed to deliver them to the British consulate in Barcelona in return for a promise that the consulate would pay him a fee of FF24,000 for his troubles. Finally, in January 1942, having climbed through remote mountain passes in the dead of winter dressed only in light clothes, James and McGrath arrived in Barcelona, from where they went down to Gibraltar and then back to Britain. McGrath, who died in 2011, won the Military Medal for his exploits in occupied Europe. His father had been awarded the same medal in the First World War.

***

On 24 January 1941, less than a fortnight after James Joyce's death in Zurich, O'Kelly wrote a long letter to Seán Murphy in Vichy. The letter accompanied a mishmash of documents that O'Kelly had received at the *chancellerie provisoire* of the Irish Legation installed in the premises of the count's wine business on the place Vendôme. In the letter, O'Kelly mentioned that a trip he had planned to the internment camp in Besançon would have to be delayed until the beginning of February. Nonetheless, he was happy to report that a number of people had already been released from the camp, 'not because they are Irish, but because they are over 60, or the mothers of children under 15 or seriously ill'. He added that he planned to visit the internment camps at Saint-Denis and Drancy as well and said he had high hopes that he would manage to 'obtain the release of practically all our people there'.[31] O'Kelly finally made it down to Besançon in February 1941, accompanied by another Irishman (probably his businessman friend John Francis Keane). The count spent ten days at the internment camp and managed to interview 170 internees, 'of whom 70 definitely established claims to citizenship', he wrote in his report to Vichy.[32] A number of parties handed over identity papers to O'Kelly, which he brought back to Paris for verification, and it was hoped that all people with claims to Irish papers would be quickly released, he wrote.

During the summer of 1941 Seán Murphy, in a report to Dublin, provided further details of O'Kelly's work securing the release of Irish nationals from internment camps earlier that year. Most people had been very quickly released after his intervention, Murphy wrote, but:

> ... a very large number (perhaps 200 at least) of persons (mainly religious) of Irish birth or descent ... was also interned in November and December last ... Many of these have since been released on obtaining limited-validity passports approved from the Legation that they are of Irish origin [*sic*]. It would seem, however, that the German authorities are not ill-disposed to find an excuse for releasing internees.[33]

Among those held at Besançon whom O'Kelly managed to have released in the early months of 1941 were a number of Irish nuns, including Isabella Keenan (whose religious name was Sister Angèle de Saint Paul) and Sister Mary Kevin O'Brien. Evelyn Murrough O'Brien Toulmin, a well-known cricketer, born in 1877, the son of Rev. Frederick Bransby Toulmin and Katherine O'Brien (sister of the 13th Baron Inchiquin, Lucius O'Brien of Dromoland Castle), was also freed. Toulmin apparently was the Germans' principal point of contact with the Irish internees at

Besançon before he was released because of his age. He died in Paris in January 1945.

Also released from Besançon in early 1941 was Bluebell, aka Margaret Kelly. Even without O'Kelly's intervention, her pregnancy meant she had a good excuse to be sent home. On 19 April 1941 Bluebell's second child, christened Francis, was born. Six weeks later, her husband, Marcel Leibovici, fearful of the gathering crackdown on foreign Jews, left Paris with false papers for Marseille in the *zone libre*, leaving Bluebell alone with two babies to look after. Bluebell needed money to do this, so she decided to return to the cabaret scene. According to her authorised biography, she was unwilling to go back to work at the Folies Bergère, where she had been choreographer before the war, because of the anti-Semitism of the theatre manager and the large number of off-duty German soldiers that went to shows there.[34]

Fortunately and quite unexpectedly, she was approached by the manager of a small cabaret called the Chantilly in the rue Fontaine, close to where she lived in the 9th arrondissement. Her biographer states plainly that the Chantilly's 'patrons were mainly French, rather than the German military occupiers of Paris'.[35] But that hardly does justice to the establishment, which was one of the main meeting points of Parisian gangsters and Gestapo agents (often one and the same) during the Occupation. It was also often the scene of score settling between Corsican gangs who controlled the prostitution and drug scene around the Pigalle area where the Chantilly was situated. 'Every second day,' according to Pierre Bourget, 'the owner of the Chantilly had to have his maître d' evacuate wounded parties wrapped up in table cloths to the Marmottan hospital … The fights provoked by the aggressiveness of local mobsters in the pay of the Gestapo and the mafia from Ajaccio were such that the Kommandatur had to issue appropriate warnings.'[36]

One of the most (in)famous *habitués* of the Chantilly during those years was Pierre Loutrel, also known as Pierrot le Fou, a murderer and mythical figure of the French underworld who worked for the Gestapo before switching sides shortly before the Liberation and meeting a violent end during an armed robbery in 1946. The dark side of the Chantilly is hinted at by Bluebell in her 1985 biography, in which she admitted that the place, 'while not German, was very definitely shady. It was a favourite haunt for black marketeers, who would openly conduct their transactions over drinks.'[37] She herself was present one night during a gun battle in the cabaret between what she described as collaborationists and black marketeers. After this incident, the Chantilly was closed by the police – but it reopened three days later, no doubt thanks to the pulling of some appropriate strings.

One day in 1941 Bluebell was summoned to meet a German colonel called Feldman, who asked her if she was interested in staging the show she put on in the Chantilly in Germany. As she was Irish, there could be no 'conflict of interest' or of loyalty, Feldman argued. But Bluebell pointed out that she held a British passport and that many of her relatives were fighting against the Germans, so it would be inappropriate to take up such an offer, which was dropped.

Count O'Kelly was deeply concerned about cases of distress among the Irish population in occupied France and the lack of any formal Irish structure to help them. For release from captivity was not the end of the Irish internees' woes. As Con Cremin wrote after O'Kelly's expedition to Besançon, while Irish identity papers may have got Irish people out of prison, now 'a number of them … will be destitute but will no longer be able to count on assistance from the Americans'. Up to that point the Americans had shown a certain amount of leeway, but by early 1941 the rules had been tightened, 'presumably on instructions from London', Cremin explained, and aid channelled through the US embassy was limited 'strictly to holders of British passports, thus leaving a number of indigent Irish to fend for themselves'.[38] In the absence of any help from the Irish government, O'Kelly wrote in his letter of 24 January to the Legation, 'the choice before many of them is to stick to their British passports, receive relief, and be interned, or else obtain the Irish passports to which they are perfectly entitled, go free and starve'. This, according to O'Kelly, was 'a deplorable situation, but it is quite obvious that these people are our responsibility in the last analysis and I stay awake nights thinking what can be done to help them. If one thing is more certain than another it is that, if we have not succeeded in doing something effectual soon, starvation will face many of the people whom I hope to have released within the next few weeks.'[39] O'Kelly wondered whether some sort of relief might be organised via the US-based Knights of Columbus, which had the triple advantage of being Catholic, mostly Irish and wealthy.

O'Kelly was right about the extent to which Irish people stranded in France had to depend on foreign charity: in the early part of the Occupation, many Irish stuck in France – some with Irish passports and others with British ones – were helped by British charitable institutions. In sharp contrast to the attitude of the authorities in Dublin, which fumbled to come up with an adequate arrangement for stranded Irish nationals, the British in France could also benefit from welfare provided by US charities.

Writing from Marseille in February 1941, Howard Kershner, director of relief for the American Friends Service Committee, a Quaker charity, wrote that it had been advised by its Paris representative that 'three hundred Irish people have been released from the prison camps in the occupied zone of France and are now without any possible means of support or permission to work. We have the possibility of opening a canteen for them if money to purchase food is available.' However, the committee also wanted to know whether the Irish were 'entitled to the allocation being paid to English prisoners through the medium of the American Embassy in Paris'.[40]

The news on that score was not good, as holders of Irish passports – and that included people who had exchanged their British passports for Irish ones – were not entitled to benefit from the allowances paid through American consulates to British subjects in France. This explains why a number of Irish people initially hesitated before giving up their British passports. Like Fr Monaghan before him, Fr O'Grady had been briefly detained at the end of 1940 because he held a British passport. Yet, in spite of this ordeal, in an August 1940 letter to Vichy, O'Kelly had explained that O'Grady was reluctant to exchange his British passport (even if now expired) for an Irish one because the British document enabled him 'to get funds from members of the Congregation from the American Embassy (as representing British interests) whereas this recourse would be closed to him if he held an Irish passport'.[41]

Largely based on O'Kelly's reports from Paris and knowledge of the arrangements the British had put in place, Seán Murphy and Con Cremin in Vichy took up the case of Irish citizens in distress with Dublin. On 4 March 1941 the Legation sent a terse telegram to the DEA stating: 'financial position of nationals daily growing worse demands for assistance increasing please reply urgently on proposals my telegrams n 68 and 106'. There followed a febrile exchange of messages between Vichy and Dublin. In one cable, the Legation wrote:

> … the number of Irish citizens and those of Irish birth now requesting passports who are or soon will be destitute is about 300 (not including religious). A great many of these have been interned and are gradually being released. In the majority of cases savings have been already spent. Employment is impossible and their relatives in Ireland are not in a position to assist. While holding

British passports they received through the American consulates subsistence allowances up to a maximum of £10 per month with little or no regard to their ability to repay. In present circumstances 1,000 francs per month would seem to be the minimum on which these persons could live.[42]

But Murphy had to whittle the number of potential aid recipients down from 300 when the DEA told him, in a cable dated 8 March 1941, that it would only assist 'actual Irish citizens'. He was also told to ensure that any full citizens in France requiring assistance furnished a list of relatives in Ireland in a position to guarantee funds provided by the department. Also to be excluded from Murphy's list were Irish citizens who were members of religious communities (these were supposedly self-sufficient). In his reply to the DEA cable, Murphy wrote that, while he agreed that the 'great majority sought Irish passports to avoid internment or secure release therefrom (rather than financial help)', the department's decision 'will cause very great disappointment' among Irish passport holders. He argued that 'in majority of cases holders of passports who are not actual citizens were born in Ireland and may consequently claim repatriation'.[43] Murphy evidently felt he would get no further with the mandarins in Dublin because he wrote to the department again on 12 March to say that the number of 'full Irish citizens' who would require special assistance would now be 'about 100', each of whom would be liable to receive a FF1,000 per month allowance (or rather 'advance', backed by guarantees from relatives back in Ireland), a figure equivalent to about €340 today.[44] The maximum amount that the DEA was prepared to allow per individual was quickly revised a little higher to be in line with the maximum amounts decreed by the British for their citizens, but still proved inadequate.

On the DEA's instructions, somebody in the Legation – possibly Count O'Kelly – finally drew up an actual list of Irish citizens destitute in Paris and occupied France in May 1941. Despite Murphy's estimate two months before that about 100 would require assistance, it contained just six names, including that of Robert Armstrong, a First World War veteran born in Newbliss, County Monaghan in 1894, who lived in Valenciennes, close to the Belgian border. Armstrong, who worked for the Imperial War Graves Commission in Valenciennes and was married to a Frenchwoman, had been granted an Irish passport in January 1936. The other five on the list were all female – Mary Collins, her flatmate Bridget Hughes, Arabella D'Arcy Hayden, Sarah Lawrence and Hannah Mulligan. Two months later, in another list, the Legation identified just three Irish citizens with full (as opposed to one-year) passports in Paris 'in financial need'. These were Collins, Hughes and Hayden. In January 1942 the Legation had just one new name, Moira Perry, to add to the list from the previous July, and Sarah Lawrence and Robert Armstrong no longer appeared.[45] What had happened? Lawrence, in spite of her advanced years, had for some reason been deemed not to be a 'full Irish citizen', but the case of Armstrong is more mysterious. Perhaps he went to ground and lost contact with the Legation, or found a more effective source of help. After the war's end a friend, Eugène Dennis, wrote to the American military attaché in Paris to relate Armstrong's wartime activities and describe how the Irishman, cut off from his usual source of income in the United Kingdom, 'had to fend for himself at the start'. But 'it was really in this period that he came to appreciate his good friends and the Valenciennes municipal authorities, who helped him as best they could'. Armstrong found refuge at the home of one of these friends in Valenciennes, 'where he was treated like a son of the family'.[46] Armstrong was arrested for Resistance activities in November 1943 and deported to Germany, where he died a year later.

Mary Collins, who appeared in the May and July 1941 lists,

felt that she was very poorly treated by the Irish authorities and short-changed when compared with her flatmate Bridget Hughes. In early 1945, by now reinstalled in Paris, the Legation told the DEA that Mary Collins had informed it that 'her circumstances (were) little better than they were during the German Occupation' and that she earned 'a very meagre living by working as a nurse who is paid by the hour'. Collins was 'very irate' to learn by letter from the Legation that she was expected to repay the maintenance allowance she was supposed to have been accorded by the DEA during the Occupation – an allowance she claimed she never received, while her flatmate, Bridget Hughes, did. The difference in treatment seems to have stemmed from Collins' unwillingness to give the names of references in Ireland 'who would then become aware of her poor circumstances'. Collins told the Legation that she intended to write to an Irish newspaper at the earliest opportunity to protest the shabby treatment she'd received at the hands of the Legation and the DEA.[47]

There were more Irish in need of help than the handful of people that appeared on the Legation lists of spring and summer 1941, but 'it was extremely difficult to get this information', according to a note from the Legation to Dublin. Fr O'Grady at St Joseph's had suggested that some Irish were reticent to have their names on any official list. Murphy explained that he thought this might be because some Irish were already receiving assistance from British sources via US consulates in France. A case in point was May Nolan, who wrote to the Legation from the girls' hostel run by Irish nuns in rue Murillo in Paris in October 1941 to state that she didn't want her parents to send her any money from Ireland, as she was getting a 'monthly loan' from the government in London.

One person initially overlooked as a candidate for a DEA remittance was John Pilkington – perhaps because he had approached neither the Legation nor Fr O'Grady at St Joseph's by the time the May and July 1941 lists were drawn up. Pilkington stands out as a rare case of a young, able-bodied Irish male who was not a priest and lived right throughout the Occupation in Paris. Born in Dún Laoghaire in 1904, he is described as a 'man of letters' in his file at the Service historique de la Défense and appears to have been making a living as a translator when war broke out.[48] As a British-passport holder, he was detained for several months in 1940 at Saint-Denis, where, according to himself, the Germans broke some of his teeth. On the intervention of O'Kelly, who probably issued him an Irish passport, he was released sometime before June 1941. Writing from an address at 47 rue Erlanger in the 16th arrondissement in the same month, he asked his mother to send him £15 each month (the maximum DEA rules would allow per individual, similar to the amount that the British authorities were prepared to give to subjects of Her Majesty) 'because life is so dear here'. But his allowance does not seem to have reached him on a regular basis, or was grossly insufficient, because just over a year later the Legation in Vichy informed the DEA in Dublin that Pilkington 'owes a considerable amount of money and is in very great need of funds'.[49]

Pilkington's money problems persisted throughout the Occupation and he wrote to Vichy to explain that as a foreigner it was impossible for him to find work and that inflation had eroded the value of the money he received from Ireland. But in December 1942 the Legation told him it was unable to help him find a job and that it could not increase his monthly allowance because he was already receiving the maximum amount authorised by the DEA. Worse, his mother back in Ireland intimated that she might not be in a position to continue to send the £15 per month he was receiving up to then. In July 1943 he joined a long line of Irish citizens complaining to the Legation that his allowance had not been increased to keep pace with inflation. 'The cost of living has more than doubled ... Also, the exchange rate has increased, but the *traitement* has always remained the same,' he wrote.[50] 'Do your best, as life here is not *drôle*.'[51] Pilkington's money problems persisted until after the end of hostilities in Europe. In June 1945 he complained again in a letter to the Legation that he was finding it very difficult to live on the few pounds that his mother had been sending him each month.

***

Unlike some Irish nationals, Ireland's representative in Paris, Count O'Kelly, was not in danger of falling into destitution. Apart from paying himself a regular wage from his own business, Vendôme Wines, he was in receipt of a salary from the DEA for his work for the Legation, as well as the pension to which he had been entitled since being forced to retire as Ireland's minister to France in 1935. The funds ensured that the count continued to mix with the *crème de la crème* of French society and was able to keep up his membership of the Travellers' Club. But some of his upper-class friendships were strange, not least that with Michel Dassonville, son of a textile-factory owner in Lille, who was a notorious profiteer and German agent during the Occupation.

Dassonville first appeared in O'Kelly's life when the Germans put pressure on the latter to sideline some of Vendôme Wines' original company shareholders because they were enemy nationals based in London. Dassonville stepped in to take their place on the occasion of the capital increase of September 1941. The Frenchman had much bigger fish to fry – notably, he was a fence for the fictitious aryanisation of companies belonging to the Jewish oligarch Worms. Yet Dassonville proved decisive in keeping Vendôme Wines afloat financially and quite possibly recruited some big clients for the company among the occupying forces, hence ensuring that the claim that Vendôme Wines' clientele was '75–80% allemande' was actually not far from the truth.

It is possible that Dassonville was returning a favour that

he owed to O'Kelly. Dassonville's British wife, Florence, had approached O'Kelly in the months following the Germans' arrival in Paris to request an Irish passport. She found he was happy to help as far as he could. In September 1940 O'Kelly sent her passport application and photos to the Legation in Vichy, along with a note that explained that Florence's father, Richard Owen, had been born in Dublin. As 'the Dassonvilles are personal friends of mine … I would [be] very grateful if the case would be expedited as much as possible as the young woman is scared stiff that she may get into trouble'.[52]

In reality, Florence Dassonville had no connections to Ireland. Nor did her father, Richard Owen, in spite of O'Kelly's claim that he was born in Dublin. In fact, Richard Owen, a fine art dealer, was born in Dulwich, England.[53] Florence's mother was a Franco-American and Florence was born in Paris. None of Florence's grandparents had an ounce of Irish blood, according to family sources.

Florence Owen had married Michel Dassonville in April 1939. During the 1930s Dassonville had made the acquaintance of Helmut Knochen, who was sent to Paris in June 1940 on an intelligence-gathering mission before rising to become head of the security police in Paris in 1941. Thanks to his friendship with Knochen, Dassonville – who was a member of a cartel of pro-collaboration industrialists – took control of a number of companies previously owned by Jews. In return, Dassonville became a *Vertrauensman*, gathering intelligence for the Gestapo under the code name T 531. Numerous contacts in Spain and Portugal meant he travelled there frequently, using his trips to infiltrate Allied intelligence networks, while apparently also finding time to denounce people who hid Jews in Paris. A couple of months before D-Day in June 1944, he is alleged to have brought back information to Knochen from Madrid that included the precise date and location of the Allied landings in June 1944. Fortunately for the Allies, Dassonville's tip-off was ignored by the German high command.[54]

The Dassonvilles lived at 9 square du Bois de Boulogne (now square de l'Avenue Foch) in the 16th arrondissement, the most upscale neighbourhood of Paris. This street, still isolated today from the surrounding neighbourhood by a closed, gated entrance, was almost entirely requisitioned by various branches of the German occupying forces between 1940 and 1944. Number 8 housed the security police, the SIPO-SD, headed by Dassonville's friend Helmut Knochen. Number 21 was the headquarters of Dienstelle Otto, responsible for buying French goods (including textiles, precious metals and wine) at knockdown prices and shipping them back to the Reich.

Interrogated by the French intelligence services in November 1944, Dassonville stated that after Knochen had turned up by chance one day at his villa outside Paris in July 1941, they renewed their friendship from before the war. 'In the course of this first visit,' Dassonville said, 'I impressed on him the difficulties in which my wife found herself on account of her British citizenship and Knochen told me right away not to worry. It was after this meeting that Count O'Kelly de Gallagh, Ireland's minister, granted my wife an Irish passport. I kept the authorities at the British embassy in Madrid informed ... of this fact, which they approved.'[55] In line with most of the statements of this untrustworthy individual during his interrogations in 1944–1945, Dassonville's implication that the Germans somehow played a part in obtaining an Irish passport for his wife may be without foundation. Nevertheless, Dassonville was able to peddle his friendship with Knochen – as well as with O'Kelly – to save Florence from being sent to an internment camp. Dassonville used his connections with the Legation to try to obtain Irish papers for some of his pals as well, including one A. P. Burke, resident in Cannes, who was invited to apply for an Irish passport in February 1941.[56]

Michel Dassonville's marriage to Florence went downhill quickly. By 1941 she had a baby boy to look after and decided she wanted to leave Michel and sit out the war in Madrid. Michel was not against separation but would not countenance Florence leaving Paris with his son. In the end, the couple came to some sort of working relationship that meant that Florence stayed in their luxury apartment in the 16th arrondissement while Dassonville continued to live a dissolute life, marked by affairs with other women and crooked business deals with the Germans.

***

By early 1941 the Home Office in London, which wanted to interrogate Desmond Nolan for suspected espionage, considered it had enough evidence to request his extradition from Portugal based on the pre-war rape charges against him. A basis for British suspicions about Nolan's spying was found in a statement from a double agent in Lisbon called Snow ('not one of our most reliable' agents, according to a British security service note). He told MI5 that the Germans 'asked me to make arrangements for him to work in Ireland, where they want to send a lot of agents ... They have arranged with him that he goes to Ireland and his wife and two children with him, and I have to contact him there and send agents through.' But by May 1941 the pressure the British were putting on the Portuguese authorities had convinced the Nolans to leave Lisbon. They next turned up in Madrid. There, Nolan told the Irish ambassador, Leopold Kerney, that 'in consequence of his difficulties with the British Consul in Lisbon, he had been imprisoned for a few days by the Portuguese authorities', but that while in jail he had met a German who introduced him to a branch of the Nazi Party in the Portuguese capital.[57]

The Nolans next made it to Berlin. The security service file kept on Desmond Nolan at Kew contains some discrepancies in the account of how they arrived there. However, it seems that from Madrid they made their way by train to the German capital, courtesy of visas provided by Desmond Nolan's Abwehr contacts in Lisbon. When they were in Berlin in June 1941, they went without much delay to see William Warnock at the Irish Legation there to exchange their single joint Irish passport for two separate ones: these were granted – but only for the time left to lapse on the joint one-year passport granted in November 1940 when they were still in Nice. Indeed, a note from MI5 from this time confirmed that 'instructions have been issued that the Nolans' Irish passports are not to be renewed after this date'.[58] No doubt the British had by now managed to inform the DEA in Dublin that, apart from the rape charges facing Desmond Nolan in the United Kingdom, he had abandoned an infant child in Nice and was wanted for embezzlement by the French police.

The Nolans did not stay long in Berlin. One report suggests that, shortly after arriving in the German capital in June 1941, Nolan's wife decided she wanted to travel to Cap d'Ail (outside Nice) in the south of France, where they had left one of their children the previous year. In September 1941, according to an account by Henry William Wicks, Nolan and his wife were issued diplomatic passports by the German foreign ministry and 'sent to Paris where they were guests in a military hotel … situated in the rue Lafayette, where his two children were brought to them. He and his wife went to race meetings and indulged in "black marketing" etc.'[59] From Paris, Nolan was to be sent to Ireland via Bilbao, 'to carry on German propaganda'. But, according to Wicks' account, 'something went wrong. The passages for Ireland were already booked and the Nolans were about to leave when they were arrested early one morning by the Gestapo and interned.'[60]

Whether or not the Nolans were confined in Paris because they got cold feet about their mission to Ireland, by November 1941 they were back in Berlin where they were both arrested upon expiry of their Irish passports (Wicks suggests that Nolan had gotten into trouble in Berlin 'through his making false statements ... over the matter of food rations'[61]). Desmond Nolan was sent to an internment camp for British civilians in Upper Silesia, while his wife was sent to a camp in Liebenau, close to Lake Constance in southern Germany, and two of the couple's children were sent to a foundling home in Nanterre in the Paris suburbs.

Nolan's file in the United Kingdom National Archives contains yet another version of events. According to this version, while in Lisbon and then Madrid, Nolan had negotiated a deal to work with German military intelligence, who provided him with a ticket and all necessary visas for the trip to Berlin via Paris to see his taskmasters. But, during the stopover in Paris, Nolan and his family went to ground until they were discovered and arrested by the German authorities in September 1941.

Meanwhile, in spite of British efforts to deprive the Nolans of the protection provided by an Irish passport, a note from the DEA to William Warnock shows that as late as October 1942 he saw grounds for renewing passports to the couple. Nolan's father, Patrick Joseph Nolan, with an address at Cabra Park in Dublin, had, Desmond Nolan claimed, served in the Free State army, while the parents of Nolan's wife, Elizabeth, born Brodie-Browne, came from Cork and were both domiciled in Ireland in December 1922. But the DEA stood firm and reminded Warnock that instructions had been issued to all offices abroad not to renew Desmond Nolan's passport and to have it impounded if presented for renewal. Officially, the Irish authorities had ascertained that Nolan had 'no claim whatsoever to Irish citizenship'; as it turned out, contrary to what he had claimed, both his parents had been born in Great Britain, just like Nolan himself.

***

A woman called Susan Hilton turned up in Paris in early 1941 and was lucky to call upon Count O'Kelly at a time when he was still liberally handing out temporary, one-year passports. Hilton herself felt her claim to an Irish passport 'was not very good because my husband is British'. But obtain it she did and she immediately used her new papers to obtain travel visas to Spain and Portugal.[62] In the Declaration of Nationality form that O'Kelly made her fill out in February 1941, Hilton said that she was a journalist and that her full name was Susan Dorothea May Thérèse Moore Hilton, born in India in 1915. She stated her father to be Cyril Edward Sweeney, born in County Donegal in 1890, and her mother to be Dorothy Tower Bellini-Barter, born in the same year in Ootacamund in southern India. She also had a brother who lived in Oldcastle, County Meath.

Hilton had quite a tale to tell. In her declaration for O'Kelly, she gave her date of departure from Ireland as 1938. This information was used to determine whether the applicant had been present on Irish soil on the day the Irish Free State officially came into existence on 6 December 1922. She chose to interpret the question in a way that served her application and her reply that she had left Ireland in 1938 was strictly true. But Hilton was nowhere near Ireland in 1922 and was only in Ireland in 1938 to seek refuge after coming under increasing pressure from the British authorities because of her membership of the British Union of Fascists. She moved back to the United Kingdom after a few weeks, when her comrades-in-arms sounded the all-clear.

Hilton decided to leave England again to join her husband in India in May 1940, just a couple of weeks after the Germans had launched their Blitzkrieg in the west. Her ship, the *Kemmendine*, slipped anchor from Glasgow but was captured and scuttled in the Indian Ocean by the German surface raider *Atlantis* in July 1940. Hilton was placed by the Germans on a captured Norwegian ship, the *Tirranna*, but a British submarine sank the *Tirranna* in September 1940 off the French coast. Hilton was picked up a second time, along with an Irishman, Thomas Cormac McGowan (or MacGowan) from Sligo, who had been medical officer on board the *Kemmendine*. In her July 1945 interrogation by the British, Hilton described McGowan as 'over sixty years old and one could see at a glance that he was an old drinker. I was sorry for him because everyone laughed at him, and because he talked to himself.'[63] No doubt her own predilection for alcohol helped her sympathise with McGowan. Hilton was detained at the German naval base in Royan until December 1940 and during the couple of months she spent there, whether because of her drinking or because of the friendship she had struck up with McGowan, the Germans came to consider Hilton as Irish – with fateful consequences.

Fellow British survivors of the *Kemmendine* were sent to an internment camp that month, but since Hilton was by that point deemed to be Irish (her British passport had gone down with the *Tirranna* in the Bay of Biscay), she was released with the *Tirranna*'s Norwegian crew members. She and McGowan were put on a train to Paris, where they arrived in December 1940. She did not (or could not) use the travel visas to Iberia she obtained after her visit to the Legation shortly thereafter, for in the summer of 1941 Hilton was staying, courtesy of the German authorities, at the Hôtel Cavour at 86 rue de Lafayette in the 9th arrondissement. As a 'journalist', she soon was convinced by them to write and broadcast about her adventures for Radio Paris and other German-controlled media.

In 1942 Hilton had a book published in Hamburg entitled *Eine Irin erlebt England und den Seekrieg* (an Irishwoman's experiences of England and the war at sea), in which she outlined her misadventures on the high seas. She also explained how she had been converted to the fascist cause in 1930s England after she had witnessed the sheer poverty and hardship that the majority of the British population lived in under a benighted upper-class plutocracy. *Eine Irin* also contains some useful insights into Hilton's life in Paris:

> On December 14, 1940, the Norwegians, the Irish doctor [Thomas McGowan] and myself travelled as far as Paris … Our luggage was very basic. It consisted of two blankets and a cardboard box, as well as food for two days … We arrived late in the night in Paris, half dead from the cold. There at the railway station, the German Red Cross took care of us. We received soup, bread and coffee.[64]

But the account of her arrival that Hilton gave to the British when she was interrogated in July 1945 was much less upbeat. She told them that she and Dr McGowan had indeed made their way to Paris, but once they were there they were cut loose 'early in the morning, without proper clothing, no money and no food cards. Added to that it was Sunday and the snow was lying on the ground. It was pitch dark and neither of us knew our way around.'[65]

She continued in *Eine Irin*:

> The doctor and I received a document that authorised us to seek out the diplomatic representatives of our country. We spent the night at the Red Cross outpost; black coffee helped us through the hours. Representatives of the Norwegian Red Cross gave us cigarettes and informed us where we had to go the following morning.
>
> It was still pitch dark when we made our way through knee-high snow; we felt thoroughly exhausted after the long journey and sleepless night.
>
> Our new freedom brought with it new worries, the first of which was where to find food and lodgings. We finally found refuge in a hotel until the return of our diplomatic representative, who unfortunately was away on official business.
>
> The winter of 1940/1941 was unusually hard, with lots of snow

and biting winds. I became sick. I lay two months in bed, cared for by the Irish doctor who expected no payment in return.[66]

Again, the account that Hilton gave of her first hours in Paris to her British interrogators in July 1945 was slightly different:

Dr McGowan felt the urgent need of cognac and I could not wait for more than two or three minutes without wanting to disappear because my kidneys were so bad. Eventually, we reached the American Embassy where we were fortunate as Mr Cross, together with his wife, paid an unexpected Sunday visit … He was very good to us – had us put in a hotel, got our food cards for us and generally bothered.[67]

If one is to believe the account that Hilton gave in 1945, the Americans even issued her with papers that would have permitted her to enter the United States. But she was too weak to avail of the opportunity, and money she requested of her father-in-law via the Legation arrived too late.

Hilton had broached her financial difficulties in *Eine Irin*:

Money remained the most delicate question … There was certainly the possibility of receiving small amounts of money from Ireland; but that was a very tortuous process, with relatives over there having to be informed and long and detailed formalities undertaken before money could be transferred. Should I have had to wait for everything to be sorted out, I would have died of hunger.[68]

She described how she went to see O'Kelly about her dilemma. The count, although he had issued her with a one-year passport ('I don't know why he gave it to me, as it was not true that I was Irish'), does not seem to have had too much sympathy for Hilton's poor state of health or her financial difficulties. When she asked him what she was meant to do given she had no money, he simply answered, 'Starve!'[69] 'And so,' she continued in *Eine Irin*:

> I went to the German authorities and laid out my predicament. I was immediately sent to the National Socialist People's Welfare (NSV) office, where I was given a small amount of money and ration cards. From this moment on, things began to go better for me. I frequently received news of the other survivors from my ship. They naturally had to be interned. I received a postcard that was typical of man's inextinguishable courage in the face of misfortune: it read 'we consider ourselves lucky and happy'.[70]

Brought back to strength, Hilton soon infiltrated the Irish community in Paris. Her dealings (real or imagined) with that community are described at length in *Eine Irin:*

> At this time I came into contact with the Irish colony in Paris, They had been left to fend for themselves when the Germans occupied France. The majority of them had no means at their disposal. The Irish consulate could provide little help. Ireland is a poor country and is not able to send limitless amounts of currency abroad, especially as there are more Irish outside Ireland than on the island itself. The exiles nonetheless remain just as good Irishmen as those that have never left the hills of Donegal or the shores of Killarney and Dublin.
>
> Some of the shipwrecked sailors grew close to the Irish colony. Since they were in a bad way, the consulate sought to get them back to their homeland. In the meantime, they wandered around Paris without speaking or understanding a sole word of French.
>
> One day one of them had a huge appetite for oranges. He asked a policeman where he could buy some. When the policeman heard him, he could hardly believe he was dealing with an Englishman. So he accompanied him to a German military post. When the

Irishman saw German soldiers, he thought he was going to be thrown into prison, and took to his heels. The French policeman ran after him, blowing his whistle, chasing him from one café to the next as the fugitive shouted 'I'm Irish! I'm Irish!' The officer of the peace finally caught up with him and the whole situation was cleared up to the general satisfaction of both sides.

The Irish colony had two meeting places: one was a café on the Place Victor Hugo and the other was a house on the Avenue Carnot. There we used to sit to chat and curse Paris, our poverty and the war. Most of us didn't have any work. The fact that the French never managed to make a distinction between the Irish and the English was a frequent topic of conversation. Over centuries of war, any time there has been conflict between France and England, the Irish have given the French their support and expect the same in return. But today the French don't recognise any difference between Ireland and England. This just shows how far English propaganda has penetrated since the days when the Irish fought on the side of the French against England.

But our compatriots in Paris would sooner be out of the war altogether. They may curse heaven and earth about their current circumstances, but when the war is over, they will remember this time as a huge adventure that they will tell their children and grandchildren about. It has always been thus with the Irish. Ireland lives wherever its people gather together. Ireland lives so long as her people are able to accept their misfortunes with good humour, and it will live as long as its people sing songs in its honour.

Lots of exaggerated rumours went through Paris; but I became thoroughly convinced that all these rumours, without exception, emanated from Jews. Just as in London, there seemed to be a limitless number of Jews in Paris.

I thought with increasing interest of those who had been left behind on the rescue ship. It was difficult to find out anything about what became of it. But one day, I came across three press cuttings from English newspapers. The name of our ship was the *Kemmendine*, and its commander was Captain Reid.

The reports on our scuttling were generally correct, with the exception of the account that appeared in 'The Daily Telegraph'. This newspaper wrote that the captain [of the German raider *Atlantis*] had ordered eight of the prisoners on board to come out on deck to see the end of their ship along with him. In actual fact, we all stood out on deck, and we were lavished with whiskey, cognac and cigarettes.[71]

During one of her interrogations by the British authorities in 1945, Hilton mentioned or was asked about Frederick (actually James) Blair, whom she said she met in Paris in 1941. 'He was down and out and running errands for the Irish embassy,' she told her interrogators.[72] Blair was born of a Scottish father and an Irish mother and had lived in Paris for many years, working for a US newspaper. Like Hilton, he later turned up in Berlin, where he became one of the speakers on the Irland-Redaktion, using the pseudonym Pat O'Brien. Blair was sacked from the Irland-Redaktion in 1942. According to another stalwart of German radio's Irish service, John O'Reilly, Hilton and Blair were sacked together 'following a scene in which Susan Hilton used endearing terms to Blair while he was in the announcing box, and still on air'.[73]

In the meantime, Hilton's companion in misfortune from the *Kemmendine*, Dr Thomas McGowan, had found refuge – along with Sarah Lawrence, one of the six people named in the Legation's May 1941 list of destitute Irish – in an old-persons' home at Noisy-le-Grand, a poor eastern suburb of Paris. McGowan, suffering from alcoholism, found himself cut off from any means of subsistence. Relatives back in Ireland had been contacted about sending him money each month, but on 9 September 1941, the Vichy Legation wrote to William Warnock in Berlin (at this

stage looking after Irish affairs in occupied France) that 'no definite arrangements' had yet been made to grant financial assistance to McGowan. At the end of the previous year, McGowan's
brother, Fr P. J. McGowan of Tulsk, County Roscommon, had
made a one-off payment, but nothing had been received from an
outside source since then. McGowan claimed to be owed money
by the Henderson Line, the owner of the *Kemmendine*. After the
Henderson Line informed the Irish Legation in Vichy that it was
not prepared to come to McGowan's assistance, Count O'Kelly
somehow made arrangements for FF850 to be paid each month
for his room and board. The Legation suggested to the DEA
back in Dublin that McGowan should be included among those
deserving of assistance from public funds 'if and when any arrangement in that matter is made', and he was eventually granted
a 'shipwreck indemnity' worth FF5,280 in December 1941.

The authorities in Dublin often proved slow in organising a
systematic flow of assistance for Irish citizens without a means
of subsistence of their own and without relatives back in Ireland
who could keep them afloat. Thomas McGowan may have paid
the price for this slowness, for he died in April 1942.

***

By early 1941 O'Kelly, even with the assistance of Louise Froc,
was faced with an increasing workload and he was finding it
'impossible to deal with enquiries and visitors', the numbers of
which had grown significantly since late 1940. Mme Froc had
been a secretary at the Legation almost continuously since it
had opened it in 1931. She had found herself out of a job when
the Legation departed Paris in June 1940, only to be taken on
again by the count in November that year. Given the rise in the
workload, Froc was joined in early 1941 by a younger woman,
Lucienne Marquetout, who also had previously been employed as
a junior shorthand typist at the Legation for several years. Mlle

Marquetout had been displaced by the arrival of Mary (or Ina) Foley from County Galway, who had turned up in Paris to take up her position as 'foreign service clerk' with the Paris Legation in the inauspicious month of May 1940, when she turned twenty-three. Foley's displacement to Vichy along with Con Cremin and Seán Murphy and the heavy work burden facing O'Kelly and Froc in Paris had enabled Marquetout to claim back her old position. But it was not to last.

O'Kelly's 'temporary chancery' operated initially from the premises of Vendôme Wines on place Vendôme, before moving back to the Legation premises in rue de Villejust in March 1941. However, the chancery's activities came to a halt on 10 June, when it was closed down by order of the German and French authorities.

The previous month O'Kelly had received a circular from the German authorities that was sent to all foreign diplomats left in Paris. It stated that the German government was no longer willing to tolerate the continued presence of diplomatic representatives in Paris when the seat of the French government was now in Vichy. In late May 1941 Seán Murphy had a long telephone conversation with O'Kelly in which the latter explained that the German authorities 'would definitely not' accept his continuing as consul in Paris. Pressure was coming from the Pétain regime in Vichy, which felt its legitimacy remained in doubt as long as countries continued to have representatives in occupied France. The Vichy authorities decided that international law allowed them to decree that any diplomats accredited to France who remained in occupied territories would simply not be recognised as accredited by the French Foreign Office. Thus, all diplomats were to leave Paris by 10 June 1941 at the latest and diplomatic premises there were to be closed. After that date, all matters involving foreign nationals in occupied France were to be dealt with by diplomatic missions in Berlin.[74]

Four days later, the Legation in Vichy informed the French

government that O'Kelly was being transferred from Paris to Vichy, with his wife and personal staff to follow in July. A notice was placed in the main Paris dailies to inform the Irish colony that the 'temporary Chancery' O'Kelly had been running since August 1940 was closing and that future correspondence should be addressed to the Legation in Berlin. During the course of the summer, O'Kelly placed a second notice in the Paris press looking for a place to rent on the Côte d'Azur for the summer holidays (while Seán Murphy and his family managed to make it back to Ireland for their holidays in June 1941).

O'Kelly left Paris in mid-June but travelled back there to pick up his sickly wife and household. Problems in obtaining the relevant travel papers meant he and his entourage did not leave Paris 'definitively' until July 1941. Over the next three years, however, the count was not content with living out a dull existence in remote Vichy. Instead, he periodically returned to Paris, both on behalf of the Legation and to look after the affairs of Vendôme Wines.

Although Seán Murphy had supplied Dublin with a full report of O'Kelly's activities in Paris in July 1941, the DEA asked for a further account of him in a memo of January 1942, requesting a precise report 'having regard to the date on which he took up official duty, the nature of this duty while there, expenses involved in connection with his duties and any other information which might be helpful to an understanding of his position generally in regard to the period of his service in Paris'. Was it possible that Dublin had no idea what O'Kelly had been doing in Paris in 1940–1941? Or were the mandarins at the DEA again quibbling over money? The DEA had already written to the Legation in Vichy in October 1940 to state that it 'wasn't aware that O'Kelly de Gallagh was in Paris looking after affairs'.[75]

In his reply to the January 1942 request from the DEA, Murphy explained that a major part of O'Kelly's tasks had 'entailed the obtaining of exit permits for Irish citizens desirous of leaving occupied France. Every conceivable difficulty was put in the way of obtaining these permits from the German authorities and only by repeated visits to the embassy, the consulate and the military police, combined with repeated invitations to meals to all concerned, could any results be achieved.' O'Kelly had requested that he be reimbursed for all the out-of-pocket expenses he had incurred, as well as removal costs to Vichy. 'Count O'Kelly does not claim,' Murphy explained, 'any extra remuneration in respect of this work, though it is obvious that such work was never contemplated in the arrangement concerning the Special Counsellorship. A claim would also appear to lie for the damage done to the carpet and walls by the constant flow of people crowded together in the corridor and on the stairs [of his premises at Vendôme Wines].'[76]

Both Louise Froc and Lucienne Marquetout lost their poorly paid jobs again when the Legation was forced to close its Paris premises. Froc wrote to Murphy in Vichy on 13 June 1941 asking for the indemnities that she was due and voicing the hope that the Legation in Paris would soon be able to reopen its doors to provide 'moral as well as material' comfort to the Irish community. 'How many poor girls have I seen distraught at the idea that they will no longer have any protection close by,' she wrote.[77] Con Cremin in Vichy replied to Froc very quickly, offering her a position at the Irish Legation in Berne, which she could not accept because of her husband's ill health. Marquetout was offered the same job, but she too declined, explaining that her brother was a prisoner of war, which meant there was nobody left to look after their aged mother. In any case, Marquetout had found a temporary job at the town hall of her local village outside Paris – appropriately enough managing ration cards – before being employed in a 'big radio business'. Froc also landed on her feet very quickly, joining a chemical company. 'However,' Marquetout wrote touchingly to Cremin on 10 August, 'we both regret the Legation and we think often of our poor Irish friends. How many of them must find themselves now in a very sad situation without the material and moral support the Legation provided.'[78]

***

By July 1941 the fate of the 'destitute Irish' had come to Susan Hilton's attention. Indignantly, she wrote to Warnock at the Legation in Berlin to state that 'there are more than 2,000 Irish here in occupied France, without the support of the Legation – and no Consul. Of those, 50% are comparatively poor, while some are entirely without funds. Many poor old women returned from Besançon imagining that they would have the support of their government, only to find that they had left one hell for another.'[79]

It is likely that Hilton picked up her information from spending time with the Irish community, or from the Irish priests at St Joseph's. She certainly knew Fr Monaghan. After the war she claimed she had helped him organise the escape of British merchant seamen. Fr Monaghan did indeed help Allied escapees during the war. Ironically, he was also approached for help by the Germans (and not just by people in their pay, such as Susan Hilton). In November 1943 Fr Monaghan met Oskar Pfaus, an Abwehr agent who had met IRA leaders in Dublin just before the war. Pfaus wanted the priest's help in finding an Irish girl in Paris willing to spy for the Germans in return for helping her to return home. Fr Monaghan apparently did put the German in touch with an Irish girl sufficiently desperate and homesick to contemplate a very uncertain trip back to Ireland at the Reich's expense. But Pfaus's efforts came to nought when Monaghan told him that the girl had been killed (although it is more likely that the Irishwoman had second thoughts or was talked out of the madcap scheme).[80]

As for Hilton, given her subsequent wartime 'career', it is not outside the realm of possibilities that her July 1941 missive was written at the behest of her German paymasters to embarrass the Irish government. By the time she wrote to the Berlin Legation in July 1941, Hilton was working for the Germans as a translator and propagandist and she was on the point of moving to Berlin to broadcast on Irland-Redaktion (Germany's wartime Irish propaganda service). Continuing her damning indictment, Hilton stated:

> … the British are getting support through the American authorities, while the Irish, who have nothing to do with the war, are left destitute. Apart from the utter cold-blooded cruelty of leaving one's nationals to starve, there is the political aspect to consider. The British are now jeering and saying: 'See now what your freedom means.' And certainly they have their justification. I myself feel that this state of affairs has arisen because Dublin is not fully aware of the appalling distress amongst the nationals in occupied territory. It would be a good thing therefore if you would inform them, making it clear that something must be done immediately.[81]

This was a hard-hitting letter, and one that left Warnock in Berlin asking his counterparts how he should respond. He also asked Dublin to spell out what funds were available for the destitute Irish in occupied France.[82] The answer at this stage in the war was that there were no funds available for the relief of Irish nationals who could not claim support from relatives or friends back in Ireland. Warnock wrote to Seán Murphy that there had 'as yet been no arrangement made for paying relief, in the ordinary sense of that term, to these or any other nationals in France. It would seem that the Department proposes to exhaust every alternative means before agreeing to support destitute nationals abroad from public funds.'[83]

After Hilton left Paris to embark on her short-lived career at Irland-Redaktion, along with Francis Stuart and a few others, the DEA in Dublin deemed that O'Kelly should not have granted her a temporary passport and instructed William Warnock in

Berlin not to renew it.[84] The Irish authorities decided not to aid Hilton in her attempts to return to Ireland and stopped handling money she received from her husband's bankers in England. At the end of April 1945, deprived of a passport and being held at a German internment camp in Liebenau on Lake Constance, she applied via the Swiss authorities for the replacement of her original British passport that she had lost when the *Kemmendine* went down in 1940. After the war, Hilton was indicted by the British authorities on ten charges of aiding the enemy and subsequently sentenced to eighteen months' imprisonment in Holloway prison. After her release she held a number of jobs, ending her days as a pet-shop owner in southern England.

Susan Hilton was not the only one to complain about the stinginess of the Irish authorities. Four years after Hilton's missive, the Legation found out, via the DEA, that Rose O'Donoghue, resident in Paris throughout the Occupation, had been telling her friends back in Ireland that there was no one to look after holders of Irish passports, even after the war.[85] Writing from rue du Dragon in the 6th arrondissement to Kathleen Barton in Dublin, she complained:

> The Irish colony thought the Legation through the Irish Red Cross would do something for them, at least since Liberation, either in the way of clothes or food, as some of them were sorely hit, and in fact some died of hunger as they had no money to buy a little extra food in the Black Market and their rations weren't sufficient. It is too bad no one looks after the colony holding Irish passports. I could write you a book about this question.

The DEA obtained this letter from the Ceann Comhairle in Dublin, whose wife was related to Kathleen Barton. Alarmed by the claim that Irish people had 'died of hunger', the DEA forwarded O'Donoghue's letter to the Paris Legation for a suitable reply. Seán Murphy was so incensed that O'Donoghue was summoned to the Legation in the rue de Villejust. There, as Murphy explained in a revealing letter back to the DEA, O'Donoghue stridently defended her position. 'What she meant,' wrote Murphy, 'was there was no one to give Irish people clothes and food like the British do. I explained to her that we had tried to get Irish Red Cross parcels but without success. She then said it was strange that Mr De Valera could offer food and clothing to the distressed countries of Europe, but could not give anything to the few Irish in France. I replied that the distressed people of Europe could not help their plight whereas the Irish in France could have returned home if they had wished.'

Murphy probably knew this argument was disingenuous. But at the end of what may have been a highly charged encounter, Murphy assured Dublin that he had managed to demolish O'Donoghue's credibility. 'I then asked her,' Murphy wrote:

… who were the Irish people who had died of hunger and she replied that she did not know but that she had heard it said that some Irish people had died of hunger. She added that she was not surprised as she had been so hungry herself. I asked her if she could find out the names of the people who had died and the dates of their death. She promised to do this but I should be surprised if I hear again from her. I made enquiries of the priests at Avenue Hoche and they were not aware of any Irish persons who had died of hunger and I think they would certainly have known any case of great distress. I formed the conclusion that Miss O'Donoghue made these statements to make her letter more interesting and to give the impression that she herself had been a bit of a martyr. She, like a great number of the Irish colony, only changed her British passport in 1940 to escape internment.[86]

***

Of course, Irish people in Paris during the Occupation not only faced money problems – even after the initial, somewhat indiscriminate round-ups of 1940, there was also still the risk of detention if they did not have irrefutable proof of their nationality. This was the case for Edward Byrne, born in Martinstown near Kilmallock, County Limerick in 1884. Byrne worked on a stud farm in Maisons-Laffitte outside Paris. Since he had a British passport, Byrne was briefly interned in Drancy in early 1941. Like many others, Byrne had to depend on his family contacting the Legation in the hope that it would take up his case. His daughter wrote to the Legation enquiring about his release (ultimately granted on age grounds), since the Legation had been good enough to issue him with a short-term Irish passport because of his Irish birth.

Many other Irish people worked in the horse industry around Paris before the war and found themselves stranded in France at the start of the Occupation. Johnny Mills, who described himself as a horse trainer and lived in Saint-Maurice, just beside the horse course at Vincennes in the inner eastern suburbs of Paris, left it a bit late to apply for an Irish passport, only doing so on 30 May 1940, less than a fortnight before the Wehrmacht strode into the capital. He had been born in Hamburg in 1893 and had been granted a British passport in March 1940. Although his only claim to Irish nationality was a father who had been born in Dublin in 1847, Mills was granted a one-year temporary passport. By late 1941 O'Kelly – as generous as ever in his distribution of documents – seems to have 'upgraded' Mills' passport to a five-year one.[87]

Also working in the horse industry around Paris was John Swaine from Dublin, who described himself in his Declaration of Nationality as a son of Michael J. Swaine, a Dublin city councillor. Swaine, who'd left Ireland at the end of the First World War, had previously worked in Chantilly in prime horse country north of

Paris, but in 1940 was 'head man' at stables in the heart of the French horse-breeding country at Maisons-Laffitte. In a letter to the Legation on 1 December 1941, William Warnock in Berlin frowned on Swaine's application because, he wrote, 'if he should lose his present employment, which is quite possible, he would be without subsistence'. Remembering the disquiet caused in Dublin by the liberal distribution of temporary passports a few months earlier and the DEA's tight-fisted approach to destitute nationals, Warnock wrote that he was reluctant to grant Swaine a passport 'unless he can show that it is most improbable that he will become a public charge'.[88] There is no record of what happened to Swaine after this.

Patrick Fenton, born in Knocklyon, County Limerick in 1896, had come to France to work as a jockey in Maisons-Laffitte in 1920 and was still there twenty years later. Having been freed from internment at the beginning of 1941, thanks to the intervention of O'Kelly, Fenton, who was possibly ill from tuberculosis, made it back to England, but had to leave his French wife, Marie, and family behind in France. In March 1942 the Legation in Vichy tried to pass on a message to Fenton from his wife, stating that the only financial assistance she was receiving came from the meagre income earned by her seventeen-year-old son, Patrick Francis, as an apprentice chartered surveyor. 'Two daughters are at school and the eldest daughter is at home as I am no longer in good health,' wrote Mrs Fenton to the Legation. 'I do a little sewing and am in great financial difficulty. We live on vegetables only. I would be very comforted if my husband could send me some money and parcels if possible. Ask him to give me news of him and of his relatives and of where they are. I am very uneasy.' Mrs Fenton ended her message saying: 'Without news since June 1940.'[89] But Patrick Fenton never received this message, for he had died in a sanatorium in Preston in northern England in November 1941.

Mary Catherine Reid, born in County Roscommon in 1904, was also involved in the horse industry there. Reid left Ireland in January 1921 for Argentina. In 1930 she married a Dutchman, Willem van Heemstra, in London. He was a member of an aristocratic Dutch family – his older sister, Ella, was the mother of Audrey Hepburn – but he and Mary Reid divorced in Paris less than seven years after their marriage. On her marriage she had acquired a Dutch passport, which she had to give up when she applied for an Irish one in September 1940. She gave her address as 4 rue Louis Codet, in the plush 7th arrondissement, with a second address at La Mare Colin, a stud farm near Montfort-l'Amaury west of Paris.

***

On 22 June 1941 Germany and her allies took the war to a new level when they invaded the Soviet Union. By the end of October, when Murphy sent a new update on the situation in France back to his superiors in Dublin, the Germans were advancing rapidly on Moscow. While French communist resistance to the German Occupation had been muzzled by the German–Soviet pact of August 1939, the German invasion of the Soviet Union led to an upsurge in guerrilla attacks by communist groups, which in turn produced a round of fearsome reprisals by the Germans. On the morning of 21 August 1941 communists gunned down a German naval adjutant as he boarded a metro train at Barbès-Rochechouart station in Paris, the first in a wave of attacks and reprisals over the following months. Communist commandos also gunned down Lieutenant-Colonel Karl Hotz in the centre of Nantes on 20 October and, a day later, another German official in Bordeaux. These attacks led the Germans to execute almost one hundred of their prisoners, many – but not all – connected to the Communist Party.

In his October 1941 report to Dublin, Seán Murphy indicated

that the attacks had 'caused a good deal of excitement' in France but were 'generally deprecated by all sections of opinion here'. That didn't mean that the French population was enamoured with the collaborationist tendencies manifested to varying degrees by members of the Vichy government. According to Murphy, 'Public opinion is, to put it at the lowest, extremely sceptical of the policy of collaboration which has brought few tangible results.' Marshal Pétain's conservative 'Révolution nationale' had not been embraced by the general population, and in the *zone libre* it was 'generally agreed', according to Murphy, that 'the population is up to 80% anti-German and in the occupied zone 85% very definitely anti-German'. Anti-German feeling was due to the food situation, according to Murphy, 'which the population attributes solely to the demands of the occupying authorities', with this feeling 'very greatly accentuated' by German reprisals. The worsening food situation was causing 'great discontent', and the secretary-general of food and supplies, Monsieur Archard, had been arrested because he had been discovered 'to be hand in glove with the black market out of which he had made several million francs'.[90]

Despite the growing hardships, Count O'Kelly had not lost his penchant for high living, as can be judged by the number of domestic servants he kept, even after he was banished to Vichy. The secretary to the Legation, Con Cremin, had two servants to look after himself, his wife and his two children. Childless O'Kelly had four, including Mme de Rougement, a *sécretaire-dame de compagnie*, Mme Vacheon, a maid, and Mme Bard, a cook, all at the service of his wife, Marjorie.[91] He also had a driver at his disposal, a Spaniard by the name of Francisco Gomez Collado. Cremin and his superior, Seán Murphy, lived in modest two-storey houses; the count lived in a manor house called Château de Beauregard just outside Vichy on the south bank of the Allier river, near the racecourse where he spent much of his not inconsiderable free time (while Murphy spent his time playing golf, using golf balls supplied by the Washington Legation). The count also continued his literary pursuits. His French translation of *Messr. Marco Polo*, a novel by the Irish writer Donn Byrne, was published with the aid of his friend John Francis Keane in Paris in September 1943.

Armed with some of the Legation's fuel allowance, O'Kelly visited his seventy-seven-year-old mother, Mary, who had been stuck at her ancestral home, Château de Rabastens near Toulouse, at the outbreak of the war and had been unable to travel back to Ireland since. During her enforced exile, Mrs O'Kelly received regular payments from her relatives that allowed her to survive. On at least one occasion, in September 1942, O'Kelly brought her from Rebastens to stay with him in Vichy.

But scarcities were spreading and did not spare the count. One of his first acts when he got to Vichy was to write to Peugeot in Paris to explain that, as the Legation's cars were often immobilised for want of petrol, he would be interested to know whether the company was in a position to supply four bicycles ('including two ladies' bikes') for his entourage.[92] It is not clear whether one of these diplomatic bikes was meant for him. He initially asked for two tonnes of coal to heat his manor house in the winter of 1941–1942, but obtained only one and a half. The indignities grew. In February 1942 he asked for and was granted a gun licence to go hunting, but in December of the same year was informed by the Vichy authorities that all gun licences were being withdrawn. Most humiliating of all, he had to request vouchers to allow him to buy goods, such as a new suit, shoes and bathroom linen. With food shortages the order of the day, O'Kelly's rural background may have been useful, for in March 1942 he requested, via the Legation, material to finish the construction of animal shelters and a hay barn at his residence.

The whole Legation, not just O'Kelly, was confronted with

wartime shortages. Fuel was indeed in very short supply. In mid-1943 Vichy was allocating the Legation fifty litres of petrol and one litre of oil per month for its needs, with a further twenty litres of petrol available on a discretionary basis. This paltry ration – reduced steadily to forty litres plus ten litres on a discretionary basis by December 1943 – was supposed to keep the Legation's three cars on the road. Yet, while a number of Irish people were facing destitution, at least Murphy and Cremin could count on Irish diplomatic outposts elsewhere to step in from time to time. Leopold Kerney in Madrid (who often drove a car and trailer as far as Lisbon to find food supplies for his family) served as a conduit for tea and coffee, as well as Carroll's cigarettes, and Robert Brennan, the minister plenipotentiary in Washington, was solicited to supply anything from coffee to large quantities of Camel cigarettes as well as the aforementioned golf balls. All these items were sent via the diplomatic bag. Even parcels of veal and ham were sent from Lisbon via Madrid to Vichy.[93] These international supply routes were undoubtedly slow, but the alternative was probably to do without.

In March 1941 the Vichy government's Ministry of Foreign Affairs had sent out a long circular to all diplomatic missions to explain how requests for new shoes had to be sent to the protocol service of the foreign ministry run by the Baron Petit de Beauverger (who employed an Irish maid called Mary Kelly and who had the good sense to switch camp by the end of 1942, when he joined the provisional government of the French republic in Algiers). In October 1941 Murphy wrote to de Beauverger looking for a coat and dress for two of his daughters, and in March of the following year he requested coupons to purchase three children's coats. In December 1941 de Beauverger had to deal with two requests on behalf of O'Kelly: one concerned a new set of wheels for his car and the other coupons to buy a new suit for him and his wife, Marjorie. O'Kelly even needed special authorisation to deliver three litres of milk each day from his residence at the Château de Beauregard to Murphy's house behind the Hôtel Gallia.

Food requests for official dinners also had to be sent to the head of protocol. One dinner at the Hôtel Gallia was organised by the Irish Legation in November 1941 for sixteen people. On 10 November the Irish requested for this dinner 'four poultry and, if possible, fish in sufficient quantity'. But the head of protocol replied that he needed at least five days' notice before being able to meet such a request.[94] A lunch for twenty people was hosted by the Legation on 8 July 1942, and another in December of that year.

As well as dealing with their own troubles, the closure of the Irish chancery run by O'Kelly in Paris in the summer of 1941 had left the Legation in a quandary. The Berlin Legation might be able to handle some high-level matters with the German military authorities in occupied France, but it would hardly be in a position to deal with the day-to-day problems of Irish citizens. O'Kelly thus suggested a couple of people who might look after the welfare of the Irish in occupied France and proposed that his friend, John Francis Keane, be accorded consular capacity on a nominal salary (though, like O'Kelly, he would have no recognised diplomatic status). Keane would be the most suitable person for the job, not least, according to O'Kelly, because he spoke fluent German[95] and he was 'well acquainted with Germans in Paris'.[96] O'Kelly had sprung the London-Irish businessman from the internment camp in Saint-Denis in October 1940 and, in turn, Keane had placed first FF10,000 and then a further FF30,000 at his disposal to help out the Paris Irish, especially Irish internees. He had also invested in Vendôme Wines.

Keane was a well-off international business executive, with plenty of managerial experience. Born in London of Irish parents in 1892, Keane had lived in France since 1919, bar periods spent in the United States and Germany. He had spent some time in New York, where he rose to the rank of director general of International Chemical Corporation (ICC). But before war broke out, Keane left ICC to found Expert Publicité Internationale (EPI), an agency that specialised in the *étude et organisation de publicité pour tous produits de commerce* (research and placement of advertisements for all commercial products). In 1933 he was living on the swanky avenue Foch in Paris, but by the outbreak of war he had decamped to the Moulin de Busagny, a manor house in Osny, thirty-five kilometres north-west of Paris (now transformed into a holiday centre for children with intellectual disabilities). Although Keane seemed, on the surface at least, eminently suitable to look after day-to-day business for the Irish, the DEA proved reticent about taking up O'Kelly's suggestion – not least, one assumes, because of Keane's lack of diplomatic-service experience and because he held only a limited-validity Irish passport.

Keane did occasionally act as a go-between between the occupied zone and Vichy. On 1 July 1943, for example, he wrote to Seán Murphy in French (as required by the authorities) to inform him of work he had carried out for members of the Irish community and of his latest meeting with O'Kelly, who was on one of his regular visits to Paris from Vichy. But Keane does not seem to have been accepted by the mandarins in Dublin or the Legation in Vichy as 'one of us'. He may not have had all that much time to look after consular affairs anyway, for he already had his own company to take care of. In any case, by mid-1941 the Legation in Berlin was officially in charge of Irish affairs in occupied France.

The presence of enemy nationals among the shareholders of EPI, John Keane's company, was a major cause of disagreement with the Germans during the Occupation, especially as the real ownership of the company was concealed behind a Guernsey-based holding company called Benison. Keane was a wealthy man thanks to Benison and, apart from dividends from his shareholding in the company, was still declaring FF315,000 (the equivalent of €107,000) in earnings to the Germans as late as 1941, when business had taken a considerable downturn. But the opaque nature of the holding company did not appeal to the authorities. Keane argued that Benison did not conceal enemy interests but was merely a screen of Guernsey-based accountants and lawyers that was designed to conceal real ownership of the company by Keane (no doubt for tax reasons). According to Keane, the share certificates that proved his direct ownership of Benison had been lost when his manor outside Paris had been raided during 1940. Worse, in June 1940 the company secretary had fled Guernsey, where Benison was registered, with all documents relating to the company. 'And so it is up to you to determine under these conditions whether the shares of which Benison Ltd. has ownership are enemy property.'[97]

The Germans remained suspicious. Why should Keane have sought to hide his ownership of the company in this way? To try to get the German authorities off his back, Keane wrote to them again at the end of October 1941 to explain that he had established Benison in 1937 as a trust to protect the interests of his wife and his two children in the case of his death. In his will, he left to them all shares in Benison – a name he had chosen because it was the name of the house near Castlepollard in County Westmeath where his mother had been born and which he had owned since 1935.

In April 1941 Keane wrote to Seán Murphy in Vichy to outline the rather complicated saga surrounding Benison/EPI and to ask him to contact the accounting firm Hughes & Allen in London to send him legal documents that proved his ownership of Benison. The Irish high commissioner in London, John Dulanty, took up the matter with Hughes & Allen, but the accountants only got around to supplying an answer towards the end of 1942, as 'their premises in the City had been bombed out and they had to transfer their papers in a very mixed condition to offices in the West End'.[98] Eventually, the papers to which Keane had referred were located, but there was not much that Hughes & Allen could do for Keane, because the Trading with the Enemy Act prevented it from transmitting documents or affidavits to persons in enemy territory.

On 16 March 1942 the German military authorities wrote to Keane to tell him that 'as long as relevant documents cannot be presented that proves the purely French character of the company Benison Ltd., 6, New Street, Guernsey, this is to be treated as an English company'.[99] In particular, the Germans were vexed to see a dividend being paid by EPI to Benison each year. These payments were stopped, while Keane had to confirm to the German military authorities that other shares on which dividends had been paid out belonged 'neither to an enemy nor a Jew'.[100]

Keane's business also suffered from the disruption caused by the hostilities. The scope for newspaper advertising – one of EPI's main business lines – was progressively narrowed by the shortage of paper, and radio advertising disappeared in May 1940 (in any case, there was little to advertise). However, EPI was still a more profitable affair than Vendôme Wines: in 1940 it made a net profit of FF950,000 (equivalent to €360,000 in today's money), of which FF800,000 was distributed in the form of dividends to the company's shareholders, including the famous Benison. Profits increased closer to FF1 million in 1941 and declined only slightly to FF936,000 in 1942.

***

During the summer of 1941 a Mayo man named Patrick Sweeney wrote a startling letter to the Legation in Vichy upon the advice of the American consulate in Marseille.[101] He said that he was being interned at Le Vernet concentration camp in Ariège, close to the Pyrenees. The Legation up to this point had no inkling that an Irishman was being held in le Vernet. Sweeney explained that he was a citizen of the Irish Free State, born in Dooreel West, Ballycroy, County Mayo on 17 March 1915, and that he had been interned since December 1939 for lack of proper papers.[102] 'I am completely destitute, having no money, unable to receive money, food or clothing from any source and in a very weak condition physically.' Sweeney asked if the Legation could provide material assistance, 'but in case I am asking too much regarding some food and clothing which I am in very dire need of at this time, as we receive very little solid food under present conditions here and in France, will you be so kind as to place my case in the hands of the American Red Cross in Vichy for consideration?' Sweeney mentioned that he was the only Irishman in Le Vernet and hoped at least that the Irish authorities could intervene to have him moved to another camp in the Vaucluse region that was 'reserved for English'.[103]

After the outbreak of the Second World War, Le Vernet was used to hold people the French deemed as 'undesirable aliens', including the writer Arthur Koestler, who in *Scum of the Earth* left a precious account of his stay in the detention centre set up in the Roland-Garros tennis grounds on the western edge of Paris before a four-month stay in Le Vernet.[104] Koestler was released from the camp in January 1940 after strong British pressure, although he only finally made it to the United Kingdom via a tortuous route after the defeat of France in June 1940.

Although Sweeney was interned in Section A, a part of the camp reserved for *interpellés de droit commun* (those arrested for common-law offences), his presence in an internment camp originally associated with Spanish anarchists led to a considerable degree of confusion and may have contributed to his eventual deportation to Buchenwald. Sweeney possibly came into contact with the American consulate in Marseille during or after a visit by an American journalist to Le Vernet. On 27 April 1941 an article appeared in *The New York Times* entitled 'Problem Offered by French Camps – Many Persons Could be Set Free if Each Individual Case Could be Checked up' in which the journalist, Lansing Warren, described his visit there. Warren explained that the Vichy government 'some time ago gave orders that all persons confined in the camps for foreigners who could obtain permission to emigrate were to receive exit visas and every facility for leaving the country'. But if the French wanted to empty their internment camps, they overlooked the case of Patrick Sweeney, who, Warren explained, 'said he had a family in Cleveland, Ohio'.

Receiving no immediate answer to his July letter, Sweeney wrote again to the Legation on 27 August 1941. He asked again for the Legation to arrange for the American Red Cross to provide him 'food and a little money and clothing which is very much in need'.[105] The Legation may have been working on Sweeney's case, but it seems not to have replied to either of the Irishman's missives.

Then, in October 1941, Seán Murphy's team in Vichy received a short note from the Perpignan branch of the American Friends (otherwise known as the Quakers), explaining that it had received a letter from an Irishman called Sweeney who claimed he had been interned since late 1939 'because his passport was not in order'. The Quakers added: 'He states that previously he had been for 8 months in the Camp of Gurs where he was interned at the end of the Spanish War.'[106] Gurs internment and refugee camp had been set up by the French government to control the influx of anti-Franco Spanish at the end of the Spanish Civil War.

Behind this note was Mary Elmes, born in Cork in 1908, who led Quaker relief efforts in Perpignan, close to the Spanish border, after the defeat of the Spanish republic in early 1939 and was still there when Sweeney turned up in nearby Le Vernet in

1940.[107] On the same day that she wrote to the Legation to alert it to Sweeney's presence in Le Vernet, Elmes wrote to a colleague in Toulouse with a similar message – stating that Patrick Sweeney had written claiming that he had been a member of the International Brigades and had spent eight months in Gurs. It is unclear whether Sweeney claimed he had fought in the Spanish Civil War and been interned merely to provoke the sympathy of the Quakers – especially in Perpignan, which was close to Gurs internment camp – or whether he had actually been in Spain during that war. We shall never know, as the archives for Gurs for the period from April 1939 to the end of June 1940 were destroyed. But we do know that many detainees were transferred there from Paris prisons at the start of the German Blitzkrieg in May 1940, which could explain Sweeney's familiarity with the Gurs camp.

Sweeney's claim to have been in the Spanish Civil War may have been designed to elicit the sympathies of the Quakers, but it had quite the opposite effect on the Irish authorities. The Legation adopted a decidedly stand-offish approach to his predicament and telegraphed the DEA: 'Sweeney apparently in belligerent force ... parents cannot support him stop application [for a new passport] should be refused.'[108]

After prodding by the Legation, Sweeney swept the Spanish story under the carpet and again claimed that he had been arrested in Paris in December 1939 'for default of official papers'. He also claimed he had been a bricklayer in London since 1934 and had come over to Paris from the Channel Islands for a short holiday, but was arrested when he overstayed and his passport expired. It seems most likely that Sweeney was arrested in Paris having committed some misdemeanour. A circular from French Minister of the Interior Albert Sarraut, on 17 September 1939, meant that foreigners or stateless persons who had been in prison could be detained in Le Vernet camp even after the expiry of their prison sentence. Despite all the correspondence, Sweeney would remain in Le Vernet for some time to come.

***

August 1941 saw some correspondence sparked by a proposal of the French minister in Dublin to transport Irish people stuck in France back to Ireland and on the ship's return journey to transport French nationals in Great Britain and Ireland back to *la patrie*. While the offer seemed to present a neat solution to the problems of the Irish stranded in France, it was unfeasible. In a telegram dated 26 August 1941 to the Legation in Vichy, the DEA asserted that the 'German armistice commission will not grant permission for boats sailing unless our government also intervenes', while the draft of a reply, typewritten on the same page as the telegram and initialled by Con Cremin, pointed out that 'Permission had been refused 3 times already by the German Commission in the past eight months, although the Italians were agreeable.'[109]

Meanwhile, the financial and physical stress facing Irish citizens in Paris grew, with the vulnerability of the numerous Irish governesses of a certain age especially apparent. These ladies had often arrived in Paris years, if not decades, before, had no family of their own and had often been left with only tenuous links to their Irish homeland. In early August 1941, shortly after O'Kelly closed the chancery in place Vendôme, William Warnock in the Irish Legation in Berlin received an application for financial assistance from Anne Russell, a lady of over seventy years of age who lived at 43 boulevard de la Saussaye, close to the American Hospital in the exclusive Parisian suburb of Neuilly-sur-Seine. On 14 August 1941 Russell wrote again to ask for help, this time from a nursing home at a different address in Neuilly-sur-Seine, and this time addressing her missive to the Legation in Vichy. Russell repeated her story once more in a letter written in a spindly hand on 5 September 1941, in which she explained that she was unable to work, had no money, nobody to help her and that she was *tout à fait dans la gêne* (really in dire straits). Russell was not a 'full citizen', the Legation in Vichy explained in a letter to Warnock on 29 August, as she had been issued a passport with 'restricted validity'. Consequently, any assistance the DEA might be prepared to grant would be 'confined'. Indeed, unless the department altered its stance, 'it is not likely that she will benefit from whatever arrangements may eventually be made in the matter of financial relief'.[110]

But although it appears Russell did not receive any help from the Irish authorities, she did not give up asking. Two years after her first plea for assistance, she wrote to the Legation to explain (yet again) that she had lost all her savings in Austria in the First World War and that her health, 'which has never been good', meant whatever cash she had was spent on medical treatment. Russell told the Legation that she held an Irish passport and received 'no assistance from any source, nor has she any relatives in Ireland who could help her'.[111]

Teresa Mary Yourelle, originally from Dunboyne in County Meath, but living at 15 rue Maubeuge in the 9th arrondissement, was also in need of financial assistance. The fifty-eight-year-old, who described herself as a 'sales lady' in her Declaration of Nationality, had had an eventful life even before she became caught up in the German Occupation. In 1911, when she was not quite twenty-eight, she had set sail for Australia from Marseille with other members of her family, but found herself back in France by the early 1920s. In 1941 Yourelle was granted a one-year Irish passport in exchange for her British one, but was unable to get her hands on it due to 'her inability to pay the fee', according to a letter from Vichy to the DEA dated 6 November 1941. Since she held only a one-year passport, the Legation – by now well aware of the DEA's position on who should be helped and who shouldn't – did not even submit her case to Dublin until January 1942, alongside that of other candidates for special assistance.[112]

Maud White, born in Dublin in 1881, had left Ireland in 1908, never to return. She was granted a one-year Irish passport in December 1940 based on a Declaration of Nationality that included a reference to her father being born in 1847 'I think' and her mother in 'about' 1840 in Dublin. The Declaration of Nationality form asked if she intended to return to Ireland. 'That depends on work,' answered the fifty-nine-year-old, who was then living on the avenue Kléber in the 16th arrondissement.[113]

Kathleen Wright also left Ireland in her youth, following her marriage. Wright, who was a member of the Vernon family – long-time occupants of Clontarf Castle – was a sixty-nine-year-old widow living near St Malo in Brittany when she made her passport application in late 1940. Rather than hazard wild guesses about the dates and places of birth of her parents, she owned up that she didn't know. The required information was probably among her papers in her villa, which was now occupied by the Germans, she explained.

Kathleen Wright's nephew also became caught up in the war in France. Robert Vernon, born in Dublin in December 1912, son of Edward Kingston Vernon of Clontarf Castle, had been a painter in southern France before the war and became a radio operator in a French Resistance movement based in Marseille, called Alliance, which was broken up by the Germans in early 1943. Vernon was arrested in February 1943 and imprisoned in St Pierre prison in Marseille before being deported to Germany. Throughout 1944 Con Cremin, by then Irish minister in Berlin, wrote to say that he had actually managed to stave off the death sentence that hung over Vernon (whom he had seen in Paris on a number of occasions in 1940).[114] But Vernon became a victim of the mad chaos that gripped Nazi Germany in the final weeks of the war and was one of thirty victims of an SS massacre at the Sonnenberg concentration camp east of Berlin on 30 January 1945.

In a letter dated 17 September 1941 to William Warnock, Fr O'Grady painted a bleak picture of how the situation had deteriorated for the Paris Irish in the fifteen months since the German Occupation of Paris had begun:

> Many of our people are in a sad plight … work is not at all plentiful and the teaching profession, in which so many were engaged, no longer offers the possibilities it did, with the result that many cannot find posts. The younger element can still find work as governesses but there are many in their fifties and upward who having lived sparingly for over a year on their savings are now at the end of their reserves and their future is dark. St Joseph's has been doing what it can to ease the situation but its power to help is also seriously curtailed by actual circumstances.

The Passionist continued:

> The approach of winter, the high cost of living and scarcity of employment, and the lack of communication all contribute to a sad state of affairs and it is in the hope that the Irish Government may be able to do something to alleviate the distress that I feel obliged to submit this report and petition to your Excellency.[115]

5

HIDING, FLEEING, BEGGING FOR MONEY

On 21 January 1942 Dublin-born William Gibson, the second Baron Ashbourne (alias Lord Ashbourne), died at the age of seventy-four at his home in the centre of Compiègne, a town some ninety kilometres north of Paris and close to the internment camp of Royallieu where other Irishmen were held during the war. Ashbourne, a convert to Catholicism, was a fervent Irish nationalist and cultural revivalist whose political views caused him to be largely disinherited by his father. His death prompted messages of condolence addressed to his French wife from the likes of Douglas Hyde and Éamon de Valera, as well as a eulogy in the *Catholic Herald*, which told its readers that Ashbourne 'always wore the kilted Irish dress and was a picturesque figure. His green kilt, green stockings and belt with massive silver buckle always created unusual interest. Before the last war Lord Ashbourne created a mild sensation by appearing in the House of Lords in kilts and speaking in Gaelic.'[1] Ashbourne had last visited Ireland in July 1939 (when he could barely walk) and was in Compiègne when the Germans marched in. In spite of his age, he was briefly interned in December 1940, before being released on the intervention of his wife, who also managed to free 'a young Irish nun' called Soeur Cécile.[2] This nun looked after Lord Ashbourne on his deathbed.

Indirectly, Lord Ashbourne had already had a run-in with the Axis powers in the interwar years. His mentally disturbed sister, Violet Gibson, had tried to assassinate Benito Mussolini in Rome in 1926, but her revolver shot only succeeded in grazing Il Duce's nose. To avoid a diplomatic incident, Gibson's trial was quickly expedited and she was sent to a mental hospital in England. She was still there at the time of the death of her brother, who seems to have played an important role in her decision to convert to Catholicism and a form of Celtic mysticism.

According to his French widow, Marianne de Montbrison, Lord Ashbourne spent the last months of his life 'more and more withdrawn in his room, surrounded by objects which had come from Ireland or which recalled it to him and leaving his room for walks'.[3] Upon his death in January 1942, Lord Ashbourne was, according to his widow, 'clad in his kilt, the Sinn Féin ring on the collar of his shirt, his dear Irish beads entwined in his joined hands ... On the coffin was the flag of the Red Hand, at his feet the Celtic Cross and many inhabitants of Compiègne who loved and admired him came to pray for him.'[4] Lord Ashbourne was buried in the hamlet of Chevincourt, fifteen kilometres north of Compiègne.

***

At the start of 1942 Patrick Sweeney was still stuck in Le Vernet internment camp. He wrote to the Legation on 13 February 1942, again, as in previous letters, giving details of his family in Mayo and explaining that he had lost all his papers in Paris when he had been rounded up. In none of the three letters he wrote to the Legation between July 1941 and February 1942 did he mention having fought in the Spanish Civil War, contrary to what the Vichy French authorities were asserting and what he had told the Quakers. Instead, he said, 'I have never been in trouble in Ireland as I was not quite 17 years old when I left home. Anywhere I have been ... I have never been in trouble with the police or in fact any person or government.'[5]

Still not receiving a reply, Sweeney contacted the Legation again on 4 March. This time he complained bitterly at his (non-)

treatment by the Irish authorities. 'I really do not see, being the only Irish subject interned here, why the representatives of my country do nothing to get me out of here ... After 28 months of internment, my morale as well as my health is rather low.'[6] Sweeney's cries for help are not at all surprising for, according to Arthur Koestler, the internment camp at Le Vernet was 'notoriously the worst in France'. Koestler described the camp as being made up of a series of huts, in each of which 200 men were expected to sleep in rudimentary compartments that contained bunk beds. Five men were meant to sleep in each bunk bed, which was less than 270 centimetres wide. According to Koestler:

> There were no windows, only rectangular slabs cut out of the wall-planks, which served as shutters. There was no stove during the winter of 1939, no lighting, and there were no blankets. The camp had no refectory for meals, not a single table or stool in the hutments; it didn't provide dishes, spoons, or forks to eat with, nor soap to wash with. A fraction of its population could afford to buy these things; the others were reduced to a Stone Age level.[7]

Food consisted mainly of bread and a cup of coffee for breakfast, a pint of soup and poor-quality boiled beef at lunchtime, and soup again in the evening. The men in Le Vernet were put to work building or repairing roads or maintaining the vast camp. However, working hours 'were limited by the daylight and by the physical inferiority of the undernourished men', who had to accomplish their tasks 'in rags and soleless shoes, in twenty degrees of frost, and slept without blankets in their barns when even the spittle on the earth was frozen'.[8]

Finally, on either 5 or 6 March 1942, Sweeney received a standard Declaration of Nationality questionnaire to fill out, which he quickly did. His answers gave little new information beyond what the Legation already knew about him. He described himself as a bricklayer and said that he had left Ireland in 1934 (instead of 1932, as he had claimed in earlier correspondence), since when he had not been back in his homeland. He cited Harrow Wealdstone (which he spells 'Wildston') in Middlesex as his address in April 1935, when the Irish Nationality and Citizenship Act that defined what an Irish citizen was came into force. Along with his filled-out Declaration of Nationality, Sweeney sent a letter to the Legation on 6 March stating that he was 'arrested in Paris on the 1st of September 1939 for not having papers'.[9]

Sweeney wrote again on 10 March with the request that 'in case you get me to the Camp des Milles near Marseille, I assure you that from there I will be able to provide for all my travelling expenses up to Ireland … Please do your best and try to get my transfer to that camp.' The camp was close to a big city – and to the American consulate and American organisations that so far had been of greater help to Sweeney than the Irish authorities. From November 1940 the Camp des Milles had become a transit camp for detainees who had managed to collect the papers and funds necessary to leave France, so many foreign (particularly US) aid organisations concentrated much of their aid effort in southern France on this camp. Sweeney may have been anxious to tap into this extensive aid network.

The contradictions in Sweeney's biography mounted with each letter he sent to the Legation. Almost two months after he had filled out his Declaration of Nationality form, he had received no news from the Legation, prompting him to write again on 4 May 1942 to explain his disappointment at the lack of help he had received – and not just from the Irish. 'Even the Red Cross of Geneva and other countries to which I have applied have not given me any satisfactory reply,' and he continued to 'wonder why the representatives of my country cannot do more for me'.[10]

The French intervened on Sweeney's behalf, with the Vichy

Ministry of Foreign Affairs writing to the Legation on 9 May 1942 to explain that one of its citizens wished to be repatriated.[11] But the Irish authorities continued to drag their feet. In reply to the ministry on 11 May, they stated that 'research carried out had not confirmed that Mr Sweeney is eligible for intervention by the Legation'.[12] This suggests either gross ineptitude, or that grave doubts still circulated in Irish officialdom about Sweeney's identity and the reasons he had ended up in Le Vernet.

Those doubts were reinforced by a 9 May note from the DEA that affirmed Sweeney was a 'veteran of the International Brigades'. But his name is not on any roll-call of British or Irish members of the International Brigades compiled in recent years.[13] In a note from June 1942, the Vichy Ministry of Foreign Affairs stated that 'Sweeney, an ex-combatant of the international brigades, was the object of an administrative measure following on a condemnation to three months imprisonment for theft and because of the unfavourable information collected about him.'[14] Thus, while Sweeney claimed that he had been picked up simply because he didn't have the proper documents, the French contended he had been arrested for robbery as well, which would explain why he found himself in the common-law section at Le Vernet, rather than in the political-prisoner part of the camp.

Still sceptical about Sweeney's story, Seán Murphy drafted a detailed account of the case for the DEA in June 1942, stating that he had been 'unable to get in touch with Sweeney for several months'. The confusing information that he had learned about Sweeney led Murphy to judge the man 'as not being a particularly desirable citizen'. Yet he felt he might be obliged to help him because 'questionable and even criminal activities do not constitute a valid reason for disowning a national in a foreign country (cf. various cases of deportation to Ireland from the USA) nor for refusing to issue him a travel document to enable him to get home'.[15]

But doubts about his identity continued and in the same note, Murphy asserted that the question of Sweeney's identity could not be 'satisfactorily settled otherwise than by the testimony of witnesses who are familiar with his appearance or handwriting'.[16] Then there was the matter of the discrepancies in the dates of birth that Sweeney had given (while in his letters he had mentioned St Patrick's Day 1915 as his date of birth, in other places he mentioned St Patrick's Day 1916). Murphy suggested that further enquiries be made in Ballycroy parish, from where Sweeney claimed to come.

The DEA even wrote to Jack Brent, secretary of the International Brigades in London, to find out whether Sweeney had actually been in the brigades. Brent said he had received letters from an English internee in Le Vernet, who confirmed that there was an Irishman interned in the camp.[17] The internee initially gave the name of the Irishman as Ginty (a common name around Ballycroy), not Sweeney, but Brent later said that he had received letters from Le Vernet that said that the 'correct name' of the Irishman in the detention camp was Patrick Sweeney. It does not seem that Brent ever confirmed to the Irish authorities that Sweeney/Ginty had been a member of the International Brigades. In a letter dated 28 September 1942, the DEA informed Seán Murphy of the news received from Brent, and also that it had received information from the police that Sweeney had sent a letter to his parents in Ballycroy in 1940.[18]

Although Murphy had previously seemed resigned to issuing a passport to Sweeney, he quickly changed his mind. On 22 June 1942 Murphy addressed a curt, four-line message to Sweeney directly to inform him that the Legation 'cannot intervene on your behalf on the grounds that you are an Irish citizen'.[19] In spite of the information that had been dug up in London and Ballycroy, the Legation wrote to Sweeney again on 3 November 1942 stating 'once more that the Department of External Affairs

Hôtel Gallia, home of Irish Legation in Vichy from 1940 to 1944.
Author's collection

A LA LEGATION D'IRLANDE

La Légation d'Irlande en France, d'accord avec les autorités compétentes françaises, communique qu'à partir de ce jour, tous ressortissants irlandais titulaires d'un passeport irlandais en règle ou d'un certificat provisoire de nationalité émis par la Légation d'Irlande en France peuvent, en se présentant au service des étrangers de leur région, faire substituer sur leur carte d'identité ou de travail la mention « citoyen d'Irlande » à la mention erronée « sujet britannique » qui, dans certains cas, s'y trouve.

Note to Irish residents in France, *Le Matin*, 17 November 1940.
Courtesy of Bibliothèque nationale de France

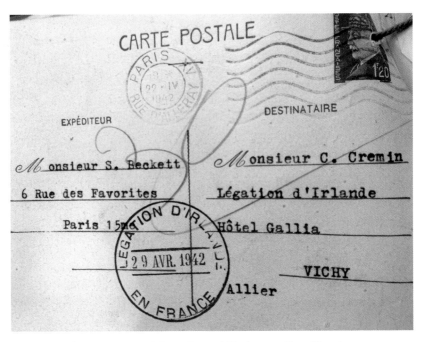

A 1942 postcard from Samuel Beckett to Con Cremin.
Courtesy of the National Archives of Ireland

Gerald O'Kelly
and his mother
in 1945.
*Courtesy of
Brendan O'Kelly*

Caserne Saint-Denis, a civilian internment camp.
Author's collection

Fr Kenneth Monaghan.
Courtesy of John Clancy

NOMS ET PRÉNOMS	DESCRIPTION	ACTES DE REMISE	TRANSCRIPTION
ÉTAT CIVIL et signalement des détenus.	DES VÊTEMENTS du détenu à son arrivée.	DES DÉTENUS au Surveillant-Chef.	DES MANDATS de dépôt et d'arrêt.

Prison admission record for Stephen Rice, 1943.
Courtesy of Archives de Paris

Stephen Rice, 1943.
*Courtesy of the
National Archives of
Ireland*

Michael Farmer and
Gloria Swanson in 1933.
*Courtesy of
Kevin Brownlow*

Robert Armstrong on his wedding day.
Courtesy of Doug Armstrong

Georgina O'Hara, 1943.
*Courtesy of the National Archives
of Ireland*

Una Whyte, 1944.
*Courtesy of the National Archives
of Ireland*

Fr Vincent Travers (top row, centre) in 1949.
Courtesy of the Irish Cultural Centre, Paris

RÉPUBLIQUE FRANÇAISE

EXTRAIT DE LA DÉCISION N° 77

Le Général de GAULLE,
Président du Gouvernement Provisoire de la République Française,
Chef des Armées

CITE À L'ORDRE DE LA DIVISION

--- --------

MAC CARTHY Janie – Forces Françaises Combattantes

« Bien que sujet irlandaise, a fait preuve au cours de l'occupation d'un magnifique
dévouement à la cause de la Résistance française. A fourni à différents réseaux dont elle faisait
partie des renseignements de grande valeur. A hébergé de nombreux aviateurs alliés et participé
à leur rapatriement. A fait preuve d'un courage et d'un sang-froid remarquables, méritant
l'estime et la reconnaissance des Français. »

Cette citation comporte l'attribution de la Croix de Guerre 1939-1945 avec étoile d'argent

A Paris, le 8 mars 1946
Par Ordre, le Général d'Armée
Chef d'Etat-Major Général de la Défense Nationale.
Signé : JUIN

A Pau, le 12 juillet 2013
Le lieutenant-colonel Michèle SZMYTKA
chef du centre des archives du personnel militaire

LE CHEF
DE CENTRE

Certificate for the award
of the Croix de Guerre to
Janie McCarthy.
*Courtesy of Centre des
archives du personnel
militaire, Pau*

Schweizerische Gesandtschaft in Deutschland
Abteilung Schutzmachtangelegenheiten

Application for $\frac{\text{issuance}}{\text{extension}}$ of passport

(To be filled out in letters)

Surname H I L T O N

Christian name Susan Dorothea

Place and date of birth 2nd. Feb. 1915

Trichinopoly. South India

Marital status Married
(single, married, divorced)

Present address Ilag Liebenau

Schloss II. Zimmer 15. Germany

Occupation none

Employed by no one

Nationality British

Native or naturalized Native

Original nationality British

Any additional nationality none

Legal home residence Chetnole. Nr. Sherborne
Dorset. England

Number of last passport

Issued at F.O. London on 2/9/36

Valid until 1941

Nationality of parents Both British

Present address of parents 42, Parkhill Rd.
Hampstead. London. N.W.3

Remarks Passport lost at sea 13/7/40
when British ship "Kemmendine" was
captured by German Raider "Atlantis"
in the Indian Ocean.

C/0594

Description

Height 5 ft. 3 ins.

Eyes Brown

Hair Brown

Distinguishing marks

Two signatures of the applicant

Susan D. Hilton
Susan D. Hilton

The undersigned authority declares that the
above description of the applicant is true and
correct and that the photograph as well as
the two signatures affixed below are genuine.

Liebenau 20 IV. 1945

Seal and signature of the authority

2

Passport application for Susan Hilton, 1945.
Courtesy of the National Archives, Kew

Desmond Patrick Nolan.
Courtesy of the National Archives, Kew

Place Vendôme, the address of Vendôme Wines.
Author's collection

as a result of enquiries in regard to your case is not prepared to authorise any action by the Legation'. Part of the reason for that might be contained in the next phrase: 'I may add for your own information that the department's enquiries tend to show that you were a member of a belligerent force in the early part of the war. The copy of your birth certificate enclosed with your letter under reference is returned herewith.' With no solid proof that Sweeney had been in the International Brigades, could the 'belligerent force' referred to be the British army?[20]

By the time of the 3 November note, Murphy knew that Sweeney was Irish and the possibility (not yet proven) that he had committed a crime of one sort or another was not enough for the Legation to deny him help as an Irish citizen. But after the controversy surrounding the granting of temporary passports to people such as Desmond Nolan and Susan Hilton, the Irish authorities had become much more cautious in handling individuals with shadowy backgrounds like Patrick Sweeney.

There is some evidence that the Germans sought to exploit the liberality with which one-year Irish passports were being granted to people in Paris. In October 1942, over a year and a half after Susan Hilton had been granted her passport, Charles Murphy, a fifty-three-year-old mechanical engineer born of Irish parents in Liverpool but living in Croix, a suburb of Lille, turned up at the Irish chancery in Paris to try to lodge his claim to an Irish passport.[21] Murphy had hitherto avoided internment by convincing the Germans that he was of Irish origin, and the local German field commander had issued a certificate to this effect to him in July 1940. But Murphy had not been able to back up his claim to Irishness with an Irish passport, telling his German contact, Dr Walter Schultz, that he had lost it. Schultz, according to Murphy, suggested that he should pay a visit to the Irish consulate to apply for a replacement.

Was this simply concern about Murphy's welfare in occupied

France, or could Schultz see some ulterior value in obtaining an Irish passport for Murphy? The latter would seem to be the case, for Dr Schultz provided not only an *Ausweis* (permit) for Murphy's trip to Paris in October 1942, but also FF2,000 for his expenses and a code name to be used in all communications with the Germans. In spite of the suspicions hanging over him, Murphy affirmed in an interrogation in January 1945 that 'my idea was, of course, all the time to get first class information and to pass it over to England whenever I got the opportunity'.[22]

Murphy's trip to Paris was not a success. Having spent a few enjoyable evenings in the French capital with friends, Murphy called at the Legation premises in rue de Villejust, 'just to satisfy Schultz that I called there in case they checked up on me', only to find that O'Kelly's one-man chancery had been closed for over a year. After returning to Lille, Murphy continued to receive money and instruction from the Germans until their departure from the city in September 1944. His contacts with the Germans earned him an interrogation by British intelligence officers in Brussels in October 1944. Murphy said the Germans had asked him whether he knew 'other' Irishmen in the Lille area but denied that he collaborated in German attempts to recruit a team of people to be trained for clandestine operations in Ireland. Murphy also denied receiving any kind of salary from the Germans and claimed that he played along with them simply to obtain 'extra ration cards'.[23] In the end, a lack of evidence prevented the British from prosecuting Murphy for his dealings with the Germans. But a confidential note from the authorities to the British Consulate in April 1947 stated that 'nobody has ever been quite convinced … that his story was the whole truth'.[24]

Early in 1942 Bluebell received word that her husband, Marcel, who had fled Paris a year before, had been picked up by the French police in Marseille and placed in Gurs internment camp. While there, Marcel regularly travelled by truck to neighbouring towns to negotiate food supplies for the camp. However, between August 1942 and March 1943, the Germans emptied the camp at Gurs, sending most of its inmates to Auschwitz via Drancy. Luckily for Marcel, before this happened one of his friends from his music academy days in Paris travelled down to south-west France, where he arranged to meet Marcel when the latter was outside the camp on his food detail. Profiting from lax security, Marcel absconded and, with false papers and a new set of clothes supplied by his friend, he headed back north, managing to cross the Demarcation Line without incident. Once they arrived back in Paris, Marcel went into hiding in an attic at 37 rue de la Bûcherie in the 5th arrondissement, close to a large police barracks.

While Marcel was in hiding, one of his Romanian cousins turned up at the Leibovicis' flat in the rue Blanche, claiming that she had escaped through the window of the lavatory in her flat during a German raid. The woman, who purported to be a daughter of Marcel's aunt, pleaded with Bluebell to shelter her, which the latter agreed to do until the girl could obtain false papers. But one sunny day, the two women were stopped by two plain-clothes policemen on the boulevard Haussmann. Bluebell was allowed to leave, but Marcel's cousin was not. At six o'clock the following morning the French police, accompanied by a member of the Gestapo, came and searched Bluebell's flat. She denied she knew the Jewess arrested the previous day and the police found nothing to incriminate her. By contrast, Marcel's purported cousin was brought to Drancy, a collecting point for the death camps in eastern Europe, and was never seen again.

Once she had learned of Marcel's return to Paris, Bluebell set about supplying him with food and reading material in his hiding place, cycling each week some twenty kilometres out to Vaucresson to buy supplies. Fears that the Germans and the French police were on Marcel's trail soon forced Bluebell to move her husband into an empty apartment on the rue Berthelot in the 5th arrondissement, not far from the Irish College. In July 1943 Bluebell was summonsed to Gestapo HQ at 84 avenue Foch, where she was asked about the whereabouts of her husband. Although she was pregnant again, she was released after an hour without having revealed anything.

***

From August 1941 to March 1942 Paul Léon was interned at the Royallieu camp in Compiègne. During this time, according to Léon's wife, Lucie Noël, Samuel Beckett often gave his bread and cigarette ration to her to send to Royallieu.[25] The Irish authorities knew about the predicament that James Joyce's friend found himself in after his arrest in Paris, with the DEA telling William Warnock in Berlin on 5 November 1941 that 'In case there is danger that Léon be shot please intervene with Foreign Office on his behalf.'[26] However, the Irish authorities were told by Warnock that any attempt to exercise diplomatic pressure on the Germans would be badly received and might actually aggravate Léon's situation. Whatever Irish intervention there was proved fruitless. In the Mémorial de la Shoah, under the name of Paul Leen, born in St Petersburg on 24 April 1893, Léon is noted as having been deported on the first convoy to leave for Auschwitz on 27 March 1942. He died there nine days later, on 5 April.

Before Paul Léon's arrest and internment, the Gestapo had paid three visits to his flat in rue Casimir-Périer. Despite thorough searches, the Germans had not seized the Joyce papers that were stored there. But there was no reason they wouldn't come knocking again, and Lucie Noël thought she might have to go into hiding herself to avoid imprisonment. In February 1942, with a suitcase full of important Joyce papers still lying in the apartment, Noël received another visit. This time there were two men, one French and one German, with the latter producing credentials showing he was a member of the Gestapo. The German said he did not know that Léon had been arrested the previous August and that they were not necessarily there for him in any case. Instead, it became apparent to Noël that they were 'starving and murdering men, but they wanted first editions'.[27] Although the two men departed empty-handed, their visit made Noël turn to the Swiss Legation, which was looking after British interests, to take custody of the Joyce suitcase until the end of the war. The cautious Swiss told her that they had nowhere to put it, so Noël turned to the lawyer Charles Gervais, while some of the more personal items were entrusted to an unnamed friend. Noël said that many months before handing the suitcase over to the lawyer, she and her husband had made a 'complete, detailed list of everything and by various channels Mrs Joyce eventually got everything back after the war was over'.[28]

In 2002 there was controversy when the Irish government acquired via Sotheby's a suitcase of Joyce manuscripts, including drafts and proofs of *Finnegans Wake*, for €12.6 million. It turned out that the vendor was Alexis Léon, son of Paul. Lucie Noël had wisely arranged to move Alexis out of Paris after the arrest of his father in summer 1941. Alexis made it down to Monte Carlo with the help of Mr Poliakoff, a friend of Spain's ambassador to the Vichy government, who was able to organise the boy's safe passage to Spain. Alexis insisted that the haul sold to the Irish had nothing to do with the material Paul Léon had collected from Joyce's flat in the rue des Vignes, which had been returned to the Joyce family at the war's end. Yet the story has refused to go away: did the material bought for the Irish government and deposited at the National Library of Ireland actually belong to the Léon family, or did Alexis Léon sell documents that his father intended only to hold in trust on behalf of James Joyce?[29]

In August 1942 Paul Léon's friend Samuel Beckett was forced to flee his apartment in the rue des Favorites when the Gloria

SMH Resistance group he was working for was infiltrated and broken up. Beckett's close friend Alfred Péron was arrested on 16 August. Péron's wife managed to send a telegram to tip off Beckett, who destroyed all incriminating documents before evacuating his residence, and to alert other members of the Resistance group, notably 'Jimmy the Greek' (Hadji Lazaro) and Suzanne Roussel (a teacher like Péron). Looking for a place to hide, Beckett and Suzanne Deschevaux-Dumesnil went to Roussel's flat, but as they climbed the staircase, Beckett claimed after the war, he was 'obsessed by a premonition of danger which caused them both to turn away'.[30] Nonetheless, Deschevaux-Dumesnil returned later the same day. Having been told by the concierge that Roussel was alone in her flat, she proceeded upstairs … only to be greeted by Gestapo officers, who were lying in wait for Roussel. Although Deschevaux-Dumesnil managed to convince the men that she was not Roussel, she was taken away for interrogation and invented a story that she had come to Roussel's flat to feed the latter's cat, a very slight alibi that did not prevent the Gestapo from searching her and Beckett's flat in rue des Favorites. But the search turned up nothing and Deschevaux-Dumesnil was subsequently released. Very quickly, she and Beckett decided it was time to disappear from circulation.

After a few days holed up in various flats and hotels across the Paris region, Beckett and Deschevaux-Dumesnil contacted Mary Reynolds, who had already helped them out in Arcachon two years earlier. Reynolds allowed them to stay a night at her house at 14 rue Hallé in the 14th arrondissement and then put them in contact with various friends of hers who kept Beckett and Suzanne overnight in a number of locations from Montmartre in the north of Paris to Vanves in the southern inner suburbs of the city. With Beckett sporting a moustache, they also stayed in small hotels under false identities before spending ten days in a 'cramped gardener's house' in which the French writer Nathalie

Sarraute and a plethora of her relations were staying in Janvry, close to the Vallée de Chevreuse, less than forty kilometres to the south of Paris.[31] But sanitary conditions were poor in the crowded house, and Beckett did not get on well with Sarraute and other members of her family. According to James Knowlson, Beckett seems to have found Sarraute 'sharp and bitchy', while she never forgave the apparent lack of gratitude that Beckett showed to her for taking him in.[32]

By the end of September 1942, with the help of smugglers, Beckett and Deschevaux-Dumesnil had crossed the Demarcation Line and made it to Vichy, where they called to the Legation at the Hôtel Gallia. However, Beckett told James Knowlson that the Irish representative he met there 'was extremely unsympathetic and unhelpful'.[33] Whoever this was, the official informed Beckett and Deschevaux-Dumesnil that they would need to go to the local police station to explain how they had travelled from Paris without valid travel documents. (Several months later, Beckett paid a fine of FF400 for crossing the Demarcation Line illegally.)

The poor impression Beckett took from his visit to the Legation in Vichy in the autumn of 1942 did not stop him from corresponding regularly with it over the next two years, writing long letters when he needed something or when he wanted to complain about his treatment at the hands of the Vichy authorities. In October 1942, for example, he wrote a long, almost indecipherable missive to the Legation to explain that he had settled in the township of Apt, some fifty kilometres from Avignon, because he had 'vague friends' in the area. After three days, he had found a house to rent called Les Roches Rouges, but the situation was far from ideal. 'The landscape is all one could desire,' he wrote, 'food all that one could not.' After the worst drought in years, no one knew where food was going to come from during the winter. Beckett explained that the local gendarmes had taken away his identity card ('I suppose to see if it had been tampered with') and that his movements were restricted 'in the extreme'. He didn't even have the right to go into Apt proper, ten kilometres from his residence, without the permission of the local police, who 'can't believe that I can be called Samuel and am not a Jew'.[34] The restrictions on his movements rankled with Beckett. He felt that as an Irish citizen he should have freedom of movement and believed that the Legation should have been doing more to promote his case.

Writing again in late 1942 from Apt (where he remained until October 1944), Beckett communicated to Con Cremin his resentment at what he saw as the lack of support from the Legation for his efforts to get the rather draconian restrictions on his movements lifted. 'If this is indeed the extent of my difficulties, in what exactly do the advantages of being of Irish nationality consist?' he asked. 'Might it not be better to be a Pole?' In a damning statement, Beckett complained to Cremin that he had 'met with no succour [from the Legation] up to the present time'. The resentment continued with an account of his efforts to obtain a residency permit in his new home – 'May I count for a little representation in this matter, please?' – and ended with a sideswipe at the measly sums he was allowed to receive from Ireland each month: 'It is certain that the Department expects us to live on our *patrimoine*'.[35] Beckett deemed that the money he received each month from Ireland (FF2,000, €565 in today's money – more than many other Irish citizens were receiving at this time) was not enough, and he asked for it to be increased to FF2,500.

Yet there is plenty of evidence to suggest that the Legation treated an obviously stressed Beckett respectfully during his two years in Apt. For example, the Legation renewed his passport rapidly and efficiently and did, in fact, help the writer in his efforts to have the very strict conditions imposed on his movements around Les Roches Rouges lifted.

On 30 June 1943 Samuel Beckett wrote again to the Legation in Vichy to complain about his treatment at the hands of the Vichy authorities since he had arrived in Apt. A summons before the prefectorial authorities for an 'examination of my situation' was just the 'latest of the innumerable petty vexations to which I have been subjected since leaving Vichy last September, not only on my way here, but since my arrival here'. This had become too much, he told the Legation:

> With regard to this constant prying into my identity, my past movements, my present movements, my means of existence, my mode of existence, why I am called Samuel etc., etc. ... when my papers are perfectly in order, when since arriving in the 'free zone' I have neglected none of the formalities of declaration, registration etc., imposed on foreigners in this area, when my only offence, I mean that of having clandestinely crossed the line of demarcation, has been judged in the police station of Apt and presumably purged by the payment of a fine of 400 francs, and when all this has been made clear time and again and apparently accepted as satisfactory in the course of repeated interrogations, I feel obliged to appeal to you to intervene. Would a Swiss citizen be baited in this manner, or a Swede? Or is an Irishman less entitled than they to the common courtesies and privileges extended to non-belligerents?[36]

But on 17 July 1943, ten days after his meeting with the prefectorial authorities, Beckett was much happier. Beckett's humour might have been lifted by the links he had established with an eccentric sixty-year-old English teacher, journalist and prolific novelist from Dublin called Anna O'Meara de Vic Beamish, who had ended up in Apt having been forced to leave her English-teaching job in Cannes. He had also learned from his visit to the local prefecture in Roussillon that, as an Irish passport holder and as stipulated in the *Journal Officiel* of 3 June, he was now allowed to travel freely in France, with no more documents needed other than his passport and French ID card.[37] The German invasion of the *zone libre* in November 1942 had paradoxically facilitated movement in France by eliminating the Demarcation Line.

***

In January 1942 the list of those in need of assistance drawn up by the Legation had grown from the initial six individuals identified in May 1941 to twenty-two. Some of the names on the January 1942 list were the same as on the earlier one – for example, fifty-year-old Bridget Hughes from Portlaoise, now described as having 'no means, work very scarce', and Mary Collins (who now shared a flat with Kathleen Doyle at 5 rue Châteaubriand beside the Champs Elysées in the 8th arrondissement), who also had 'no means and little work'. Arabella D'Arcy Hayden, who had also been on the May list, was now described as having 'no regular work'. The new names on the list included Samuel Beckett, still at that stage living at 6 rue des Favorites, John Pilkington, the eccentric art student Una Whyte, a Mrs Hyde (eighty-three) living in the town of Bernay in Normandy along with her son and daughter and described as of 'no means', Kathleen Doyle ('not a full citizen'), who had 'no means, no work', and Teresa Yourelle, described as having 'no income, slender means'.

A missive from the Legation to Dublin from the same month referred to the 'Irish Sisters' in the convent at 28 rue Murillo in the 8th arrondissement, who were 'striving to carry on a pension'. The convent was run by the Poor Servants of the Mother of God, largely composed of Irish nuns, who first established a mission in Paris in September 1890. Through the years they changed premises frequently, while concentrating on their mission of providing board and lodging to girls from Ireland and Britain who were in Paris to study or to look for work. After more than nine years in rue Ampère in the 17th arrondissement, the nuns had moved into the premises in rue Murillo, one of the most upscale neighbourhoods in the city, in December 1939.

The Poor Servants' first real taste of the Occupation had come in December 1940. After morning mass in the rue Murillo, which was read by Fr O'Grady of St Joseph's, the police rounded up all the nuns and the priest. Three nuns who held Irish passports were quickly released, but Fr O'Grady and Brigid Agnes Leahy, the superior of the convent (in religion called Sister Mary Anthony), who both held British passports, were arrested, as were twenty-two lay residents of the *pension*. They were brought by bus to the Gare de Lyon, where they were locked in a train, but Sister Mary Anthony managed to spot Count O'Kelly, who was already 'getting some other nuns released'.[38] He explained to Sister Mary Anthony that he could do nothing for her there and then, but told her she should write to him once she had reached her destination and that he would intervene forthwith. The train set off from Paris at 7.30 p.m., with its passengers – who had been given no information on their destination – fearful that they were being sent to Germany. But the terminus was Besançon, close to the Swiss border, which they reached at 4 p.m. the following day. There, the train's passengers – largely consisting of old people and religious – were placed in the internment camp for enemy nationals. Sister Mary Anthony claimed that up to 1,000 nuns, almost all English speaking, were interned in Besançon in December 1940.

O'Kelly, with the help of the Berlin Legation, proved as good as his word and Sister Mary Anthony (born in Abbeyfeale in County Limerick in 1880) was released on 23 December 1940, as was Fr O'Grady. She made it back to rue Murillo, where she was dismayed to find that the *pension* was empty but for two boarders. However, other women who were released from Besançon in the following weeks soon came to the convent.

Throughout the Occupation, a steady stream of English-speaking women, most of whom had previously worked and lived as governesses with French families, turned up at the convent looking for accommodation – the only place they could go to because 'many of the families were afraid to have an English person in the house'.[39] A number of governesses with British passports who were not released from Besançon were moved to another internment camp set up in hotels at the spa resort of Vittel, where they were 'reasonably comfortable'.[40] Many of these women were eventually released from custody in 1942 and 1943 and made their way back to rue Murillo. Some Irish nuns were also detained for a time in Vittel: at the beginning of 1942 these included Sarah O'Donnell, Bernadette McCourt and Mary Anne Laval – all of them Irish citizens with five-year passports issued by the Legation in spring 1941.

There was a constant fear at rue Murillo that the Germans could, at any moment, requisition the convent and turf out its residents. Even as that threat seemed to recede (although, according to Sister Mary Anthony, the nuns 'had the Gestapo living opposite'), the women living in the convent had to survive in an occupied city with little food and money, and scant job opportunities.[41] As Agnes Hannigan, a long-time friend of the Poor Servants (as well as a parishioner at St Joseph's and sister of the governess-cum-*résistante* Lilly Hannigan), put it many years later, 'even keeping alive was an activity in itself'.[42] The Irish residents were mostly unable to pay hostel fees during the Occupation, at least until a system of limited remittances from Ireland was put in place in the second half of 1941, and therefore led a spartan existence. Holders of British passports had a slightly easier time and were able to pay for their board and lodging in the early part of the Occupation, as they received loans via a British government fund distributed by the American consular authorities. Some money was also provided by a handful of French lodgers (including a countess). Yet, according to one nun, Sister Mary

Anthony, the mother superior, frequently 'used to go and barter for food at the public market'.[43]

By the spring of 1944 about twenty-five women (of whom four were Poor Servant nuns) were residing at rue Murillo, many or most of them Irish. Although in a smart neighbourhood, the building itself was not comfortable, as it was damp in winter and 'the water runs down the walls, the roof so bad we had the rain down, the pipes are old'.[44] But at least the Irish had a roof over their heads and they were among their own, receiving the support of Fr O'Grady and the Irish community that congregated at St Joseph's church in the nearby avenue Foch.

The large numbers of priests, seminarians and nuns in France were a constant preoccupation of the Legation. In April 1942 the mother superior of the convent of Sacré Coeur de Marie in the posh suburb of Neuilly wrote to the Legation to assure it that the convent had not been hit during the recent air raids on the Paris region. 'Given that the community is rather Irish we fear that our families and friends in Ireland might think that it was our convent that was hit by a bombardment on 3 March following an announcement on the radio.'[45] Would it be possible, the mother superior wanted to know, to put a small notice in the Irish press to reassure people in Ireland that everybody was all right?

In August 1942 Patrick Walsh of Ballintubber in County Roscommon made enquiries to the DEA about his daughter, Margaret, who had travelled to the mother house of the Little Sisters of the Poor (Bon Secours) in Brittany in May 1940. But Margaret had discovered during her noviciate that life as a Little Sisters of the Poor nun was not for her. She left in March 1942 to try a different order, which explains why, in September 1942, the Legation was able to inform the DEA that Margaret, who by then was twenty-two years old, was about to take her vows at the Bon Pasteur (Good Shepherd) convent in Angers. However, something caused her to leave this community as well, for by

September 1943 she had found refuge at the Good Shepherd
monastery at Charenton-le-Pont in the inner suburbs of Paris.
The head of the community there wrote to the Legation in Vichy
to tell it of Walsh's desire to go home to Ireland. He asked that
her father 'make the necessary arrangements' for her passage via
Portugal, but Sister Mary of St Canice, a member of the order in
Charenton-le-Pont, said the convent would cover the necessary
expenses if it were impossible to find an alternative source of
funding.[46] This letter was written in spring 1944, when it was
impossible to get out of France. Instead, Seán Murphy wrote
back to Sister Mary to say he was looking for an Irish nurse for
his fifteen-month-old daughter. 'I should be glad if you would
be so good as to let me know whether Miss Walsh has the right
capacity for such a post.'[47] Murphy's plan to employ Margaret
Walsh does not seem to have worked out, for in October 1944, he
employed a girl called O'Hanlon to look after his offspring and
Walsh disappears from the records.

As living conditions worsened and the threat of air raids
grew, many Irish tried to leave France, but it became increasingly
difficult to do so, and the Germans finally decided to stop granting
exit visas altogether in late 1943. Before then, some did manage
to make it out. Mme Lannigan O'Keeffe, who had been living
on the boulevard Magenta in the 10th arrondissement, and who
had been interned in Besançon in 1940, seems to have managed
to leave Paris for Australia via Vienna in October 1942. 'Perhaps
she was among the group of persons whose exchange at Istanbul
against German nationals was announced some weeks ago on the
Swiss wireless,' wrote the Legation to Vichy on 28 December
1942.[48]

Other Irish stuck in occupied France may have managed to
get back to Ireland via Lisbon before the end of 1943. On 8 October 1943 John Flanagan wrote to the Legation from a cheap
hotel on the rue de Vaugirard in Paris to enquire how he could get

home. Flanagan (who gave no details about where he was from in Ireland) said that he had been stranded sick in Jersey when the Germans invaded the Channel Islands in June 1940 and had then made his way to Berlin to look for work in 1941. An Irish passport had been issued to him there in May 1942. However, by 1943, he wrote, 'seeing there was no hope of getting home from Berlin and owing to air raids and a lack of work I got fed up and got in my pappers [*sic*] a complete discharge from Germany with the intention of going back to Jersey'. But he concluded that the situation in Jersey was 'very bad' and so had set his sights on getting back to Ireland instead. Through the Legation, he asked that his sister, who lived in Talbot Street, Dublin, book a passage for him via Lisbon. Flanagan explained he had papers and enough money to get him to the Portuguese capital, having worked with the German Occupation forces in France. What became of Flanagan thereafter remains something of a mystery. A registered letter sent to him by the Legation on 28 February 1944 to his hotel was returned with the mention '*parti en Irlande*'.[49]

The Irish authorities were guarded in providing help to Irish people wishing to quit France. 'We are prepared at the present to consider the question of repatriating at State expense only such of our male citizens as have qualified to receive maintenance advances under our scheme for assisting destitute citizens abroad,' wrote the DEA in a letter to the Legation in June 1942.[50] So those Paris Irish who were female and were not receiving relief from the Legation were, it seemed, to be left to their own devices. For the department, the less-than-forthright help it was willing to offer was not (or not only) about money. The DEA was willing to accept only destitute males in part for reasons of decorum. 'The Irish ships on the Lisbon–Dublin service have no accommodation for female passengers,' it explained in a June 1942 memo, 'and the only alternative route is by air, which we have had to rule out on the grounds of its cost.'[51]

Getting to Lisbon from occupied France was not easy and the process of obtaining the relevant exit and entry visa from the German, Spanish and Portuguese authorities was time-consuming. In March 1944 the Legation explained to Mary Bennett that 'the preliminary arrangements for travel normally take about three months to complete'.[52] Even when an Irish national did obtain the permission needed to travel (and by spring 1944 that was highly unlikely), he or she then had to pay upfront the cost of the train journey from Paris across northern Spain to a place like Fuentes de Oñoro on the Spanish–Portuguese border and then on to Lisbon, before finding passage on a boat or aeroplane to the British Isles. A letter from the DEA to the Legation in Berlin in October 1942 detailed how Irish people who did eventually manage to make it to Lisbon in spite of everything then had to lodge a sum in Reichsmarks to cover their cost of passage and their stay in Lisbon while they awaited passage. Intending travellers from Lisbon had a choice between an Irish ship to Ireland and a BOAC flight to southern England. Each option had its drawbacks. The trip by ship was relatively cheap (£10) but, explained the DEA, 'none of the Irish vessels … have accommodation for more than two passengers and sailings are at about fortnightly intervals'. By contrast, BOAC flights to Bristol were more regular and 'available fairly freely', but a seat cost £35 18s 6d, over twice the maximum monthly allowance the Irish authorities allowed its citizens in France to receive at this stage of the war.[53]

Seán Murphy managed to get back to Ireland for a holiday in the spring of 1942. But he was on duty in Vichy in May 1942 when Pierre Laval received him. After a period in the political wilderness because of his raw ambition, his tendency to grab the limelight and his over-enthusiasm for ever-closer collaboration with the Germans, Laval had, with the help of the Nazis, just been reappointed *chef du gouvernement* in Vichy. At their meeting, Laval told the Irishman that he knew he was unpopular, but he was not discouraged and felt 'fairly confident that he would succeed with his policy'. The two also spoke of Ireland, and Laval said 'he sincerely hoped [Ireland] would remain neutral in spite of Roosevelt's troops in Northern Ireland'.[54]

In November 1941 the DEA had informed Murphy that the Germans would grant him permission to visit Paris again, but only for personal reasons, and the permission 'did not apply to other members of family'. Murphy finally managed to stay in the French capital from 2 June to 14 June 1942, one year after O'Kelly had been forced to close down the 'provisional' chancery there. Murphy found the premises of the Legation at rue de Villejust 'very dirty, and official and personal property in bad condition due to damp caused by leak in the roof'. There was also a problem with moths. 'You are aware of course that Paris is very bad for moths even in normal conditions,' he wrote to Dublin. But he found that the concierge and his wife were looking after the place and 'are completely honest, which is of course the primary consideration'.[55] Murphy conveyed his impressions of the occupied city:

> My general impressions of Paris were sad … There is very little motor traffic except those of the occupying authority. One sees an enormous number of bicycles and cycle taxis but the general impression one has from the point of life is a deserted city. We had the chance to see the Champs Elysées about eight o'clock in the evening without a vehicle of any sort or kind from the Concorde to the Etoile … There seems to be no mixing between the French and the Germans. One thing amongst the French which is very remarkable; they talk much less to one another in the streets than they did and even in cafés conversation is very subdued.

Murphy said he met very few people because he wanted to give the impression that he was a casual visitor and not on diplomatic business, which the Germans and Vichy French would have frowned on. But the few people he did meet were 'all of the view that the war would end before the end of the winter. They could offer no reason for this view but all said they felt quite convinced it would be so.'[56] Sadly, the Second World War had three more increasingly destructive and murderous years to run.

During this June 1942 trip, Murphy called on the Irish priests in St Joseph's on the avenue Hoche and on Fr Travers in the Irish College. He reported that 'all are well and reasonably comfortable'. At St Joseph's, Murphy found that Fr O'Farrell and Fr Monaghan 'were both very much thinner' than when he'd last seen them in 1940. By contrast, Fr Travers looked 'extremely well', at least physically, a fact that Murphy ascribed to the food the priest had grown in the grounds of the Irish College. The increasingly dire food situation in Paris had forced Fr Travers to dig up part of the grounds to plant his own vegetables. The ground was barren, 'for there was little soil and it was full of stones'.[57] But using a pick and spade, and with the help of one of the gardeners at the nearby Luxembourg gardens, who supplied him with soil and manure, Fr Travers managed to grow food on the college's former croquet court. The priest started with tomatoes, lettuce, cucumber, marrows and Brussels sprouts. He also grew carrots, radishes, onions, broad beans and haricots, only later adding potatoes (it was hard to find seedlings). Fr Travers gave some of the products of his labour to his neighbours and sometimes bartered them for other items.

As a result of his gardening Travers enjoyed a healthy diet, got plenty of exercise and had something to keep him busy. For apart from saying mass at five o'clock each morning for a group of nuns, he had little to occupy his time. 'The two or three months each winter when gardening of any kind was impossible, I found hardest to bear,' he wrote. During those winter months he 'read a good deal and retired very early to bed', while at the same time he became an assiduous wireless listener. His acquisition of six hens in May 1941 had not been a success, with five of the six dying without having laid a single egg. More promising was his cook-cum-concierge's rabbit-breeding initiative. The concierge managed to breed thirty to forty rabbits at a time, ensuring a constant supply of meat, 'although one can get tired of too much rabbit for dinner'. Fortunately for Fr Travers, Mary Maher, an Irishwoman in Laval who had spent most of her life in France 'doing acts of charity', sent two geese for Christmas dinner in 1942 and continued to send parcels of eggs, meat, cheese and butter right up to the end of the war.[58]

In May 1941 Fr Travers was invited to broadcast for the Germans on Radio Paris – an offer he wisely thought 'better not to reply to at all and the matter was not pursued further'.[59] Travers thus continued his one-man vigil at the Irish College, although that did not necessarily mean he was lacking Irish company. Just around the corner from the college, at 30 rue Lhomond, was the headquarters of the Spiritans, where Fr Griffin from Kilmurry in County Clare resided. Fr Griffin, who was to rise to become head of the Spiritans in the 1950s (the first non-French member of the order to do so), kept a low profile during the war, but perhaps managed to benefit from Fr Travers' crops of vegetables.

By 1942 the main way Irish people provided financial help to their friends and relatives stuck in France was by sending money to the DEA, which forwarded the amount to the Legation in Vichy for distribution. The amounts that could be sent were rigorously capped. Until spring 1944 remittances were limited to £15 per person (the same amount that London allowed British subjects to receive), which hardly took into account the massive inflation for even the most basic items throughout the war. At the exchange rate applied, £15 worked out at FF2,640, which, according to analysis by the French national statistics agency INSEE, would have bought the modern equivalent of

€745 worth of goods in 1942 but only €491 in 1944.[60] It was only on very rare occasions – in cases of utter destitution – that the department advanced government funds not guaranteed by relatives in Ireland.

Seán Murphy continued to press the case for doing more to help the Irish stranded in wartime France, especially as inflation continued to eat away at the value of money. 'Official' inflation in occupied France is estimated to have been of the order of around 20 per cent per year from 1940 to 1944, but inflation for hard-to-get items was much higher, even before black market prices are taken into consideration. In a letter to the DEA dated 7 November 1942, Ireland's minister to France wrote that the sharp rise in inflation 'fully justifies an increase of at least 50% in … monthly payments. It will be remembered that there has been no increase in the number of francs received by … people since the system of payment was introduced in 1940 whereas the cost of living during that time has increased by at least 60%.' Given these circumstances, Murphy requested that Dublin take 'a more liberal view' to payments to Irish nationals. He also pointed to inconsistencies in the way the department dispatched money from Dublin, remarking that 'It is not easy to follow the principle which is applied in the case of these payments.' He wrote:

> On the one hand, you have pensioners of the government receiving the equivalent of 3 pounds per month while their monthly pension amounts to 20 pounds per month and on the other hand you have Lord Granard being allowed a monthly payment of nearly 19,000 francs per month for the payment of the salaries of his French servants. You will admit that there appears to be some glaring inconsistency. I merely cite this example to show that a more liberal view might be taken of the needs of Irish citizens in France without causing any great difficulty from the point of view of finance control.[61]

Indeed, a list of remittances from November 1942 shows that the Earl of Granard transferred FF8,471 via the Legation to a M. Guiot of Levallois-Perret outside Paris. This was by far the largest single transfer the Legation handled that month (but was still only about £50 at the exchange rate being used).

The DEA was not indifferent to Murphy's efforts. On 7 December 1942 it wrote back to state that the scale of allowances to people in France was under consideration. But in February 1943 it wrote again to state that it had concluded that any increase in monthly payments 'would not be justified'. It recognised Murphy's argument that prices had increased by 60 per cent since 1940. However, it pointed out 'that there has been a similar increase in the cost of living here, but that wages have been stabilised as far as possible by government order in an effort to avoid the inflation which would inevitably follow from the continuous equation of income with a rising cost of living'. As for the Earl of Granard's large payments – far larger than those authorised for 'normal' Irish people – 'these are primarily intended to protect his property in France', wrote the DEA.[62] Apart from his substantial residence at 73 rue de Varenne, the most aristocratic part of Paris, the Earl of Granard had left behind in France a substantial thoroughbred racing and breeding operation, inherited by his American wife upon the death of her father in 1929. No doubt, the earl's relative prominence in Irish politics as a member of Seanad Éireann in the 1920s and 1930s also singled him out for special treatment. (At the same time, Lord Granard's membership of the British establishment ensured that his manor house at Lamorlaye, in prime horse-breeding country outside Chantilly, was commandeered by the German military authorities in 1940.)

1942 saw the Irish authorities become increasingly inflexible in their approach to dealing with British passport holders and handling money for them, even when they were Irish born. In

July 1942 the Legation wrote to the DEA in Dublin to inform it of a letter it had received from the health clinic in Ivry-sur-Seine, where Lucia Joyce had been looked after. The clinic had written concerning a patient called Louise Scully, born in Dublin in 1878, who had been interned there since 1921. The cost of her care had been paid through a firm of solicitors in Dublin, but payments had ceased after the fall of France two years before. The clinic was now seeking back payments. But the Department of Finance in Dublin told the DEA that 'they would not be prepared to approve of any payments being made through the Department ... in view of the fact that Miss Scully is the holder of a British passport. We have, accordingly, informed Messrs Roche & Sons, solicitors, that they should pursue the matter of her maintenance with the British Foreign Office.'[63] In a letter to the Legation on 21 November 1942 the DEA reiterated the Department of Finance's stance: henceforth the department would only handle remittances for actual holders of Irish passports. Scully died penniless at the clinic in Ivry on 4 April 1944, aged sixty-six.

By September 1942 Seán Murphy was reporting discontent about Vichy's repression of growing dissent. A soccer match scheduled that month between Switzerland and France in Lyon was cancelled at the last moment because of fears it 'would lead to mass demonstrations against government', and Murphy said 'the measures against Jews seem to be fairly widely resented both on humanitarian grounds and as going unnecessarily far on German lines'.[64] Rationing was becoming increasingly draconian. On 30 June 1943 the Legation wrote to Dublin to inform it of another reduction in rations in France. While the bread ration had been maintained at 275 grams per adult per month and the sugar ration at 500 grams ('plus 250 grams for making jam'), the meat ration was reduced to 120 grams per week (with manual workers granted a monthly supplement), while fats, including butter, had been reduced to 310 grams per month and coffee mixture to 150 grams ('containing not more than 15 grams of pure coffee').[65]

By this stage, the tide of war was turning against the Axis powers. On 8 November 1942 the British and Americans launched Operation Torch, the invasion of French North Africa. In response to the new threat this posed to southern France, three days later the Germans marched into the *zone libre*, previously unoccupied. Although Pétain and his government were left in place, the unopposed arrival of German cohorts in the *zone libre* removed the last shreds of autonomy the Vichy regime liked to think it had. On 22 November the German 6th Army was encircled at Stalingrad in the war's most decisive battle. In an infamous radio broadcast on 13 December 1942, Vichy *chef de gouvernement* Pierre Laval reaffirmed 'his belief in a German victory'. But according to a message from Murphy to Dublin three days later, the diplomatic community estimated by this stage that 'at least 90% of the French population as a whole' was against Laval's collaborationist policy. Murphy could not tell 'whether he [Laval] sincerely believes in this policy, but, at any rate, he has the courage which few, if any, have here at the moment to follow his point of view to the bitter end, and it is not beyond the bounds of possibility that his point of view may cost him his life'.[66] (Laval was to be executed for treason in October 1945.)

The deadly atmosphere in Vichy at the end of 1942 was further underlined by Murphy's account of a conversation he had had with Ernest Lagarde, director of political affairs at the Vichy Foreign Office, in a dispatch to Joseph Walshe on 16 December. Murphy noted that when he had put it to Lagarde that 90% of the French population was against Laval's policies, Lagarde replied without hesitancy, 'at least that percentage'.[67]

In the same dispatch Murphy mentioned that he and his wife had been invited to dine with Marshal Pétain and his wife. Pétain was in good form and perfectly amiable with his guests.

But, thought Murphy, 'the striking thing was how all the members of his entourage flattered him and how naturally he received it, though it was at times almost silly. I must say I was confirmed in the view which I have had for some time that he is very susceptible to flattery.' Murphy had heard it said that Pétain was every day 'being pushed more and more into the background ... Nearly everyone is agreed that his prestige is a quickly diminishing asset.'[68] This was an inevitable outcome of Pétain's guarded relationship with the Germans alongside the pushiness of Laval and other hardcore collaborationists.

The German invasion of the *zone libre* on 11 November 1942 complicated matters for the French embassy in Dublin and for the French ambassador, Marie-François Laforcade, who had remained loyal to the Vichy regime. Later that month Dublin told the Legation in Vichy of the pressure that Laforcade was under to throw in his lot with the Free French, led by General Charles de Gaulle.[69] Dublin was anxious to know whether 'if such collaboration took place would Vichy disown [him]'? Even more importantly, Dublin asked Murphy, 'What do you think of future of diplomatic corps in Vichy?' An answer to this question was deemed 'very urgent'.[70] Murphy replied in a coded telegram sent via Gibraltar a week later, on 5 December (which was not decoded for another two days). He believed that in the event of collaboration with the Gaullists, Laforcade would be disowned and that it was 'impossible to say future of diplomatic corps here. Seven South American countries have decided recently to withdraw their missions in addition to those which have broken relations.'[71]

6

DIRE STRAITS

At the start of 1943 the saga of Patrick Sweeney's bid for release from Le Vernet internment camp was still ongoing. The DEA in Dublin had been in contact with his family and the parish priest in Ballycroy in a bid to establish his identity. According to the DEA in January of that year, 'This young man, Patrick Sweeney, left home for work in England about seven years ago. His sister states that the family had a letter from him stating he was belonging to the Army and was just then in hospital in France. They have no more news of him whatsoever. They made several enquiries to the English Army authorities but no definite reply.'[1] A living relative recalls that the Sweeney family – which had indeed established itself in England – had always assumed that Patrick Sweeney had been in the Irish Guards Regiment and had been captured.[2] But no regimental list for the Irish Guards for 1939–1940 includes a Patrick Sweeney.

Given that Sweeney's Irish identity now seemed beyond doubt, the DEA wrote to the Vichy Legation in January that it had 'no alternative but to authorise the issue of a passport to him'.[3] As soon as Seán Murphy could confirm that Sweeney was not a British prisoner of war, an Irish passport was to be granted. On 29 March 1943 Murphy wrote to the DEA admitting that the Sweeney affair had become buried under a thick, impenetrable fog of partial information and suppositions. He concluded that Sweeney was not a member of the International Brigades and thought that the reason 'that the French Foreign Office should describe him as such is probably due to the fact that he is interned in a camp which is, I understand, mainly occupied by former Spanish International Brigade members'.[4] Murphy also dismissed the notion that Sweeney could have been a British prisoner of war.

A letter addressed to Sweeney at Le Vernet in early April 1943 was returned with the note 'gone away'. Further enquiries showed he had left the camp on 8 January, but Murphy was 'unable to ascertain whether he was released or transferred elsewhere'.[5] Murphy eventually found out from the Vichy authorities that, since Sweeney was deemed a political prisoner (in patent contradiction with his confinement in the common criminal section at Le Vernet), he had been sent from Le Vernet to Paris, where he had been handed over to the Gestapo. The Germans then sent Sweeney to Frontstalag 122, also known as the Royallieu internment camp on the outskirts of Compiègne, north of Paris. Little or nothing is known of Sweeney's time at Royallieu, where he stayed until early 1944.

The next news of Sweeney came from William Warnock at the Irish Legation in Berlin on 29 July 1943. A German officer had informed him that the French had handed Sweeney over to the German authorities some time previously. The German officer did not know why the French had interned him, but told Warnock 'that Sweeney had volunteered for work in Germany and that they would probably send him there for that purpose'.[6] It is difficult to understand this claim, for Sweeney was still languishing in the camp at Royallieu several months after Warnock's note to Vichy.

The Legation still wanted to understand why the French had interned Sweeney in 1939 and wrote to the secretary-general of the police at the Ministry of the Interior on 1 August 1943. But the letter was transferred back to the Ministry of Foreign Affairs, which gave exactly the same laconic answer in September 1943 as it had given in June 1942: 'Mr Sweeney, a veteran of the International Brigades, had been subject to administrative measures following his condemnation to three months' prison for theft and on account of unfavourable information gathered on his account.'[7] No other information was forthcoming from the French.

One further document adds to the enigma of Sweeney's case. Vichy France drew up individual files on detainees. Among these files is an undated index card relating to Patrick Sweeney that simply states his nationality, followed by the mention *A Fresnes fait 18 mois* (i.e. he spent 18 months at Fresnes prison).[8] Perhaps Sweeney had spent some time in this prison in 1943 before being transferred to Royallieu.

***

At the end of January 1943 the Legation received a long typewritten letter from Roger Wuillaume, a senior manager at the Marseille branch of the insurance company Agrippina. It contained a detailed account of the dramatic arrest of Wuillaume's colleague and friend William O'Hea on Saturday 23 January 1943. At 5.30 p.m. that afternoon, O'Hea, who had successfully applied for an Irish passport in 1940, had been sitting on the terrace of the Café Riche on the Canebière, the main thoroughfare in the centre of the Mediterranean city, when he was whisked away by police officers who had been checking people's papers. According to Wuillaume, O'Hea 'was guarded the whole night with about one hundred other people in a room normally reserved (according to the notices on the walls) for the control of prostitutes. The heat was unbearable ... Given the number of people in the room, it was impossible for everybody to sit down, even on the ground. Mr O'Hea spent the night standing up.'[9]

O'Hea had been caught in the huge round-up of Jews and other undesirables carried out by the Germans – abetted by the French police – from 22 to 24 January 1943, three months after the Germans had invaded the *zone libre*. The police authorities estimated that 40,000 people had their identities checked in those three days, of whom 4,000 to 6,000 were taken into custody, including about 1,640 Jews who were to be deported to the death camps of eastern Europe.[10] The round-up was mostly concentrated in the infamous Vieux Port area of the city, which was quickly thereafter torn down by the authorities. O'Hea was one of about 300 people picked up in other parts of the city centre and brought to the Evêché, as the police headquarters in Marseille is still known.

After an uncomfortable wait, O'Hea was singled out for questioning at three o'clock on the morning of 24 January 1943. He was able to present a ream of official papers, including his identity card, his residence permit, his driving licence, a certificate from the foreigner section of the local police stating that he and his wife had been accorded permission to reside in Marseille, and a letter from the head office of Agrippina Insurance in Cologne attesting that O'Hea was a director for the company in the *zone libre*. But this was not enough for O'Hea's interrogators. After a few hours' rest, he was placed in a truck and transported with a number of other people to the Arenc train station.

While being led from the truck into the station between two rows of German soldiers with bayonets fixed to their rifles, O'Hea, who spoke German, asked one of them if he could speak to an officer. The request was denied. Later, according to Wuillaume's account, O'Hea found out that 'he and his companions were in the middle of being delivered to the German authorities as people who had been subject to investigation and had been recognised by the French authorities as undesirables'.[11]

At ten o'clock on the morning of 24 January, O'Hea was placed in a cattle wagon on a train marked with the Star of David and transported along with some 1,640 others to the Royallieu concentration camp at Compiègne. According to Wuillaume's account:

... the last contact [O'Hea had] with the French authorities was when a garde mobile opened the door of the cattle wagon for a split instant and threw some bread and cheese as well as a few tins of sardines onto the floor. Of the sixty people locked into the wagon, about fifty were Algerians (Jews and Arabs) who threw themselves on the food like wild animals. Being in bad health, M. O'Hea did not partake in the struggle.

O'Hea had no further access to food or drink during the two days he was on the train. Moreover:

The cattle wagons contained neither straw nor any kind of receptacle to fulfil natural needs ... as the 50 Algerian natives were not so bothered by this, it was impossible to move around the wagon without stepping on turds ... especially as there was no lighting ... The absence of straw ... made it impossible for M. O'Hea to sit down ... He thus remained standing for the entire journey, finding it impossible to sit for more than a few minutes at a time.[12]

The train arrived at Compiègne at around eight o'clock on the morning of 26 January. O'Hea was put into a dormitory with around forty other lice-covered detainees. On 30 January a German non-commissioned officer interrogated him. On being presented with the same papers O'Hea had shown to the police in Marseille, the German expressed his 'profound surprise' at O'Hea's treatment. On 1 February – a day before the official surrender of German forces at Stalingrad – after extensive enquiries to the French interior ministry, O'Hea was released (as were forty-two other people who had been on the train from Marseille) and thereafter 'treated with the utmost respect' by the Germans, who blamed his arrest on the French authorities.[13] O'Hea was given permission to spend a week in Paris before undertaking the arduous journey back to Marseille.

It seems that the Legation – perhaps alerted by Wuillaume's letter – played a role in O'Hea's release. In March 1943 O'Hea wrote to Seán Murphy to thank him for his 'prompt intervention' and asked him to help in his bid to obtain compensation for 'wrongful arrest' from the French Ministry of the Interior. 'While I am naturally interested in getting what compensation I can,' O'Hea wrote, 'I also feel that this sort of treatment should not be taken lying down, and that if compensation is insisted on, Irish citizens will be less likely to be molested by the French police in the future.'[14] By April 1943, when O'Hea next wrote to the Legation, his permanent address was 1 rue Blanche in Paris, where Agrippina's Paris branch was based.

Murphy took up O'Hea's grievance and wrote directly to Pierre Laval, the head of the Vichy government and its minister of the interior, to whom Murphy issued 'a formal protest against the disregard shown by French police officers to the rights of Irish citizens as citizens of a neutral country'.[15] The Legation also informed Laval that it supported O'Hea's claim for FF51,785 in compensation. But a year later, in April 1944, the Legation had to inform O'Hea that the French government did not accept any responsibility for his arrest.[16] Nonetheless, 'as an act of courtesy towards the Irish Government', according to Murphy, the Vichy authorities were prepared to make an *ex gratia* payment of FF10,000 (worth the modern-day equivalent of about €2,280). O'Hea accepted and gave Murphy FF1,500 of the sum 'to be devoted to any Irish charitable object at our entire discretion'.[17]

Unlike O'Hea, other relatively well-to-do Paris Irish had minimum contact with the Legation, probably, in some cases, because their finances were sufficiently solid to allow them to dispense with Legation assistance. Peter Purcell, born in Naas, County Kildare, in 1898, had joined the British army at the age of sixteen on the outbreak of the First World War, and by 1918 had risen to the rank of second lieutenant of the Royal Dublin

Fusiliers. Purcell did not return to Ireland after the war, instead staying on to work in public relations in Paris. By 1935 he was working as an executive for Paramount Films, a post he seems to have maintained throughout the Occupation (although with no American films being imported, one wonders what he had to do). He asked the Legation to send a message to Ireland on his behalf in March 1943 on the anniversary of the death of his mother. As well as paying for the cost of the telegram, by way of thanks he sent the Legation two cinema tickets for the Paramount cinema in Paris. Otherwise, Purcell, who died in Paris in 1956, seems to have had few dealings with Irish officialdom in wartime France.

By contrast, the more financially challenged Irish men and women naturally turned increasingly to the Legation for help as the Occupation dragged on. In March 1941 relatives in Ireland wrote to the Legation seeking news of Cork woman Georgina O'Hara, giving an address for her in Biarritz. Later that year O'Hara made her way to Paris and her name appeared on the list of Irish people facing difficulty that Fr O'Grady supplied to Warnock at the Legation in Berlin in January 1942. In February the Legation wrote to O'Hara to say that it had contacted her brother in Ireland to seek money for her; however, thirty-one-year-old O'Hara again appeared on the updated list of full passport holders deemed 'in need of assistance' that the Legation in Vichy supplied to Dublin in April.[18] The DEA eventually channelled her a remittance of FF2,640 per month (worth about €750 today) from July 1942 on. O'Hara's family lived in Passage West in County Cork and, according to a letter from the DEA of 5 May 1943, the family 'is in very poor circumstances and unable to provide funds for her maintenance'. Her sister, Kathleen, who was a nurse in England, was able to send to the department 'some small amounts for her sister's benefit, provided that she can obtain the permission of the British Trading with the Enemy Department'.[19]

By the end of July 1943 O'Hara had moved into the Irish convent on the rue Murillo, from where she wrote to the Legation in a bid to solicit money from her mother back in Passage West. 'I need a sum of FF5,000,' she stated, 'because I am just out of hospital; I cannot go back to work yet, and I still need medical attention, but I no longer have any financial resources at all.'[20] So urgent was her need that she hoped the Legation would be able to advance her the money she had requested from Ireland.

Just eleven days later, on 4 August 1943, O'Hara wrote from another address, in rue St Ferdinand in the 17th arrondissement. She explained that she had found a job 'working as a non-resident governess for a salary of FF1,200 and have no other source of income in France. Otherwise, I am as well as can be expected under the present conditions.'[21] Instead of reiterating her request for money, she asked for news of her parents. Over a month later, on 23 September 1943, O'Hara wrote from a 'provisional address' at 128 rue du Faubourg Saint-Honoré to inform the Legation that she was convalescing, 'as a result of complications after an operation for appendicitis'. Worse, she explained, 'I was totally wiped out by the bombing raid on Sept. 15'.[22] Factories in the industrial northern and western suburbs of Paris had been attacked that night, causing the deaths of almost 300 people and wounding more than 500 others.[23]

O'Hara next wrote to the Legation on 6 October 1943, this time from a small hotel at 10 rue Chalgrin in the 16th arrondissement, from where she had already written to Vichy in March. She wrote in detail about what had happened to her during the 15 September air raid:

In fact, I lost everything – clothes, personal effects, jewellery and even bank notes, because I had gone down to the bomb shelter in the cellar without having enough time to take anything with me apart, thankfully, for my ID card. Several floors in the building collapsed because of a bomb. I have just obtained new food ration cards but I still haven't been able to find clothes or cooking equipment and I am only able to live from what friends give me.

O'Hara was eager to explain the various difficulties she had had with the authorities since the armistice in June 1940 – including a refusal to let her work for six months – 'but such a delicate matter can wait until the end of the war'. She asked the Legation to intercede, this time with her sister, to ask her to send money and clothes. She also requested news of her family back in Ireland.[24]

The Legation took O'Hara's hardship very seriously, writing to her on several occasions between June and early October 1943 and transmitting her messages to her family by telegram. On 11 October it told O'Hara that the DEA in Dublin wanted to know whether she wished to return to Ireland. Given the hardship she was experiencing, it might appear surprising that O'Hara did not take up this offer to assist in her repatriation. But on 24 October she replied, 'upon reflection and after all I have already gone through, I would prefer to avoid the risks involved at this point in time in undertaking a journey to Ireland … My health is better now and I can resume working.'[25] O'Hara may not have agreed with Samuel Beckett's preference for France in war to Ireland in peace, but it is apparent (not least from the fact that most of her letters to the Legation were in French) that O'Hara, like Beckett and Janie McCarthy, was fully integrated into Parisian society by this stage and simply connected to Ireland by some relatives and the occasional wisp of nostalgia.

George Bradish offers a similar tale of physical and financial hardship. In August 1941 Bradish had written to the Legation in Vichy from the American Hospital in Neuilly, where he was undergoing treatment that would last several months, to ask that his monthly allowance from Dublin be sent to his wife, who lived on the rue Marbeau in the 16th arrondissement. The couple's financial situation worsened as the war progressed, and on 9 February 1943 Bradish wrote two letters to the Legation. In one of them he asked that his relations in County Wexford be approached to increase the amount they sent him from £25 to £50 per month, as he couldn't live on less, especially as his wife was in need of constant medical attention and he himself was a 'grand convalescent' having undergone surgery. Bradish needed this increased allowance as soon as possible, he explained, as he found himself in a 'critical situation'.[26] In a second, longer letter, carrying the same date of 9 February 1943, Bradish explained that he had been informed by the Swiss consulate in Paris, which had been looking after British interests since the United States entered the war in December 1941, that the aid he had been receiving from the United Kingdom was being stopped, leaving him to his own devices.

In response to a request for more details on his circumstances, Bradish wrote to the Legation again on 22 October 1943 to explain how he had spent eighteen months in the American Hospital in Neuilly after his release from internment in Besançon and how he had been forced to turn to the YMCA at the beginning of 1943 when funds from London had dried up. Bradish's rent in rue Marbeau had been FF15,000 per month before 1940, but even with the 50 per cent reduction his landlord had granted him for the duration of the war, it was still far higher than the YMCA's loan of FF1,800 per month. After three months, even the YMCA money gave out, leaving Bradish to lean on friends. His wife sold some of her jewellery to help make ends meet, but he had still not paid tax and doctors' bills. Bradish had convinced the French Red Cross to give him FF8,000 to pay for his treatment, but that was not enough. He was also awaiting the bill for the removal of a prostate gland at the American Hospital in August 1943. 'It is a nightmare trying to make both ends meet,' he wrote. Obviously desperate, Bradish complained to the Legation on 2 March 1944 that he had not received his monthly remittance for February and that he and his wife were 'absolutely dependent on friends for what we eat besides the rent'.[27] Nevertheless, George Bradish made it through the rest of the Occupation and travelled back to Ireland in April 1945.

The plight of Joseph Barrett Brandreth, a retired *Financial Times* journalist resident in France since the close of the nineteenth century, was equally acute. Even though he was in his seventies, Barrett Brandreth, along with his wife, Claire, was arrested by the Germans in 1940 in his wife's home village in the Somme, where the couple had retreated from their primary abode in Courbevoie in the inner suburbs of Paris. After their arrest, they had been sent with other British nationals to the internment camp at Besançon. When he learned of the old man's arrest, Count O'Kelly sent letters to both the German Embassy and the German military administration. Both missives contained what O'Kelly described as 'a courteous but energetic protest' against the 'unjustified' measures taken against Irish citizens and he called on the military authorities to take into account 'humanitarian considerations' when considering the fate of Barrett Brandreth.[28] He managed to have Barrett Brandreth quickly released on health grounds and issued him with a temporary passport (Barrett Brandreth's passport application of 3 November 1940 stated that his father had been born in Dublin in 1845). Although Barrett Brandreth was born in London, he had made many visits to his grandparents, who lived at the Manor House in Finglas in Dublin, and had last visited Ireland in August 1935.

While his newly minted Irish passport might have helped him in his dealings with the Germans, the old man's woes were far from over. He was admitted with serious health issues to the American Hospital in Neuilly in March 1941, the same month that his wife died. He stayed there for a year and a half – and all the time his medical bills and rent were mounting. The aged

Barrett Brandreth found it increasingly difficult to access any income, cut off as he was from his bank account, held by the Midland Bank in London, as well as his British pension, worth £300 per annum.

His circumstances did not improve in 1943, when he described himself as needing 'continual medical attention', having undergone several major operations. On 5 May 1943 he sent a letter to Seán Murphy in Vichy from St Joseph's church in the avenue Hoche, where he was staying as a guest of Fr O'Grady. In a bad way, both financially and physically, he asked Murphy to send a telegraph to his cousin in Dún Laoghaire, County Dublin, to inform her that his 'health remains precarious, no second operation possible'. He needed constant medical attention, he explained, and 'healthy abundant food, which can be obtained only after much difficulties [sic]'.[29] Worse, the taxman had come knocking, looking for payment of taxes unpaid over the previous three years. According to the Legation, by July 1943 he was seriously in arrears on his rent and taxes and risked 'having his furniture seized shortly'.[30]

Things only got worse. By November Barrett Brandreth calculated that his medical bills ran to FF40,976 and 85 centimes, the equivalent of about eighteen times the monthly allowance he was granted by the DEA.[31] Despite this, he struggled on for the rest of the Occupation, continually arguing that his sole financial resource, the FF2,260 monthly allowance from the Legation (the maximum authorised by the DEA), was not sufficient to cover both his living expenses and his medical expenses, especially in view of fast-rising inflation. He felt aggrieved that the allowance was ultimately being sourced from his own bank account in London. Yet the Irish continued to restrict the amounts they were prepared to send to France and applied for most of the Occupation a pre-war rate of exchange that bore no relation to the effectively devalued French franc and the huge rise in the cost of living.

By January 1944 Barrett Brandreth was back in the American Hospital. But at least the Midland Bank in London had by then obtained a licence from the authorities to forward him monies (however little) via Dublin for a further six months, backdated to October 1943 – although there are indications a percentage was held back to cover administrative costs. In spite of his tribulations, Barrett Brandreth managed to see Paris liberated in August 1944, only to die there some months later, on 14 March 1945.

English teacher Constance Rafroidi, a sister of Alfred O'Rahilly, president of University College Cork, wrote to the Legation on 30 August 1943, from Arpajon in the outer southern suburbs of Paris, because she hadn't received any money for several weeks. 'I am worried because with my four children (two of whom are sick, as is my husband at the moment), I really need [money] … Whoever doesn't have money dies from hunger unfortunately.' Besides beseeching the Legation to ask her family in Ireland to continue to send money (her father sent her £5 each month), she asked, 'Have you found tea for me?'[32]

On 5 November 1943 Mrs Rafroidi wrote again to the Legation to obtain money from Ireland and 'some tea'. She was, she wrote, almost penniless, and stated that the education of her children was 'costing her dearly'.[33] One of those children, Patrick, later became professor of English at the University of Lille and was one of the main instigators of the academic journals *Cahiers irlandais* and *Études irlandaises*.

The supply situation for the Legation itself was also becoming problematic. Seán Murphy wrote to the head of Vichy's Service de Protocole to inform it that his laundress would be unable to clean his family's and his personal staff's clothes unless she received supply coupons for five kilograms of soap per month. But Mme Rafroidi in Arpajon was unaware of the Legation's own supply problems, writing an angry note on St Stephen's Day 1943 in which she noted that 'it seems all British subjects in France have received *food* for themselves and their children. I have *4* children and have *almost nothing* to give them, so will you please help me, also and give me some food including *tea*, like for the English.'[34]

In the summer of 1943, undaunted by his previous failure to have the ceiling on remittances from Ireland raised, Seán Murphy again argued the case for increasing the monthly allowance for Irish citizens in France from the FF4,400 maximum for a couple (FF2,640 for a single person). Once again he pointed out that (conservative) official figures showed that the cost of living index in France had risen by 60 per cent since 1940. But the index covered only items offered publicly for sale. Given that even some quite basic items were not offered for sale publicly in sufficient quantity, and were instead available only on the black market, the real rate of inflation was undoubtedly much higher. Inflation was also being fed by the Germans, who, leaving aside the vast swathes of French economic production they simply 'requisitioned', were able to buy whatever was available on the French market thanks to the favourable rate of exchange for the Reichsmark, thus crowding out French buyers. 'I do not propose to suggest that you should increase the scale of allowances to Irish nationals to a degree which would make them ready customers of the black market,' Murphy wrote to the DEA on 21 July 1943. 'I think, however, that, if in 1940 you considered FF2,640 as only sufficient to cover the monthly needs of a single person in the conditions then prevailing, the corresponding figure now would be greater by at least 40%.'[35]

Murphy understood that the Irish authorities' determination to maintain the maximum monthly allowance at FF2,640 per month since late 1940 was 'guided to a considerable extent by the necessity of keeping the export of currency within the narrowest possible limits'.[36] However, in a further long missive to the DEA in November 1943, he argued that 'a case can and should be made to the Department of Finance for a general increase in the maximum remittances allowed to be paid to Irish nationals in France'. He said such a case could be based on the 'notorious fact' that the price of all goods and services had risen considerably since 1940. 'It would be going too far to say that people in France are starving or are unclad', not least because there was a thriving black market. Most people, Murphy said, resorted to the black market to supplement official food rations, which were insufficient. But with butter on the black market costing ten to fifteen times the official price, Irish people dependent on remittances from home were simply excluded from access to such basic items. He pointed to a stream of letters about the size of allowances sent by the Irish in France since the beginning of 1943.[37]

In 1941, with a nudge from the paymasters in Dublin, Murphy had purposefully excluded members of religious orders from the 100 or so Irish nationals in France he estimated were in need of assistance, as it was reckoned that nuns and priests benefited from the support of the communities to which they belonged. The truth was somewhat more complicated. On 29 March 1943 the Service Social d'Aide aux Emigrants (SSAE) in Lyon wrote to the Legation in Vichy to explain that May Finucane, born in Newtownsandes near Listowel, County Kerry, in 1920, had come to Paris in March 1939 to become a nun, but by 1941 she or the community in which she lived had determined that she had no religious vocation. Excluded from the community, she was now in dire need of financial assistance.

In May 1943 there was a direct exchange of letters between the Legation and Finucane, who by then was staying at 78 rue Notre Dame des Champs in the 6th arrondissement in Paris. In her correspondence, Finucane applied for assistance and passage back to Ireland. The Legation wanted more information so, in a follow-up letter, Finucane explained that she had arrived in France in March 1939 to enter the noviciate of the Soeurs du Bon Secours, further along the same street from where she was writing. By early 1941 the French nuns had determined that Finucane did not have a 'vocation for their congregation'. In spite of her protests that she was from a 'numerous, well to do Kerry family', she was 'put to live and eat with French orphan children'. Then the nuns found Finucane a job as a maid, working, she said, 'as a slave for 200 francs a month'. She had since found herself a better-paying job (earning FF600 per month) but understandably wanted to go home. Although she felt the Bon Secours congregation should pay for her fare home, she knew it would refuse. Instead, she told the Legation, she felt her family back in Ireland 'will be happy and willing to pay all expenses'.[38]

However, by the autumn of 1943, the ex-noviciate Finucane had still not made it back to Ireland. On the contrary, she had travelled east, to the heart of Nazi territory in Berlin, which by then was coming under steadily increasing Allied bomber attacks. By September 1943 – just two months before the RAF launched a series of giant, but largely unsuccessful, air raids against the German capital in the so-called 'Battle of Berlin' – Finucane was living in north-west Berlin and working at a Telefunken plant making sophisticated equipment for the Luftwaffe. Soon after her arrival in Berlin, she called into William Warnock at the Irish Legation in Drakestraße and showed him a letter from the Legation in Vichy that explained that arrangements had been made for her to return to Ireland. The Legation had booked a passage for her on a boat from Lisbon to Ireland and had already arranged for the necessary transit visas to be issued. But she had decided she was not ready to leave – her mood had changed considerably since the French nuns had thrown her out of the convent in 1941 and forced her to work as a 'slave'. She told Warnock that she had come to Berlin during the summer of 1943 with a group of French girls who had jobs in German factories. She felt very happy there and 'had not yet decided whether she would endeavour to return to Ireland'.[39] Even as he issued her a new passport, Warnock advised her she should seize the chance to go home.

That passport – issued on 15 October 1943 – was to be the last that Warnock granted before the destruction of the Legation in Drakestraße during the massive night-bombing campaign of the following month. Finucane lived through that attack and the destruction wrought on the city during the rest of the war, marrying a German and ending up in England sometime after the end of hostilities.

One of May Finucane's acquaintances also applied for help to the Irish authorities to make it home. Molly McGrath from Carrick-on-Suir, County Tipperary had been sent to France to learn French and had been unable to make her way home after the French defeat in June 1940. She ended up, she recounted in a June 1943 letter to the Legation, in the same convent in Paris where Finucane was serving her noviciate and they became friends. McGrath, who was nineteen years of age in 1943, grew tired of the nunnery and found work looking after children in a family in the 16th arrondissement. She hated the job, 'but it seems we can not do anything at this present moment'. Some of her Irish friends had made it home, and she wondered whether the Legation might be able to do something for her. If not, she had 'heard saying also that many girls return home by Germany, as they go there to work for a while and then they get home'. McGrath cited the example of her friend May Finucane. 'She seems to be very happy there, as she meets a lot of Irish boys and girls who came directly from Ireland.'[40]

But McGrath did not join Finucane in Germany. Her family back in Ireland received a letter from an American soldier based in France in December 1944 to say that all was well with Molly, but when the family wrote back to the soldier, the letter was returned to sender. In February 1945 she was discovered residing at the convent in rue Murillo along with many other single Irish girls down on their luck and unable to return home.

Finucane and McGrath were not the only Irish girls who had come to Paris to enter a religious order around the outbreak of war only to find they didn't have a vocation. Rosie O'Hanlon had adopted the name Sister Marie de Levrette and settled into life with an Augustinian community at 28 rue de la Santé in the 13th arrondissement. But in 1943 she left the convent and found employment as a children's nurse with a succession of families. In April 1944 O'Hanlon became a ward's maid at the American Hospital in Neuilly, after the Legation helped her to obtain the necessary authorisations. She remained there until October 1944 and a month later was employed by Seán Murphy as a nurse to his children. However, O'Hanlon showed little inclination for the work and left after five or six days, finding work in a maternity clinic instead. She had not liked having to live with a family and instead wanted to find a place of her own. Indeed, with the money she earned as a nurse, she had found accommodation 'in a hotel of sorts' located in Levallois-Perret in the inner suburbs that she shared with 'some friends who had left the same convent'.[41] One of these friends might have been Maureen Mooney, who had 'abandoned the religious life because her health was not equal to it'.[42] Any one of these girls could have been the one that Sister Mary Anthony mentioned in a letter dated June 1945. She wrote that she had a girl from Cahirciveen, County Kerry, to help: 'she is a good girl; she tried her vocation with the Little Sisters of the Poor, but did not go on'.[43]

While Murphy tried to keep in touch with O'Hanlon, she did not like her movements being known, and she 'did not wish her father to know that she had left the convent', according to the nuns in rue Murillo.[44] In early 1945 the Legation tried to reach out to offer to help her get home, but she came down with 'gastric troubles' in April 1945, prompting the mother superior of her former convent to advise that she postpone her return to Ireland for some time. In Murphy's view, there was more to it than a health scare: simply, O'Hanlon was 'unwilling to give details about herself to her parents' and it was useless to insist that she go home until she herself had decided the time was right.[45]

In late 1943 Anne Le Guen wrote to the Legation about Margaret Catherine Lawlor, a sixty-four-year-old Dubliner who had worked for the Le Guen family for forty years and who had remained at the family residence in Pornic on the west coast of France near Nantes after that summer. Letters had remained unanswered and Le Guen had been unable to send her wages. 'She must by now be completely without money and she has no possibility of procuring any in this country.'[46] Could the Legation step in to obtain news of '*ma chère Irlandaise*'? The Legation had already intervened on Lawlor's behalf at the beginning of the Occupation by issuing her a passport that kept her out of an internment camp. Lawlor's 1940 passport application shows she was born in Dublin in 1878, but had left Ireland for France in 1900 and had been back only twice in the intervening forty years. At the time of the application, she was living in the Le Guen's family residence in boulevard Brune in the 14th arrondissement. The Le Guen family must have made contact with Lawlor following this, but she once again came to the Legation's attention in April 1945, when Mme Le Guen wrote to state that she had once more lost contact with Lawlor, who had been staying in Pornic since the previous June.

The SSAE was a French, state-backed agency charged with the welfare of migrant workers. In November 1943 it wrote to the Legation to present the case of Catherine Stevenson, born in Dublin on 23 August 1874, who had worked as a governess and an English teacher, living with the same family for many years. Stevenson had fallen ill and had to be hospitalised. But when she was ready to leave hospital, the family she had been staying with intimated that it could not take her back because of 'lack of space'. They had found her a place in a nursing home in Neuilly-sur-Seine, an ultra-chic suburb of Paris, and agreed to pay FF500 of the FF900 monthly boarding costs. To pay the remaining FF400 owed each month to the nursing home, Stevenson sold all her personal belongings, 'but she soon will have nothing to sell', the SSAE explained. She hadn't found anybody who wanted English classes and her only income came from occasionally minding a child, which earned her FF10 per day, 'which is totally insufficient'.[47] In short, the SSAE explained to the Legation, Stevenson needed FF400 per month until she found more work. (Given she was sixty-nine, this must have been an unrealistic proposition.)

The Irish Free State had a scheme whereby it would advance a loan of FF1,000 to Irish citizens who could prove that they did not have relatives who could come to their aid. This might have helped Catherine Stevenson, or Sarah Lawrence, who had appeared on the first list of Irish people in need of financial assistance drawn up by the Legation in May 1941. Lawrence, born in Dublin in January 1890, had left Ireland in 1912 for England and arrived in France a year later. She had worked for the family of an Irishman called Stellen in Montfort l'Amaury to the west of Paris in the early 1920s, but her life was thrown into turmoil by the Occupation. By 1941 she was living, penniless and in bad health, in an old people's home in Noisy-le-Grand. François Russo, a solicitor acting on Lawrence's behalf, wrote to the Legation in June 1943 to explain that Lawrence was 'sick, half paralysed and deaf ... all these infirmities stem from a serious wound and from an operation she underwent in the theatre of war in 1914–1918'.[48] Russo mentioned that he had managed to have Lawrence admitted to a hospital in Saint-Germain-en-Laye for a few days but suggested to the Legation that it should arrange for Lawrence to stay in another old people's home.

In July 1943 the Legation sent Russo a standard question-naire asking where Lawrence was in 1922, where her parents were

born, when she left Ireland, etc. The form had to be completed before she could be deemed an Irish citizen and thus eligible for the
FF1,000 per month (worth the modern-day equivalent of €227
in 1943) in financial aid offered by the state. The solicitor was also
asked whether he knew of any old-persons' home that would be
willing to take Lawrence in. The Legation wrote to Russo again
on 5 August 1943 to ask him if he was sure that Lawrence had
nobody in Ireland who could come to her aid. 'The Department
of Foreign Affairs insists on this point before it will do anything
to come to the aid of people without means involving public
money.' Worse, it seemed that because of Russo's reply to the
Legation's questionnaire, 'Mlle Lawrence may not be considered
an Irish citizen and she may not enter into the category of Irish
people to whom the Department is ready to give advances.'[49]

Lawrence took pen to paper herself in September 1943,
'obliged almost by poverty' to explain to the Legation that she
had been unable to continue to work as a cook at a castle in
Marly-le-Roi outside Paris because her doctor had told her the
job was too hard for a woman of her age and her 'heart was very
tired'.[50] She had found a furnished room at 17 rue Bosquet in
the 7th arrondissement in Paris. But the two hours of cleaning
she did every day did not pay enough to cover her FF350 rent
and allow her to buy food. She was unable to work full time and
she had nobody who could help her. The previous week she had
only bread to eat and she was afraid of 'falling completely sick'
through lack of food. 'I am meant to buy medicine but I can't
for lack of money and I'm hungry,' she wrote on the margin of
another Legation questionnaire on 15 September 1943.[51] In a
separate blotchy letter sent later in September, she wrote, 'come
to my aid, Monsieur le Ministre, God himself will bear witness
and will prove his recognition to you'.[52]

However, the Legation was adamant. In a letter dated 1
December 1943 it informed the SSAE that 'Mlle Lawrence is

not an Irish citizen: even if she were, the Legation would like it to be known that there are no funds available that would allow it to provide material help to her on a regular basis.'[53] But while the Legation was obliged to toe the DEA line in official responses to cases of distress, the people there sometimes proved less hardhearted than their colleagues back in Dublin, and Seán Murphy himself sent the SSAE FF500 from his own pocket for Lawrence.[54] The money came too late, however, as Sarah Lawrence had died at the Hôpital Boucicaut in the 15th arrondissement on 9 November 1943.

Other members of the French nobility became anxious for their Irish governesses. On 23 July 1943 Countess Turquet de la Bossière (born Matilda O'Kelly of Newtown, County Galway in 1865), who lived on the avenue Victor Hugo in the 16th arrondissement in Paris, wrote to the Legation on behalf of her compatriot Brida Ghallahan (perhaps Callahan), 'who finds herself in the most precarious circumstances' and was desperately sick. Ghallahan/Callahan had been a nursery governess for several upper-class families. Countess Turquet, who was a relative of Count O'Kelly, explained that Ghallahan had been unable to accompany her current employer, Countess de Caumont la Force, and her family to their summer residence in the countryside. Countess Turquet had the idea that she could find for Ghallahan 'a small pension in the style of Irish social insurance so that she could move into a rented room where friends and nursing sisters could look after her needs – unless there is an Irish home or convent where she could be received and protected'.[55]

In October 1942, two years after she had first contacted the Legation about the theft of her passport, Leitrim art student Una Whyte wrote again to Ireland's diplomatic representatives from an address at 112 boulevard Malesherbes in the 17th arrondissement, asking them to send a request to her family in Ireland for money 'to buy my winter clothing'. A month later she received a letter from the Legation admonishing her for having left her passport behind at the ticket office at Montparnasse railway station – the second time in two years she had lost the precious document in Paris.

When she first arrived in Paris, Whyte had had a monthly income of £80–£100. But the cap on the amount that Dublin was prepared to allow to seep out of the closed Irish economy meant that the Irish in France – including Whyte – received far less than that during the Occupation and had to undergo increasing levels of hardship as inflation rose steeply. In late October 1943 Whyte was living at 44 rue Julie (now called rue de l'Abbé Carton) in the 14th arrondissement (her third address in four years in Paris, a feat worthy of James Joyce). From there she again contacted Seán Murphy in Vichy to ask him to cable the following message to her parents in County Leitrim:

> Get O'Flynn to transfer my bank account to Lloyds Paris. Consider me permanently residing on continent. Terrible discomfort during eighteen months for clothes, finance. Send white sweater and wool for tailor, a supply of chocolate to relieve cooking. Health medium. You won't see me again except you send cash. Una.

Whyte added an almost apologetic, but not quite logical, postscript to her message, destined for the Legation. 'Thanks for sending October allowance,' she wrote. 'Unfortunately, all disappeared, there was a queue in the bank. Evidently mishandled what was left.'[56]

It was now increasingly difficult to transfer money to occupied France. Murphy, in a curt note dated 3 November, replied to Whyte that:

> … in spite of the information previously furnished, you are still labouring under some misapprehension as to the possibility of

receiving money in France ... Even if your family were prepared to send you a limitless amount of money they could not do so because of the regulations governing the export of currency, as they are limited in the amounts they can to the figures laid down by the Department of Finance.[57]

Clothes parcels were also out of the question. Murphy saw no point in sending Whyte's message and instead suggested that if she needed extra funds, 'you would be well advised to submit a detailed statement of your requirements'. No doubt unimpressed with the Legation's reply, Whyte wrote back on 9 November 1943: 'There is nothing to add to message for F.I. Whyte, Dromahair. He can do what he likes; I am now twenty-seven years old and must have something to start on if I find work.' The work prospects for a foreigner with no skills or connections in Paris in November 1943 would have been close to non-existent, but Whyte needed money, enjoining Murphy to 'please send telegram at once, s.v.p.'.[58]

**

The misadventures of Stephen Joseph Rice from Mullaghnee, outside Castleblaney in County Monaghan, were extraordinary. Born in 1881, Rice had first left Castleblaney to go to New York before the First World War, where his brother worked as a plumber. Rice was in the United States again from 1930 to 1940. In the mid-1930s he was living in San Francisco, but by the outbreak of war in 1939 he had an address in Lower Manhattan, New York, and was making a living as a 'livestock attendant' on boats transporting cattle across the Atlantic. On 19 June 1940 he was on the *Ville de Namur*, a cargo ship transporting 400 horses from the US to Bordeaux, when it was torpedoed off the Atlantic coast of France. Thus began almost five years of struggle for Rice in a war-torn country of which he knew nothing, whose language he didn't speak, and where he was without friends or family and without any regular means of subsistence. But Stephen Joseph Rice was a tough man and he survived, living mostly on charity but also apparently finding occasional work.

Rice is first mentioned in Con Cremin's notes of his conversation with Count O'Kelly on 16 January 1941. O'Kelly asked Cremin whether the Legation 'can accept responsibility for his repatriation and maintenance pending arrangements being made ... Count O'Kelly says he thinks that Rice could be able to refund expenditure.'[59] The Legation provided Rice with some money, but it is unclear whether any efforts were seriously undertaken to get Rice back to Ireland, for almost four years later he was still pounding the pavements of the French capital. He subsequently came to the attention of the Irish authorities at the end of May 1943, when he wrote to Seán Murphy from the Prison de la Santé. Rice – by then in his sixties – was sore about how he had been fobbed off by Irish officials since 1941. 'I am in prison here in Paris. I want you to come here and get me out,' he wrote. He continued (using idiosyncratic punctuation and spelling), 'In November 1941, you sent me 500 francs you knew I wanted money I was living on charity it was not write of you to treat me like that I fought threw all the Irish trouble was wounded in Dublin 1916 on Easter weeke write at once to me and let me know what you are going to do with me.'[60]

Murphy sent Rice a Declaration of Nationality form to fill out and a letter asking about the date and circumstances of his imprisonment. In reply, Rice wrote that he had been arrested because he did not have any proper residency papers:

> I did not know where to get my papers or wher[e] to go to get them as I had no person here to helpe me to get them I cannot speak French I was in a poor way here. Am in prison since the end of May 1943. It is terrible here for me as I have no one here in Paris

to send me food. The prisoners all here there people sends them in there food, so please come here at once and get me out I would go to German Red Cross and the[y] would give me money to help me out to get food when I was hungary I was with them the day befor I was taken to prison and told me to write to you for to come here and the[y] would help you to get me to my family in Ireland as I told you befor I was threw the hole war in Ireland was wounded in 1916 Easter weeke. Yours, Rice.[61]

In Rice's Declaration of Nationality form, there are some discrepancies in his life story. No longer a livestock attendant, he gave his occupation as 'ship carpenter'. He also stated that he had returned to Ireland from the United States sometime in the late 1920s, but left Ireland for the New World for a second time in 1930. In addition, he claimed he had boarded the *Ville de Namur* in New York in 1940 in a bid to travel home to Ireland.

In a further letter to the Legation in October 1943, Rice supplied more details of his ordeal when the *Ville de Namur* sank. 'I lost all my papers when the ship was torpetoed,' he wrote. 'The ship sank in ten minutes I was in Bordaux Hospital for 6 months I was all broke up I have no papers Count O'Kelly got me a paper here it is no good it got wore out I do not know where I got it.' Rice explained that the ship he was on was originally called *American Banker* before its sale to a European company resulted in a change of name to *Ville de Namur*. He ended his letter to Murphy with an interesting perspective on the diplomat's mission in a war-torn country. 'Well, Mr Murphy,' he wrote, 'I hope that you will write to me when you get this letter and not wait so long as you did the last letters I wrote to you but perhaps you are busy man but remember you are not in prison and remember only for me and likes of me you would not be in France at all. Yours faithfully, Stephen Rice.'[62]

Murphy did what he could for Rice, putting pressure on the

French authorities to release the erstwhile seaman. Finally, in reply to enquiries, the director of la Santé wrote to the Legation on 12 July 1943 to tell it that Rice had been arrested on 30 May on foot of the 1938 decree that enabled the incarceration of foreigners found without proper papers but that he had been released on 9 July.

In that same month, Mme G. Brandt at the SSAE wrote to advise Murphy in Vichy that it had been looking after Rice, 'who is in great distress', for the past year. He had just come out of prison, Brandt explained, had a bad leg and was living in hostels for homeless people. The SSAE had tried to sort out Rice's legal situation with the French authorities, but that had proved impossible because Rice was seen 'very irregularly', according to Brandt. 'He disappears for three months, comes back, tells us that he has been in Germany or interned (because he didn't have any ID) and that he didn't have any money.' In the opinion of the SSAE, 'the best solution … would be to repatriate this man'. The SSAE wondered whether the Legation had set up a fund to help send Irish citizens back home and, if not, whether it could provide Rice with an allowance 'from time to time'. Rice, who was sixty-two years of age, was clearly unable to continue working for a living, even if there were work to be had. 'For a long time,' explained the SSAE, 'Mr Rice was able to work, but unfortunately, while engaged in some contract work for the Germans, he seems to have had an accident and now he limps. I should add that Mr Rice speaks English badly, he is terribly hard to understand.'[63]

Curiously, although the Legation had known of the circumstances in which Rice had found himself since 1940, and Rice had filled out a Declaration of Nationality while incarcerated in la Santé, Con Cremin in Vichy replied to the SSAE on 3 August to request Rice's birth certificate to see whether he was eligible for an Irish passport. In her next letter to Cremin, ten days later,

Brandt suggested that any money destined for Rice should be sent to the SSAE rather than to Rice directly, since a couple of letters the Irishman had been expecting at the Salvation Army hostel where he was staying had already gone missing. In any case, according to Brandt, 'from our experience of dealing with him over the past two and a half years, when he has pocket money, he spends it without thinking. We were therefore very happy to see that he himself asked that any money allowance should be channelled through us.'[64]

But there seems to have been a communication problem. Either that or the Legation did not send money as quickly as it was needed, for a couple of weeks after Brandt's second letter, Rice himself wrote to Seán Murphy to find out whether funds had been sent to the SSAE:

> If you sent me money to there pleas let me know at once how much yous sent me and when did yous for I want money just now very badly I am asking yous people of the Irish Legation to get me home to my family in Ireland yous can get me home now it is different now nor it was 2 years and a half ago so let me know if yous are going to do anything about me home I hardly walke now at the present time with my knee and ankle that I got broke when the ship was sank I got a letter from my familey in Ireland a few months ago they are all alive thanks be to God for goodness to us all – write as soon as yous get this letter.[65]

In a postscript, Rice dismissed Brandt's suggestion, asking that any correspondence should be sent to him directly at the Salvation Army hostel rather than to the SSAE.

It sounds like Rice was vexed with the SSAE for not handing over all that he was due as speedily as he wished. On 29 August 1943 the SSAE wrote again to Vichy to confirm that it had received from the Legation FF500 (equivalent to about €113) for Rice. Mme Koechlin, social assistant at the SSAE, told the Legation somewhat laconically that 'we gave him 300 francs from the remittance so that he could buy shoes for himself and we will give him the rest bit by bit so that he isn't able to spend this money unwisely'.[66] Koechlin reiterated that it would be better for the SSAE to serve as an intermediary for any further monies from the Legation destined for the Irishman. The Legation seems to have followed the SSAE's advice, thereafter transferring FF1,000 per month to it on Rice's behalf until the Irishman was able to leave France.

On 28 October 1943 Rice wrote again to Murphy: 'Hoping the erival of this letter will find you enjoying good health as for myself I am just alive and no more,' he writes. 'Well Mr Murphy the reason I am writing to you this letter I was told here that Count O'Kelly comes here to Paris every month so he is coming here to Paris the 3 of November could you pleas send me an old over coat if any kind and a pair of pants and a old pair of shoes as I have none send them with Count O'Kelly.'[67] It seems, therefore, that the FF300 he received from the SSAE in August had not gone towards footwear.

The SSAE had other desperate cases to deal with in late 1943. Charles Edward Joy was born in Dublin on 16 September 1885. He had been a lieutenant in the Royal Navy in the First World War and afterwards married a Frenchwoman, had two daughters and settled in Paris. By 1943 one of his daughters was a pharmacy student and the other was studying music at the Paris conservatory. Joy had worked for Chase National Bank in rue Cambon in the centre of Paris since 1927 and followed most of the Chase staff to Châteauneuf-sur-Cher in the centre of France after the German invasion. He was still there in 1941 when the bank dismissed most of its staff, himself included.[68] Joy had applied for an Irish passport to replace his British one in August 1940 and in January 1941 he wrote to the Legation about the formalities involved in crossing the Demarcation Line. After losing his job Joy eventually found a way to get back to Paris, where he tried to earn a living as an English teacher at the École de Navigation. But that job did not last, as it was reserved for French nationals, so he turned to giving private lessons. However, by November 1943, when the SSAE brought his case to the attention of the Irish authorities in Vichy, 'he was having less and less students'. His daughter Geneviève had been awarded a first prize at the Paris music conservatory and earned money for the family by giving music lessons, but the Joys, according to the SSAE, 'obviously are finding it difficult to live on the fluctuating earnings of a single daughter and thus find themselves in a precarious situation'. Although Charles Joy had already approached the Legation, according to the SSAE, and had been told that nothing could be done for them, the SSAE made a renewed plea for financial help to the Irish authorities, saying the family 'has a lot of dignity. One feels that they must have been really pushed by necessity to ask for help.'[69]

A month later, Charles Joy wrote directly to the Legation in Vichy. He had met Seán Murphy some months before and explained that he wanted to take up the minister's suggestion that he and his family should leave France and try to get to Ireland via Portugal. His funds were low, he wrote, but he wanted the Legation to forward a letter to his brother Samuel, who lived on Lower Baggot Street in Dublin, to ask him to reimburse the Irish government for the expenses involved in repatriating him. However, on 8 May 1944 the DEA informed the Legation 'that no further passages will be available from Lisbon for the present'.[70] In any case, Joy still had not obtained a Portuguese transit visa for himself or his family by this stage and his request for one was turned down on 7 June 1944, a day after the Allied landings in Normandy.

Nonetheless, the Joy family survived the turmoil of the

closing phase of the German Occupation. In March 1945 they sent a message to their relatives in Ireland to tell them they were doing 'quite well', while a letter from the Legation to Dublin on 12 March stated that Charles Joy was working for the US Red Cross. Geneviève Joy, the sole breadwinner for the family during the Occupation, went on to become a renowned pianist and teacher at the Paris conservatory. She married the French composer Henri Dutilleux and died, aged ninety, in Paris in 2009.

In Maisons-Laffitte, outside Paris, the family of Patrick Fenton, the Limerick-born jockey who had died in Preston in 1941, seems to have had no news of him after the Germans interned him in June 1940. By 1943 his eldest son, Patrick Francis Fenton, was approaching an age when he risked being caught up in the STO scheme, whereby the Vichy authorities obliged young men to make themselves available for work in Germany instead of military service. A promise by the Germans to release French prisoners of war proportionate to the number of workers recruited was trumpeted by Vichy as a way of drumming up popular support for the scheme. But as the war progressed, many young men joined the Maquis in forests and mountains to avoid having to go to Germany.

Patrick Francis Fenton's mother tried a different ploy. She wrote to the Legation in May 1943 to see if her son could opt for Irish nationality. Seán Murphy took up Fenton's case with the DEA. Whether Patrick Francis, born in Maisons-Laffitte near Paris in 1925, could claim a *certificat de nationalité* depended on whether his father was an Irish citizen under the terms of the constitution. The DEA confirmed that Patrick Francis Fenton could indeed be considered 'a natural-born citizen' unless he forfeited his right to Irish citizenship upon his twenty-first birthday. In Murphy's view, Fenton therefore did not need to do anything to assert his Irish citizenship, but he also thought 'the French government may in any event, in present circumstances, refuse to waive their earlier rights to his services if he is a French citizen'.[71]

A Mme Hennessy who lived in the town of Bailleul on the Belgian border faced a similar challenge in protecting her adolescent son from the vagaries of the German Occupation. At the beginning of 1944 she wrote to the Legation to inform it that her son, Jacques Hennessy, had been arrested on 22 January 1944, following a house search, and thrown into prison in the town of Loos. This house search had followed a series of anonymous letters sent to the local *Kommandatur* denouncing Jacques as a 'dirty Englishman', according to Mme Hennessy, who pleaded with the Legation to help her because of the Irish birth of her husband, Patrick Francis Hennessy. In a letter, she told the Legation that 'while it is true that Patrick Francis's four children were all born in France, they are all included on his Irish passport'.[72] Whether because of the Legation's intervention or whether the Germans simply could pin nothing on him, Jacques Hennessy was released on 1 March 1944.

Other Irish citizens were troubled by Vichy's attempts to press-gang people into the STO or other work schemes (half-hearted though these attempts often were). For example, a twenty-seven-year-old Irish student called James Fox was summoned by the Secrétariat Général à la Main d'Oeuvre and by the German military authorities in June 1944 with a view to sending him to work in the factories in Germany. In parallel, as the war went on, French nationals were required to make themselves available to protect installations – especially rail tracks – against sabotage. James Boyle, born in Belleek, County Fermanagh in 1893, worked as a stud-farm manager at Mortefontaine, near Chantilly, north of Paris. The owner of the farm, Paul Duboscq, contacted the Legation in April 1943 to find out whether the local authorities had the right to 'ask him [Boyle] to take up guard duties like French citizens'.[73] The Legation's reply to Duboscq was simple and to the point: as an Irish citizen, Boyle could not be press-ganged into guarding rail tracks and if the local authority in question pressed the Irishman further, then the Legation promised to take the matter up with the Ministry of Foreign Affairs in Vichy.

But just as some French families hoped to exploit their Irish links to benefit from the protection afforded by a neutral country, other French nationals found their Irish origins vexatious. A radiologist called Jean-Paul Brennan wrote to the Legation from the Parisian suburb of Neuilly to inform it of 'the difficult situation I find myself in from the application of the recent laws on the medical profession'. Back in August 1940 the Pétain regime had passed legislation that stipulated that all practising doctors had to be French citizens born of a French father. Brennan was, he explained, the son of a County Armagh man who had been brought to France three years after his birth in 1853. Brennan had spent six years in the French army, 'including 48 months at the front during the Great War'. In spite of his services to his country, he had been granted only a 'provisional authorisation' to exercise the medical profession, an annoyance that he ascribed to the nationality of his father.[74]

In September 1943 the Legation sent the French foreign ministry a list of four Irish citizens who were requesting exit visas to allow them to return to Ireland via Lisbon: Sister Philomena O'Driscoll, who was living in a convent in the Loire *département* in central France, and three Paris Irish: William D'Esterre Darby, Elizabeth Mary McConville and May Finucane (who by then had actually left Paris for Berlin). The Legation had already made several appeals to the German consulate in Vichy to obtain exit visas – at least on behalf of McConville, who had been confined in the civilian internment camp at Vittel. McConville's relatives had made representations to Frank Aiken, de Valera's minister for 'coordination of defensive measures' as far back as 1941. Prodded by Aiken, the Legation leaned on the Germans and she was eventually released from Vittel in March 1943. No doubt penniless and friendless, McConville made her way to the hostel run by Irish nuns in rue Murillo. But the Irish authorities had less luck when it came to getting her out of occupied France. Before the Legation in Vichy had sent its repatriation list to the French authorities, the German consulate wrote on 13 July 1943 to state that authorisation for McConville's journey to Ireland could not be given,[75] and by October 1943 William Warnock in the Legation in Berlin was informing Dublin that exit visas from France to Portugal 'were no longer being granted' to anybody.[76] McConville was still in the Irish convent in rue Murillo in December 1946, when she applied for a Red Cross food parcel.

As the Occupation progressed, the civilian internment camp at Vittel was partially cleared to make way for Jews from eastern Europe whom the Germans hoped to exchange for German civilians held by the Allies. But at least one unfortunate Irishwoman was still interned in Vittel in April 1944 – County Donegal woman Margaret Gallagher, who had left Ireland in 1912 at the age of twenty-one and had worked in Germany and Argentina before arriving in Paris, where she was caught by the war and interned because of her British passport. After she was granted a temporary Irish passport in the spring of 1944, she was released from Vittel and thereafter seems to have followed her fellow Vittel detainee McConville to the Irish convent in rue Murillo.[77]

***

Janie McCarthy, involved in helping downed Allied airmen and generally abetting the Allied cause since 1940, showed more mettle than most people, Irish or French. The range of her Resistance activities is breathtaking and her work for the Allied cause was possibly the most consistent and lengthy of any Irish person in Paris during the Occupation. Between 1940 and 1944 she worked for at least four different Resistance networks, all the time making a living as an English-language teacher and residing at her small flat in rue Sainte Anne.

The height of her involvement came in 1943. As that year wore on, the Allied bombing campaign in western Europe grew in intensity, with the US army air forces joining the RAF to pummel the German war machine. The increased activity meant that increasing numbers of aeroplanes were being shot down and their crews were either killed or sent to prisoner-of-war camps. However, a number of airmen shot down over France and the Low Countries were hidden by the local population or Resistance groups and evaded capture. While McCarthy was involved in monitoring German installations and troop movements in the early years of the Occupation, by 1943 helping some of these downed Allied airmen seems to have consumed an increasing amount of her attention. She was particularly busy in the second half of 1943, working for a succession of ephemeral exfiltration lines.

Escape reports written by three US airmen, who had to make a forced landing east of Paris in December 1942, described McCarthy's role in a shadowy escape line that eventually got them as far as the Spanish border almost five months later. One of those airmen, Iva Fegette, recounted how one day in early 1943 he and his compatriot William Whitman set out on foot to cross Paris in search of the American Hospital in Neuilly. Unable to find the place, they turned back towards Paris, but as they walked down the Champs Elysées, somebody threw a grenade into a café full of Germans, causing mayhem. The Americans were able to make it back to their respective hideouts, where they had to hole up for several weeks before arrangements could be made to spirit them out of Paris to Bordeaux and then to St-Jean-de-Luz and the Spanish border. Fortunately, during those long weeks, McCarthy paid the men frequent visits and, according to Fegette, 'kept us laughing all [the] time'.[78]

McCarthy, along with friends from her early Resistance days, Natacha Boeg and Elisabeth Barbier, is further mentioned in the escape file of Allen Robinson, who was shot down over western France in early 1943.[79] By then, Barbier had structured a network to help downed Allied airmen, called the Réseau Vaneau, with McCarthy acting as one of her faithful lieutenants. Robinson spent some time holed up in Barbier's flat at 72 rue de Vaneau in the 7th arrondissement, finally making it over the Pyrenees in September 1943, after months of hide-and-seek with the French and German authorities.

Barbier and McCarthy also worked for an escape network called the Réseau Comète, whose members were described as coming predominantly from a *milieu bourgeois et catholique*. The testimony provided after the war by one of its members, Pierre Robert, gives an idea of the feverish activity of the Réseau Comète and related escape lines:

> From 1941 to 1944 [a Brussels branch of the Réseau lasted until February 1944], there were around 4–5 exfiltrations organised each month, each time with 4–5 aviators involved. The official list shows 288 military men were exfiltrated (mostly aviators, mainly RAF men, some Americans, some civilians), to which one must add 111 civilians (mostly Belgians on the run from the Gestapo), without forgetting hundreds of others that were not recorded for one reason or another.[80]

Janie McCarthy was involved in many of these exfiltrations and one can imagine that the other networks she worked for had a similar work rate.

At the beginning of June 1943 the Germans penetrated the Réseau Comète. Once they had managed to close it down, they moved swiftly on to Elisabeth Barbier's Réseau Vaneau. McCarthy miraculously avoided capture when Barbier, her mother and Natacha Boeg were arrested by the Gestapo at the rue Vaneau flat on 18 June 1943. After the war McCarthy claimed that the unexpected arrival of one of her language students at her apartment in rue Sainte Anne caused her to miss a dinner that Barbier had organised at her home that evening. The Irishwoman was lucky, for a stake-out of rue Vaneau enabled the Gestapo to capture a number of airmen and French helpers in the days following Barbier's arrest. Barbier herself was sent to the Ravensbrück concentration camp for women in northern Germany, where she was to remain until the camp's liberation at the end of April 1945. Shortly after the war, she gave a series of statements to the French and American authorities about her activities, making several references to Janie McCarthy.[81]

McCarthy must have been scared by the arrest of Barbier and Boeg, but she did not try to leave the capital. Instead, after the organisation centred around Barbier was broken up, McCarthy continued to work with other nebulous escape lines. The Irishwoman appears in the escape report of Canadian airman Clarence Witheridge, who was shot down over France in mid-August 1943 on the way back from a bombing run over Milan.[82] After several weeks on the run, Witheridge related how he was brought by two women, one of whom was McCarthy, by train from the town of Vernon, west of Paris, to a safe house in the French capital, where he stayed before making it across the Spanish border at the end of the year. In her deposition to the Americans after she was liberated, one of McCarthy's closest comrades-in-arms, Lucienne Bodin, described their train journey to Vernon on 1 November 1943. They went there, she said, 'to collect three aviators from the graveyard keeper there, one Canadian and two Americans. The two Americans were arrested two days later with Doctor Morin in St Cloud.'[83]

Another of McCarthy's closest associates, still at large in late 1943 despite German crackdowns, was a nurse called Marie-

Thérèse Labadie. McCarthy and Labadie passed Allied airmen in need of hiding between each other according to circumstances. In late 1943 McCarthy fetched two US Air Force men, Andrew Hathaway and Sidney Casden, from outside Paris. McCarthy briefly housed Hathaway, who had bailed out of a B-17 bomber over Beauvais, in her own small flat on the rue Sainte Anne, before passing him to another safe house and then getting both Hathaway and Casden into hiding in the homes of Labadie's mother and brother in Ecouen, a town north of Paris. In late November 1943 McCarthy fetched Casden and Hathaway from Ecouen and guided them through Paris as far as the Gare d'Austerlitz, where, she claimed after the war, she pretended they were deaf mutes when confronted at a German checkpoint. It is hard to believe the Germans would have been so naïve, but McCarthy managed to pass Casden and Hathaway on to other *résistants*, who spirited them out of France via Spain in January 1944. Casden described McCarthy in his escape report as 'old 45 … greying hair, plump'. According to Casden, she mentioned to him that 'she was comparatively new to the org'.[84] (This was a strange thing to say: McCarthy was by this stage a veteran *résistante*. She may have meant that she was 'comparatively new' to the precise escape line that was organising Casden's escape from France.)

Like McCarthy, Marie-Thérèse Labadie was a member of a number of fast-changing evader networks, including the high-profile Réseau Shelburn. After the war, McCarthy confirmed the role of Labadie and her brother who, she stated in her deposition to the American authorities, 'also provided me with important military information on V1 rocket launch pads'.[85] This indicates that over three years after she first went to spy on German train movements in northern France in the early days of the Occupation, McCarthy was still involved in information gathering as well as helping airmen. Labadie provided further confirmation of McCarthy's activities, telling the Americans during her 1945 de-briefing that she had entered into contact with McCarthy in June 1941 and that, on the request of the Irishwoman, she 'procured some clothing and a little money destined for the escape of several British prisoners of war'. When it came to helping Allied airmen, Labadie said that McCarthy, who apparently was also known as 'Miss Mack', was responsible for 'supplies, conveying, interpreting and liaising'.[86] McCarthy was mentioned too in the 1945 deposition of Frank Bulfield, who lived in Le Vésinet in the western suburbs of Paris. According to Bulfield, McCarthy was often 'called in to question aviators for identification by radio from London'.[87]

Lucienne Bodin and her husband, Jean, both hairdressers, were friends and neighbours of McCarthy's in the centre of Paris and worked closely with her. The Bodins were zealous in their efforts for Allied airmen, working for the Shelburn, Samson, Vengeance and Défense de la France escape lines. After the war, the Americans reckoned that Mme Bodin had 'sheltered about 30 airmen and helped 40 others'.[88] In her deposition to the Americans, Lucienne Bodin described McCarthy as a 'person who was very devoted to the aviators, spoiling them a lot. She made three trips [with me] for the purposes of reconnaissance or to bring back aviators.'[89]

Having avoided capture by the Gestapo when Elisabeth Barbier was arrested, McCarthy had another scare in late 1943, shortly after putting Sidney Casden and Andrew Hathaway on a train out of Paris. On the morning of 21 November Lucienne Bodin was arrested in a café along with two other Réseau Shelburn operatives, Suzanne Bosnière and Marie Betbeder-Matibet. As was frequently the case, the network had been infiltrated. It is quite possible that one or other of the two US airmen arrested in Vernon on 1 November helped put the Germans onto the scent. All three women were sent to Ravensbrück. Jean Bodin was arrested on the same day as his wife and sent to a separate concentration camp – the couple were lucky to survive. By contrast, Betbeder-Matibet died in Ravensbrück in 1944. Like McCarthy, she was an English teacher and worked at the prestigious Catholic secondary school the Lycée Fénelon. Betbeder-Matibet made regular trips throughout the Occupation to the military barracks at Saint-Denis to bring supplies to the British and Irish who were interned there.

Probably alarmed by the arrests of her friends, McCarthy went to ground, leaving her flat in the rue Sainte Anne for a while and booking into a small guesthouse on the other side of the city. She sent a one-line telegram via the Legation to her sister in Killarney, County Kerry in late November 1943 from the Pension Port Royal in rue Berthellot in the 5th arrondissement, close to the Irish College: 'Well but anxious about you all.'[90]

McCarthy was not the only Irish person engaged in Resistance activity in northern France at this time. Having briefly appeared in the Legation's list of Irish in financial need in January 1942, Robert Armstrong seems to have managed to find support in his local community in Valenciennes. He too became involved in Resistance activities and in helping downed Allied aviators, resulting in his arrest in November 1943 and imprisonment in Loos. In May 1944 the Vichy delegation in occupied France alerted the Legation that Armstrong had been sentenced to death by a German military tribunal in Lille for helping American airmen. A local lawyer called Delcourt and Ireland's diplomatic representatives successfully intervened to save Armstrong's life at this time. The efforts of the legations in Berlin and Vichy on Armstrong's behalf were supported by the DEA in Dublin, which informed them that Armstrong was 'well known' to Seán MacEoin, a hero of the War of Independence and Armstrong's local Fine Gael TD in Longford.[91] However, neither his lawyer nor the legations were able to stop the Irishman's deportation to Germany via Brussels. In Berlin, Ireland's minister to Germany, Con Cremin, who had been sent to replace William Warnock in 1943, was informed that the German authorities were willing to consider exchanging Armstrong as well as two other Irish internees (Mary Cummins and Robert Vernon) for German 'political prisoners' held by the Irish.[92] But by the second half of 1944 such a scheme was logistically impossible and, just as importantly, could have been seen as compromising Irish neutrality.

Instead, a letter from an anonymous Dutchman dated 31 May 1945 gave extensive details of Armstrong's peregrinations and eventual death in Germany. Armstrong was, wrote the Dutchman, initially imprisoned in a camp called Rheinbach, close to Bonn, but in September 1944 was transferred to another camp in Kassel before being sent to Waldheim, a camp for political prisoners in Saxony, in December 1944. While in Kassel, Armstrong and his comrades had been forced to work in the fields. As autumn had turned to winter, Armstrong's health declined drastically. 'He had a huge carbuncle on his leg that was poorly looked after and day after day he became thinner. Because he was not able to work as much as he was meant to, he was often pushed around by the prison guards.' Armstrong was in a desperate state. 'The day before we left for Waldheim he had been knocked about again by a guard because he had not eaten his meal quickly enough. He had to be helped to walk; he could barely move on his own anymore.' On 14 December 1944 Armstrong left Kassel for Waldheim (close to the much better-known Colditz), where he died about two days later for 'he was already too weak and his leg was no more than an open sore'.[93]

Dubliner William O'Connor, born in 1893, lived in Douai in the north of France, just over forty kilometres from Valenciennes, where Robert Armstrong resided. O'Connor's life story was not dissimilar to Armstrong's. Like Armstrong, O'Connor had served in the British army in the First World War, had been appointed gardener at his local imperial war cemetery and had married a

Frenchwoman. O'Connor became involved in the French Resistance and, like his fellow Irishman, was arrested and deported to Germany; however, unlike Armstrong, O'Connor lived to tell the tale. French files show that O'Connor (who had three children) started working for the Voix du Nord Resistance movement in February 1942, helping to transport arms, distributing leaflets and clandestine newspapers, cutting telephone lines, providing assistance to shot-down Allied airmen and acting as a liaison officer.[94] He was arrested by Gestapo agents at his place of work in Douai cemetery on 1 September 1943 and sent before a military court in Arras. There, he was condemned to eighteen months' hard labour for *Engländerbegünstigung* (aiding and abetting the British), first in Rheinbach and then at another camp in Siegburg, from where he was repatriated to France on 24 May 1945. O'Connor told French officers who debriefed him after the war that he had been tortured by the Germans before being brought to trial and that he had contracted typhus while in Siegburg.[95]

While Janie McCarthy avoided Ravensbrück, other Irish *résistantes* did not. Agnes Flanagan, born in Birr, County Offaly in 1909, was a nursing sister working for an order based in Tournai, close to the French border in Belgium. She was arrested first in September 1941 for helping British escapees, then a second time a year later for destroying documents that might have compromised the local Resistance. She was sent to prison in Aachen and then hauled before the *Verfassungs Sondergericht* (special constitutional court) in Essen on 30 November 1942 and transported as a political prisoner to Ravensbrück five days later. After the camp's liberation in April 1945, Flanagan was evacuated to Sweden. From there, she made her way to 4 rue de Neva, close to the Arc de Triomphe in Paris, in autumn 1945, before moving back to Belgium. She married a local man called Depret in St Piat's church in Tournai in 1948 and lived in a very modest house in that Belgian town until her death in August

1986. On 21 August she was buried in a communal grave plot in the Cimetière du Nord in Tournai. Her remains were removed and incinerated ten years later when the lease expired.

While interned, Flanagan may have come across Kate McCarthy from Drimoleague in County Cork, who had been arrested in Béthune in August 1941 for helping Allied airmen and had been brought to Ravensbrück around the same time as Flanagan.[96] McCarthy, a nursing sister like Agnes Flanagan, had assumed the name of Sister Marie Laurence on taking her vows. She had already served in the British military hospital in Béthune during the First World War and returned to Béthune before the outbreak of the Second World War after a number of years in the United States. McCarthy became involved in Resistance activities after the German invasion. According to her Resistance file, she organised 'the sheltering and the passage to England of 200 British officers and soldiers from the Dunkirk pocket' in May 1940.[97] Shortly after the downfall of France in June, she worked closely with Sylvette Leleu to organise the escape of British and French soldiers from the local hospital and from provisional prisoner-of-war camps that had been set up near Béthune.

In October 1940 McCarthy joined the Musée de l'Homme network, of which Leleu was an important lynchpin, while all the time continuing to work at Béthune hospital. Contact with the Musée de l'Homme network in Paris meant that the *résistants* in provincial Béthune were able to increase and diversify their activities. However, the Musée de l'Homme network was soon penetrated after the capture of a courier, resulting in the arrest of about twenty people, including Leleu and McCarthy, in June 1941. They were both condemned to death but then had their sentences commuted to deportation in August 1942 and spent time in a succession of camps, eventually ending up in Ravensbrück, from which they were liberated in April 1945. At the time of her liberation, McCarthy weighed twenty-seven kilograms.

While in Ravensbrück, McCarthy met Germaine Tillion – a renowned author and ethnologist, and a fellow member of the Musée de l'Homme network. After the war, Tillion furnished a character reference for the Irishwoman, stating that 'During her trial and during all the time of her very hard captivity, her courage, her goodness, her good humour were never lacking. She was a help and an example for all those around her.'[98]

7

DARKNESS BEFORE THE DAWN

By the beginning of 1944 Marshal Pétain's État français was in its death throes, and although Pétain retained a measure of personal popularity, his government lost whatever faith the French had placed in it three years earlier. 'Criticism' of the Pétain regime, Seán Murphy had written to Dublin in August 1943, was 'much more open and more widespread' and the position of the government was 'becoming more and more difficult'. And while the Germans feared an Allied invasion of France, Murphy opined that at least 80 per cent of the French population was 'waiting impatiently' for it. 'They are quite convinced that Germany is beaten and with typical French shrewdness they think it is a good thing to get in early and well with the opponents.'[1]

With an Anglo-American invasion looming, tensions between various right-wing factions within the Vichy regime increased. Hardliners grew in influence as the less committed drew back or changed sides, culminating in the appointment (on German insistence) of Joseph Darnand, head of the dreaded Milice, as secretary-general in charge of maintaining order. Murphy wrote to Dublin on 1 February 1944 to report a considerable increase in police activity 'and it appears in growth of resistance movements'. He also said that many civil servants and government secretaries had been forced to resign 'and had been replaced by *persona grata* with German authorities', which helped to improve relations with the Germans, at least for the moment.[2]

The continued existence of the Irish Legation in Vichy was coming increasingly into question. The number of foreign diplomatic missions to Vichy had dropped steadily since 1940, and by January 1944, only eighteen were left, many belonging to satellite countries of Nazi Germany. The DEA in Dublin considered closure of the Legation likely – if only on account of the deterioration of relations between Pétain's government and the Germans. (In September 1943 Pétain had unsuccessfully tried to sideline Pierre Laval and nominate a new government to negotiate peace with the Allies.) If Murphy and his staff had to leave precipitously, the DEA advised that they 'go to Lisbon not Switzerland to avoid being cut off for the rest of the war'.[3]

Should the Legation be forced to leave, Murphy informed Dublin, the Irish community would be able to rely on Count O'Kelly, who was willing to stay in France 'in a private capacity' and ensure that financial aid continued to be distributed to the Irish community. Possibly worried about the direction Vendôme Wines was taking since he had been forced to move to Vichy, O'Kelly had by this time become more involved again in the running of the company. In November 1943 he had himself nominated as *gérant* (manager/administrator) alongside his office manager, Maurice Prévost. Coincidentally (or not), after a first business trip to Spain and Portugal as German administrator of Vendôme Wines in autumn 1943, Hans Gechter did not represent Vendôme Wines on his second journey to Iberia in March 1944.

The Legation was facing ever-greater restrictions. At the beginning of June 1943, the German military authorities decreed that, without special permission, the movements of all diplomatic missions in Vichy would be limited to a fifty-kilometre radius around the town. Yet O'Kelly continued to be granted a degree of favour. Benefiting from his ownership of Vendôme Wines and the rather ambiguous title of 'special counsellor', he made frequent visits to Paris, with his friend John Francis Keane reporting that he was 'very busy in Paris' in June 1943.[4]

While life had become extremely hard for many Parisian Irish by the beginning of 1944, it was not too bad for O'Kelly, at least from the point of view of public recognition. The Vichy government awarded him the Légion d'Honneur in February 1944 – a 'courtesy' that the French had first proposed back in 1935. For some reason, perhaps due to hostility towards O'Kelly from inside the DEA at that time (1935 was the year of his forced retirement from his position as Irish minister in France), Irish officialdom did not reply to the offer until spring 1940, when Seán Murphy took up the matter. But then the defeat of France intervened. The issue of O'Kelly's Légion d'Honneur remained in abeyance until 30 December 1943 when – perhaps after some post-Christmas prodding from the wine-merchant-cum-special-plenipotentiary – Murphy sent a handwritten letter to the Vichy authorities to inform them that the 'Irish government would view the conferral of this honorary distinction on Monsieur O'Kelly de Gallagh with great pleasure'.[5] So on Valentine's Day 1944, the État français informed the Legation in Vichy that 'Marshal and Chief of State Pétain has agreed to raise Count O'Kelly de Gallagh et [de] Tycooly to the dignity of Grand Officer of the Légion d'Honneur'.[6]

***

On the morning of 17 January 1944, along with 1,946 other men, Patrick Sweeney was deported from the Royallieu internment camp in Compiègne to Buchenwald in Germany. The packed train stopped on several occasions during the two and a half days it took to reach its destination, following successive escape attempts by prisoners.[7] In reprisal, the Germans ordered the prisoners crowded into one cattle truck to undress in freezing winter temperatures. Only once during the journey, just inside the German border at Trier, was food distributed.

Buchenwald – where Sweeney was to spend six months – was a camp for political prisoners. Sweeney is listed as *politisch Iren* – an Irish political prisoner.[8] His registration card (no. 40903) describes Sweeney as 'a farmer, Catholic, single, probably has never been seriously ill'.[9]

Sweeney was transferred from Buchenwald to another camp at Kreuzberg in Upper Silesia (now in Poland) in July 1944. The internment camp at Kreuzberg (Ilag VIIIZ, also designated Oflag VI/Z) was mainly used by the Germans to confine civilian citizens of their western enemies. From the summer of 1944 on, a number of these civilians were repatriated to the United Kingdom as part of an exchange programme between the Allies and the Germans. The living quarters at Kreuzberg, which consisted of an old, hastily adapted three-storied convent, were described by neutral inspectors in 1944 as 'satisfactory' and the recreational facilities as 'excellent'.[10] According to the Red Cross, of 442 prisoners held in Kreuzberg in May 1944, just twenty-three had volunteered to participate in work details.

While it is not known whether Sweeney was moved by the Germans ahead of the Soviet capture of the Kreuzberg camp in February 1945 or whether he was still there when the Soviets arrived, he made it back to England at war's end and thereafter worked on trawlers based in the port of Fleetwood on the Irish Sea. He died in Fleetwood in 1999, seemingly without leaving a complete account of his extraordinary misadventures.

Another Irishman, Cecil Francis Atkinson, was on the train that left Compiègne for Buchenwald on 17 January 1944. Atkinson was born in Dublin in July 1905. He was a music teacher, but of poor health, with a paralysed leg. In 1940, when he applied for an Irish passport in exchange for his British one, he was feeling the pinch financially. But that did not stop the Legation insisting he repay the cost of a telegram sent to his solicitor in Dublin,[11] and informing him that the DEA was 'not prepared to arrange for the payment of more than the equivalent of £15 per month'.[12] At least until 1942 – and in contravention of regulations that forbade foreigners from residing on the coast

– Atkinson had lived in Cassis, near Marseille in the south of France. But when he was arrested on 26 March 1943, some five months after the Germans had invaded the *zone libre*, he was living in the centre of Marseille. After his arrest, Atkinson was sent to the Royallieu internment camp to await his deportation to Buchenwald. In January 1944 Con Cremin in Berlin found out that he had been arrested 'when illegally crossing into Spain'.[13] But protected by his Irish passport and with a crippled leg, why would Atkinson have risked his life escaping to Spain?

The real reasons for Atkinson's arrest and deportation to Buchenwald are unclear. According to a letter from the British authorities in Berlin in January 1947, a witness who saw him in Cassis in April 1942 said, 'he was then in possession of his Eire passport and in touch with Mr Murphy, Eire Minister to Vichy'.[14] Nor is it clear why Atkinson did not benefit from the same largesse that had helped curtail William O'Hea's stay in Compiègne, or why intervention by the Legation proved less effective than it had been in the case of O'Hea.

Categorised as a political prisoner by his German gaolers, Atkinson's profession was given as *Privatier*, a gentleman of independent means. He did not stay long in Buchenwald, for on 22 February 1944 he was sent, along with 700 other prisoners, to the concentration camp at Flossenbürg, a little further south and close to the Czech border. Atkinson died in Flossenbürg on 13 April 1944, with the cause of death given by a German doctor as 'cardiac insufficiency as a result of pneumonia'.[15] It should be noted, however, that false medical reports were frequently drawn up by concentration camp doctors to disguise the murder of sick inmates. After his death, an SS officer wrote on Atkinson's file that his 'clothes were brought to the clothes-recycling point for they were in tatters and unusable. Transport and packaging costs do not seem to be justified.'[16]

In January 1944 the Legation again became anxious about

Stephen Rice and it finally issued him a new passport to replace the one he had lost when his ship sank in 1940. The SSAE believed that the best solution for Rice was his repatriation to Ireland. 'Do you believe there is any hope to reach a result in this regard?' Mme Brandt asked the Legation in February.[17]

During the spring of 1944, without waiting for the Legation to act, the resourceful Monaghan man pushed ahead with his attempts to get out of France. On 29 April he wrote to Seán Murphy to announce the good news that he was 'getting back home to my wife and children I have got my French passport and my Spanish passport and my German passport. But I have not got my Portegal passport yet it takes two months to get it but the Portegal councelate told to write to you to Vichy and for you to telephone to Lisbon to the Irish Legation in Lisbonn.'[18]

On 4 May, just over a month before D-Day, Mme Brandt of the SSAE confirmed to the Irish Legation that Rice had shown her the exit visa he had obtained from the German authorities. This document apparently allowed him to leave France for Ireland via Hendaye on the Franco-Spanish border. How he managed to obtain an exit visa at a time when the Germans were on high alert ahead of an Allied invasion and had stopped issuing exit visas to other Irish people remains a mystery. The only problem was that the German exit visa expired on 20 May. Could the Irish authorities look after these formalities and pay for Rice's journey home, Brandt enquired in her 4 May letter?[19] Clearly the Legation failed to do so, as when the 20 May deadline expired, Rice was still in Paris.

By the time of the Allied landings in Normandy on 6 June 1944, Rice was *still* stuck in Paris, in spite of the impressive list of exit and entry visas he had obtained. But he did not despair. On 20 June he wrote to Count O'Kelly, who was in Paris and unable to get back down to Vichy because of the breakdown in transport links following D-Day. Writing, as usual, on cheap school-copy-book paper, Rice said he was aware there were no more ships running between Dublin and Lisbon. Not to worry. He didn't even want to go to Dublin at that juncture in time. Instead, he told the count, 'I want to get back to New York to get my money that is coming to me there is boats running from Lisbon to New York or if not I can get to England and from England to New York I have got my French passport and my German passport all I want is my Portugal passport. The Legation in Vichy will have to write to the Legation in Lisbon.' Across the top of this letter, somebody, presumably from the Legation, wrote the words 'no action'.[20]

Rice was still in Paris on 18 July when he wrote his next missive, this time to Seán Murphy in Vichy. Again he wanted the Legation to write to Lisbon to obtain a 'Portugal passport' (in other words an entry visa to Portugal). 'You cannot blame me to get away from France the Portugal councelate says here in Paris that I should get away and that you should do your best to get me away.'[21] But Rice's long, unplanned sojourn in Paris was to last until December 1944.

***

Irishman Michael Farmer had a very different experience of wartime France to most of his compatriots. He was engaged in a series of drunken escapades around the town of Brive in central France that almost caused him to be executed by the French after the Liberation. Farmer, born in County Cork in 1902, had at various times of his existence been an actor, a toy boy and the head of his own car rental company – but his main claim to fame was his marriage to the American film actress Gloria Swanson. According to a 1946 press cutting, 'no party, dîner or ball worth going to, from Palm Beach through Bermuda to the Lido, was without Michael Farmer. He was handsome, he was rich, and pretty women adored him.'[22] At the time of his marriage to Swanson, an American magazine wrote that Farmer attended 'the most magnificent parties held in the most magnificent homes in Paris' and that he mixed with 'the most sophisticated, highly placed nobility of England, of France and Italy and the social registrites [*sic*] of America fortunate to be numbered as friends of the most exclusive set on the Continent'.[23]

The same, uncritical article provides some valuable information on Farmer's background, explaining that while he had been born of poor parents in Ireland, he had moved to London in his youth, where he had come to know a rich elderly American lady called Mrs Edmund Hubbard, who wished to adopt him as her son, 'but he could not consent to it'. Through Hubbard, Farmer was introduced to another American called Hogan, and together they established a car insurance business, progressively branching into other parts of the auto business, 'arranging for cars to meet ships on cabled requests from America, providing reliable chauffeurs etc., and acting as a "man of affairs" … that is, the agent who inspects, buys and sells motors'. Farmer eventually set up his own business. But he did not need to play the entrepreneur for long, as, upon her death, Mrs Hubbard left him a fortune 'estimated at eight or nine millions of dollars', and his high life moved up a notch. Moving to Paris during the 1920s, he dated a succession of young American debutantes and actresses and lived 'in a beautiful apartment which he bought and furnished in the most exquisite taste with rare and lovely antiques'.

With *Motion Picture* describing him as 'a dashing Irishman of a breed that is the darling of the world of men – as well as women', it is perhaps not surprising that Gloria Swanson was one of those who fell for his charms.[24] Noël Coward and the British film director Edmund Goulding introduced her to him one evening in 1931. A one-night-stand on a boat on the Côte d'Azur resulted in Swanson becoming pregnant and a hastily arranged (and stormy) wedding. She landed him a role in a film called *Perfect Understanding* in 1932 but, deciding that acting was not for him, he branched into film production – although with limited success. His marriage to Swanson quickly went downhill, with Swanson filing for divorce (her fourth) in 1934. No doubt, Swanson had had enough of Farmer's drinking and gambling, as well as his jealousy at her flirting with other men. Farmer, who spoke with a lisp, was described as 'pleasant enough but very self-centred and opinionated'.[25] On the set of *Perfect Understanding*, he was said to have been 'so jealous he carried a revolver to dispose of possible rivals'.[26]

Residing in Paris at 9 avenue Bugeaud in the plush 16th arrondissement, Farmer spent much of his ample free time in the 1930s gambling and going to nightclubs in Paris and the Côte d'Azur (aptly called 'a sunny place for shady people' by Somerset Maugham). In 1935 he managed to crash his car into the Hollywood, one of the casinos he frequented in Juan-les-Pins, between Nice and Cannes. He conveniently blamed a defect in the steering gear.[27] He was in Cannes when the war broke out and was still in southern France in 1941.

Farmer was a violent drunk who got into frequent altercations, and in August 1941, in the bar of the Hôtel des Noailles in Marseille, one of those quarrels involved officials from the German and Italian consulates, who subsequently put pressure on the Vichy authorities to banish him from the Mediterranean coast.[28] Representations made on his behalf by the Legation in Vichy meant that he avoided an internment camp, but he still had to submit to *résidence forcée*, a regulation that obliged foreigners to reside in certain areas and evacuate others (especially areas close to the coast). After the war, without referring to the brawl in Marseille, Farmer proved to be economical with the truth when he claimed he was confined to residence simply because the Germans considered him a 'London Irishman'.[29]

Farmer was confined first to the village of Uzèrche in Corrèze and then to the village of Beaulieu-en-Dordogne. In Beaulieu, he stayed at a manor house called Château de Loubs until 1943 and spent his money freely. 'He was always accompanied by numerous women and he drank prodigious amounts of cognac ... Drinking seems to have been his main occupation', according to a letter of 5 June 1945 from the state commissioner in Brive to the state prosecutor.[30]

During his internal exile, Farmer applied to leave occupied France via Lisbon. Arrangements had actually been made to repatriate him to the United Kingdom in 1943, but the scheme fell through when his relatives on his mother's side, the Goods, 'decided not to extend the required facilities because they thought somebody might be impersonating him'.[31] As Farmer would have been well able to refund any sum he received, it seems harsh for his relatives not to have advanced the price of Farmer's ticket from Lisbon, but it seems that relations between Farmer and the Good family had broken down a long time before. Even if his relatives had been willing to pay for his fare from Lisbon, the chances of leaving occupied France became ever slimmer as the Allied invasion of France approached. The British and Americans, ahead of D-Day, subjected whole towns and cities to aerial bombardment day and night, so the Germans stopped issuing exit visas, and by May 1944 sea links between Ireland and Lisbon had been suspended. Fate had a few more tricks to play on Farmer before he was able to make it back to Britain.

A hell-raiser like Farmer inevitably became bored in the rural hamlet of Beaulieu. Upon his request, the prefect for the Corrèze *département* gave him permission to move to Meyssac, another village closer to Brive, in November 1943, and a month later he was allowed take up residence in Brive itself. It would have been unusual for a 'London Irishman' with a history of violent behaviour to gain such favourable treatment, leading to accusations that Farmer offered something to the police or Germans in return for permission to reside in Brive. But until his departure from there in early June 1944, he was required to report once a week at the *Kommandatur* in the nearby garrison town of Tulle.

Staying in a hotel called La Truffe Noire (which still exists), Farmer spent his time drinking, fornicating and spending freely, with one of his mistresses estimating that he spent FF5,000 per day (one recalls that, before an increase in May 1944, Irish citizens in France could receive from Ireland a maximum of FF2,640 *per month*). His behaviour might have earned him a few nights in the local jail in peacetime, but by June 1944 his reputation was such that, after the Liberation, a local state commissioner wrote to the state prosecutor that 'if Farmer is brought before the Court of Justice in Brive, he will receive the death penalty; as far as I'm concerned, this is neither a hypothesis nor a prediction, but a certainty'.[32] Such was the contempt that his volatile nature (especially when drunk), combined with the company he kept, had earned him.

One incident related in the thick dossier kept on Farmer in the regional archive in Limoges relates how a drunken Farmer 'boasted' in front of the clientele of a restaurant called Chez Paul that he informed on *maquisards*. A local member of the Resistance called Albiat or Lieutenant Celerier (nicknamed 'Le Tigre') took Farmer outside and threatened him with a gun and grenade, but was restrained by another man. Another version of this incident was more nuanced, recounting that the dispute broke out between Farmer and Albiat that evening because the latter accused Farmer of 'frequenting the Germans too often'. The next day the Germans came looking for Albiat, who was forced to go into hiding in the surrounding countryside. He believed that Farmer was behind this raid, although the Irishman denied it.

On another occasion in May 1944, while under the influence, Farmer became vexed when he saw his girlfriend, Liliane Tabar, in the company of three men in the bar at La Truffe Noire. He was doubly peeved because he was not invited to have a drink with this party, so he stormed out and immediately telephoned the *Feldgendarmerie* (military police) to tell them that three individuals carrying a suspect package were in the hotel. The *Feldgendarmerie* arrived and brought the three men away for interrogation, but found that the 'suspect package' only contained paintings the men were hoping to sell. All three were quickly released. When they went back to La Truffe Noire, they found Farmer, who, having sobered up, tried to apologise for what he had done, explaining that his action was simply a joke. According to Farmer's statement, given during his detention after the war, he and the men he falsely accused 'ended the evening drinking champagne'.[33]

After the Liberation, the French authorities heard other accusations against Farmer. In 1943, while still in Meyssac, he was implicated in the arrest by the Gestapo of an architect called Clauzade, who resided at the same hotel. Later, while living in Brive, Farmer and his girlfriend were accused of being sent by the local Gestapo to gather information on two individuals (they apparently came back empty-handed). Farmer was also accused of driving around the countryside in his big car firing randomly at *maquisards*. However, not enough evidence was found in any of these cases to bring charges against him.

The Corrèze *département* was extremely tense and it was also a hive of Resistance activity ahead of the D-Day landings. On 7 June 1944, the day after the Allied landings in Normandy, the Resistance briefly took control of Tulle, thirty kilometres down the road from Brive. The infamous SS Das Reich Panzer Division, on its way to the Normandy Front, took back possession of Tulle on 9 June and killed 100 male members of the local population in reprisal for Germans killed during the Resistance capture of the town.

From early in the Occupation, the Germans had employed gangs of dangerous Parisian delinquents, collectively called the 'Gestapo française'. One such group was the 'Carlingue', also called the 'bande de la rue de Lauriston' (the Lauriston Street gang) and the 'Groupe Bonny-Lafont'. These gangs carried out dirty work for the Germans (often involving torture and murder), in return for which they were allowed to pillage at will. Members of the Carlingue were sent to the Corrèze *département* in February 1944 to sow terror and bring it back into line.[34] Initially headquartered in Tulle, they were reinforced in April and progressively extended activities throughout the Corrèze *département*. Farmer would have known some of these representatives of French lowlife from the Parisian nightclubs he'd frequented before the war. These reprehensible individuals, and quite probably some of the German occupiers as well, became good drinking companions. A number of names recur in the Farmer dossier held in the Limoges archive, including that of a Becker and Roger Marfaing, while others are known simply as 'Paul', 'Axel' and 'Eddy'. (The last was probably Eddy Pagnon, who owned a garage in the 17th arrondissement in Paris and who was executed by the French authorities at the end of 1944.)

Among the welter of events in which Farmer became caught up during the spring of 1944, one strange incident stands out. The Germans apparently arrested him on 5 April. According to his own deposition, he was suspected of belonging to the British intelligence service and of supplying money to the Maquis. He was held in Tulle for ten days and received frequent beatings. During interrogation after the war, Farmer claimed he was released after one of the members of the French Gestapo, Becker, recognised him as the husband of Gloria Swanson. Whether true or not, Farmer's story afterwards was that Becker and he struck up a friendship. Thereafter, as the report of the French state commissioner put it in June 1945, 'he [Farmer] maintained contact with the French agents of the German police and invited them and their mistresses to his table on many occasions'.[35]

But the atmosphere in Brive was becoming very heated and few people there regretted Farmer's departure on 5 June (the eve of D-Day). Thanks to the intervention of the Legation, he managed to wrangle authorisation to return to Paris 'to do an inventory of his apartment' in the 16th arrondissement. In reality, it is likely that Farmer knew he risked assassination by the local Resistance if he stayed in Brive any longer.

***

Life in occupied Paris grew even more difficult in the year before liberation. Food and heating fuel became scarcer, the German occupiers were more oppressive and air raids over industrial areas grew more intense. Penniless, in poor health and with her small apartment destroyed in an air raid, Cork woman Georgina O'Hara likely came to regret her decision to turn down the DEA's offer to help get her out of France the year before. Writing in impeccable French from the home of friends in rue Chalgrin in the 16th arrondissement on 1 March 1944, O'Hara thanked the Legation for having transmitted her latest message to Dublin.[36] But since she had been bombed out of her home the previous September, she had to borrow toiletries and clothes from friends. She had no money to buy new clothes and no clothing coupons. O'Hara, who came from a modest background, had lost the 'small reserve of bank notes' she had left and had to borrow money. She therefore repeated her request that the Legation contact her sister in England for funds to pull her out of her difficulty. She also asked for news of her sick father in Ireland.

In May 1944 O'Hara received a letter from Roland Atkinson in Gibraltar, via the SSAE, that informed her that her mother was willing to pay for her repatriation back to Ireland. In a reply by telegram to Ireland that was never sent, O'Hara said she had finally 'applied for repatriation', reversing her earlier decision to stay in France. But it was too late to hope to get back to Ireland (as the Legation informed her on 5 June). Then, on 14 June, O'Hara was arrested by the Germans and brought to Fresnes prison outside Paris, where she was kept and interrogated for three days. 'An anonymous letter had been sent to the German authorities to inform them that I must be involved in espionage, which would afford me plenty of means to live the high life!' she wrote.[37] Once the calumny was revealed to be just that, O'Hara was released, with the authorities' apology.

After the Liberation, O'Hara found a job as a cashier in a hotel near the Opéra (but was 'normally a teacher', according to her passport application). On 12 January 1945 she applied for her passport to be renewed, with Fr O'Grady of St Joseph's cited as sponsor. By this time she had again changed address and was living at rue du Bois de Boulogne on the city's western limits, close to where her flat had been destroyed in September 1943.

The surge in Allied air attacks on industrial areas and marshalling yards around Paris in the months leading up to D-Day in June 1944 was witnessed by Fr Travers, who saw several aircraft shot down. He remembered one night in April 1944 when the Allies attacked the marshalling yards at Porte de la Chapelle on the northern edge of the city (which caused the death of well over 600 civilians). Travers immediately made his way to the college cellar, which doubled as an air-raid shelter. 'My heart was thumping against my ribs, my tongue was stuck to the roof of my mouth and I felt weak at the knees. The shrapnel from the bursting anti-aircraft shells was falling in showers. The college seemed to be rocking above me. Though the target must have been nearly two miles away, as I learned later, I was convinced that the place attacked was not more than half a mile away.'[38]

Fr Travers continued to dawdle around the Irish College, with little to do except tend his vegetable garden. Yet he never sought to abandon his post and request a safe passage out of France, no doubt conscious that, should he leave, the college might fall into the wrong hands. In February 1943 the Legation wrote to the DEA in a telegram: 'Travers in residence consider advisable remain in interest of property unless circumstances oblige otherwise'.[39]

Threats of a takeover came exclusively from the French. The Vichy government's Ministry of Foreign Affairs wrote to the Legation that since buildings housing the École nationale de la France d'outre-mer (a training college for the French colonial administration) were about to be requisitioned by the Germans, the said establishment had thought of moving into the Irish College.[40] 'It seems to me,' Travers wrote on 7 March 1944, to the new secretary of the Legation, Denis McDonald, who had replaced Con Cremin, 'that passing out of Irish control, it [the college] would be liable to requisition by any military authority – a thing I would wish to avoid if at all possible'.[41] Travers and the Legation tried to fob the French off by telling them that the college was not available, as it was being used for emergency food supplies. But the French did not buy the argument, with the political section of the Ministry of Foreign Affairs pointing out in a letter in April 1944 that only part of the college was being used as a food depot and that the École nationale de France d'outre-mer, 'currently much reduced, could be entirely housed in that part of the building that has remained vacant'.[42]

The Irish changed tactics. Although permission to occupy the college would have to come from the Irish bishops, who, in the view of Fr Travers, were unlikely to give it, the Legation wrote to Dublin on 23 May 1944 recommending that the French request for daytime use of some of the college classrooms be accepted by the bishops, 'if only to avoid full requisition later by occupying authorities'.[43] Travers was aghast at the prospect of having to host aspiring colonial administrators on the premises and he fired off a missive to the Legation on 25 May stating that the Ministry of Foreign Affairs was 'under a misapprehension' if it thought the college could accommodate a school. 'The whole of the ground floor of the college with the exception of the kitchen, the chapel, and two small rooms occupied by the Défense Passive, are occupied by the Commission de Ravitaillement [supplies commission],' he wrote. 'Even the college is filled with the tables, benches, forms and chairs taken from the classroom, the recreation room and the refectory.'[44] Travers invited the Ministry of Foreign Affairs to see for itself. But in less than two weeks the D-Day landings occurred, leading to the final collapse of the État français and any ambitions it had for its aspiring colonial administrators.

On 1 May 1944 Seán Murphy had informed Dublin that 'in very near future very serious situation likely to occur' and that the position of the diplomatic corps still in Vichy might be at issue. 'It is well to foresee the danger of hurried departure in the near future,' he wrote, not least because the 'present situation between Marshal and German authorities can hardly continue'.[45] On 9 May the Legation reported that two days earlier the Germans had forced Marshal Pétain to leave Vichy for his own safety, on the pretext that an Allied landing or a general uprising was imminent. Pétain, according to Murphy, 'took leave in an emotional atmosphere and was obliged to forego his wish to be taken in a German car'.[46] The head of the État français took up residence in the Château de Voisins near Rambouillet but only stayed until 19 May when the Germans – in a sign of their increased nervousness – ordered him back to Vichy. In an encrypted cable, Murphy rightly surmised that 'his departure [from Vichy] met with Hitler's disapproval'.[47] Although Pétain's government and the remaining diplomatic missions to the État français were still in Vichy, Murphy wrote that the 'future seems more uncertain than ever'.[48]

***

On 1 June 1944 an Avro Lancaster bomber of the RAF was shot down during an air raid on rail-marshalling yards in the Paris region. Three of the seven-man crew died when the aircraft crashed in the vicinity of Poigny-la-Forêt, two were quickly captured by the Germans, but two (Flight Sergeant Robert Davidson and Sergeant T. P. Starling) were taken in by a group of local Resistance workers. The group included one Elizabeth 'Lilly' Hannigan, who looked after them and helped them avoid capture until the area was overrun by advancing Allied troops in August 1944.[49]

Lilly Hannigan (1919–1992) worked as a governess for wealthy families in and around Paris, and at the outbreak of war she was with the Le Bret family at their mansion at Poigny-la-Forêt to the west of Paris. She became involved in a Resistance unit based in Saint-Germain-en-Laye and periodically cycled the forty-five kilometres from Poigny-la-Forêt to Paris with secret messages, while also helping downed Allied aircrew. One of her main contacts was Fr Kenneth Monaghan at St Joseph's church on the avenue Hoche, whom she frequently met after Sunday mass to pass on important messages. Hannigan explained in a 1950s article in the *Irish Independent* how she found herself rescuing airmen:

> It happened quite accidentally she insists, with a modesty that seems to run in the family. An American plane came down in the garden of the house where she was governess to a family of six boys. The crew was unhurt, and she directed them to a hiding place in the forest nearby. By devious means, she got in touch with Resistance personnel who arranged for the Americans to be smuggled out.[50]

For her actions, Hannigan was awarded a certificate from the Americans after the war.

Hannigan's older sister, Agnes, had also been working as a teacher and governess in France when war broke out. For many years, Agnes worked for a well-to-do French family in Angers, returning once to Dublin for three weeks in 1928, when her mother was dying. Sometime after 1935 she moved to Paris, where she formed a close association with the Irish nuns in rue Murillo. Agnes told writer David O'Donoghue of her meetings with Fr Monaghan at St Joseph's during the war.[51] Living in the centre of Paris (69 avenue Victor Hugo in the 16th arrondissement), Agnes was more liable to be hit by food shortages than her sister Lilly, who lived in the countryside. At some stage, Agnes wrote a laconic note to the Legation that stated she required 'food, any sort'.[52]

***

On 6 June 1944 the Allies made a series of successful landings in Normandy and the liberation of western Europe began. According to Fr Travers, news of the landings did not seem to change life in Paris much at first: 'The German soldiers did not give any outward sign of being perturbed by the situation, and the French population as a whole, in my experience, awaited passively their own liberation'. Down in Vichy, there was no change to daily life either. Murphy reported on 8 June that 'here is quite calm', although the food situation was becoming more difficult. After the Allies broke out of Normandy at the end of July, 'the number of rumours of all kind grew', wrote Fr Travers. 'The ARP [air-raid protection] men were practically continuously on duty, though very few bombs fell on Paris. The head of the ARP in the college had given utterance for a couple of years to pro-German sentiments and he was cordially disliked by all the others.'[53]

One of the last reports from Hans Gechter to the German authorities concerning Vendôme Wines was dated 22 June 1944. He included the balance sheet for 1943 when, he explained, the company had made a net loss of almost FF94,000. The problem was that the authorities had set an official rate for bulk wine purchases, Gechter wrote, but wine growers preferred not to sell at this rate, 'hoping to get a better price in the future'. Gechter remained upbeat, arguing that business had stabilised somewhat in 1943 and that the managers 'have the satisfaction of noting that our customers have remained faithful while a lot of interesting personalities figured among our new customers in 1943'.[54]

While Vendôme Wines seemed to manage to stay afloat, by mid-1944 John Francis Keane's company, EPI, was in crisis. At the outbreak of the war, EPI had employed fifteen people and had a turnover of FF5–7 million. But by spring 1944 turnover had fallen by two-thirds and a large part of the workforce had been let go. Only one accountant was left in the firm, forty-four-year-old Pierre Georges Bezos, a married man with two children. Alarm bells started ringing violently when the Vichy authorities summoned Bezos to a medical test with a view to press-ganging him to work in the factories in Germany as part of the STO. Fortunately, Count O'Kelly sprang into action, although it appears incongruous that he should have addressed his plea on behalf of Keane/Bezos to Vichy's notorious Minister of Information and Propaganda, Philippe Henriot (who was assassinated in his bed by the Resistance in June 1944).[55] Nonetheless, O'Kelly's intervention yet again brought quick results. On 31 March 1944, three days after O'Kelly had written his letter, Henriot's head of staff drafted a reply, informing the Irishman that measures had been undertaken 'immediately' to ensure that Bezos did not have to leave his job.

EPI paid no dividends in either 1942 or 1943, and on 20 January 1944 Keane informed the military authorities that the company 'has been forced to cease all advertising business, as our retail sellers are not even able to fulfil the orders of their usual customers'.[56] EPI still made a net profit of FF421,000 in 1943, the equivalent of about €96,000. EPI also appears to have run a chemical business, in keeping with Keane's pre-war experience as director general at ICC. However, despite his best efforts, the lack of raw materials drove this side of Keane's business into the ground.

In spite of all the financial and legal difficulties facing his company, Keane was not facing personal financial distress, for by the spring of 1944 his city address was 53 avenue Montaigne, one of the most expensive streets in Paris (he was still living there in 1950). Although the war was reaching its climax, Keane, like a true businessman, was still on the lookout for opportunities. Five weeks before the Liberation of Paris, he wrote to Seán Murphy in Vichy from a water mill he was renting in Levimpont, outside Paris, to ask him whether Irish suppliers would be able to supply 3,000 kilograms of concentrated liver extract to some of his business friends. No doubt Keane was hoping to get in early on a post-Liberation deal.

***

As the Battle of Normandy raged in June 1944, restrictions on traffic in and around Vichy became even more draconian. Having already been restricted to a fifty-kilometre radius around the town in June 1943, a year later motor vehicles and foot traffic were restricted even more tightly, to a radius of twenty kilometres. Any journeys beyond that required a *Sonderausweis* from the German authorities. Finally, from 24 June 1944 on, motor and foot traffic around the town was forbidden between 10.30 p.m. and 5.30 a.m.[57] Nevertheless, the Legation announced to the authorities that Count O'Kelly intended to leave Vichy by car on 1 August 1944 for a ten-day trip to Paris, along with his Spanish driver Francisco Gomez, and his friends Jacques Noailly and Pauline de Villaine from outside Vichy. With Allied aeroplanes strafing French roads at will, this was a dangerous journey. Field Marshal Erwin Rommel had been seriously wounded when his car was strafed in western France less than two weeks before. Despite the chaos, O'Kelly and his party seem to have made it to the French capital and back in one piece, for over a month later, on 25 September, he set out again from Vichy in his Studebaker – although this time to a liberated Paris.

Even as fierce fighting continued in western France, the DEA in Dublin muscled in on the case of Stephen Rice. On 4 August, just three weeks before the Liberation of Paris, the department wrote to the Legation in Vichy to inform it that, having granted Rice a passport and financial assistance, the department now had 'very grave doubts as to the *bona fides* of this applicant, both in regard to his true identity and the story'. They wanted to know what Rice had been doing for three years in Paris, and why he had asked for a copy of his birth certificate in September 1941 but waited over two years more before he put in an application for a new passport. In addition, the decision to grant Rice financial assistance in September 1943 – before he was actually granted a passport – was 'unprecedented and would not be in accordance with the Department's practice'.[58]

Another regular client of the Legation, Una Whyte wrote to it again in early July 1944, this time to ask its help in obtaining clothes coupons and the name of a dentist. With the Allies advancing on Paris, the Legation had other concerns and wrote back to tell her it could not help her on either count. Then, on 16 August 1944, she wrote to the Legation from Briare on the Loire river, south of Paris. On that same day, General Patton liberated the city of Orléans, just seventy kilometres upstream, although Briare itself had to wait until 25 August, the day that the last German forces in Paris surrendered. With fighting raging in the region, how and why did Whyte go to Briare? In her letter, she excused herself for the lateness of her acknowledgement of receipt of her latest monthly payment from Ireland. This, she explained, was because she had left Paris with the intention of 'going for a cycle tour, which is now impossible'.[59] But her planned cycle tour had been to Brittany, and Briare is some 400 kilometres from the Breton city of Rennes.

As the Allies approached Paris and the Germans progressively evacuated the city in August 1944, Bluebell's car, parked in a garage close to her home in rue Blanche since her family had returned to Paris from Bordeaux in 1940, was discovered by the Germans, who took its tyres. Intent on filing a claim for compensation, Bluebell set off on her bicycle early one morning to the Champs Elysées, possibly to the Wehrmacht-Reifenstelle (tyre service) at number 123. There she found the Germans busily packing their bags and destroying documents. Compensating Parisian motorists for the 'requisition' of their rubber tyres was the least of their worries. A major who was present did listen to Bluebell's grievance and asked to see the certificate of ownership for the car in question, but Bluebell had left it at home. The German told her to go fetch it, but to be back by eleven o'clock, as the Wehrmacht was in the process of evacuating the city.

Bluebell raced down the Champs Elysées on her bike as far as the place de la Concorde. When she reached it, she heard a series of 'sharp popping noises' that she took to be sounds coming from the charcoal converter of a car.[60] But looking around, she saw that other cyclists on the large square had dismounted and had fled for cover. Bluebell realised that she had stumbled into a Resistance attack on the Naval Ministry, a German strongpoint on the north-east side of the square at the entrance to rue de Rivoli. She got off her bicycle and lay flat on the ground as the gun battle raged around her. After about half an hour, the shooting stopped. When a young German soldier clutching a sub-machine gun approached to see if Bluebell was all right, she yelled at him in English, 'Get away, for Christ's sake, get away from me,' causing the startled German to retreat.[61] A friendly tobacconist escorted Bluebell (and her bike) back to rue Blanche, where some days later Marcel turned up. Having had to remain hidden for two and a half years, the Liberation of Paris meant that he could venture freely around the city and for the first time see his third child, a daughter, who had been born in October 1943.

As the Americans approached Paris, the remaining Germans (mostly administrative staff and stragglers) began blowing up ammunition dumps and reinforcing a number of strong points. The police went on strike on 15 August and then, on 19 August, barricaded themselves inside the city's main police station, beside Notre Dame, thus triggering a week-long insurrection – although it was far from the heroic affair portrayed in French propaganda. Unlike the pitched battles and wanton destruction visited on Warsaw during the uprising that same month, the fighting in Paris consisted of disparate groups of *résistants* firing a few shots at the weakly armed remnants of a German garrison that made few and feeble attempts to take back control of insurgent positions. 'They [the Germans] were interested mainly, I think, in keeping their lines of communication open for their retreating armies,' wrote Fr Travers.[62]

On 20 August 1944 Resistance policemen took over the town hall of the 5th arrondissement, just 200 metres from the Irish College, provoking an attempt by three German tanks parked in front of the building on the place du Panthéon to dislodge them. Local residents were terrified by the din of firing, 'and some of those who were most vociferous about what the French would do when the time of liberation came were arrant cowards when brought up against actual fighting,' according to Fr Travers. Instead 'most of the French civilian population were wishing that the rising of the police had not taken place'. At one stage, the police wanted to place their German prisoners in the Irish College, but Travers refused to become involved, pointing out that 300 tons of food were stored there. Elements of a French armoured division penetrated the city on 25 August, having to deal with isolated pockets of resistance and snipers as they advanced. But these last shreds of resistance – mostly the work of collaborationists, according to Travers – were quickly swept away and the *collabos* rounded up and frequently lynched. He remembered seeing two 'terrified Asiatics', handcuffed, being marched down the rue des Irlandais by some armed civilians. 'I heard later that they were perfectly innocent students who had nothing at all to do with the war.' At last the Americans arrived to restore some order and, on the place du Panthéon, Travers got chatting with a GI whose parents were from County Roscommon.[63]

Despite the Liberation, Fr Travers did not make it home right away, instead living through another cold winter in Paris in 1944–1945. At the end of November 1944 the ARP was still using two small rooms, while the rest of the ground floor was given over to an emergency food store. But at least the foundation that administered the college managed to channel about FF6,000 per month to Travers for the upkeep of the premises.

Bluebell became indirectly involved in the score settling against alleged collaborationists in the days following the Liberation of the city. The granddaughter of the concierge of the building in rue Berthellot where Marcel had been hiding called Bluebell to ask her to intervene with the police to have her grandmother released. Bluebell did as was requested, vouchsafing for the kindness of the old lady during Marcel's enforced confinement, and the concierge was let go. But she was rounded up again a couple of hours later by the authorities, who had serious reasons to investigate the old woman. She had, it was alleged, betrayed several people who had hidden in her building during the Occupation, often selling them to the Germans or the French police for a reward of as little as FF50. The only reason she had not betrayed Marcel was because Bluebell regularly brought her some extra food and paid her FF60 a week. Bluebell subsequently heard that the concierge was found guilty of the charges brought against her and died in prison.

French justice also caught up with Michael Farmer and his ex-girlfriend Liliane Tabar in the autumn of 1944.[64] The latter proved more than willing to sell out her erstwhile Gestapo friends, supplying her interrogators with all the names and addresses of the *collabos* she knew. She had fallen out with Farmer and was particularly happy to talk of his activities during the few weeks she had known him in Brive. She revealed that the last time she had seen Farmer had been at a cabaret called the Perroquet au Nid, close to the Champs Elysées, on 4 September 1944 (Edith Piaf played a series of concerts there in early 1943).[65] Paris having been liberated ten days earlier, the pair needed to come up with a strategy for dealing with the French police, which Tabar and Farmer knew were looking for them both. But the conversation between the two former lovers must have become heated, for Tabar said that Farmer threatened to have her arrested by the Americans if she gave him away.

Despite her estrangement from Farmer, Tabar did not try to present him as a fully paid-up member of the Gestapo française. She told her interrogators that, after the savage beatings he had received during his ten-day imprisonment in Tulle in early April 1944, the Cork man had meekly agreed to do the Germans' bidding. But she also stated that she did not 'believe he was an agent of the Germans … Farmer, who was not very courageous, simply wanted to do anything to be in their good books and to be left in peace. He never carried an arm.'[66]

On 8 November 1944 Michael Farmer was finally arrested in Paris. Giving '*cinéaste*' (film maker) as his profession, he was sent down to Brive, where he was officially accused of '*intelligence avec l'ennemi*' and incarcerated on 10 November 1944. In the following months, the wheels of diplomacy worked in Farmer's favour. In early 1945 an official at the Irish Legation in Paris concluded that Farmer was even more harmless than Tabar had suggested. 'The accusations made against Farmer are centred on his habit of associating with German officers and Gestapo officials at Brive during the latter days of the German occupation. I have pointed out that Mr Farmer's personal habits of intemperance might have led him into strange company in public bars.'[67] Given this view of Farmer as nothing more than a harmless drunkard, the Irish authorities had no qualms about defending him against the accusations brought by the French, with the Legation arguing in a letter to the Prefect of Corrèze dated 21 February 1945 that Farmer's story showed that 'he was an unhappy individual because of his intemperance, but he was not somebody to get mixed up in politics'.[68]

The state commissioner in Brive and the state prosecutor were also willing to give Farmer the benefit of the doubt, with the former mentioning that Farmer was 'a charming man when he was sober, which he sometimes was, but he was the greatest hell-raiser one could ever meet when he had drink taken – which was often – and then he was capable of the worst acts of stupidity'.[69] In the end, the state prosecutor felt there was not enough evidence to accuse Farmer of espionage, which would have made him liable for the death penalty. He instead suggested Farmer should be pursued for the lesser charge of 'harming the external security of the State'. But tempers had cooled since the *épuration sauvage* of the first weeks of the Liberation, when people were executed by kangaroo courts and countless women who had fraternised with the Germans were humiliated by having their hair shorn off in public. In addition, by the time Farmer was due to stand trial in September 1945, the Legation had further leaned on the French to avoid a diplomatic incident. He was released from prison on 12 September 1945, the day before it was decided that his dossier should be *classée sans suite* (filed away) by a court in Limoges.

Of course, Farmer's own version of his life in central France during the Occupation was slightly different. In 1946 he explained to a British journalist that the Germans had begun to suspect that he was supplying money to the Maquis and locked him up in a château 'with several other forgotten people'. According to Farmer, he was only let go 'after some "rough stuff" by the Gestapo' and thereafter he made it back to Paris in time for the Liberation in August 1944.[70]

Farmer left France sometime after his release and spent his declining years in the United Kingdom. In 1958 he was found guilty of drink-driving by a court in southern England. Farmer died in Chester in 1975.

***

Farmer was not the only Irishman to feel French justice breathing down his neck after the Liberation. On 22 August 1944 the Germans evacuated the town of Biarritz after over four years of Occupation. Two of the town's residents, Denis Corr and his wife, Marie-Louise Rousse, were immediately arrested by the French police and brought with a number of other suspected *collabos* to the detention centre set up at the Beyris polo grounds on the outskirts of the nearby town of Bayonne. (The stables at Beyris had previously served to house refugees from the Spanish Civil War and then prisoners of the Germans.)

Denis Corr was born in Seatown, Dundalk, County Louth on 12 January 1876, son of Lawrence Corr and Anne Kelly. A cousin (and namesake) who contacted the authorities in Dublin to ascertain his whereabouts in 1939 explained that Corr had lived in the Irish capital before moving to Glasgow and then Lourdes, where he had been working as a baker in 1932.[71] After the death of his first wife, he married a much younger Frenchwoman, Marie-Louise Rousse, with whom he ran a general provisions store called the Maison Jeanne-Anne at 9 bis avenue Maréchal Foch in the centre of Biarritz. Biarritz was occupied by the Germans from June 1940. Upon the Germans' departure on 22 August 1944, the local police arrested the Corrs for 'placing a sign in their shop window that forbade Jews from entering' and for 'propaganda in favour of the LVF'. The Légion des Volontaires français (LVF) was a contingent set up by various collaborationist factions to fight for the Germans on the Eastern Front. As the war wore on, it was progressively integrated into the Waffen SS.[72]

Whether these charges were sound or not, it is quite possible that the Corrs turned themselves in on 22 August, fearing a public lynching. The power vacuum that existed in France in August and September 1944, before De Gaulle's provisional government had installed its authority, facilitated the *épuration sauvage*, and the Corrs would have been a likely target. Indeed, a day after his internment, Denis Corr's shop in Biarritz was 'destroyed by the crowd'.

On 17 September 1944 Marie-Louise Rousse pleaded with the local Comité de Libération to release her and her husband, as she 'could not understand why I and my husband are detained. Both of us, so confident that we rushed into your arms for protection, are now treated as vulgar assassins.'[73] But the Comité de Libération turned down her plea because the couple had carried out a *grosse activité pro-allemande*. She had to wait until February 1945 before she was released from the camp and placed under house arrest in her hometown of Bagnères-de-Bigorre in the foothills of the Pyrenees, while her husband remained interned.

Minutes from the formal police interrogations of Rousse in January 1945 reveal that she claimed Denis Corr had posted the notice barring Jews from his establishment right from the start of the German Occupation in 1940 only to deflect German suspicions of him. Although he held an Irish passport, he had been warden at the Anglican church in Biarritz and as a result had been obliged to present himself to the local *Kommandatur* every morning. The Germans were willing to let Corr avoid this inconvenience and to allow him to travel as far as the Demarcation

Line as long as he placed the offending sign in his shop window. However, Rousse was also willing to recognise that Corr was anti-Semitic 'because he had been the victim of Jewish manoeuvring in commercial matters when he was still in Scotland'. She was also prepared to admit that she supported the Vichy regime and that her anti-Communism pushed her to support the LVF and the Parti populaire français of Jacques Doriot. But she maintained that her involvement never went beyond using LVF literature to wrap up goods for her customers, while her Irish husband's involvement in collaborationist activities was even slighter, for 'he speaks French badly'. She also claimed that the couple helped a Jew called Klein to escape across the Spanish border, and even listened to the BBC during the Occupation, though it was strictly forbidden.[74]

Having heard a number of witnesses, the police concluded that Rousse, who had a drink problem, was 'a simple woman of modest origins who seems to have taken her opinions from her husband. These opinions were largely shaped by commercial opportunism.'[75] The police file on Rousse is much thicker than the one for her Irish husband – possibly because of his poor state of health, which ensured he avoided more vigorous questioning.

Although his wife was released from Beyris in February 1945, Denis Corr had to wait several more months before he was judged, despite the April 1945 request from the Legation that his case 'at least be brought to trial with the minimum delay'. Count O'Kelly visited Corr in detention and the Legation felt that, given his age and 'lack of intelligence', his lawyer would be able to make a 'reasonably good case' in his favour.[76] But Corr faced the serious charge of 'espionage' when he was finally brought before the Court of Justice in Pau in December 1945. Jurors were asked to consider two main questions and one subsidiary question: first, had Corr 'as a foreigner, entertained intelligence with a foreign power in time of war … with a view to favouring the enterprises of this power against France?' Second, had he exposed French people to reprisals for the same end? And third, did Corr knowingly undertake actions that would have endangered national defence? Corr benefited from the cooling of passions in the fifteen months since France's liberation and the ransacking of his business in Biarritz and was found not guilty of the two main counts against him. However, he was found guilty of the subsidiary charge of endangering national defence, albeit with undefined 'attenuating circumstances'. He was sentenced to six months' imprisonment, fined FF3,000 and ordered to pay court expenses of FF369.[77]

It seems that Corr did not serve much prison time after his condemnation. After his spell in detention at Beyris, he had been hospitalised in Bayonne, and by the time of his trial he was under house arrest in Pau with the requirement to report weekly to the local police station. On 13 December 1945, the day after the court in Pau handed down its judgment, he was described in a hospital note as 'afflicted by paraplegia of the lower limbs that prevents him from walking', and in January 1946 he was given leave to go home to Biarritz in view of his 'poor state of health'.[78] Denis Corr died in Biarritz in October 1952, at the age of seventy-six.

Michel Dassonville was also going through a difficult time at the hands of the French authorities. Dassonville – collaborationist, alcoholic, adulterer (and a major shareholder in Count O'Kelly's Vendôme Wines) – was officially arrested on 27 November 1944 and subjected to a series of police and intelligence service interrogations.[79] For some reason – which even the Minister of Justice in a note to the police said he could not comprehend – Dassonville was paroled in spring 1946, when he bolted for Brazil with a tidy fortune and the intention of founding a publishing company. The French tried in vain to have him extradited, but ended up condemning him to death in absentia. Michel Dassonville died of liver failure in Rio de Janeiro in 1948.

Dassonville's estranged wife, Florence, set sail for New York with her five-year-old son in December 1945, still making use of the Irish travel documents originally supplied by O'Kelly. In November 1944, when she had been interrogated by the French intelligence services, she claimed she had obtained an Irish passport thanks to a putative Irish grandfather. A police report from the same month mentions that Michel Dassonville approached O'Kelly on his wife's behalf.

***

In October 1944 Samuel Beckett returned to his flat at 6 rue des Favorites. Miraculously, in spite of the Gestapo raid two years earlier, the small studio flat was intact, with nothing removed apart from some papers and books. Beckett was anxious to visit his ill mother, whom he had not seen for close to six years, and left for Dublin via London in April 1945 after his brother Frank in Ireland had contacted the DEA for assistance with the travel arrangements. Just before he left, the provisional French government awarded Beckett the Croix de Guerre, stating that he had 'carried out his task to the extreme limit of audaciousness'.[80] During his stopover in London, Beckett appeared in the War Office in London for questioning about the Gloria SMH Resistance network he had worked for in 1941 and 1942.

Beckett remained in Ireland until early August 1945, when he left to work as 'interpreter-storekeeper' in the Irish Red Cross Hospital that had been set up in Saint-Lô, a town in western France that had been almost completely obliterated by Allied bombers just ahead of the D-Day landings. His decision to volunteer to work for the Red Cross was hardly (or not totally) motivated by altruism. 'This is the only way in which I can return to France with the certainty of being able to keep on my flat,' he wrote on 21 June 1945. There were still draconian controls on the export of currency from Ireland, while high inflation was eating into the value of the allowance he received each month from his father's estate. 'It is impossible to get sterling out of here to France for any other than strictly commercial purposes,' he wrote.[81] The hospital in Saint-Lô quickly ran into administrative difficulties, but given the financial issues Beckett was facing, what was he to do? For, as he wrote to a friend, 'Life in Paris is pretty much impossible, except for millionaires.'[82]

Beckett made a number of brief visits back to Paris during the second half of 1945, sometimes acting as an impromptu tour guide for fellow members of the Irish Red Cross team from Saint-Lô. One member of that team, Jim Gaffney, described how one Saturday:

> Sam took me into Notre Dame which was magnificent. Sam has an assistant storekeeper here named Tommy Dunne, a very decent little Dublin chap. Sam is a TCD graduate, interested in writing and in letters generally; he has lived in Paris for the last 6 or 7 years. He is a most valuable asset to the unit – terribly conscientious about his work and enthusiastic about the future of the hospital, likes a game of bridge and in every way a most likeable chap, aged about 38–40, no religious persuasion; I should say a free thinker – but he pounced on a little rosary beads which was on a stall in Notre Dame to bring back as a little present to Tommy D. It was very thoughtful of him.[83]

Beckett resigned from his position with the Irish Red Cross Hospital at the end of 1945. One of his last assignments was to obtain poison from Paris to rid the children's and maternity wards of a rodent infestation.

In the months following the Liberation of Paris, designer and architect Eileen Grey made her way back to her flat at rue Bonaparte. She had managed to stay in Tempe a Païa, on the heights above Menton, until April 1942, when she was forced to leave on foot of the regulation forbidding foreigners from living near the coast. She went instead to an artists' colony in a castle in Lourmarin, north of Aix-en-Provence. She briefly stayed in another flat she owned at the harbour in Saint Tropez in September 1942, but since that too was on the coast, she was told to move back to Lourmarin. 'Life in Lourmarin,' she wrote, 'was very solitary. Being continuously underfed makes one feel down.'[84] In September 1943 she ended up in Cavaillon, about thirty-five kilometres further west, staying there until the liberation of southern France in August 1944. Grey was distressed to learn that her Saint Tropez apartment had been destroyed when the Germans mined the harbour before their retreat, and she was unable to get back to her house in Menton for some time, as the Germans continued to occupy the heights above the town until the last days of the war. She summed up the state of her various southern French properties thus: 'I have saved nothing from Roquebrune, Tempe a Païa has been looted, the little flat on the port [of Saint Tropez] was blown to bits by the Germans. There is nothing else worth keeping.'[85] Grey decided to return to her residence in the rue Bonaparte in Paris in late 1944, living largely on potatoes, and suffering, like most other Parisians, from constant power cuts. She eventually sold Tempe a Païa to the British painter Graham Sutherland in 1954.

***

The Irish Legation made its official return to Paris in the autumn of 1944 and immediately ran into a diplomatic tiff about the future of Seán Murphy as Ireland's minister to France. Members of the French provisional government were none too happy that Murphy had been Irish plenipotentiary in Vichy for four years and had not been replaced by somebody less tainted. On 23 August 1944 the provisional government in Algiers sent an encrypted message to the French Legation in Dublin (decrypted by the British) that read, 'it is obvious – without questioning Mr Murphy's personality – that the maintenance as representative to the provisional government of a minister of Ireland currently accredited to Vichy hardly appears suitable'.[86] The controversy rumbled on for a few weeks, in spite of Joseph Walshe's insistence that Murphy should stay on, 'at least until a successor can be found', and the DEA secretary's argument that Ireland had a very shallow pool of suitable diplomats to send to Paris.[87] Back in Paris, Seán Murphy confirmed to Walshe on 4 October that 'I was very coldly received and roughly received by Secretary General [of French foreign ministry] who stated they wanted no heads of missions who served in Vichy.'[88] According to Robert Patterson, the French foreign ministry manifested its hostility by making sure that 'Murphy was constantly reminded that his presence was no more than tolerated in the French capital and that he was allowed to remain there only with great reluctance on the part of the French authorities.'[89]

Nonetheless, the Legation was able to officially open for business in Paris on 25 October 1944, although, because of damage to the electrical installations and the unavailability of heating oil at the Legation's pre-war premises in rue de Villejust, its members had to be housed at the Hôtel Bristol on the rue du Faubourg Saint-Honoré for several months.

By the end of 1944 the DEA had received confirmation of Stephen Rice's identity from the US authorities. Evidently tired of doling out FF1,000 per month to this man, the Legation later reported that it strove to impress on Rice 'the desirability of finding an early means of travelling to Great Britain'.[90] The Monaghan man finally managed to leave France in December 1944. In a January 1945 letter, Rice told the Legation that he had obtained a lift 'on American truck to Kong [Caen in Normandy] and we got a train from Kong to Sherbo [Cherbourg] the following night and the next day we got a boat to Portland England'.[91] When Rice reached London, he found that the American shipping company he had worked for knew all about his case, since the Legation had contacted the United Kingdom authorities. But Rice's letter to the Legation was not just a courtesy: he again needed cash, this time to tide him over while he pressed the shipping company for the back money he was owed. He explained that the FF1,000 per month allowance he had received from the Legation was useless in the United Kingdom unless he could get it changed into sterling, and for that, he needed the Legation to write to the Irish high commissioner in London.

Stephen Rice eventually moved back to Castleblaney, where he died in a nursing home in the late 1950s. That other Irish sea-dog who had wandered around Paris for the duration of the Occupation, John McKelvey, also made it out of Paris alive, leaving the city by aeroplane in October 1944.

8

HELPING JEWS

In the run-up to the outbreak of war, one can detect a certain coldness in official Ireland's approach to the Jewish question. On 22 August 1939 a message came through to the Legation in Paris from the DEA's legal advisor, Michael Rynne, that an application from P. Harrison, living in Dublin, for a study visa for his Romanian niece Ites Cogen was to be refused. 'The applicant is a Jew and, as it is thought that his real motive is to gain admittance to this country for his niece with a view to establishing her permanently here, the Department of Justice has refused the application,' wrote the legal advisor.[1] During the Occupation the attitude among Ireland's diplomats, in France at least, could at times be flippant – as revealed in an episode from the early months of 1940.

From 49 rue Victor Hugo, an elegant Art Nouveau house in Brest at the tip of Brittany, René Rothschild, who had been director of Brest's municipal theatre before the war, submitted his application for an Irish passport to Count O'Kelly in October 1940. The Germans were detaining Rothschild as a British subject even though 'he apparently has never been out of Brest in his life and speaks no language but French', according to O'Kelly. While the man's *livret de famille* showed that Rothschild's father had been born in Dublin, 'nothing seems to be known about the father's antecedents, but I doubt if the family is connected with Brian Boru'.[2] The Legation wrote to Rothschild in November 1940, explaining that he would need to produce a document of an 'official character' issued by the Irish authorities that proved his father was born in Dublin before he could be entered on the register of nationals.[3] Such a document must have been forthcoming, for by January 1941 Rothschild's Irish nationality had been recognised and a one-year passport was issued, contributing to Rothschild's release from detention.[4]

By August 1941 Rothschild was living in a hotel in Montpellier in the *zone libre*. But when we last hear of him in the Legation archives, an obviously anxious Rothschild was still waiting for a decision on his application for a full passport from the Minister for Justice according to the terms of article 2 (4) of the 1935 law on nationality and citizenship. Meanwhile, a 'provisional administrator' had been appointed by the Germans to take over Rothschild's estate.

O'Kelly's initial, sceptical approach to Rothschild's application for a passport in 1940 was not necessarily characteristic of his own approach to Jews in general. Back in 1932 he had taken pen to paper in defence of Robert Briscoe, then Fianna Fáil TD for Dublin South. *L'Ami du Peuple*, a right-wing daily belonging to the French cosmetics king and anti-Semite François Coty, and generously subsidised by fascist Italy, had run a series of front-page articles entitled, 'The financiers that lead the world'. One of these articles, published on 20 April 1932, caught O'Kelly's attention because it suggested that international Jewish finance was behind the Irish struggle against Great Britain. Newly elected Taoiseach Éamon de Valera was engaged in an attempt to make a 'complete break' with London, wrote *L'Ami du Peuple*. 'Nobody would think of seeing in this attempt the work of a secret agent of Kuhn, Loeb & Co.' (a prominent Jewish-owned New York bank), but agent there was, according to the newspaper, and he was 'a Zionist Jew called Robert Briscoe'. This Jew, of Lithuanian origin, 'brought up in the Dublin ghetto', according to *L'Ami du Peuple*, had become 'very well versed in banking affairs, and had become a kind of treasurer for M. De Valera's party. Soon, it counted entirely on him to procure the resources necessary for the troubles then well underway.' Briscoe became responsible for raising money for the cause of Irish independence in the United States. Officially, explained the daily, the money raised by de Valera came from fundraising in the Irish-American community, 'but its exceptional abundance and the regularity with which it arrived coincided with the moment the Lithuanian Jew made contact with the banks of his co-religious in America. Thanks to Kuhn, Loeb & Co., it was possible for Briscoe himself to organise massive smuggling of arms and ammunition from Germany that enabled the Irish nationalists to sustain the insurrection.' Briscoe, 'one of the most ardent opponents' of the Anglo-Irish Treaty, also managed to find funding for the anti-Treaty side during the Civil War, claimed *L'Ami du Peuple*. Calling Briscoe an 'occasional Irishman', *L'Ami du Peuple* wondered whether the British 'sometimes suspected the role that the financiers who rule the world played in the sudden worsening of the wound in the Empire's side'.[5]

This was too much for Count O'Kelly. In a right to reply (no doubt dictated by Dublin) that appeared on the front page of *L'Ami du Peuple* on 28 May 1932, he put it on record that neither Robert Briscoe nor any of his family had any contact with Kuhn, Loeb & Co. The money that Briscoe used to buy arms in Germany was supplied by the late Michael Collins, 'at the time minister of finance in the republican government' and came 'directly from subscriptions among the Irish people'. In addition, the links established in the 20 April article between Irish politics and international Israelite finance were 'just as tendentious' as the allegations concerning Mr Briscoe himself.[6]

But *L'Ami du Peuple* stood its ground, stating in the same issue that 'the funds collected in Ireland were tiny' and that in reality the IRA 'depended on the considerable sums that came to it from the U.S.: more precisely, these sums came largely via American Express, which had opened an account for the Irish revolutionary government ... Mr Robert Briscoe's financial trips to America cannot be denied. On the same trips, he led a number of propaganda rallies.' *L'Ami du Peuple* even went so far as to claim that Briscoe was a member of the extremist faction that had condemned Michael Collins to death and had had him executed.[7]

The Briscoe family had other connections to France, apart from appearing in the headlines of an extremist newspaper. Robert Briscoe's brother, Herbert David ('Bert') Briscoe, who was born in Dublin in August 1896, ran a company called Cinéco at 72 avenue des Champs Elysées with other members of his family. Up to the outbreak of war, this company supplied technical equipment to the film industry. But by the end of 1939 Herbert had left Paris for his native Dublin, with the intention of founding a bed-wadding factory. He was able to obtain a visa to take one of his family's domestic helps, a Czech national called Paula Cermac, back with him to Ireland. Considered a Jewish enterprise, Cinéco was taken into German administration after the French defeat in June 1940. In November 1940 O'Kelly found out from the local manageress, Mrs Shumaker, 'that the material [belonging to the firm] had been confiscated and that she cannot even receive a receipt therefore'. She had been informed by Herr Ebel of the German military administration 'that if the Briscoes were Jews, they did not stand a chance of getting their stuff back'.[8]

Some of the Briscoe family's Paris acquaintances tried to contact Herbert during and after the Occupation, and vice versa. On 4 January 1941 Marie Bloch, living at 21 avenue des Villiers in the 17th arrondissement in Paris, wrote a note to the Legation in Vichy (probably in response to an enquiry from Dublin) asking it to tell 'Monsieur Briscoe that I am well and am not wanting for anything'.[9] In September of the same year, Robert Briscoe tried to intervene in the case of a family friend called Fay Abruech. After the war, in August 1946, a Mr Tsygalnitzky wrote to the Legation for help in tracing Herbert Briscoe, who, he said, had lived in the western suburbs of Paris (the Briscoes had lived at 34 boulevard d'Auteuil in Boulogne-Billancourt).

***

Throughout the autumn and winter of 1940 Seán Murphy produced a series of long, highly informed reports for Dublin. In one of them, sent from Vichy to Dublin on 29 August 1940, Murphy mentioned the repeal of a 1939 decree (called the 'décret-loi Marchandeau') that threatened the press with legal action for 'slander and insult of a racial and religious nature'. He surmised that the repeal of the decree 'may give rise to a press campaign of an anti-Semitic character'. Apart from traditionally anti-Semitic organs such as the weeklies *Je suis partout* and *Gringoire*, Murphy had yet to see many such articles in the general press. But he remained convinced that 'the latent tendency towards anti-Semitism in France is clearly enhanced both by the present circumstances and the fact that the Popular Front government, which is almost universally represented as the beginning of the end for the country, was very largely composed of Jews and seems to have favoured their appointment to important positions'.[10]

Murphy's report did not refer to the full range of measures taken against Jews in the early weeks of the Occupation, most notably the 22 July 1940 decree that withdrew French citizenship from Jews who had been naturalised since 1927. Two months later, in September, the Germans ordered the first census of Jews in occupied France. In October the Vichy government published a law on the status of Jews, excluding Jews from the civil service (including teaching) and from working in the press. A day after the October 1940 status of Jews law came into effect, local prefects were accorded the power to intern 'foreigners of Jewish race'. Not to be outdone, the Germans decreed a census of all Jewish-owned companies in the occupied zone. These same companies were then ordered to display prominently a sign with the words

'Jüdisches Geschäft' (Jewish business). In the autumn of 1940 Jews were also told to turn up at their nearest police station to have the word 'Jew' stamped in red on their identity cards. But all these measures, shocking as they were, constituted just the beginning of the calvary that Jews in France were to experience in the years 1940 to 1944.

After the invasion of western Poland in September 1939, Nazi Germany had herded Polish Jews into a number of ghettos. Less than two years later, in June 1941, the German invasion of the Soviet Union triggered the mass slaughter of Jews throughout the newly conquered territories. Then, in January 1942, the Wannsee conference resulted in a detailed plan for the 'final solution' of the Jewish question in Europe. It involved the deportation of Jews *en masse* from Germany and occupied countries and their subsequent destruction in special camps in eastern Europe. The head of the SS, Heinrich Himmler, set massive quotas for deportations of Jews from individual countries: the French target, including the *zone libre*, was 100,000. The Germans expected cooperation from the Pétain government in Vichy in meeting this target. Pierre Laval and his lackeys decided initially to hand over foreign and stateless Jews, while Jews with French nationality were only to be troubled if the quota was not met. To avoid having to round up French nationals, Laval ended up proposing that stateless children be deported, even though the Germans had initially demanded only the handover of Jews over sixteen years of age.

The first Jews deported by the Germans from occupied France left in a train convoy from Compiègne on 27 March 1942. Then, on 12 July, when the Germans ordered all Jews in occupied France to be arrested, the French decided to collaborate – but only in the round-up of foreign Jews. On 16 July a vast dragnet called *Vent printanier* (spring wind) was unleashed by the French police in Paris, resulting in the arrest of almost 13,000 foreign Jews over two days. Some 6,000 were sent directly to Drancy in the Parisian suburbs before being packed into cattle trains bound for the east. Drancy was the site of important rail-marshalling yards, making it convenient as a departure point for trains heading to Auschwitz and other death camps. The remaining people rounded up on 16–17 July were kept initially at an indoor cycling arena (since demolished) near the Eiffel Tower called the Vél' d'Hiv and were subsequently sent to camps in Pithiviers and Beaune-la-Rolande, not far from the capital, before they too were deported to eastern Europe.

At the beginning of August the Vichy authorities extended their round-up of foreign Jews (as well as Roma and gypsies) to the *zone libre*, resulting in the deportation of another 9,000 people. Further round-ups followed. Although primarily aimed at foreign Jews, numerous French Jews were needed to meet German quotas, and between 1942 and 1944 almost 76,000 Jews in all, including 11,000 children, were deported from France to Auschwitz and other camps. Only 2,000 returned in 1945.

On 18 August 1942, a month after *Vent printanier*, Seán Murphy wrote to Dublin to assert that the population in the occupied zone had been horrified by 'very severe measures taken against the Jews and the internment of large numbers of women and children in concentration camps under appalling conditions'.[11] Although the infamous Commissariat général aux Questions juives was just a stone's throw from the Hôtel Gallia, where the Legation was housed in Vichy, it is a telling reflection of the lack of information supplied by the Vichy regime on its anti-Semitic measures that on 25 September 1942 Murphy told Dublin that he had learned the substance of fresh anti-Jewish legislation, not from the Vichy government, but from the secretary to the papal nunciature, Monsignor Carmine Rocco, and from the Swiss Legation. Murphy was able to inform Dublin that 'these regulations apply only to Jews (whether French citizens or not) who came to France, more or less as refugees since about

1936 (i.e. since about the time at which the Popular Front – regarded as Jewish – came to power)'. 'The exact nature of the regulations in question is not known as they have not been made public', although two circulars had been communicated to local prefects outlining the measures to be taken against the Jewish population. Murphy had not seen the circulars, but, he wrote, 'it seems certain ... that the French government has undertaken to hand such persons over to the German authorities'. Even more damningly for Vichy, Monsignor Rocco had told Murphy that Laval (who had returned to power as government head in April 1942) 'at least to some extent took the initiative in this matter, i.e. that the regulations in question are not purely the result of German pressure'.[12] This last phrase would seem to be a reference to Vichy France's decision to deport children as well as adults. This decision was taken, as Laval put it to a council of ministers meeting on 12 July, 'with humanitarian intentions' to ensure that children were not separated from their parents.[13]

As the French were further pressed to meet their quota of Jews to deport, Murphy's reports became more alarming. In August 1943 he told the DEA that the Germans were now asking Vichy that all Jews naturalised before 1927 be handed over and that 'all those naturalised since 1933 have already been handed over and a great deal more who were full French citizens by birth'. It appeared that Pétain had been so outraged by the new German demands that 'up to the moment nothing has happened'.[14]

Murphy's reports coincided with attempts by Jewish organisations to leverage Ireland's neutrality to rescue Jews from the Nazis' clutches. In May 1943 Harry Goodman, a prominent member of the Jewish community in the United Kingdom, travelled to Dublin and met the secretary of the DEA, Joseph Walshe, to thrash out a series of initiatives that the Irish government could undertake to help European Jewry.[15] These proposals included allowing the Irish legations in Vichy, Rome and Berlin discretion in granting a limited number of visas to Jews. It was proposed to begin by issuing visas to 100 people. Once these 100 people had left for Ireland, another 100 visas could be granted. Furthermore, the legations were to grant an unspecified number of transit visas to Jews who had a reasonable hope of finding refuge in the United Kingdom, US or Palestine. Walshe also suggested that the Irish authorities would be open to the idea of admitting Jewish orphans for adoption, while another proposal that the Irish charter a ship to transport Jewish children from Bulgaria to Palestine and/or Turkey needed further examination.

On 25 August 1943 Murphy was told that the Irish government had been approached with a view to obtaining visas for certain eminent members of the Jewish community in German-occupied Europe. At the same time the DEA was aware that there was very little hope the Germans would grant the corresponding exit visas. Asked to investigate, Murphy came to the same conclusion. He was told in December 1943 that an entry visa for Ireland would grant no protection whatsoever in the absence of a prior agreement with the Germans.

Yet, word got around that even if there was little hope for Jews to leave continental Europe, the mere granting of an entry visa by a neutral government might be enough to stop their deportation to the death camps of eastern Europe. Thus, at the end of 1943 Jewish authorities based in the United Kingdom pleaded with the de Valera government to grant entry visas and residence permits to 200 eastern European Jewish families, mostly with South American passports, who had been sent to the internment camp at Vittel in eastern France. Dublin once again instructed the Legation in Vichy to make enquiries. In a (slightly cryptic) telegram to the Irish Legation in Vichy at the end of 1943, Joseph Walshe at the DEA wrote that 'two hundred Polish Jewish families at present at Vittel. If we could provide for these families in Ireland would Germans allow them to leave

France. As French are naturally interested [how] would they find Germans attitude [?].'[16] But even if the French authorities were willing to grant exit visas to enable the Jews to leave Vittel for Ireland, it was the Germans – not the French – who were in full control in Vittel, and they told Vichy they were unwilling to accept any French interference in their treatment of foreign Jews.

Since it was useless to involve Vichy France, the Irish decided to approach the Germans directly. Con Cremin in Berlin was instructed to find out whether the Germans would allow the 200 Jewish families in Vittel to leave with Irish visas if transport could be provided, and whether they would allow a further 500 Jewish children to find shelter in Ireland for the duration of the hostilities. Nothing came of this initiative. The German officials whom Cremin met were perplexed about Irish motivations for wishing to save foreign Jews. 'If it was intended that these families should become Irish citizens the German authorities would, I was given to understand, "gladly save us the inconvenience of having so many Jews",' Cremin wrote on 24 March 1944.[17]

The Irish kept trying, especially when word filtered out that at least some of the Vittel Jews were on the point of being deported east. But Ireland had little diplomatic muscle and on 18 April 170 Jews were transported from the Vittel internment camp to Drancy, where, eleven days later, they were placed on a train bound for Auschwitz. A further sixty followed on 16 May.

The Irish continued in their attempts to intervene. On 5 July Cremin sent an encrypted message to Joseph Walshe saying that the German Foreign Office had told him that 'the 200 families you have in mind cannot be traced'. As if to put a final stop to Irish badgering, Cremin reported that 'the German authorities have treated this application with all possible goodwill because it came from Ireland instead of refusing it out of hand in the usual way'.[18]

A nun from Northern Ireland, Sister Mary Ina Begley, who was interned at Vittel and who worked in the camp hospital, told the *Manchester Guardian* newspaper in September 1944, shortly after the camp's liberation, that 'Last May 400 to 500 Jews … were taken away, and there were fifteen cases of suicide. They threw themselves out of the train and others threw themselves from windows, while some cut their veins. We did not know what became of the others.'[19]

***

Amid the tragedy that hit Jews in France, there were a number of individual cases with special connections to and resonance in Ireland. Although she had been born in Czechoslovakia, Ettie (Esther) Steinberg lived in Dublin with her family from 1926 until her marriage to Vogtjeck Gluck in the Greenville Hall Synagogue on the South Circular Road in Dublin in the summer of 1937. She was considered an Irish citizen. After their marriage, the couple moved initially to Antwerp, where Vogtjeck worked as a goldsmith, and then to Paris, where their son, Leon, was born on 28 March 1939. The French defeat in June 1940 forced them to leave the French capital and to move from place to place to avoid arrest. But in the summer of 1942 the French police finally caught up with them in a hotel in Toulouse, immediately marking them for deportation to the east. They were deported in convoy 27, which left Drancy on 2 September 1942 and arrived in Auschwitz two days later. Nothing more was ever heard of them. Ettie Steinberg is believed to have been the only Irish citizen to die in Auschwitz.

On 29 November 1943 Sophie Philipson wrote to the Legation in Vichy from the Hôtel Cosmopolitain in Nice to ask for news of her husband, Serge, whom she had not seen since the outbreak of the war. She wanted to know whether Serge had moved to take out Irish nationality, 'given that a change in my nationality would considerably reduce the considerable danger of being deported that I and my daughter face'.[20]

Warsaw-born Serge Philipson had arrived in Ireland in 1937 as part of an early drive to attract foreign investment to Ireland. An Irish delegation, spearheaded by Minister for Trade Seán Lemass, had gone to France, where they had met Henri Orbach (Sophie Philipson's brother), who ran a small hat factory called Les Modes Modernes. Orbach agreed to install his factory in Galway, which became the Galway Hat Company, and persuaded his partner and brother-in-law Serge Philipson to run it for him. Philipson failed to obtain Irish visas for his parents, his niece and his sister, who all eventually perished in the Holocaust.[21] But he had been able to bring his wife, Sophie, and their daughter, Rachel, with him to Galway. Unfortunately, Sophie made the tragic decision to return to Paris to be with her elderly mother and so that Rachel could go to a French school. She, her daughter, her brother and her mother were still in France in June 1940.

The DEA pointed out in a memo to the Legation on 26 February 1944 that Serge Philipson 'is not a naturalised citizen and in fact has never made any application for naturalisation'.[22] (Philipson only became an Irish citizen in 1946.) The implication was that Sophie Philipson could not take it for granted that the department would help with her predicament. In contrast to the discouraging tone adopted in this memo, Dublin wrote to the Legation a month later, on 27 March, to say that the Department of Justice 'had no objection to the grant or renewal of visas to Mr Orbach, his wife and son and Mrs Philipson and her daughter'.[23] But Dublin was out of touch with the situation on the ground, for since her November 1943 letter the Legation had lost trace of Sophie Philipson.

In February 1944 a certain Paul Durant wrote to the Legation from Paris in reply to the latter's request for news on the whereabouts of Sophie Philipson, her brother, Henri Orbach, and her mother, Gitla Orbach. According to Durant, Sophie Philipson had been picked up in Nice on 31 January 1944, along with Gitla and Henri. All three had been sent to the internment camp in Drancy.[24] But her daughter, 'Mme Laly' (Rachel), and her nephew, Stéphane Orbach (Henri's son), had not been arrested (perhaps because they were French born). On 28 February Aline Rilly, mother-in-law of Henri Orbach, travelled from Paris to Vichy to seek advice about Rachel Philipson and Stéphane Orbach, whom she had been sheltering since the arrest of Sophie and Henri at the end of January. Seán Murphy had to tell Mme Rilly that he could see 'no hope of sending child [Rachel] to Ireland to join her father, and as Mme Rilly fears that she herself may be interned I advised her to endeavour to place the child with friends somewhere in the country'.[25] Murphy wrote to Sophie Philipson at Drancy on 14 March 1944, asking her to send news that could be sent on to her husband in Galway. But Sophie Philipson was probably dead at this stage. Records show that the forty-two-year-old was deported from Drancy to Auschwitz on convoy 68 on 10 February 1944. Her file card from Drancy gives her nationality as Irish.[26]

On the same day it tried to contact Sophie Philipson in Drancy, the Legation sent Aline Rilly a message from Serge Philipson looking for news of Rachel and Stéphane. But one month later, on 14 April 1944, one Jacques Darbly, a neighbour, wrote to the Legation in Vichy to explain that Rilly had been unable to reply because of illness. Fortunately, the children had been dispatched to other families 'where a close eye is kept on them', Darbly wrote. Rachel Philipson's father could be reassured that she was receiving the best of care and that news could continue to be sent to Rilly's address at 36 rue des Archives in the heavily Jewish Marais district of Paris.

In November 1944, after most of France had been liberated, fourteen-year-old Rachel Philipson wrote to the Legation in Paris with a request to join her father in Ireland and – not knowing that Sophie Philipson had died in Auschwitz – asking for news of her mother, whom she had last seen the previous January. Rachel survived the war, eventually settling in Canada. Back in Ireland, Serge Philipson became a successful businessman, maintaining close contacts with France, and was for many years president of the French Benevolent Society, which helped French citizens stranded in Ireland. He was also a good friend of Louis Jammet of the restaurant of the same name, and a prominent patron of Irish art. He died in 1988, but not before revealing to one of his friends that 'the greatest sadness of his life was the realisation that his life and involvement in Ireland during the last war prevented him from sharing the tribulations of his people during the Nazi atrocities. He had to endure this anguish in isolation.'[27]

At the end of 1943, almost two years after Marie Bloch had sent her reassuring message to the Briscoes, the Legation again became involved in seeking information on the Bloch family. On 20 December 1943 it sent a fresh letter addressed to Anna Bloch at 19 rue de Rivoli in Nice to ask for news of her and her two daughters, Marie and Clara. But the letter was returned to sender with an anonymous, typewritten note explaining that Anna and one of the daughters, Clara, had been arrested as Jews in November 1943 (there was no mention of Marie). The Legation understood the difficult situation that Jews in France faced, but was powerless to intervene in any meaningful way. On 18 February 1944 it was reduced to writing to the rue de Rivoli address in the forlorn hope that the same person who had typed the anonymous message on the returned letter of 20 December would do the same again. Then, on 2 March 1944, Murphy wrote a note to Anna Bloch at the 'camp de concentration Drancy' to inform her that enquiries had been made by her relatives in Ireland to the DEA in Dublin 'as to the present health of herself and her daughter Clara'. The only reply the Legation received was a curt eight-word phrase written on the margin of Murphy's letter: '*Obengenannte Person befindet sich nicht in Lager Drancy*' (the above-cited person is not in the Drancy camp).[28] Irish efforts were too little and too late.

The list of deportees kept by the Mémorial de la Shoah in Paris shows that Anna Bloch (born in Kiev in 1879) and Clara Bloch (born in Minsk in 1897 and described in her Drancy file as a secretary) were deported to Auschwitz in convoy 62, which left Drancy on 20 November 1943.[29] As for the other Bloch daughter, although the Legation told Dublin that she was 'believed to be at liberty in Paris', Marie Bloch, born in Moghilev in Belorussia in 1903 and residing at 24 rue Leibniz in Paris, had been deported from Drancy to Sobibor death camp in Poland on 23 March 1943.

9

THE SKIES BRIGHTEN ... FOR SOME

Having finally moved back to the Legation premises in rue de Villejust, in January 1945 Seán Murphy received an invitation from Frank McDermott to tea at the British Officers' Club in the rue du Faubourg Saint-Honoré, right beside the British embassy. McDermott, who had been a senator in Seanad Éireann from 1938 to 1943 – and a persistent critic of Ireland's neutrality during the war – was now working as a correspondent for *The Sunday Times*, but he told Murphy that his reasons for coming to Paris were strictly personal. While McDermott was one of the few Irish politicians who had argued in favour of Ireland joining the war alongside the British, Murphy was still astounded to see him dressed in the uniform of a British war correspondent and mentioned the fact twice in an 18 January letter to Dublin. Murphy said McDermott explained that the military attire was 'a means of facilitating his movements'. (McDermott returned to Paris in the early 1950s as French correspondent for *The Irish Times*.) Murphy also mentioned that staying at the Hôtel Scribe, beside the Opéra Garnier, was the Dublin-born writer Denis Johnston, 'who prepares material for broadcasts about air force stations in France'.[1]

Murphy met Johnston on the second of the latter's visits to recently liberated Paris. Johnston, who worked as a war correspondent for the BBC, had already covered Winston Churchill's visit to the city on Armistice Day (11 November) in 1944, when he noted that there were 'plenty of luxuries and good clothes in the shops – but all at fantastic prices'. (During this short stay, another BBC war correspondent, Robert Barr, told Johnston that he had come to the conclusion that the Germans had been 'unobtrusive and well behaved' during the Occupation and that 'many Parisians hardly ever saw them and complained of the Resistance movement causing unnecessary trouble'.)[2] Johnston joined the Allied push across the German border, reporting from newly captured Aachen, but he was brought back to Paris for ten days when he broke a leg. New Year's Day 1945 saw him in Brussels, but he returned to Paris later in January, when his meeting with Murphy took place, before moving on to Alsace to cover the Allied advance again.

Una Whyte continued to keep the Legation busy following the Liberation. In November 1944 a telegram was received at the Legation from her mother, urging her to come home and informing her that a personal application by Una through Lloyds Bank in London was necessary to release funds from her account there. But by this stage her latest *fait d'armes* had seen her thrown into prison for cycling in a restricted military zone on the Atlantic coast without a permit. When she was stopped in October 1944, she was found to be in possession of sketches she had made of German soldiers sitting in cafés in Paris. The French authorities thus suspected her of spying. She was imprisoned in Nantes, from where she harangued the Irish embassy to get her out. 'You are cruel to have left me three months in this dreadful place,' Whyte wrote to Murphy on 19 January 1945. 'They haven't the slightest reason for detaining me. I'd rather have spent the winter in the Conciergerie.' But Whyte attached one important proviso to her demand for help: 'I hope repatriation is not the condition of my release.'[3] Five years of war and deprivation had not inculcated any longing for the bogs of County Leitrim.

The DEA in Dublin considered that Whyte's long detention through the winter of 1944–1945 was a very steep price to pay for simply cycling through a military zone, leading it to conclude that 'if she is still in prison the Department feels that there must be something else wrong'. Whyte was eventually released on 22

February 1945, over four months after her arrest on the Atlantic coast. On 5 March she turned up at the Legation in Paris 'dressed as habitually in trousers and jacket and her appearance was dirty and neglected'. She was still suffering from toothache, but otherwise did not appear the worse for wear after her time in prison. And she was anxious to quash any suspicions that she had collaborated with the Germans. Although it had been her habit to sketch people sitting in cafés in Paris, including German soldiers, she claimed that 'she had never fraternised with the Germans'.[4]

Having sprung Whyte from prison, Irish (and French) officials were anxious that she should go home, as she had come to the attention of the French police on several occasions in the period 1940–1944. When Whyte told the officials she only wanted to go back to Ireland for a ten-day holiday, the Legation informed her that 'she might discount the possibility of returning to France' thereafter and told her to make up her mind definitively on where she was going to live.[5] However, nothing could persuade her to return home for longer than a short holiday, and she insisted instead on getting herself into further trouble in continental Europe. In September 1945, for example, she was hospitalised, having been knocked off her much-used bicycle in Paris. In a note dated 27 February 1946 she declared that she had applied for a visa to Switzerland with the intention of 'spending five years in Geneva'. Whyte had a sponsor, Mr Per Jacobson, who worked at the Bank for International Settlements. (In fact, her father was a personal friend of Jacobson's, whom he tried to contact via the Berlin Legation in February 1944 with a view to sending Una clothes and other items.) It was not exactly that she wanted to leave Paris, but, as she explained to the Legation, the intelligence section 'at the prefecture cannot let me sojourn in this country for more than two months. They account this to two prosecutions in 1940 amounting to the sum of 500 francs fine then for internment at Nantes last year.'[6] Perhaps Una

Whyte did get to Switzerland. Perhaps she did not. In any case, her continental escapade came to an end at some stage, for she died a spinster at home in Dromahair in 1963, leaving behind £19,000 in an account at Lloyds Bank in England – perhaps the same account that she had tried to access while in occupied Paris in 1944.

The British intelligence services caught up with convicted sex offender and putative German agent Desmond Nolan after the liberation of the internment camp in Vittel in September 1944. Although he appears initially to have escaped their vigilance, the British found him in the French capital in December 1944. Nolan made a statement admitting that he had been approached by the Germans in Madrid in 1941 to undertake espionage but claiming that he had refused, and the British secret services were unable to disprove his version of events. Perhaps, somewhere between Lisbon and Berlin in mid-1941, Nolan had gotten cold feet about working for the Germans. As a result, they had thrown him into internment camps after his temporary Irish passport had expired in November 1941 – first in Upper Silesia and then in Vittel, where he was reunited with his wife, who had initially been placed in a different camp in Germany. Yet Nolan's case is a decidedly murky one, and the British authorities continued their investigations into his wartime activities, in spite of the patchy evidence. There was, for example, the February 1945 statement from MI5 informer Henry William Wicks that the Nolans had spent time in Paris, 'guests of the German Army of Occupation'. But the Foreign Office stated that Wicks 'need not be considered too reliable'.[7]

In May 1945 the American embassy in London added to the accusations piling up against Nolan, sending a letter to the British Foreign Office stating that Nolan was 'suspected of being a collaborator with the German officers at the internment camp at Vittel' and that he was considered a 'squealer who listened to what the internees would say and then notify the camp commander'. Nolan, according to some internees, was seen 'as a German collaborator who passed out German newspapers and other German propaganda'.[8]

Janie McCarthy was of a different moral standing. She went back to her home town of Killarney several times after the war, with the story of her exploits making its way into the local press, including her claim to have lost a sole escapee in her care – a French medical student who fell victim to a French double agent. An article appeared in *The Kerryman* in December 1954 describing McCarthy's exploits thus:

> For devotion to duty and service in the educational field during the First World War, she received the Palmes d'Académie in 1918, a very rare distinction for a foreigner to receive. She was teaching in Paris when the Germans occupied the city during the last war and within two months was a member of the resistance. She visited at least once a week the civilian camp at Saint-Denis near Paris, the Military Hospital Val de Grace and the Sanatorium at Brevannes outside Paris. The money she earned, except just sufficient to pay for the bare necessities of life, she devoted to the welfare of the internees, young Frenchmen in hiding to escape working for the Germans or trying to get to England or the Maquis, and Allied airmen who had been shot down. She engaged in many dangerous missions fetching parachutists into Paris to safe hide-outs or guiding them from one refuge to another in the city.[9]

McCarthy gained a series of accolades from the French, American and British authorities. The French awarded her the Croix de Guerre and the Médaille de la Résistance; from the British she received the Tedder Certificate for assisting British personnel to escape; and from the Americans the Medal of Freedom and a citation from President Dwight Eisenhower.

On 12 December 1945 the chef de service de la France combattante wrote the following text to justify why McCarthy should receive the Médaille de la Résistance:

> Miss McCarthy is of Irish nationality. Having resided in Paris for the past 25 years and having become an admirable friend of our country, Miss McCarthy painfully felt the rigours of the defeat of 1940. Completely devoted to the national cause since the armistice, she dedicated herself unreservedly to the Resistance from its birth in September 1940.
>
> Miss McCarthy entered into service with the St Jacques network in October 1940, and transmitted all types of information of great value to it. Later becoming an agent for the Vaneau network, she participated with great self-denial and unshakable courage in the sheltering and repatriation of Allied airmen. She undertook several liaison missions between various clandestine organisations, miraculously escaping Gestapo searches.
>
> After the arrest of the head of the Vaneau network, she joined the Samson network, where she continued her devotion to the national cause until the Liberation.[10]

The Médaille de la Résistance was granted to Janie McCarthy by decree on 24 April 1946.

To people who had helped their downed airmen during the Occupation, the Americans gave out not only medals but also monetary awards. Files were drawn up for each person who could claim to have helped an American airman. These helpers were graded on a scale from 1 to 5 according to the number of airmen helped and the degree of risk and hardship the helper had experienced. Lucienne Bodin, a 'Grade 1' who was in the Réseau Shelburn with McCarthy before being arrested and sent to Ravensbrück, was awarded FF40,500 (the modern-day equivalent of just over €5,000) in 1945, as well as the Medal of Freedom. Marie-Thérèse Labadie and her brother, with whom McCarthy had worked in 1943, each received FF7,500 from the Americans. However, when Labadie went back to the Americans looking for more, presenting them with an itemised bill for the clothing, food and cigarettes her family had given the escaping airmen, they sent her packing.

The Americans did not give any money to Janie McCarthy. Some observers suggested they were uncomfortable with McCarthy's ability to avoid arrest while those around her were being picked up. Was McCarthy deliberately let free to roam Paris so that she could unwittingly guide the Gestapo to the heart of the various networks she worked for? This is hardly likely. The Americans still awarded her the Medal of Freedom, yet – given her length of service and the breadth of her activities in the Allied cause – it seems surprising that she was classified as only Grade 5 in the Americans' scale. Grade 5 was, according to its compilers, the 'lowest grade, covering the majority of helpers such as the ones who had helped just one airman, who had given shelter to an airman shortly after his landing, or who had given help to six or seven men during short periods of time'.[11] It may be that McCarthy owed her low grade to the fact that she did not actually give shelter to US airmen. There is no mention in escape reports of her having provided accommodation, at least for any length of time (she briefly put up Andrew Hathaway and possibly Sidney Casden in November 1943) – perhaps because her apartment was too small or because she felt it inappropriate to have unknown men there. The Americans may also have felt that, as a citizen of a neutral country, she did not run the same risks as French people.

In her deposition to the Americans, McCarthy mentioned that she often 'received either Americans or British for dinner and supper' and that she fetched shot-down aviators from various locations around Paris to bring them to hiding places. The opinion of the American officer looking into her case was that she 'convoyed some aviators in Paris, accompanied by other persons (10 aviators). Made the trip from Paris to Vernon once.' The officer also stated that 'her place seems to have been a rendezvous for helpers and a center to establish contacts every time the organisation was broken'.[12]

In spite of failing health, McCarthy continued to conduct language classes at her apartment until just before her death on 20 December 1964, at the age of seventy-nine, at the Hertford British Hospital in the suburb of Levallois-Perret. She was buried in the local cemetery eight days later. (McCarthy was sufficiently well known by this stage to earn an obituary in *The Irish Times* on 2 January 1965.) The grave plot was leased for ten years to Cornelius Healy. The lease was not renewed, so, as per French custom, McCarthy's remains were unearthed and incinerated before the plot was leased out to another party in 1975. *Sic transit Gloria.*

***

On 24 March 1945, at a time of lingering diplomatic tensions between Dublin and Paris, Seán Murphy finally met General de Gaulle 'in private audience' at his hotel in Paris. His impression of de Gaulle was that 'he is rather cold in manner, possibly due to shyness; that he is of nervous temperament and that he is rather touchy. He gives one the impression that he considers he has a mission towards France. I can imagine that he might be very difficult in negotiations.' In spite of French displeasure at Murphy's reappointment as Ireland's minister to France in the immediate aftermath of the Liberation in 1944, and the minister plenipotentiary's mixed impressions of the general, Murphy thought that 'one could say, on the whole, that the interview was cordial'. During it de Gaulle expressed his great admiration for

Taoiseach Éamon de Valera 'and the manner in which he had kept his country neutral'.[13]

Just as the French were initially unhappy with the maintenance of Seán Murphy at his post in Paris, so the Irish authorities were vexed by the Gaullists' appointment of Jean Rivière as the French ambassador to Ireland. Rivière, who arrived in Dublin in March 1945, was not a Hibernophile, and frequently underlined the French foreign ministry's displeasure at Murphy's reappointment to the new provisional government.

The simmering tensions between Dublin and the French provisional government came to a modest head on 8 May, the day of Germany's capitulation, when a group of protesters (including Charles Haughey) made a failed attempt to burst into Trinity College and confront those who had both hoisted the Union Jack over the front gate and burned the Irish tricolour. The protesters then broke three windows in Jammet's Restaurant in nearby Nassau Street, probably because the place had staunch ascendancy associations.[14] The owner of Jammet's, Louis Jammet, who had been an ardent Gaullist throughout the war, prevailed on the newly arrived Rivière to 'formally complain' to the DEA and to report the incident back to the new regime in Paris. Jammet's move to involve the unloved French ambassador in the window-breaking incident led DEA secretary Joseph Walshe to fire off a letter dripping with irony to Seán Murphy. 'We are definitely convinced that Jammet wants to give himself the position of a local Führer. He was actually given the title during the last six or eight months of the war of "Chef de la Résistance en Irlande". Our sense of humour sometimes appears to fail even the French.' Walshe had had enough of Jammet's antics and told Murphy that his department was 'taking steps to inform members of the government and their friends who frequent this restaurant of his despicable action'.[15]

The Jammet incident provided more ammunition to those in

the new French regime who wanted Murphy recalled from Paris, and sniping between the French and the DEA continued into June, when an indignant Walshe sent a cutting to Paris from *The Irish Times* dated 2 June 1945, relating to an 'informal tea party' given at the French Legation in Dublin by Ambassador Rivière. Provoking Walshe's ire was the list of guests invited by the French ambassador, which included the Dean of St Patrick's and Christ Church, as well as a Colonel and Mrs Delemere and the Lieutenant-General, Sir James and Lady Hartigan.[16] According to Walshe, the list 'consists of the most anti-Irish and the most collaborationist elements in the ascendancy class. The same crowd has not appeared together at any Legation since the inception of the State ... Some people here think that Mme Rivière has already got the ascendancy bug so badly that her opinion of the ordinary Irish has become assimilated to theirs.'[17] Walshe was not impressed and had grave doubts about the prospects of Rivière being 'a valuable intermediary between this country and France'. Already, wrote Walshe, 'his egregious faux-pas in relation to the Jammet affair revealed an immaturity of judgement and outlook which raises considerable doubts about his future'. Walshe wanted Murphy to find out whether Rivière was involved in some officially sanctioned ploy to humiliate the Irish ('if the present symptoms do in effect indicate a fundamental disease') and explained that 'there is a general feeling here that, after the dose we had to tolerate during the war from certain Legations, it is time to warn the heads of foreign missions who play fast and loose with our sentiments that they are no longer welcome.' Walshe felt that Murphy should impress on the French 'how much harm can be done to good relations by entrusting French interests here to people who put the attractions of snobbery and flattery before their country's interests'.[18] Rivière lasted in Ireland less than two years and was replaced by Count Stanislas Ostroróg in November 1946.

In contrast with Rivière's brief stint as French ambassador to Ireland, Murphy stayed on in his position in Paris until 1950, when he was appointed Ireland's first ambassador to Canada. He later became secretary of the DEA in Dublin, before retiring in 1957. Murphy died in July 1964, aged sixty-eight.

***

Even after the Liberation, times remained hard for the twenty-four women residing at the Irish convent at rue Murillo. In June 1945, while praising the continuing help provided by Fr O'Grady in nearby avenue Hoche, the superior at the convent, Sister Mary Anthony, wrote that the community 'are only struggling on, waiting for help to come'.[19] Among several other Irish residents of rue Murillo who applied for a Red Cross parcel in 1945–1946 was 'trained Irish nurse' Eleanore Bonasse, aged sixty-two, who said she was 'quite alone over here and cannot get anything sent over from Eire'.[20] Anne Doyle, aged sixty-five, also staying at the hostel run by the nuns, asked for shoes as well as a food parcel.[21] Sister Mary Anthony herself applied for help, explaining that 'rations are insufficient'.[22] Ellen Comerford, born in 1875 in Ballyfoyle, County Kilkenny, likewise requested help, stating that 'I am married to a Frenchman. Even so, my heart is Irish.'[23] Comerford's request was refused, the Legation explaining that 'having abandoned her Irish nationality upon marriage' she could no longer benefit from Irish Red Cross help.[24]

Inevitably, the provisional government in France turned its attention to raising taxes. In the autumn of 1945 the nuns in rue Murillo, who had given shelter to so many Irish girls in their hostel during the war, received a demand from the provisional government for sums due on 'tourist accommodation' from the years 1940 to 1942, forcing the Legation to intervene to explain that the mainstay of the convent's clientele were mostly penniless British and Irish governesses who had all been interned at some stage during the Occupation. The Poor Servants remained in rue Murillo until 1960, when they moved to premises at rue Lübeck in the 16th arrondissement. By then the practice among French bourgeois families of employing British and Irish governesses for their children was in decline. The Poor Servants turned to catering for au pairs, working closely with Agnes Hannigan, who ran a placement agency (as well as the Franco-Irish Cultural Exchange organisation, which arranged student exchanges). The Poor Servants left Paris in September 1997.

As the Allies advanced into Germany in spring 1945, Fr Travers consented to the use of the Irish College as a transit centre for newly freed prisoners of war ('on condition that certain repairs were carried out to electrical and plumbing installations').[25] The first arrivals were Dutch and they remained in the college for a fortnight before being sent elsewhere. They were followed by a group of Polish officers ('very good Catholics all of them'). Then, in June 1945, the college became, for six months, a centre for displaced persons claiming US citizenship. Shortly afterwards, Travers received a letter from Brigadier General Allen of the US army headquarters:

> It is appropriate at this time that I should again express to the Irish bishops through you the sincere and warm appreciation of the U.S. Army for their generosity in permitting us the use of the College as a centre for displaced persons claiming American citizenship. The premises have been ideal for the purpose. The loan of them was made to us at a time when it was next to impossible to find suitable alternative accommodation subject to requisition. No question of compensation was ever raised.[26]

After his six years of exile, Fr Travers made it back to Dublin in the summer of 1945, leaving the college in the care of a Sister Rafferty of the Daughters of Charity order. In August 1949

Travers, then in Maynooth, was reappointed rector of the Irish College. But by then the Irish College had slipped *de facto* out of Irish hands. During the summer of 1945 Sister Rafferty had had a conversation with a Polish nun who alerted her to the plight of a group of Polish priests and clerical students who had been imprisoned in Dachau and other concentration camps in Germany. They had been transported to Paris after the liberation of the camps, but with the communist seizure of power in Poland, the prospects of continuing their priestly studies back home seemed dim. Moved by their story, Sister Rafferty arranged for the Poles to occupy the empty Irish College for a modest monthly rent. The Poles remained untroubled at the college until the late 1980s, when the Irish progressively reclaimed the place. The Polish community finally left for the Paris suburb of Issy-les-Moulineaux in 1997.

***

Irish writer Francis Stuart had travelled to Paris on several occasions before the war. He had last passed through the city in December 1939 on his way to take up a position teaching English at Berlin University, managing to obtain a transit visa from the Legation in Paris on the understanding that he was heading for Switzerland.[27] Stuart spent the first part of the war in the Irland-Redaktion, broadcasting propaganda on behalf of the Germans as well as teaching English, but he fled bomb-shattered Berlin for southern Germany in 1944. He and his girlfriend, Gertrud (known as Madeleine) Meissner, were to remain there and in Dornbirn across the Austrian border until the war's end, no doubt hoping to make it to safety in neutral Switzerland. But the Swiss border was firmly closed and Stuart experienced significant hardship before managing to find a place on a French freight train that travelled from Bregenz in Austria to the French capital. Stuart eventually arrived at the Gare de l'Est on 14 August 1945.

An ex-lover of his in Berlin, Róisín Ní Mheara, had pre-
ceded him. In June of that year, she wrote a letter (signed Mrs
R. O'Mara) from les Annonciades in Melun to the Legation,
inquiring whether Francis Stuart 'has arrived in Paris yet from
Germany, or whether you have news of his whereabouts'.[28] Ní
Mheara, who had also worked for the Reich in Berlin during
the war, was born Rosaleen James in London in July 1918. She
claimed her parents were Irish but she was adopted when still a
baby by General Sir Ian Hamilton and his wife. In March 1945, a
few months after Stuart, she fled Berlin with her young daughter
and ended up in Heidelberg in western Germany. Ní Mheara
claimed in her forthrightly pro-German (not to say Hitlerian)
Recollections that she and her daughter were brought from Heidelberg to Paris by a US army adjutant who had instructions
from the British secret service 'to deliver me personally into the
hands of the British ambassador in Paris'.[29] Ní Mheara wrote
that she somehow managed to escape British custody in Paris
and travelled out to Rueil-Malmaison in the city's suburbs, where
she entrusted her four-year-old daughter to the parents of a girl
she had known in Berlin. Alone, she then marched into the Red
Cross offices near the Arc de Triomphe, where the British authorities caught up with her again.

A relatively plausible account of what happened next to Ní
Mheara appears in Stuart's *Black List Section H.* In the novel, Ní
Mheara tells H (Stuart's alter-ego) that her grandfather (actually
it was probably her stepfather, Sir Ian Hamilton) intervened and
'though he didn't want her back in England, had her sent to the
English hospital in Paris'.[30] After some time recovering from her
ordeals, she was sent to les Annonciades ('a refugee camp of sorts
... a dilapidated house belonging to the British government'),
from which she tried to contact Stuart.[31]

Stuart himself was initially sent to a reception area for displaced persons at the villa Rothschild in the rue Leonardo Da

Vinci (16th arrondissement) and took his meals around the corner in rue Leroux. His state of mind is revealed in his diary (but only to a certain extent, since these diaries were heavily redacted by Stuart). On 15 August 1945, the day after he arrived in Paris, he noted:

> What a ceaseless swarming of this city! How alone and flooded over in it am I! But that too had to be so that I begin to see how to live not only in the outer peace of Dornbirn, not only as a hermit in poverty, hunger, danger, but in the midst of this great worldly mode. This first day of peace I am here in this 'camp' in Paris, separated from S (Madeleine), the immediate future uncertain, bitten by vermin, alone, with nothing to do but wait. And at the same time I am infinitely better off than I ever was before in my days of 'success' in the old place.[32]

The next day, Stuart noted that he was writing 'lying in my bunk in the very dirty repatriation centre. This forced inactivity is not my way, it is something quite different, but how beautiful it is … Later: a day of intense loneliness, anxiety, apprehension about S, like that first evening in Bregenz.' During his first lonely few weeks in Paris, Stuart took a trip down memory lane, writing one day that he had gone by metro to Montparnasse, where he 'sat at the deserted terrasse at the Dôme and drank a coffee'. Stuart had frequented the Dôme on a previous trip to Paris in 1937, meeting two ladies there one evening with whom he 'indulged in an orgy of drinking and sexual activity', according to one biographer.[33]

Stuart moved into the cheap Hôtel Copernic in the street of the same name (also in the 16th arrondissement), where he occupied 'a dark little room', but he continued to take his meals at the villa Rothschild.[34] He was given a fawn raincoat by the Quakers in rue des Martyrs (9th arrondissement), but a visit to the Irish Legation proved frosty. An Irish diplomat told him that 'his appearance in Paris wasn't a matter of official rejoicing for the representatives of his native land'.[35] According to another account, he was informed by the Legation's first secretary, Denis McDonald, that 'his presence in Paris was an embarrassment', and that he was best advised to go back to where he had come from.[36] Stuart had already been given the cold shoulder by the Berlin Legation in August 1942, when Con Cremin (who had temporarily taken Warnock's place while the latter recovered from a car accident) told him he had received instructions not to renew Stuart's passport. A further visit to Cremin in June 1944 – possibly with a view to arranging his and Madeleine's repatriation to Ireland – had also yielded nothing.[37]

Still, the Irish authorities in Paris provided some money for Stuart when he turned up there in 1945, and his passport was renewed. Later, via the Legation and after much bureaucratic delay, he got further handouts from his extended family, including Seán MacBride, half-brother of Stuart's estranged wife, Iseult, and from Iseult herself.

On 23 August 1945 Stuart went to visit Róisín Ní Mheara ('Susan' in *Black List Section H*) in Melun, when she told him she had ambitions to become an actress. He found Ní Mheara desperately unhappy, perhaps thinking of the threat of a trial for treason in the United Kingdom, or of the daughter she had had to abandon on the other side of Paris. His meeting with Ní Mheara did nothing to lift his own spirits, as she told him that during her interrogations by the British his name had cropped up. She also told him that Robert Brasillach, one of France's best-known writers, had been executed in February 1945 for his 'intellectual crimes' in the service of the Nazi cause during the Occupation. 'If you'd been a Breton, they'd have shot you too,' Ní Mheara suggested.[38] Stuart himself summed up his mood as a combination of 'apprehension, an acute sense of my own wretchedness, fear and longing for S and even, lest anything should be wanting, physical misery from having over-eaten of the good food'.[39]

Stuart spent the next couple of weeks moping around Paris, giving the occasional English lesson. At the end of August he decided to return to Madeleine in Dornbirn, but his papers were not in order, and in Strasbourg, on the border with Germany, he was told he could not continue his journey. He went back to the Hôtel Copernic in Paris and began to complain a bit less. 'I have my work. I have time to do it. A room, a bed, enough to eat, no bombs and health,' he wrote on 27 September.[40] Stuart had heard about the sniper(s) that had fired on the crowd as General de Gaulle approached Notre Dame for the *Te Deum* arranged on 26 August 1944 to celebrate the Liberation of Paris the previous day. While staying in the Hôtel Copernic, he made use of this incident to concoct a story about a Latvian SS soldier and Sam Morrison, citizen of a neutral country, who moved around liberated Paris sniping from rooftops.[41]

In November 1945, still in danger of being arrested and tried by the British but with his papers in order and with a forged letter purporting to come from the Irish Legation, Stuart made it back to Austria on his second attempt. But both he and Madeleine Meissner were soon locked up by the French forces of occupation and kept under surveillance in the French-occupied part of Germany. After waiting seven months for an exit visa, Stuart finally made it back to Paris at the beginning of July 1949. Madeline followed him a month later. They found lodgings in the attic of an apartment belonging to a Hungarian writer called Ladislas Dormandi, at 20 avenue de Breteuil (7th arrondissement), where Madeleine started to work as a *domestique* for the family. Stuart and Madeleine struck up a friendship with the writer and horse punter Liam O'Flaherty and his partner, Kitty Tailer, before moving to England in 1951 and then to Ireland. By that time, Stuart had convinced himself that the coast was clear and that neither the British nor the Irish authorities were likely to give him much stick for his wartime activities.

***

The tea-deprived Constance Rafroidi loomed into view again in April 1945, when her brother, Alfred O'Rahilly, turned to Seán Murphy via the DEA. He needed help in tracing Maureen, Constance's eighteen-year-old daughter, who had run away to Paris from home in Arpajon after a quarrel with her mother. O'Rahilly, in Cork, described Constance as 'odd' and Maureen as 'more stable and reliable than the mother', but there were grounds for worrying about Maureen's 'moral and material welfare' in the big city.[42] However, Maureen called into the Legation to explain that she had found a job as a clerk at the US army's Paris headquarters and was renting a room for herself. The argument with her mother seemed to be over Maureen's wish to marry her boyfriend.[43]

Constance Rafroidi wrote again to the Legation on 1 February 1946 to ask if it could help her to organise travel for another of her offspring, her nine-year-old daughter, whom she wanted to send to one of her sisters in Dublin. 'She will be much better fed in Dublin than in France just now and the doctor recommends the change as soon as possible for the child's health.'[44] Five days later Seán Murphy wrote to suggest she contact the Red Cross instead.

On 2 October 1945 Murphy received a letter from Passage West in County Cork from Georgina O'Hara's mother, who hadn't seen her daughter for seven years. Georgina was urgently needed at home, for 'her father asked me to beg you to help her quick journey home, it being his dying wish to see her again, being confined to bed for 17 years. There is very, very little strength left him now and closing on to his 82nd year, I will trust in God that we will not fail him now.'[45] Murphy received a letter in a similar vein from O'Hara's sister, Kathleen, who was serving as a nurse at a British military hospital in Germany and offered to pay all expenses involved in getting Georgina home to see her father one last time. The Legation established contact with Georgina but again she dragged her feet. In spite of the urgent request from her sister and mother, Georgina told the Legation she wouldn't go back to Ireland until early December, and 'she was rather obstinate about her decision'.[46]

Early in 1948 Bluebell was asked to choreograph for the Lido (situated at 76–78 Champs Elysées, 8th arrondissement), which had opened two years earlier. To be close to her new place of work, Bluebell and her family moved to 27 rue Marbeuf (8th arrondissement), right beside the Champs Elysées, where they resided until 1972. Her husband, Marcel Leibovici, ran the business side of the Bluebell Girls and looked after the musical orchestration. His constant womanising meant Bluebell increasingly distanced herself from him until he was killed in a car crash near Sens in March 1961 – not far from where Albert Camus had met his death (also in a car crash) a year earlier. In 1972 Bluebell moved to a penthouse apartment in a newly built block in rue de la Faisanderie (16th arrondissement). She died in August 2004 and is buried in Montmartre cemetery, right beside the writers and critics Edmond and Jules de Goncourt. A bronze bust of Bluebell placed on her headstone was stolen in 2008. But her wartime experiences of sheltering her Jewish husband were not entirely forgotten: the story of theatre owners Marion and Lucas Steiner in the classic François Truffaut film *Le Dernier Métro* (1980) was in part inspired by the story of Bluebell during the war.

In 1946 Robert Fox of MIS-X, a section of the US War Department that aided US prisoners of war and those evading capture in enemy territory, began an investigation into the help provided to Allied soldiers and airmen by the Passionist priests on the avenue Hoche. But while Fox concluded that the priests had done some sterling work during the Occupation, he determined that 'they want no reward. They work for God and humanity, not for medals.'[47] In particular, the leader of the community, Fr O'Grady, was 'staunch in his refusal of any recognition for his work'.[48]

After the war, Fr O'Grady's colleague, Fr Kenneth Monaghan, was posted to the British Army of the Rhine in Germany. A newspaper article mentions that on 19 December 1948 he helped organise a Christmas party for over 500 German orphan and refugee children, at which the children 'had a substantial Christmas tea, a Punch-and-Judy show and a Christmas parcel on leaving. The children in their turn gave their benefactors a musical entertainment.'[49] Fr Monaghan continued working as an army chaplain in the United Kingdom and Germany until 1951 and died in Wales in 1969.

Still living in Switzerland, Nora and Giorgio Joyce visited Paris in late 1948 and again in 1949 to sort out the property salvaged by the late Paul Léon in 1940. Giorgio in particular was anxious to raise money quickly, and so books, manuscripts and pictures that Léon had retrieved at considerable risk to himself from James Joyce's flat in the rue des Vignes in late 1940 were exhibited for sale from 8 to 25 October 1949 at the Left Bank bookshop and gallery La Hune.[50] With so many matters needing attention in Paris, there was little time to visit Lucia Joyce, who was back at the clinic in Ivry-sur-Seine in the Paris suburbs. Giorgio went out to Ivry for an hour, but he found Dr Delmas' clinic so unkempt and was so unsettled by Lucia's condition that he decided Nora should not see her.

Nora Joyce became involved in a bid to have James Joyce's body repatriated from Zurich to Ireland, following the example of William B. Yeats, who had died in the south of France in January 1939 and whose body was brought home by the Irish Naval Service in September 1948 for reburial in Drumcliffe, County Sligo, replete with state honours.[51] Pushed by Nora

Joyce, Harriet Weaver (Joyce's long-time sponsor) and family friend Maria Jolas brought up the possibility with Count O'Kelly of something similar being organised for the author of *Ulysses*. But having made the relevant inquiries among the ranks of Irish officialdom, O'Kelly came back with the news that there was no popular support for a Yeats-like reburial of Joyce in Ireland.

***

Count O'Kelly earned contempt in some quarters because of Vendôme Wines' customer profile during the Occupation – although he later claimed he never sold Germans 'the good stuff' and he used his contacts with them to gather information on behalf of the British.[52] Whether this was true or not, Vendôme Wines resumed normal service for a while after the Liberation, selling wine to the upper echelons of British society. In February 1945 O'Kelly decided to step back again from running the company, saying that he was 'liable in the near future to be called away for long periods'.[53] But his company provided wines for a lavish reception organised in June of that year to celebrate the return of the Duke and Duchess of Windsor to Paris after their wartime exile to Bermuda.[54] For a few more years O'Kelly continued to live with his wife and various servants in the large first-floor apartment on the rue du Général Appert in the upscale 16th arrondissement that had been his residence since the 1930s. During his Parisian years he had surplus funds to send to his Swiss bank account, held by Crédit Suisse in Geneva. He also had a bank account at JP Morgan in Paris, which, when the taxman started to make enquiries at the beginning of the 1950s, contained FF1.1 million.[55]

O'Kelly's love of cars continued into the early post-war period. By late 1946 he was travelling around France in a very swish Buick Super Convertible sedan with his ever-faithful Spanish driver, Francisco Gomez, at the wheel. Although there was still little motor traffic, the count managed to ram an ancient Citroën driven by a local farmer at a crossroads outside Orléans in July 1948.

O'Kelly began to ease out of Paris in the late 1940s, as he was tired of the French capital and was looking for a sunnier European city where he and his frail wife could live cheaply. He went to Switzerland for three weeks in November 1945 and again in June and September 1946. In October 1946 he stayed a month in Lisbon. He finally sold the Buick and left Paris to take up a position as *chargé d'affaires* in Lisbon in the summer of 1948. Vendôme Wines was wound up in May that year.

O'Kelly may have had a bellyful of post-war France, but there was no escape from the infamous French tax authorities, known colloquially as *le fisc*. In January 1951, well after the count had left Paris, *le fisc* sent him a demand to pay a 'national solidarity tax' on French assets that he had not declared, including Vendôme Wines. He refused to pay as a matter of principle and wrote to Con Cremin (who was then Ireland's ambassador to France), 'I've suffered a severe *revers de fortune* and there is not the least likelihood of me being *matériellement* in a position to pay anything. This is just a try-on.'[56] O'Kelly pleaded in a further letter to his Paris Legation colleagues dated 24 July 1951:

> [Vendôme Wines] may have been a small source of revenue at the beginning [but] was completely knocked out by the war and was, so far as I remember, in permanent deficit from the very beginning thereof ... Far from being a source of revenue, much less of enrichissement to me, it was I who during the war had to bring it money in an attempt to keep it afloat ... When the company was finally liquidated in 1948 to the best of my recollection the shareholders – of which I was the principal – lost four-fifths – if not nine-tenths – of their capital. I cannot remember the exact figure, but it was a disaster.[57]

His friend John Francis Keane was also hassled for taxes owing on his participation in Vendôme Wines, and was fined by the tax authorities for valuing his stake at below par.

Once firmly established in Lisbon, O'Kelly soon had the title of 'minister plenipotentiary' bestowed upon him and began sending enthusiastic reports home to Dublin on the delights of the regime of Antonio Salazar. In the arcane language of diplomatic etiquette, minister plenipotentiaries are ranked below full ambassador and O'Kelly became 'probably the worst paid in Lisbon's diplomatic corps' simply because the count had been 'denied ambassadorial status and the salary that goes with it'.[58] Though he served there until his death in 1968, O'Kelly was never appointed to the rank of ambassador to Portugal, a point that clearly rankled with him and that he traced back to his sacking from the position of Irish minister to France in 1935. In an October 1965 memo to Hugh McCann, secretary to the Department of Foreign Affairs, he argued:

> [My] nomination as ambassador here would constitute for me a rehabilitation, in my eyes and in the eyes of all my colleagues, after over 30 years – half a life time – of wandering in the wilderness under a contentious cloud. Were you to say at this point that personal considerations should have no place in civil service transactions, I couldn't agree more. But alas! Personal considerations were the only ones that operated to break my career in the first instance.[59]

The death of O'Kelly's wife, Marjorie, in December 1957 left the count without any immediate family. Yet he maintained his life-long love of high society, establishing a wide array of contacts in Lisbon who still remembered the count fondly many years afterwards. In 1965 he was upset with Nigel Dempster of the *Daily Express* – to the extent that he wrote to the secretary of the Department of Foreign Affairs in Dublin to deny he had even talked to the journalist. In a somewhat racy article (for the time) on the Dublin Horse Show in August 1965, Count O'Kelly is quoted by Dempster in the *Daily Express*'s William Hickey column as saying that 'too many people come to the Dublin Horse Show who don't know one end of a horse from another'.[60] Pretty undiplomatic stuff for a diplomat, but probably very much to form for Gerald O'Kelly.

Despite the controversies surrounding Vendôme Wines, Count O'Kelly de Gallagh managed to survive the war, during which he rendered useful service to Ireland and the Paris Irish. Aptly enough, Éamon de Valera is said to have admitted after the war that 'we have done wrongly by this man'.[61] But perhaps the greatest wrong of all is that he is now almost completely forgotten.

ENDNOTES

Introduction

1   Paris Legation files, P49/21, Vichy Legation to DEA, 5 February 1941, National Archive of Ireland (NAI).

2   De Valera Papers, P150/2571, University College Dublin Archives. Note from Joseph Walshe, secretary of the DEA, to Éamon de Valera, 28 November 1941. See also Paris Legation files, P49/21, Susan Hilton quoted in Warnock to Murphy, 12 July 1941, NAI.

3   Samuel Beckett in an interview with Israel Shenker, *The New York Times*, 5 May 1956.

4   Paris Legation files, P26/2, Whyte to Murphy, 15 February 1945, NAI.

5   'Diplomat's Diary Reveals Joyce's Attachment to Ireland', *RTÉ News*, 13 January 2016, www.rte.ie/news/special-reports/2016/0112/759567-james-joyce/.

6   One case involves Jack Parken (sometimes referred to as Jack Parker or Parke), described by Patrice Miannay in *Dictionnaire des Agents Doubles dans la Résistance* (Le Cherche Midi, 2005) as an Irishman 'born around 1905', who worked as an accountant and spoke flawless French. Parachuted into occupied France as a radio operator, Parken (alias Jacques Dufresnes) was arrested in the rue Miromesnil in the 8th arrondissement of Paris during the summer of 1943. Under torture, he agreed to infiltrate a Resistance group in Lyon. Parken disappeared in Normandy in July 1944, 'perhaps the victim of the sabotage of his train'. He is mentioned in the biography of one of the most effective German secret agents active in France during the Occupation, Hugo Bleicher – see Hugo Bleicher, *Colonel Henri's Story* (William Kimber & Co., 1962), pp. 123–6. In judicial files held at the Archives Nationales outside Paris, Bleicher mentions that he last heard of Jack Parker in the Montélimar area in southern France in the summer of 1944 (see judicial files for Suzanne Laurent, Z/6/862–863).

7   Dermot Keogh, *Jews in Twentieth-Century Ireland: Refugees, Anti-Semitism and the Holocaust* (Cork University Press, 1998), p. 191.

1 Trouble at the Legation

1   Donal O'Kelly, *My Brother Jack* (Donal O'Kelly, 1968), p. 14.

2   Jacques Dumont de Montroy, *Mes Voyages en Angleterre et en Irlande de 1947 à 1993* (Jacques Dumont de Montroy, 2006), p. 21.

3   The Royal University was the precursor to the Irish university colleges.

4   In consideration of his services, the title of Count of the Holy Roman Empire was conferred on Dillon O'Kelly in 1767 'by Imperial letters patent,

with special remainder to all descendants in the male line and females in the male line (until married)'. O'Kelly, a general in the Imperial Army, distinguished himself in the defence of Konopiště Castle in Bohemia. Since Dillon had no issue, the title reverted to his father, Festus, who lived in Tycooly, County Galway.

5   O'Kelly (1968), p. 14.

6   O'Kelly de Gallagh's war service record is held at the National Archives, Kew (NAK) War Office (WO) file 339/1448.

7   *Omar Khayyam* (Librarie Le Triptyque, 1933); *Trois poèmes de Kipling* (Imprimerie A. Sirot, 1945).

8   The term used by the DEA was 'compulsory retirement from the public service'.

9   Dermot Keogh, *Ireland & Europe: A Diplomatic & Political History, 1919–1989* (Hibernian University Press, 1989), p. 52. There might be some justification in this claim. In one report he sent to Dublin on 3 April 1935, Count O'Kelly wrote: 'It is very difficult to obtain first-hand information from the Quai d'Orsay, who are extraordinarily reticent on the whole' (Paris Legation files, P19/28, NAI).

10   Department of Foreign Affairs (DFA), file EA 3–1, O'Kelly to Walshe, 13 April 1926, NAI, quoted in Michael Kennedy and Joseph Morrison Skelly (eds), *Irish Foreign Policy, 1919–1966: From Independence to Internationalism* (Four Courts Press, 2000), p. 38.

11   Brian P. Murphy, *John Chartres: Mystery Man of the Treaty* (Irish Academic Press, 1995), p. 117.

12   Art Ó Briain letter to Leopold Kerney, 23 September 1935 (private collection).

13   *Ibid.*, undated 1935.

14   Charles Bewley, Ireland's plenipotentiary in Berlin until 1939, provided a summary of Ó Briain's short stint in Paris: 'He continuously protested against the government's pro-British policies. De Valera, who had appointed him, refused to go to the Legation during any of his frequent stays in Paris "as long as that man is there". In 1938 he received invitations from British diplomats to various British colonial events that he turned down each time, in line with instructions. Then [DEA] secretary Walshe telephoned to tell him he must accept the invitations. When he refused, he was sent on holiday and soon thereafter removed from the position.' Charles Bewley, 'Der irische Ministerium für Auswärtige Angelegenheiten', memo to Reich foreign ministry, 11 October 1940, R 101.083, Reichssicherheitshauptamt-Inland, Politisches Archiv des Auswärtigen Amt, Berlin.

15   According to Charles Bewley, 'Murphy was deputy secretary at the Department for a year. He is a relation of Walshe's and is under his influence. He distinguishes himself more by his kindness than by any particular ability.' *Ibid.*

2 All Quiet on the Western Front

1   A piece in the 2008 issue of the Rockefeller Archive Center newsletter states, improbably, that 'Daniel O'Brien was at the Paris Office throughout the War, even when the office moved to Lisbon ... [Thanks to] O'Brien and other RF [Rockefeller Foundation] staff, many scholars and their families were able to make their way out of Europe to England and America through the RF field offices in Paris and Lisbon.'

2   Letter dated 26 September 1939, Martha Dow Fehsenfeld and Lois More Overbeck (eds), *The Letters of Samuel Beckett, vol. 1, 1929–1940* (Cambridge University Press, 2009), p. 667.

3   Peggy Guggenheim, *Out of this Century: Confessions of an Art Addict* (Universe Books, 1979), p. 208.

4   Letter dated 6 December 1939, Fehsenfeld and Overbeck (2009), p. 669.

5   Richard Ellmann, *James Joyce* (revised edition, Oxford University Press, 1983), p. 728.

6   Fr Patrick Travers, 'Some Experiences during the War Years: The Irish College in Paris 1939–1945', republished in *Colloque*, the quarterly review of the Irish Vincentians (no. 18, autumn 1988), p. 442.

7   *Ibid.*, p. 443.

8   George Perry, 'Fifty Years in the Front Line', *The Sunday Times* magazine, 23 August 1981.

9   Paris Legation files, P2/11 (8), Bergin to Paris Legation, 6 March 1940, NAI.

10   In 1930 James Joyce wrote to his son, Giorgio: 'Some days ago I had to renew my passport. The clerk told me he had orders to send people like me to the Irish delegation. But I insisted instead and got a British one.' See 'James Joyce Chose a British Passport', Letters page, *Financial Times*, 15 May 2014.

11   Ellmann (1983), p. 738.

12   Paris Legation files, P1/6–2/9, Mulcahy to Paris Legation, 23 December 1939, NAI.

13   Scoop!, www.scoop-database.com.

14   Paris Legation files, P2/11 (8), McMorrow to Paris Legation, 15 October 1939, NAI.

15   *The Irish Times*, 2 January 1965.

16   Correspondence between Lord Halifax and Lord Granard, 12 December 1939, NAK Foreign Office (FO) file 371/2/2942.

17   Lord Granard did serve Great Britain, acting as an air advisor to the Minister of State for the Middle East during the war.

18   Guggenheim (1979), p. 209.

19   Ellmann (1983), p. 732.

20   Carol Loeb Shloss, *Lucia Joyce: To Dance in the Wake* (Bloomsbury, 2004), p. 394.

3 Detention and Destitution

1   An open city was one that would not be defended.
2   Niall Keogh, *Con Cremin, Ireland's Wartime Diplomat* (Mercier Press, 2006), p. 18.
3   Paris Legation files, P1/6-2/9, letter from D. McAllister to Murphy, December 1940, NAI.
4   *Ibid.*, P19/34A, confidential report from Seán Murphy to Joseph Walshe, 18 June 1940, NAI.
5   Literally, Castle of the Great Butcher – in fact the Château du Grand Bouchet.
6   Armand Ziwès, secretary-general of the Bordeaux prefecture and nephew of the Irish Legation architect whom Murphy referred to a few lines earlier.
7   Travers (1988), pp. 444–5.
8   Paris Legation files, P19/34A, Murphy to DEA, 28 June 1940, NAI.
9   German ordinance of 27 September 1940.
10 Letter dated 10 June 1940, Fehsenfeld and Overbeck (2009), p. 683.
11 James Knowlson, *Damned to Fame: The Life of Samuel Beckett* (Bloomsbury, 1996), p. 303.
12 *Ibid.*, p. 302.
13 Brenda Maddox, *Nora: A Biography of Nora Joyce* (Houghton Mifflin, 1988), p. 448.
14 Lucie Noël, *James Joyce and Paul Léon: The Story of a Friendship* (The Gotham Book Mart, 1950), p. 37.
15 'No Love Letters in Joyce's Secret Trunk', *Irish Independent*, 16 December 1991.
16 Paris Legation files, P2/112, also P33/14, undated memo, August 1940, NAI.
17 *Ibid.*, Seán Murphy to James Joyce, 26 November 1940.
18 Joyce had known O'Kelly for several years and believed that the count could be relied upon to intervene in his favour. As far back as 1933, Joyce claimed in a letter that he had convinced the count to adopt a beverage appropriately named Clos Saint Patrice as the Legation wine. See Richard Ellmann (ed.), *Selected Letters of James Joyce* (Faber & Faber, 1975), p. 368.
19 Paris Legation files, P2/112, James Joyce to Seán Murphy, 1 December 1940, NAI.
20 See Seán Cronin, *Frank Ryan: The Search for the Republic* (Repsol Publishing, 1980).
21 Enno Stephan, *Spies in Ireland* (Four Square Books, 1965), p. 145.
22 *Ibid.*
23 Guy Vissault de Coëtlogon Security Service file, NAK KV2/303.
24 Kurt Haller Security Service file, NAK KV2/769.
25 Guy Vissault de Coëtlogon Security Service file, NAK KV2/303.
26 Abwehr dossier, Service historique de la Défense (SHD), Vincennes, GR 28 P7, 164 and 165.

27 'A Digest of Ham – Volume Two', Security Service file, NAK KV4/14.

28 *Ibid.*

29 Joseph Lenihan Security Service files, NAK KV4/14 and KV4/60920.

30 Joseph Lenihan Security Service file, NAK KV4/14.

31 Guy Liddell diary, vol. 6, 4 July 1942, Security Service Policy (Pol F series), NAK KV4/190.

32 Joseph Lenihan Security Service file, NAK KV4/14.

33 Secretary's files, Paris series, P12/1, telegram 152, Seán Murphy to DEA, 23 August 1940, NAI.

34 Typewritten obituary dated 1 December 1958, signed Sister Bonaventura CP, kindly supplied by Alan Randall, Menevia Diocesan Archivist, Carmarthen, Wales.

35 Typewritten document signed Alfred CP, Rector, kindly supplied by Alan Randall, Menevia Diocesan Archivist, Carmarthen, Wales.

36 According to St Joseph's parishioner Agnes Hannigan, cited in David O'Donoghue's *Hitler's Irish Voices* (Beyond the Pale Publications, 1998), p. 196, and an article by P. D. Thomas, 'A Catholic Father Operated as British Contact in Paris in WWII', in *OSS Society Newsletter*, Summer/Fall 2007.

37 Secretary's files, Paris series, P19/34, Murphy to DEA, 8 July 1940, NAI.

38 Paris Legation files, P48/18-49/3, Murphy to DEA, 27 August 1940, NAI.

39 *Ibid.*, Secretary's files, Paris series, P12/1, telegram from Joseph Walshe to Seán Murphy, 22 July 1940, NAI.

40 Nubar Gulbenkian, *Pantaraxia: An Autobiography* (Hutchinson, 1965), pp. 193–4. The multi-millionaire oil financier Calouste Gulbenkian ('Mr. 5%') was Iraqi minister in Paris at the outbreak of the war and then became Iranian ambassador to Philippe Pétain's government in Vichy before moving to Lisbon in 1942. From there, he sent regular packages to his friends in the Irish Legation in Vichy via the diplomatic bag. Gulbenkian was also a friend of the Irish ambassador in Madrid, Leopold Kerney, helping to arrange for Kerney's son, Éamon, to take a trip to Paris and stay in the Ritz Hotel in the summer of 1942.

41 Secretary's files, Paris series, P19/34, Murphy to DEA, 27 August 1940, NAI.

42 *Ibid.*

43 Travers (1988), p. 447.

44 *Ibid.*, p. 448.

45 See www.rootsweb.ancestry.com/~irlcar2/Knockbeg_College_04.htm.

46 Travers (1988), p. 448.

47 Secretary's files, Paris series, P12/1, Murphy to Joseph Walshe, 23 August 1940, NAI.

48 *Ibid.*

49 In September a telegram was received in Dublin from the Berlin Legation stating that 'The German Army strongly opposed diplomats travelling to and from occupied territory. All small countries in the same position.' Paris

Legation files, P48/19, 13 September 1940, NAI. Subsequent visits by Seán Murphy to Paris were made to look as if they were being undertaken in a personal capacity.

50 Paris Legation files, P33/3–34/2, handwritten memo of conversation with O'Kelly de Gallagh, 8 January 1941, NAI.

51 *Ibid.*, P1/6–2/9, Count O'Kelly to Vichy Legation, 27 August 1940, NAI.

52 *Ibid.*, P49/21, O'Grady to Murphy, Vichy Legation, 7 October 1940, NAI.

53 *Ibid.*

54 *Ibid.*, P33/3–34/2, O'Kelly to Vichy Legation, 24 September 1940, NAI.

55 Fichier du camp d'Argelès, 1260 W 51, Archives départementales des Basses-Pyrenees, Perpignan.

56 A strange parallel with Lang's case is that of William Coman from County Tipperary, who was serving in the BEF when he was separated from his unit during the German bombardment of Rouen. He managed to get as far as a town called Vermelles, near Lille, and avoided capture for two years (see *History Ireland*, vol. 23, no. 3, May/June 2015).

57 Paris Legation files, P2/9, undated letter (end August or early September 1940) from Lang to Legation, NAI.

58 *Ibid.*

59 *Ibid.*

60 *Ibid.*, Legation to Lang, 11 September 1940.

61 *Ibid.*, Lang to Legation, 24 September 1940.

62 Admiralty file, NAK ADM 1/10902.

63 From typescript of notes made by Confrey for RTÉ radio broadcast, kindly supplied by Jean Confrey O'Hara.

64 Paris Legation files, P49/4, Vichy Legation to DEA, 5 March 1942, NAI.

65 *Ibid.*, P49/18, letter from Kerney to Irish Legation, 21 October 1940, NAI.

66 *Ibid.*

67 Correspondence with Éamon Kerney (son of Leopold Kerney), April 2015.

68 Paris Legation files, P48/18–49/3, message from O'Kelly de Gallagh to Seán Murphy, 22 October 1940, NAI.

69 *Ibid.*, P49/18, O'Dare to Vichy Legation, 17 November 1942, NAI.

70 *Ibid.*, P49/19 (3)–49/22, Daniel McAllister to Seán Murphy, 9 December 1940, NAI.

71 *Ibid.*, letter from Hélène McAllister to Legation, December 1940.

72 McAllister returned home in March 1943, after the abolition of the Demarcation Line.

73 *Ibid.*, P49/24, O'Kelly de Gallagh to Murphy, October 1940, NAI.

74 Article 4 of the 1935 Irish Nationality and Citizenship Act stated that 'Every person who is not a citizen of Saorstát Éireann by virtue of Article 3 of the Constitution but was born before the 6th day of December, 1922, either in Ireland or of parents of whom at least one was born in Ireland shall: (a) if such person is at the passing of this Act or becomes thereafter

permanently resident in Saorstát Éireann be deemed to be a natural-born citizen of Saorstát Éireann; or, (b) if such person at the passing of this Act is permanently resident outside Saorstát Éireann and is not a naturalised citizen of any other country, be deemed upon being registered in accordance with the next following sub-section of this section, to be a natural-born citizen of Saorstát Éireann.'

75 Paris Legation files, P49/18, O'Kelly de Gallagh to Murphy, Vichy Legation, undated (late 1940), NAI.

76 *Ibid.*, 13 November 1940.

77 *Ibid.*, P33–34/2, Vichy Legation to William O'Hea, 6 August 1940, NAI.

78 *Ibid.*, O'Hea to the Perpignan police prefect, 10 January 1941.

79 *Ibid.*, Vichy Legation to John Keane, 21 October 1940.

80 Report to Colonel T. D. Drake on board SS *Gripsholm* (9 September 1944) by Canadian doctor Reuben Rabinovitch, who met Dawson-Buckley in Drancy in January 1941, when the latter was 'in charge of camp contacts'. Report kindly supplied by Michael Moores Leblanc.

81 Paris Legation files, P33–34/2, Fenton letter to O'Kelly de Gallagh, 26 October 1940, NAI.

82 *Ibid.*, P49/34 (A), Irish Legation Vichy to Berlin chargé d'affaires, 17 July 1942, NAI.

83 *Ibid.*, P1/6 (2), Murphy to O'Kelly de Gallagh, 19 March 1941, NAI.

84 Security Service file for Desmond Patrick Nolan, NAK KV2/6349.

85 Security Service file for Desmond Patrick Nolan, NAK KV2/6347.

86 *Ibid.*

87 *Ibid.*

88 DFA, Berlin letter books, letter from DEA first secretary to Berlin Legation, 29 October 1942, NAI.

89 Paris Legation files, P49/6 (a)–49/9, Murphy letter to DEA, 23 January 1941, NAI.

90 *Ibid.*, P33/13, O'Kelly de Gallagh to Vichy Legation, 11 October 1940, NAI.

91 The barracks, located near the centre of Besançon, still stood in autumn 2015 but was slated for destruction to make way for an 'eco-neighbourhood'.

92 Undated memo, reproduced in George Perry, *Bluebell: The Authorised Biography of Margaret Kelly, Founder of the Legendary Bluebell Girls* (Pavilion, 1985), p. 106.

93 Paris Legation files, P19/34, telegram 336, Murphy to Walshe at DEA, 19 November 1940, NAI.

94 In a letter addressed to the Washington Legation in June 1941, Murphy asked for golf balls to be sent over in a diplomatic bag, as golf was 'one of the few distractions in Vichy'.

95 Secretary's files, Paris series, P12/1, coded telegram from Murphy to DEA, 13 January 1941, NAI.

96 Aengus Nolan, *Joseph Walshe: Irish Foreign Policy, 1922–1946* (Mercier Press, 2008), p. 162.

97 DEA Secretary files A2, Joseph Walshe memorandum to Éamon de Valera, 21 June 1940, NAI, Dublin, quoted in Catriona Crowe *et al.* (eds), *Documents on Irish Foreign Policy, vol. VI (1939–1941)* (Royal Irish Academy, 2008), p. 249.

98 Secretary's files, Paris series, P12/1, Murphy to Walshe at DEA, 1 March 1941, NAI.

4 Organising Help

1 Paris Legation files, P33/14, Murphy to F.T. Cremins, Berne Legation, 13 January 1941, NAI.

2 *Ibid.*

3 Shloss (2004), p. 407.

4 (Mr Beckett is in excellent health and is not wanting of anything.) Paris Legation files, P49/4, letter from Samuel Beckett to O'Kelly de Gallagh, 4 June 1941, NAI.

5 Martha Dow Fehsenfeld *et al.* (eds), *The Letters of Samuel Beckett, vol. 2, 1941–1956* (Cambridge University Press, 2011), p. xvii.

6 *Ibid.*, p. xvi.

7 SHD, Vincennes, Bureau Résistance, file number 16 P 42711.

8 Beckett report (original reference PF 601.715) contained in Security Service report on Gabrielle Cecile (Jeannine) Martinez Picabia, NAK KV2/1313.

9 In *The Secret War: Spies, Codes and Guerillas* (William Collins, 2015), pp. 262 and 281–2, Max Hastings argues that 'sigint' (signals intelligence) was immeasurably more important in World War Two than 'humint' (intelligence gathered from human sources of the kind that Beckett was involved in). In Hastings' view, the main value of 'humint' was that it provided *résistants* with the sentiment that they were 'doing their bit' for the Allied cause and helped boost national self-esteem after the war.

10 Martinez Picabia Security Service file, NAK KV2/1313.

11 Maddox (1988), p. 340.

12 Noël (1950), p. 38.

13 *Ibid.*

14 Bewley said of O'Kelly: 'He was very popular in diplomatic and French circles. His popularity and his title led to his dismissal, for which no reason was given by the Ministry. He is efficient and energetic; he has no outspoken political opinions and showed unquestioning loyalty to all Irish governments. His mother was Austrian [*sic*].' Bewley, memo to Reich Foreign Ministry, 11 October 1940, R 101.083, Politisches Archiv des Auswärtigen Amt, Berlin.

15 Leyba turned up in Lisbon in 1943, when he asked for a loan of £20 (then

raised to £80) from Ireland's representative there, Colman O'Donovan. The latter wrote in a letter to Seán Murphy (Paris Legation files, P33/19A, O'Donovan to Vichy Legation, 21 June 1943, NAI) that he couldn't understand why Leyba didn't ask the Gulbenkians, 'who are closer friends than I am'.

16 Dossier Hans Gechter, Archives Nationales, Pierrefitte-sur-Seine, AJ/40/580.

17 *Ibid.*

18 *Ibid.*

19 *Ibid.*

20 Members of the ultra-right Iron Guard that attempted to seize power in Bucharest in January 1941 were known as 'Greenshirts' in reference to the colour of their uniform.

21 Paris Legation files, P49/32 (9), Ambrose O'Kelly to Count O'Kelly, 21 November 1941, NAI.

22 *Ibid.*, P20/3, telegram from Murphy to Ambrose O'Kelly, 2 May 1942, NAI.

23 The story of Romanian oil supplies for the diplomatic corps in Vichy was told by Nubar Gulbenkian: 'The Rumanian Military Attaché was highly popular when he succeeded in getting a twenty-ton tank-car, full of petrol, sent from Rumania for his own use and that of his friends. However, not surprisingly, that supply did not last as long as he had hoped it would; others, not in the privileged circle, decided to take a share without his permission and the petrol "leaked" away.' Gulbenkian (1965), p. 194.

24 Paris Legation files, P20/3, letter from Murphy to Krug von Nidda, 26 October 1942, NAI.

25 Témoignage de Mme Barbier-Campbell, dite Marie Ange ou Elisabeth (Réseau Vaneau), Archives Nationales, Pierrefitte-sur-Seine, 72AJ/81/II Pièce 3.

26 'Flight to Freedom', BBC Northern Ireland, first broadcast on 21 June 2005.

27 Escape report to MI9 for Oliver James, NAK WO 208/3308.

28 James's account differs from McGrath's on this point. The former stated in his 1942 escape report that they approached an 'old lady' who took them to her home 'where her son and his wife gave up their bed for us'.

29 Again, James's version – given just four months after these events – differs from McGrath's account. According to James, the lady they had met at the Red Cross 'led us to the Irish Catholic church near the Etoile'.

30 The Bishop of Nevers was Patrice Flynn, a man of Irish origin and an arch defender of the régime of Philippe Pétain.

31 Paris Legation files, P49/21, letter from Count O'Kelly to Murphy, 24 January 1941, NAI.

32 *Ibid.*, P49/13 (21)–49/19, telegram from Vichy to DEA in Dublin, 19 February 1941, NAI.

33   *Ibid.*, Murphy to DEA, summer 1941 (date illegible).

34   Perry (1985), p. 113.

35   *Ibid.*, p. 114.

36   Pierre Bourget, *Histoires secrètes de l'occupation de Paris* (Hachette, 1970), p. 135.

37   Perry (1985), p. 114.

38   Paris Legation files, P33–34/2, Con Cremin minutes from conversation with Count O'Kelly, 22 January 1941, NAI.

39   *Ibid.*, P49/21, Count O'Kelly to Murphy, Vichy Legation, 24 January 1941, NAI.

40   *Ibid.*, P49/21, Kersher, American Friends Service Committee to Vichy Legation, 7 February 1941, NAI.

41   *Ibid.*, P19/34A, Count O'Kelly to Vichy Legation, 27 August 1940, NAI.

42   *Ibid.*, Vichy Legation to DEA, 5 February 1941.

43   *Ibid.*, Vichy Legation to DEA, 12 March 1941.

44   According to calculations made by French statistical agency INSEE – see www.insee.fr/fr/information/2417794.

45   Paris Legation files, P49/19 (3)–49/22, letter from Vichy Legation to Berlin Legation, 26 January 1942, NAI.

46   Letter from Eugène Dennis to Major John White, 20 June 1946, contained in the file for Robert Armstrong in the Bureau des Archives des victimes des conflits contemporains (BAVCC), Caen, AC 27 P 8898.

47   Paris Legation files, P49/32 (10)–49/85, letter from Paris Legation to DEA, 28 February 1945, NAI.

48   File for John Pilkington, Bureau Résistance et Seconde guerre mondiale, SHD, Vincennes, 16 P 478119.

49   Paris Legation files, P49/13, also P49/4, note from Vichy Legation to DEA, 30 July 1942, NAI.

50   According to the French statistical agency, INSEE, prices in the city of Bordeaux increased by a compound rate of 250% between 1939 and 1945, representing an annual inflation rate of 20% per annum.

51   Paris Legation files, P49/4, note from Pilkington to Vichy Legation, July 1943, NAI.

52   *Ibid.*, P49/5–49/6, Count O'Kelly to Murphy, Vichy Legation, 24 September 1940, NAI.

53   Information supplied by Florence Dassonville's nephew Jonathan Owen, New Zealand, July 2014.

54   According to Knochen, interrogated after the war, 'Our general staff do not seem to have taken it seriously.' Depositions d'Helmut Knochen 1131–1135, dossier Helmut Knochen, ancien chef du SD en France, Archives nationales, Pierrefitte-sur-Seine, 3W/77–3W/105, Haute Cour de Justice, Vol. 2.

55   Dossier de procédure contre Michel Dassonville, Archives Nationales, Pierrefitte-sur-Seine, Z/6/822–823 dossier 5691.

56 Paris Legation files, P49/6 (a)–49/9, Vichy Legation note to A. P. Burke, 24 February 1941, NAI.

57 Security Service file for Desmond Patrick Nolan, NAK KV2/6349.

58 *Ibid.*

59 *Ibid.*, Testimony of Henry W. Wicks, 16 February 1945.

60 *Ibid.*

61 *Ibid.*

62 Defendant: Hilton, Dorothea May Theresa. Charge: Doing an act likely to assist the enemy, 8 January 1946, NAK CRIM 4/1745.

63 *Ibid.*

64 Susan Hilton, *Eine Irin erlebt England und den Seekrieg* (Falken Verlag, 1942), pp. 141–2.

65 Susan Hilton, Security Service personal file (pf series), statement to British interrogators, 1 July 1945, NAK KV2/423.

66 Hilton (1942), p. 142.

67 Hilton statement to British interrogators, 1 July 1945, NAK KV2/423.

68 Hilton (1942), pp. 142–3.

69 Defendant: Hilton, Dorothea May Theresa. Charge: Doing an act likely to assist the enemy, 8 January 1946, NAK CRIM 4/1745.

70 Hilton (1942), p. 143.

71 *Ibid.*, pp. 143–5.

72 Hilton statement to British interrogators, 1 July 1945, NAK KV2/423.

73 DFA file A521 G2 interrogation of John O'Reilly ('Notes on John Fras. O'Reilly's activities in the Channel Islands and Germany'), quoted in O'Donoghue (1988), p. 97.

74 Paris Legation files, P48/19, circular to diplomatic services in Paris, 20 May 1941, quoted in Murphy cable to DEA, 21 May 1941, NAI.

75 Secretary's files, Paris series, P12/1, Joseph Walshe to Murphy, 1 October 1940, NAI.

76 *Ibid.*, P100/2, Vichy Legation to DEA, 24 February 1942, NAI.

77 *Ibid.*, P100/5, Froc to Murphy, 13 June 1941, NAI.

78 *Ibid.*, P14/1, Marquetout to Cremin, 10 August 1941, NAI.

79 Paris Legation files, P49/21, quoted in William Warnock to Vichy Legation, 12 July 1941, NAI.

80 Mark Hull, *Irish Secrets: German Espionage in Wartime Ireland, 1939–1945* (Irish Academic Press, 2003), p. 59.

81 Paris Legation files, P49/21, Warnock to Vichy Legation, 12 July 1941, NAI.

82 *Ibid.*, Warnock to DEA, 26 July 1941.

83 *Ibid.*, P49/21–33/17, Warnock to Murphy, 28 July 1941, NAI.

84 *Ibid.*, P49/32 (10)–49/85, DEA to Warnock, 27 August 1942, NAI. Hilton slipped further into the depths of alcoholism and was removed from her role at the Irland-Redaktion in 1942. For details of Hilton's activities in Berlin, see O'Donoghue (1988).

85   Paris Legation files, P49/7 (2), DEA to Irish Legation, 12 June 1945, NAI.

86   *Ibid.*, Murphy to DEA, 27 June 1945.

87   Johnny Mills was the younger brother of Charlie Mills, a famous pre-war racehorse trainer who owned a stud farm at Schloß Staffelde, outside Berlin. When the Irish Legation was bombed out of its premises at Drakesstraße in the centre of Berlin in late 1943, Charlie Mills made his facility available to the Irish authorities.

88   Paris Legation files, P33/17, Warnock, Berlin Legation to Vichy Legation, 1 December 1941, NAI.

89   *Ibid.*, P49/3(2), Fenton to Vichy Legation, 6 March 1942, NAI.

90   *Ibid.*, P19/34, letter from Murphy to Dublin, 25 October 1941, NAI.

91   *Ibid.*, P20/2, note to head of coal services in Vichy from Murphy, 11 November 1941, NAI.

92   *Ibid.*, P107/1, O'Kelly de Gallagh to S.A. Peugeot, 24 July 1941, NAI.

93   *Ibid.*, P20/2, letter from Colman O'Donovan, Lisbon Legation to Seán Murphy, 5 May 1943, NAI.

94   *Ibid.*, P19/34, Vichy Legation to Directeur du Protocole, Ministère des Affaires etrangères, 10 November 1941, and reply, 11 November 1941, NAI.

95   *Ibid.*, P33/17, letter from Murphy to Warnock, 29 July 1941, NAI.

96   *Ibid.*, P33/13, memo written by Murphy of call between him and Count O'Kelly, 25 May 1941, NAI.

97   Reports to Militarbeféhlshaber in Frankreich; Division Wi. I Allgemeine Wirtschaftsangelegenheiten – Expert Publicité Internationale (EPI) file, letter dated 16 June 1941, Archives nationales, Pierrefitte-sur-Seine, AJ/40/720 (1415).

98   Paris Legation files, P49/6 (a)–49/9, Dulanty letter to Murphy, 3 December 1942, NAI.

99   Reports to Militarbeféhlshaber in Frankreich, letter dated 16 June 1941, Archives nationales, Pierrefitte-sur-Seine, AJ/40/720 (1415).

100 Paris Legation files, P49/6 (a)–49/9, letter from Keane, 5 November 1942, NAI.

101 The American vice-consul in Marseille, Hiram Bingham, visited a number of internment camps in southern France.

102 In French and German documents, his date of birth is given as 17 March 1916.

103 Paris Legation files, P49/13 (21)–49/19, letter from Patrick Sweeney to Vichy Legation, 25 July 1941, NAI.

104 See also Bruno Frei's account of his internment in Roland-Garros and Le Vernet at the same period in *Die Männer von Vernet: Ein Tatsachenbericht* (Deutscher Militärverlag, 1961).

105 Paris Legation files, P49/18, letter from Patrick Sweeney to Vichy Legation, 27 August 1941, NAI.

106 *Ibid.*, letter from American Friends Service Committee, Perpignan, to Vichy Legation, 17 October 1941.

107 In January 1943 Elmes was arrested by the Gestapo on suspicion of helping Jewish children escape from the Riversaltes internment camp into Spain. She spent six months in Fresnes prison near Paris before being released.

108 Paris Legation files, P49/18, telegram 250, DEA to Vichy Legation, 2 April 1942, NAI.

109 *Ibid.*, P2/9, Vichy Legation to DEA, 25 August 1941, NAI.

110 *Ibid.*, P49/21, Vichy Legation to Warnock, 29 August 1941, NAI.

111 *Ibid.*, P2/9, Russell to Vichy Legation, 14 August 1943, NAI.

112 *Ibid.*, P33–34/2, letter to Dublin, 26 January 1942, NAI.

113 *Ibid.*, P2/9, Declaration of Nationality form registered by Count O'Kelly, 31 October 1940, NAI.

114 Keogh (2006), pp. 86–7. Of Vernon, Cremin wrote to Joseph Walshe in December 1944 (Paris Legation files, P49/13, NAI, Dublin) that 'my impression is that if he was guilty of espionage activities it was without any deliberate intention to work against Germany but probably because of the system governing allowances to Irish nationals in France during the war. His monthly allowance which may have been sufficient for the first year or so after the armistice was inadequate later on to keep him in the lifestyle which he was used to. Vernon's temptation was on financial grounds.'

115 Paris Legation files, P49/19 (3)–49/22, O'Grady to Warnock, 17 September 1941, NAI.

5 Hiding, Fleeing, Begging for Money

1 *Catholic Herald*, 30 January 1942.

2 Paris Legation files, P49/4, note from Vichy Legation to DEA containing translation of letter from Lord Ashbourne's widow, Marianne de Montbrison, 5 June 1942, NAI.

3 *Ibid.*

4 *Ibid.*

5 *Ibid.*, P49/18 (4), letter from Patrick Sweeney to Irish Legation at Vichy, 13 February 1942, NAI.

6 *Ibid.*, 4 March 1942.

7 Arthur Koestler, *The Scum of the Earth* (Eland Publishing, 2012, ebook edition).

8 *Ibid.*

9 Paris Legation files, P49/18 (4), letter from Patrick Sweeney to Irish Legation at Vichy, 6 March 1942, NAI.

10 *Ibid.*, 4 May 1942.

11 *Ibid.*, P49/18, note 6463, Pol from Ministère des Affaires etrangères, direction politique to Irish Legation at Vichy, 9 May 1942, NAI.

12 *Ibid.*, Vichy Legation to Ministère des Affaires etrangères, 11 May 1942.

13 See, for example, list contained in Appendix D of Robert A. Stradling, *The Irish and the Spanish Civil War 1936–1939* (Manchester University Press, 1999).

14 Paris Legation files, P49/18 (4), Ministry of Foreign Affairs note translated and quoted in letter from Irish Legation in Vichy to DEA, Dublin, 20 June 1942, NAI.

15 *Ibid.*, letter from Seán Murphy to DEA, 20 June 1942.

16 *Ibid.*

17 *Ibid.*, letter from DEA to Irish Legation at Vichy, 28 September 1942.

18 *Ibid.*

19 *Ibid.*, P49/21, Vichy Legation to Patrick Sweeney, 22 June 1942, NAI.

20 *Ibid.*, P49/18, letter from Irish Legation at Vichy to Patrick Sweeney, 3 November 1942, NAI.

21 Security Service file, Charles Murphy, NAK KV2/2739.

22 *Ibid.*, interrogation of Charles Murphy, 19 January 1945. A British investigation after the Liberation claimed Murphy was actually given FF60,000, equivalent to almost €17,000 today, a considerable sum when one remembers that Irish nationals were restricted to receiving FF2,640 per month via the Legation.

23 Security Service file, Charles Murphy, NAK KV2/2739.

24 *Ibid.*, Wakefield to Willoughby, 17 April 1947.

25 Knowlson (1996), p. 304.

26 Keogh (1998), p. 164.

27 Noël (1950), p. 42.

28 *Ibid.*, p. 40.

29 See 'Irish Historical Mysteries: The Trade in Joyce Manuscripts', 21 January 2012, homepage.eircom.net/~Seanjmurphy/irhismys/joyce.htm.

30 Mentioned in a copy of a Beckett report (original reference PF 601.715) contained in a report on Gabrielle Cecile (Jeannine) Martinez Picabia, NAK KV2/1313.

31 Knowlson (1996), p. 316.

32 *Ibid.*

33 *Ibid.*, p. 321.

34 Paris Legation files, P49/4, Samuel Beckett to Vichy Legation, 11 October 1942, NAI.

35 *Ibid.*, Samuel Beckett to Con Cremin, undated letter, late 1942.

36 *Ibid.*, P49/17, Samuel Beckett letter to Vichy Legation, 30 June 1943, NAI.

37 *Ibid.*, 17 July 1943.

38 File IIF/54/2/3/2/1 (pt), documents relating to the internment of Sister Mary Anthony, letter from Sister Mary Anthony to Sister Germanus, 29 April 1945, Archives of the Poor Servants of the Mother of God, Brentwood, UK.

39 *Ibid.*

40   'Poor Servants of the Mother of God, Paris 1890–1990', article by Sister Kathleen Grimes contained in St Joseph's church weekly bulletin, 1 July 1990, Archives of the Poor Servants of the Mother of God, Brentwood, UK.

41   File IIF/54/2/1/1/2 (pt), letter from Sister Mary Anthony, January 1945, Archives of the Poor Servants of the Mother of God, Brentwood, UK.

42   File IIG/3/1, '1930 rue Ampère', undated article, Archives of the Poor Servants of the Mother of God, Brentwood, UK.

43   Quoted in 'In Paris the nuns can give a good cup of Irish tea', *The Universe*, July 1969, Archives of the Poor Servants of the Mother of God, Brentwood, UK.

44   File IIF/54/2/1/1/2 (pt), letter from Sister Mary Anthony to Sister Germanus, 29 April 1945, Archives of the Poor Servants of the Mother of God, Brentwood, UK.

45   Paris Legation files, P49/4 (3), postcard to Vichy Legation, 8 April 1942, NAI.

46   *Ibid.*, letter to Vichy Legation, 14 March 1944.

47   *Ibid.*, letter from Murphy to Sister Mary, 5 May 1944.

48   *Ibid.*, P49/3 (3), telegram from Vichy Legation to DEA, 28 December 1942, NAI.

49   *Ibid.*, P49/54–49/85, John Flanagan to Vichy Legation, 8 October 1943, NAI. Other Irish nationals who had been in the Reich passed through Paris. In May 1945 Niall Bonass and Arthur Purtill arrived at the Irish Legation in Paris saying they had been held in prison in Germany. They were each granted passports and subsistence money before continuing their journey home.

50   *Ibid.*, P49/19A–49/32, DEA to Vichy Legation, 15 June 1942, NAI.

51   The lack of ships under an Irish flag was a major concern for the Irish, who could not depend on British merchant vessels to continue supplying needed imports as the war wore on. In July 1942 Seán Murphy was instructed by Dublin to find out whether there were any neutral ships in French ports, or French ships in neutral ports, 'which we might buy or charter from the owners'. See decrypt of intercepted diplomatic communications, 1–31 July 1942, NAK HW 12/278 (107342).

52   Paris Legation files, P49/6 (a)–49/9, Vichy Legation letter to Mary Bennett, 9 March 1944, NAI.

53   *Ibid.*, P49/13 (21)–49/19, DEA to Berlin Legation, 27 October 1942, NAI, letter setting out the logistics of repatriating sixty-six Irishmen who had been working in the Channel Islands until the German invasion and had subsequently been employed in Germany.

54   Secretary's files, Paris series, P12/1, also Paris Legation files, P48/17–48/18, telegram 195, Murphy to DEA, 9 May 1942, NAI.

55   Although Murphy mentioned the concierge being paid off when they left the Legation (see p. 34), a caretaker must have been appointed.

56   Secretary's files, Paris series, P12/1, also Paris Legation files, P48/17–48/18, Murphy to Joseph Walshe, DEA, 22 June 1942.

57   *Ibid.*

58   Travers (1988), p. 448.

59   *Ibid.*, p. 451.

60   *Convertisseur franc-euro: pouvoir d'achat de l'euro et du franc*, https://www. insee.fr/fr/information/2417794.

61   Paris Legation files, P49/12A, Murphy letter to DEA, 7 November 1942, NAI.

62   *Ibid.*, DEA to Vichy Legation, 22 February 1943.

63   *Ibid.*, 21 November 1942.

64   *Ibid.*, P19/34, Vichy Legation to DEA, 22 September 1942, NAI.

65   *Ibid.*, P48/16, also P10/2, 30 June 1943, NAI.

66   *Ibid.*, P19/34, Murphy to Joseph Walshe, DEA, 16 December 1942, NAI.

67   *Ibid.*

68   *Ibid.*

69   Laforcade eventually did change his allegiance to Free France in September 1943.

70   Secretary's files, Paris series, P12/1, coded telegram 763, Joseph Walshe, DEA to Murphy, Vichy Legation, 27 November 1942, NAI.

71   *Ibid.*, Murphy to Walshe, 5 December 1942.

6 Dire Straits

1   Paris Legation files, P49/18 (4), DEA to Vichy Legation, 22 January 1943, NAI.

2   Correspondence with David Sweeney, October 2014.

3   Paris Legation files, P49/18 (4), DEA to Vichy Legation, 22 January 1943, NAI.

4   *Ibid.*, P49/18 B, Vichy Legation to DEA, 29 March 1943, NAI.

5   *Ibid.*, 10 June 1943.

6   *Ibid.*, Vichy to DEA, quoting Warnock letter, 29 July 1943.

7   *Ibid.*, Ministère des Affaires etrangères, section politique, to Vichy Legation, 2 September 1943.

8   Patrick Sweeney file, AC 27 P 7995, BAVCC, Caen.

9   Paris Legation files, P49/18E, Wuillaume undated letter to Vichy Legation, February 1943, NAI.

10   Maurice Rajsfus, *La Police de Vichy. Les forces de l'ordre françaises au service de la Gestapo 1940–1944* (Le Cherche Midi, 1995), p. 213.

11   Paris Legation files, P49/18E, Wuillaume undated letter to Vichy Legation, February 1943, NAI.

12   *Ibid.*

13   Beate Husser, Jean-Pierre Besse and Françoise Leclere-Rosenzweig, *Frontstalag 122, Compiègne-Royallieu: Un camp d'internement allemand dans*

l'Oise, 1943–1944 (Archives départementales de l'Oise, 2008).

14 Paris Legation files, P49/18E, O'Hea to Murphy, 16 March 1943, NAI.
15 *Ibid.*, Murphy to Pierre Laval, 15 April 1943.
16 *Ibid.*, Murphy to O'Hea, 20 April 1944.
17 *Ibid.*, O'Hea to Murphy, 27 April 1944.
18 *Ibid.*, P49/21, Vichy Legation to DEA, 22 April 1942, NAI.
19 *Ibid.*, DEA to Vichy Legation, 5 May 1943.
20 *Ibid.*, P49/15, O'Hara letter to Vichy Legation, 24 July 1943, NAI.
21 *Ibid.*, 4 August 1943.
22 *Ibid.*, 23 September 1943.
23 See Philippe Boiry and Gaëtan de Salvatore, *Paris Auteuil sous les bombes, Septembre 1943* (L'Harmattan, 2000).
24 Paris Legation files, P49/15, O'Hara letter to Vichy Legation, 6 October 1943, NAI.
25 *Ibid.*, 24 October 1943.
26 *Ibid.*, P49/5, Bradish to Vichy Legation, 9 February 1943, NAI.
27 *Ibid.*, P49/4–49/13, 2 March 1944, NAI.
28 *Ibid.*, P49/18, Count O'Kelly to German military administration, 22 November 1940, NAI.
29 *Ibid.*, P49/15, Barrett Brandreth to Vichy Legation, 5 May 1943, NAI.
30 *Ibid.*, Vichy Legation message to DEA, 21 July 1943.
31 *Ibid.*, Barrett Brandreth to Vichy Legation, 24 November 1943.
32 *Ibid.*, P49/13 (13), Rafroidi to Vichy Legation, 30 August 1943, NAI.
33 *Ibid.*, 5 November 1943.
34 *Ibid.*, 26 December 1943.
35 *Ibid.*, P49/13, Murphy to DEA, 21 July 1943, NAI.
36 *Ibid.*, Murphy letter to Charles Brennan, Washington, 24 September 1943.
37 *Ibid.*, P48/16–49/12A, Murphy to DEA, 12 November 1943, NAI.
38 *Ibid.*, P49/32, Finucane to Vichy Legation, 6 May 1943, NAI.
39 *Ibid.*, P49/19, Warnock to Vichy Legation, 16 September 1943, NAI.
40 *Ibid.*, Molly McGrath to Vichy Legation, June 1943.
41 *Ibid.*, P49/32 (10)–49/85, Murphy to DEA, 25 February 1945, NAI.
42 *Ibid.*, Murphy to DEA, 6 April 1945.
43 File IIF/54/2/3/2/1 (pt), letter from Sister Mary Anthony to Sister Germanus, 21 June 1945, Archives of the Poor Servants of the Mother of God, Brentwood, UK.
44 *Ibid.*
45 Paris Legation files, P49/32 (10)–49/85, Murphy to DEA, 10 April 1945, NAI.
46 *Ibid.*, P49/21, Murphy to DEA, 22 October 1943, NAI.
47 *Ibid.*, SSAE to Vichy Legation, 25 November 1943.
48 *Ibid.*, Russo to Vichy Legation, 21 June 1943.
49 *Ibid.*, Vichy Legation to Russo, 5 August 1943.

50 *Ibid.*, Lawrence to Vichy Legation, 6 September 1943.

51 *Ibid.*, 15 September 1943.

52 *Ibid.*, undated letter, September 1943.

53 *Ibid.*, Vichy Legation to G. Koechlin, SSAE, 1 December 1943.

54 Other individuals also helped their compatriots. On at least one occasion, the Benedictine nuns at rue Tournefort in the 6th arrondissement received money from the Archbishop of Dublin and the taoiseach, Éamon de Valera, who in 1941 organised a joint transfer of £20 according to one of the regular lists of remittances.

55 Paris Legation files, P49/3, Turquet to Vichy Legation, 23 July 1943, NAI.

56 *Ibid.*, P49/12A–15, letter (undated) from Whyte to Murphy, Vichy Legation, October 1943, NAI.

57 *Ibid.*, Murphy to Whyte, 3 November 1943.

58 *Ibid.*, Whyte to Murphy, 9 November 1943.

59 *Ibid.*, P48/18–49/3, handwritten notes of conversation between Count O'Kelly and Cremin, 16 January 1941, NAI.

60 *Ibid.*, P49/21 (10), Stephen Rice to Murphy, undated letter (received 4 June 1943), NAI.

61 *Ibid.*, P49/18, Rice to Murphy, 15 June 1943, NAI.

62 *Ibid.*, P49/21, Rice to Murphy, 28 October 1943, NAI.

63 *Ibid.*, Brandt, SSAE, to Murphy, 23 July 1943.

64 *Ibid.*, Brandt, SSAE, to Cremin, 13 August 1943.

65 *Ibid.*, Rice to Vichy Legation, letter received 26 August 1943.

66 *Ibid.*, Koechlin, SSAE, to Cremin, 28 August 1943.

67 *Ibid.*, Rice to Murphy, 28 October 1943.

68 Chase Bank remained in business in Paris throughout the Occupation. According to Fabrizio Calvi, the bank 'enabled the laundering in the U.S. of huge amounts of money linked to the spoliation of property belonging to Jews and victims of the Holocaust'. See *1944 – Débarquements, Résistances, Libérations, Le Monde*, hors-série (May–July 2014), p. 75.

69 Paris Legation files, P49/21, SSAE to Vichy Legation, 25 November 1943, NAI.

70 *Ibid.*, P49/18 (8), DEA to Vichy Legation, 8 May 1944, NAI.

71 *Ibid.*, P49/3 (2), Vichy Legation to DEA, 26 May 1943, NAI.

72 *Ibid.*, P49/17, Hennessy to Vichy Legation, 27 January 1944, NAI.

73 *Ibid.*, P49/18 (8), Dubosq to Vichy Legation, 14 April 1943, NAI.

74 *Ibid.*, P49/9 (4)–49/12 (15), Brennan to Vichy Legation (letter undated), NAI.

75 *Ibid.*, P49/20 (bis), letter from German consulate to Vichy Legation, 13 July 1943, NAI.

76 *Ibid.*, P49/13 (21)–49/19, Berlin Legation to DEA, 18 October 1943, NAI.

77 *Ibid.*, Gallagher Declaration of Nationality, dated 22 April 1944.

78 Escape and Evasion Reports 1942–1945, E&E 31, Iva Lee Fegette and

William A. Whitman, https://catalog.archives.gov/id/5554673, National Archives and Records Administration (NARA), Washington DC.

79 Escape and Evasion Reports 1942–1945, E&E 103, N. Allen Robinson, https://catalog.archives.gov/id/5554743, NARA, Washington DC.

80 Témoignage de M. Pierre Robert (Réseau Comète), Archives nationales, Pierrefitte-sur-Seine, file 72AJ/45.

81 Témoignage de Mme Barbier-Campbell, dite Marie Ange ou Elisabeth, recueilli par Mlle. Patrimonio le 12/3/1946 (Réseau Vaneau), Archives nationales, Pierrefitte-sur-Seine, file 72AJ/81/II Pièce 3. Records of Headquarters, European Theater of Operations, United States Army (World War II), case files relating to French citizens proposed for awards for assisting American Airmen, compiled 1945–1947, Record Group 498: Elisabeth Barbier, Box 919, NARA, Washington DC.

82 Escape report SPG 1665, Clarence Howard Witheridge, www.cometeline.org/fiche230.html.

83 Case files relating to French citizens, Record Group 498, Jean and Lucienne Bodin, Box 935, NARA, Washington DC.

84 Escape and Evasion Reports 1942–1945, E&E 355, Sidney Casden, https://catalog.archives.gov/id/5554995, NARA, Washington DC.

85 Case files relating to French citizens, Record Group 498, Janie McCarthy, Box 1097@290: 55/30/5, NARA, Washington DC.

86 *Ibid.*, Pierre and Marie-Thérèse Labadie, Box 1065, NARA, Washington DC.

87 *Ibid.*, Frank Bulfield, Box 949, NARA, Washington DC.

88 *Ibid.*, Jean and Lucienne Bodin, Box 935, NARA, Washington DC.

89 *Ibid.*

90 Paris Legation files, P49/8, handwritten note for transmission to Dublin, November 1943, NAI.

91 Government code and cypher school, decrypt of intercepted diplomatic communications, 1–31 August 1944, NAK HW 12/303/4.

92 Government code and cypher school, diplomatic section and predecessors, decryption of intercepted diplomatic communications (BJ series), September 1944, NAK HW 12/304/8 (Ireland 136384, 136134).

93 Letter from an anonymous Dutchman to Madame Debrabant, primary school teacher in Douai, 31 May 1945, contained in file for Robert Armstrong AC 27 P 8898, BAVCC, Caen.

94 William O'Connor AC 21 P 606 328, BAVCC, Caen.

95 William O'Connor 18 P 44 8836, SHD, Vincennes.

96 Dubliner Mary Cummins, another Irish *résistante* active in Belgium, also ended up in Ravensbrück. Cummins appears to have been repatriated via Paris in spring 1945 and may have spent time at the Irish convent in rue Murillo. Sister Mary Anthony mentions in a letter from June 1945 that an Irish girl who had spent years in a German prison camp had arrived.

'From Belgium she was taken. Most of her companions died or were shot. Mr Cremin (of the Irish Legation) told her to come here when she would arrive in Paris.' (File IIF/54/2/3/2/1, letter from Sister Mary Anthony to Sister Germanus, 21 June 1945, Archives of the Poor Servants of the Mother of God, Brentwood, UK). Cummins was the subject of an RTÉ radio documentary in January 1993, 'In the Shadow of Death'.

97 File for Katherine Anne McCarthy, 16 P 381550, SHD, Vincennes.

98 *Ibid.*

7 Darkness before the Dawn

1 Secretary's files, Paris series, P12/1, Murphy to DEA, 22 August 1943, NAI.

2 *Ibid.,* Vichy Legation telegram to DEA, 1 February 1944.

3 *Ibid.,* Walshe to Vichy Legation, 6 January 1944.

4 *Ibid.,* P19/34, Vichy Legation to DEA, 2 June 1943 and P49/9, Vichy Legation to DEA, 19 June 1943, NAI.

5 *Ibid,* P100/2, Murphy to Service de Protocole de l'Etat Français, 30 December 1943, NAI.

6 *Ibid.,* letter from the Service de Protocole de l'Etat Français to the Irish Legation, 18 February 1944.

7 Mémorial de l'internement et de la déportation, Camp de Royallieu. List des convois, www.memorial-compiegne.fr/iso_album/14._convoi_du_17_janvier_1944.pdf.

8 *Neuzugänge vom 19 January 1944,* List of new arrivals at Buchenwald from various locations, Doc. 5267739#1, International Tracing Service (ITS) archives, Bad Arolsen, Germany.

9 Registration card for Patrick Sweeney, 19 January 1944. Doc. 72233730#1, ITS archives, Bad Arolsen, Germany.

10 Prisoners of War, Germany: Ilag VIII, Tost; Ilag VIIIZ, Kreuzberg; Ilag Lebebau; Ilag Biberach, NAK WO 361/1849.

11 Paris Legation files, P2/9, Vichy Legation to Atkinson, 18 September 1940, NAI.

12 *Ibid.,* 2 October 1940.

13 Government code and cypher school, diplomatic section and predecessors, decryption of intercepted diplomatic communications (BJ series), May 1944, NAK HW 12/300/12.

14 Letter from Frank Fulham, HM Consul General, Berlin to Central Tracing Bureau, British Army of the Rhine (BAOR), 21 January 1947, Cecil Atkinson file, ITS archives, Bad Arolsen, Germany.

15 *Ibid.*

16 *Ibid.*

17 Paris Legation files, P49/21, SSAE to Vichy Legation, 22 February 1944, NAI.

18 *Ibid.,* Rice to Vichy Legation, 29 April 1944.

19   *Ibid.*, SSAE to Vichy Legation, 4 May 1944.

20   *Ibid.*, Rice to Vichy Legation, 20 June 1944.

21   *Ibid.*, 18 July 1944.

22   'Playboy Who Set Europe Talking', unknown British newspaper report, dated 1 January 1946, Gloria Swanson papers held at the University of Texas, Austin (supplied by Tricia Welsch, Professor of Cinema Studies, Bowdoin College, Brunswick, Maine).

23   'The Man that Gloria married', *Photoplay Magazine*, February 1932, p. 29.

24   'Retire? Gloria Swanson wouldn't think of it!', *Motion Picture,* May–June 1933, p. 83.

25   Rowland V. Lee, 'Adventures of a Film Director' (unpublished manuscript, copyright American Film Institute, 1970), p. 333.

26   Matthew Sweet, *Shepperton Babylon: The Lost Worlds of British Cinema* (Faber & Faber, 2005), p. 124.

27   Stephen Michael Shearer, *Gloria Swanson: The Ultimate Star* (Thomas Dunne Books, 2013), p. 272.

28   Writing to a friend from the bar at the Ritz Hotel in Paris in 1945, Farmer gave his slightly different version of events. He had been living in Biarritz until August 1940, when he was forced out by the Germans. He travelled to Cannes in the *zone libre* but was thrown out of there after he refused to shake the hand of the local Italian consul, Signor Giglioni. He went to Marseille, where his attempts to arrange a US visa and a Clipper ticket across the Atlantic came to nothing. While in Marseille, he became involved in the famous brawl in the Hôtel des Noailles in August 1941. See Shearer (2013), p. 306.

29   'Playboy Who Set Europe Talking', 1 January 1946.

30   Dossier judiciaire Michael Farmer, 184 W 160, Archives départementales de la Haute-Vienne, Limoges.

31   Paris Legation files, P49/18 (5), DEA note to Paris Legation, 28 July 1945, NAI.

32   Dossier judiciaire Michael Farmer, 184 W 160, Archives départementales de la Haute-Vienne, Limoges.

33   *Ibid.*

34   Grégory Auda, *Les Belles Années du Milieu* (Editions Michalon, 2013), p. 169.

35   Dossier judiciaire Michael Farmer, 184 W 160, Archives départementales de la Haute-Vienne, Limoges.

36   Paris Legation files, P49/12, letter from O'Hara to Vichy Legation, 1 March 1944, NAI.

37   *Ibid.*, P49/13 (12), O'Hara to Vichy Legation, 23 June 1944, NAI.

38   Travers (1988), p. 452.

39   Paris Legation files, P49/4 (4), Vichy Legation to DEA, 4 February 1943, NAI.

40 *Ibid.*, Section politique, Ministère des Affaires etrangères to Vichy Legation, 4 March 1944.

41 *Ibid.*, Fr Travers to Vichy Legation, 7 March 1944.

42 *Ibid.*, Section politique, Ministère des Affaires etrangères to Vichy Legation, 21 April 1944.

43 *Ibid.*, telegram from Vichy Legation to DEA, 23 May 1944.

44 *Ibid.*, letter from Travers to Seán Murphy at Vichy Legation, 25 May 1944.

45 *Ibid.*, P48/2, Murphy to DEA, 1 May 1944, NAI.

46 *Ibid.*, Murphy to DEA, 9 May 1944.

47 Murphy to Walshe, 26 May 1944, Government code and cypher school, diplomatic section and predecessors, decryption of intercepted diplomatic communications (BJ series), May 1944 (decrypt 131938), NAK HW 12/300/20.

48 Paris Legation files, P48/2, Murphy to DEA, 9 May 1944, NAI.

49 Davidson, Robert and Starling, T P., Prisoners of War Section. Escape/ Evasion Reports: Code MI9/SPG: 2345, NAK WO 208/3322/95.

50 'An Irish Club in Paris', *Irish Independent*, 6 October 1956.

51 'Irish heroes of the French Resistance', *The Sunday Business Post*, 22 July 2001.

52 Paris Legation files, P49/12 (16)–49/13 (17), handwritten note from Agnes Hannigan to the Vichy Legation, undated, NAI.

53 Travers (1988), p. 452. Paris Legation files, P48/18, Murphy to DEA, 8 June 1944, NAI.

54 Dossier Hans Gechter, Archives Nationales, Pierrefitte-sur-Seine, AJ/40/580.

55 Paris Legation files, P49/9, Count O'Kelly letter to Philippe Henriot, 28 March 1944, NAI.

56 Letter of 20 January 1944, Archives nationales, Pierrefitte-sur-Seine, file AJ/40/720 (1415) – Expert Publicité Internationale (EPI).

57 Paris Legation files, P100, note from Service de Protocole to Vichy Legation, 22 June 1944, NAI.

58 *Ibid.*, P49/21 (10), DEA to Vichy Legation, 4 August 1944, NAI.

59 *Ibid.*, P49/12, Whyte to Vichy Legation, 16 August 1944, NAI.

60 Perry (1985), p. 138.

61 *Ibid.*

62 Travers (1988), p. 453.

63 *Ibid.*

64 Dossier judiciaire Michael Farmer, 184 W 160, Archives départmentales de la Haute-Vienne, Limoges.

65 During the war, Edith Piaf lived in an apartment above a high-class brothel on rue de Villejust, the same street as the Irish Legation. See Robert Belleret, *Piaf: Un mythe français* (Fayard, 2013).

66 Dossier judiciaire Michael Farmer, 184 W 160, Archives départementales de la Haute-Vienne, Limoges.

67 *Ibid.*

68 *Ibid.*

69 *Ibid.*

70 'Playboy Who Set Europe Talking', 1 January 1946.

71 Paris Legation files, P10/92, also P43/48, DEA to Paris Legation, 15 August 1939, NAI.

72 Police files for Denis Corr and Marie-Louise Corr, 77 W 89 and 77 W 99, Archives départementales des Pyrénées-Atlantiques, Pau.

73 Police file for Marie-Louise Corr, 77 W 99, Archives départementales des Pyrénées-Atlantiques, Pau.

74 *Ibid.*

75 *Ibid.*

76 Paris Legation files, P1/5 (2) C, Paris Legation to DEA, 20 April 1945, NAI.

77 Cour de Justice du Département des Basses-Pyrenees, Deliberation of 12 December 1945, 1257 W9, Archives départementales des Pyrénées-Atlantiques, Pau. In April 1945 the Irish Legation had mentioned that the case against him was that he had 'belonged to an information network which operated under German control'.

78 Police file for Denis Corr, 77 W 89, Archives départementales des Pyrénées-Atlantiques, Pau.

79 Cours de Justice du Département de la Seine: Dossiers de procédure contre Michel Dassonville, Archives Nationales, Pierrefitte-sur-Seine: a) Z/6/822-823 dossier 5691; b) Z/6/895.

80 Citation dated 31 March 1945 contained in Samuel Beckett's file, 16 P 42711, Bureau Résistance et Seconde guerre mondiale, SHD, Vincennes.

81 Letter to Gwynedd Reavey, 21 June 1945, in Fehsenfeld *et al.* (2011), p. 15.

82 Letter to George Reavey, 31 October 1945, in *Ibid.*, p. 24.

83 Quoted in Eoin O'Brien, *The Beckett Country* (The Black Cat Press, 1986), pp. 326–7.

84 Letter to Prunella Clough, 19 September 1942, in Caroline Constant, *Eileen Grey* (Phaidon, 2000), p. 161.

85 Peter Adam, *Eileen Grey, Architect, Designer: A Biography* (Thames & Hudson, 2000), p. 323.

86 Letter from Algiers government to French Legation in Dublin, decrypt of intercepted diplomatic communications, 1–31 August 1944, NAK HW 12/303/4 (135497).

87 Message from Marie-François Laforcade, French minister to Ireland, to Algiers, decrypt of intercepted diplomatic communications, 1–31 August 1944, NAK HW 12/303/4 (135724).

88 Keogh (1989), p. 184.

89 Robert Patterson, 'Ireland, Vichy and Post-Liberation France, 1938–1950', in Kennedy and Skelly (2000), p. 113.

90 Paris Legation files, P49/21 (10), Murphy to DEA, 6 February 1945, NAI.

91 *Ibid.*, Rice to Denis McDonald, 14 January 1945.

8 Helping Jews

1   Paris Legation files, P2/9, Rynne to Murphy, 20 August 1939, NAI.

2   *Ibid.*, Count O'Kelly to Murphy, 22 October 1940.

3   *Ibid.*, Vichy Legation to René Rothschild, 11 November 1940.

4   *Ibid.*, letter from René Rothschild to Vichy Legation, 4 January 1941.

5   *L'Ami du Peuple*, 04/1932–06/1932, MICR D–10033, Bibliothèque Nationale de France, Paris.

6   *Ibid.*

7   *Ibid.*

8   Paris Legation files, P33–34/2, Count O'Kelly to Vichy Legation, 22 November 1940, NAI. Herbert Briscoe served his commercial apprenticeship in Wilhelmine Berlin before going to the United States, where he first worked as a salesman and then ran a business that imported light bulbs. He and his brother Wolfe ran the Briscoe Importing Company in Dublin and then a succession of businesses in continental Europe between the world wars. See Robert Briscoe, *For the Life of Me* (Longmans, 1958).

9   *Ibid.*, P49/4, Marie Bloch to Legation, 4 January 1941, NAI.

10 *Ibid.*, P19/34, Murphy to DEA, 29 August 1940, NAI.

11 *Ibid.*, P48/17, Murphy to Walshe, 18 August 1942, NAI.

12 *Ibid.*, 25 September 1942.

13 Quoted in Serge Klarsfeld, *Vichy–Auschwitz: Le rôle de Vichy dans la solution finale de la question juive en France, 1942* (Fayard, 1983), p. 108.

14 Secretary's files, Paris series, P12/1, Murphy to DEA, 23 August 1943, NAI.

15 Dermot Keogh, 'La neutralité irlandaise, la Shoah et la Seconde Guerre Mondiale' part of 'Les neutres européens face au Génocide', in *Revue d'Histoire de la Shoah*, n. 203, October 2015.

16 Department of Foreign Affairs files, P419/44, telegram (n. 869) from DEA to Vichy Legation, 18 December 1943, NAI.

17 Berlin Legation files, Cremin to Walshe, Department of Foreign Affairs file 419/44, quoted in Crowe *et al.* (eds), *Documents in Irish Foreign Policy vol. VI (1941–1945)* (Royal Irish Academy, 2010), p. 405.

18 Cremin to Walshe, 5 July 1944, Government code and cypher school, diplomatic section and predecessors, decryption of intercepted diplomatic communications (BJ series), July 1944, NAK HW 12/302/7 (decrypt 133385).

19 'Repatriates return home – stories of internment conditions under the

Nazis', *The Manchester Guardian*, 11 September 1944, quoted in Keogh (1998), p. 185.

20 Paris Legation files, P49/20 (1), letter from Sophie Philipson to Vichy Legation, 29 November 1943, NAI.

21 Keogh (1998), p. 162.

22 Paris Legation files, P49/20 (1), DEA to Irish Legation Vichy, 26 February 1944, NAI.

23 *Ibid.*, DEA to Vichy Legation, 27 March 1944.

24 *Ibid.*, Durant letter received by Vichy Legation on 11 February 1944.

25 *Ibid.*, note of interview with Aline Rilly, signed Denis McDonald, 28 February 1944.

26 Fichier du camp de Drancy, Sophie and Rachel Philipson, F/9/5720, Mémorial de la Shoah, Paris.

27 'Serge Philipson – an Appreciation', *The Irish Times*, 22 October 1988.

28 Paris Legation files, P49/20 (1), Irish Legation Vichy to Bloch, 2 March 1944, reply received from Judenlager Drancy on 8 March 1944, NAI.

29 Fichier du camp de Drancy, Clara and Anna Bloch, F/9/5681, Mémorial de la Shoah, Paris.

9 The Skies Brighten ... for Some

1 Paris Legation files, P19/34, also P16/45, Murphy to DEA, 18 January 1945, NAI.

2 Bernard Adams, *Denis Johnston: A Life* (The Lilliput Press, 2002), p. 269.

3 Paris Legation files, P49/13, Whyte to Irish Legation Paris, 19 January 1945, NAI.

4 *Ibid.*, P49/13 (10), DEA to Paris Legation, 5 March 1945, NAI.

5 *Ibid.*, Paris Legation to Whyte, 10 March 1945.

6 *Ibid.*, Whyte to Irish Legation Paris, 27 February 1946.

7 Security Service file, Desmond Patrick Nolan, NAK KV2/6349.

8 *Ibid.*

9 'McCarthy, Miss Janie', *The Kerryman*, Golden Jubilee supplement, 11 December 1954, p. 52.

10 Citation supplied by the Grande Chancellerie de l'Ordre de la Libération, Paris.

11 Case files relating to French citizens, Record Group 498, Janie McCarthy, Box 1097@290: 55/30/5 NARA, Washington DC.

12 *Ibid.*

13 Secretary's files, Paris series, P97, Murphy to DEA, 26 March 1945, NAI.

14 'Report on Skirmishes on VE Day, including Breaking of Window at Jammet's', *The Irish Times*, 9 May 1945.

15 Secretary's files, Paris series, P12/1, Joseph Walshe to Murphy, Paris Legation, 24 May 1945, NAI.

16 'Social & Personal', *The Irish Times*, 2 June 1945.

17 Secretary's files, Paris series, P12/1, Walshe to Murphy, 7 June 1945, NAI.

18 *Ibid.*

19 File IIF/54/2/3/2/1 (pt), letter from Sister Mary Anthony to Sister Germanus, 21 June 1945, Archives of the Poor Servants of the Mother of God, Brentwood, UK.

20 Paris Legation files, P49/21, Bonasse to Paris Legation, 12 July 1946, NAI.

21 *Ibid.*, Doyle to Paris Legation, 2 September 1946.

22 *Ibid.*, Sr Mary Anthony Leahy to Paris Legation, 27 November 1946.

23 *Ibid.*, Comerford to Paris Legation, 23 July 1946.

24 *Ibid.*, Paris Legation to Comerford, 24 September 1946.

25 Travers (1988), p. 454.

26 *Ibid.*

27 Breton nationalist and German intelligence service operative Guy Vissault de Coëtlogon mentioned during his 1944 interrogation by the British that he 'thought' he had seen Stuart 'at an Irish meeting held at the Cité Universitaire, Paris in 1939'. Security service file, Guy Vissault de Coëtlogon, NAK KV2/303.

28 Paris Legation files, P49/5, O'Mara to Paris Legation, undated note, June 1945, NAI.

29 Róisín Ní Mheara, *Recollections* (Xlibris, 2015 ebook edition).

30 Francis Stuart, *Black List, Section H* (The Lilliput Press, 1995), p. 386.

31 Ní Mheara (2015), Kindle ebook location 2336.

32 Stuart diaries, University of Ulster, Coleraine, entry for 15 August 1945.

33 Kevin Kiely, *Francis Stuart, Artist and Outcast* (The Liffey Press, 2007), p. 75.

34 Stuart diaries, University of Ulster, Coleraine, entry for 25 August 1945.

35 Stuart (1995), p. 380.

36 Geoffrey Elborn, *Francis Stuart: A Life* (Raven Arts Press, 1990), p. 181.

37 Stuart diaries, University of Ulster, Coleraine, entries for 23 August 1942 and 30 June 1944.

38 Stuart (1995), p. 387.

39 Stuart diaries, University of Ulster, Coleraine, entry for 24 August 1945.

40 *Ibid.*, entry for 27 September 1945.

41 Stuart (1995), pp. 383–8.

42 Paris Legation files, P49/17, DEA to Murphy, Paris Legation, 26 April 1945, NAI.

43 *Ibid.*, Paris Legation to DEA, April–May 1945.

44 *Ibid.*, P49/13 (13), Rafroidi to Paris Legation, 1 February 1946, NAI.

45 *Ibid.*, P49/13 (12), letter from O'Hara to Paris Legation, 10 October 1945, NAI.

46 *Ibid.*, letter from Paris Legation to DEA, 18 October 1945.

47 Case files relating to French citizens, Record Group 498, Fr Kenneth Monaghan, Box 1115@290: 55/31/1, NARA, Washington DC.

48 *Ibid.*

49 'Catholics Give Party to 500 German Children', *Catholic Herald*, 31 December 1948.

50 Maddox (1988), p. 365.

51 There is much debate as to whether the remains brought back to Ireland were Yeats's. See 'Yeats: papers confirm bones sent back to Sligo were not poet's', *The Irish Times*, 18 July 2015, www.irishtimes.com/news/ireland/irish-news/yeats-papers-confirm-bones-sent-to-sligo-were-not-poet-s-1.2288662.

52 Henry O'Byrne (related to O'Kelly via the latter's mother, Mary O'Byrne), who spent the period 1942–1950 in Paris, also relates that the count used his position in Paris to communicate with the Intelligence Service. Email exchange with the author, 28 January 2013.

53 Vendôme Wines 277.602 B, 277.650 B, D33U3 1348, Registre de commerce, Archives de Paris.

54 Anthony Beevor, *Paris after the Liberation 1944–1949* (Penguin Books, 2007), p. 154.

55 Paris Legation files, P100/10–102/15, Count O'Kelly letter to Paris Legation, 24 July 1951, NAI.

56 *Ibid.*, O'Kelly to Cremin, 21 January 1951.

57 *Ibid.*, O'Kelly to Con Cremin, 24 July 1951.

58 'Worst Paid Diplomat', *Irish Independent*, 5 January 1968.

59 Department of the Taoiseach, private office records, S 12639 B, O'Kelly memo to Hugh McCann, 1 October 1965, NAI.

60 'I call you today from Dublin', William Hickey column, *Daily Express*, 5 August 1965.

61 Conversation with Count O'Kelly's nephew, Brendan O'Kelly, Connecticut, April 2013.

BIBLIOGRAPHY

PRIMARY SOURCES

IRELAND
National Archives of Ireland (NAI), Dublin
Quotations from files of the Department of Foreign Affairs (DFA) – previously the Department of External Affairs (DEA) – at the National Archives in Dublin have not all been separately referenced, but parameters for finding the various boxes of material held at the archives are provided below.

Paris Legation files (P series)
Within the P series, there are fifty sub-series covering the period 1932 to 1945 and designated P1 to P50. The sub-series files most consulted were: P1/9–P1/10; P2/9–10; P2/22; P12/1–12/3 (Secretary's files, including communications between DEA and Vichy); P13; P17/22 (Credentials and appointments); P19/34 (including P19/34A, confidential report from Seán Murphy to Joseph Walshe, 18 June 1940); P20/3; P21/9; P33/3–34/2; P33/13; P33/17; P46/15–P48/17 (including P48/17, letter from Seán Murphy to Joseph Walshe, 18 August 1942); P48/18–49/3 (including message from Murphy to Walshe, August 1940); P49/3 (2)–49/4; P49/5–49/6; P49/6 (a)–49/9; P49/9 (4)–49/12 (15); P49/12 (16)–49/13 (17); P49/13 (21)–49/19 (30); P49/22; P49/25; P49/32 (9); P49/86–50/4; P100–105 (including files for 100/2 [Count O'Kelly], 100/5 [staff 1941–1952] and 100/9 [Ina Foley]); P107/1–108/1 (including repatriation files); P118/2 (SS *Luimneach*, 1940–1948); P141H (Louise Froc, 1931–1938); P141T (Lucienne Marquetout, 1936–1940); P141F (Ina Foley, 1939–1940); P143, 122/19–324/24 (J. F. Keane); P106/3–12; P118/119 (Death of Count O'Kelly de Gallagh).

Department of Foreign Affairs files
Letter books Berlin, 1940–1941 and 1942–1944

Department of the Taoiseach, private office records
O'Kelly de Gallagh files (restricted) S 5734 A; S 5735 A; S 12639 B (1935), B067, 15106, 2149, 2159 (1960s)

Trinity College Dublin, Manuscripts & Archives Research Library
Denis Johnston diaries & notebooks, 10066/57–246

University College Dublin Archives
Papers of Éamon de Valera (1882–1975), IE UCDA P150

FRANCE

Archives de Paris
Prison records for Stephen Rice
Prison de la Santé, D 2Y14
D Y14/301 registre d'écrou
3136 W 1 mises en liberté

Registre de commerce
Expert Publicité Internationale (EPI) 217.514B, D31U3 1298
Vendôme Wines 277.602 B, 277.650 B, D33U3 1348

Archives départementales de l'Ariège, Foix
5W 128 Le Vernet/organisation, fichier

Archives départementales de la Haute-Vienne, Limoges
Dossier judiciaire Michael Farmer, 184 W 160
Registre d'écrou Michael Farmer, 2293 W 9

Archives départementales des Basses-Pyréneées, Perpignan
Fichier du camp d'Argelès, 1260 W 51

Archives départementales des Pyrénées-Atlantique, Pau
Cour de Justice du Département des Basses–Pyrénées
Arrêt du 12 décembre 1945 concernant Denis Corr, 1257 W 9
Police files for: Denis Corr, 77 W 89; Marie-Louise Corr, 77 W 99
Deliberation of 12 December 1945, 1257 W9

Archives Nationales, Pierrefitte-sur-Seine
Sous série AJ/40: Archives allemandes de la Seconde Guerre mondiale
AJ/40 579–773: Rapports au Militarbefëhlshaber in Frankreich; Division Wi. I
    Allgemeine Wirtschaftsangelegenheiten
AJ/40/580: Dossier Hans Gechter
AJ/40/680 (611): Vendôme Wines
AJ/40/720 (1415): Expert Publicité Internationale (EPI)

Sous série 72/AJ Archives du Comité d'Histoire de la Deuxième Guerre mondiale,
fonds privés et documents divers relatifs à la période 1939–1945, 72AJ/35–72AJ/89
Résistance intérieure
72AJ/45/IV: témoignage de M. Pierre Robert (Réseau Comète)

72AJ/80/VIII: rapport Marie-Rose Zerling dite 'Claudette' (Réseau Shelburn)
72AJ/81/II Pièce 3: témoignage de Mme Barbier-Campbell, dite Marie Ange ou Elisabeth (Réseau Vaneau)
72AJ/81/II/Pièce 7: témoignage de M. Paul Maury, dit Henri (Réseau Vaneau)
618/MI/1–3 Prisons françaises, prisons allemandes: fichiers et dossiers des internés, 1939–1945
'Prison de Fresnes, classement alphabétique du nom d'interné' – Service central d'identification et sûreté nationale, 1888–1944
Z/6 – Cours de Justice du Département de la Seine
Dossiers de procédure contre Michel Dassonville: a) Z/6/822–823 dossier 5691; b) Z/6/895
Fonds bleuet, October 1948–October 1949, Compte rendu de l'audience de la Cour de Justice de la Seine, 22 décembre 1948; 334AP/29 (Dassonville)
Judicial files for Suzanne Laurent (née Renouf): Z/6/862–863, dossier 5790
3W/77–3W/105, Haute Cour de Justice, Vol. 2
Depositions d'Helmut Knochen 1131–1135, dossier Helmut Knochen, ancien chef du SD en France

Bibliothèque Nationale de France, Paris
La Gazette de l'Hôtel Drouot, 1940–1944
MFilm Fol–V–2712 Annuaire du Commerce Didot-Bottin (1943), site François Mitterrand, under reference M18000–788, T2/2 (Paris professions) (bobine 788 = 1943)
L'Ami du Peuple, 04/1932–06/1932, MICR D–10033

Bureau des Archives des victimes des conflits contemporains (BAVCC), Caen
Robert Armstrong, AC 27 P 8898; Cecil Atkinson, AC 27 P 8910; Mary Cummins, AC 27 P 2506; Agnes Flanagan, AC 27 P 3466; William O'Connor, AC 21 P 606 328; Patrick Sweeney, AC 27 P 7995; Robert Vernon, AC 21 P 547 361

Grande Chancellerie de l'Ordre de la Libération, Paris
Janie McCarthy citation, décret du 24 avril 1946, Journal officiel du 17 mai 1946

Mémorial de la Shoah, Paris
Fichier du camp de Drancy
Clara and Anna Bloch, F/9/5681
Paul Leen (Léon), F/9/5710
Famille Orbach, F/9/5719
Sophie and Rachel Philipson, F/9/5720
Cahier de mutation du camp de Drancy du 28/1/1944 au 11/08/1944, F/9/5785

Service historique de la Défense (SHD), Vincennes
Bureau Résistance et Seconde guerre mondiale:
Dossiers administratifs de résistants: Robert Armstrong, 16 P 17321; Samuel Beckett, 16 P 42711; Katherine Anne McCarthy, 16 P 381550; Janie McCarthy, 16 P 381551; William O'Connor, 18 P 44 8836; John Pilkington, 16 P 478119; Robert Vernon, 16 P 590803
Section spéciale Allemagne de la DGER, GR 28 P7 (Abwehr dossiers 164 and 165)

UNITED KINGDOM
Archives of the Poor Servants of the Mother of God, Brentwood, Middlesex
IIF/54/2/3/2/1 (pt), Documents relating to the internment of Sister Mary Anthony
IIF/54/2/1/1/2 (pt), Letters from Sister Mary Anthony, Sister M. Loyola, Sister M. Kevin, Sister M. Bernarde, 1944–5
III (Paris) (42), Letter from the Archdiocese of Paris, February 1944
IIG/3/1, '1930 rue Ampère', undated article
'Poor Servants of the Mother of God, Paris 1890–1990', article by Sister Kathleen Grimes contained in St Joseph's church weekly bulletin, 1 July 1990

National Archives, Kew
Admiralty file, ADM 1/10902
CRIM 4/1745, Defendant: Hilton, Dorothea May Theresa. Charge: Doing an act likely to assist the enemy, 8 January 1946
FO 371/2/2942, correspondence between Lord Halifax and Lord Granard, December 1939
FO 561/123, British Societies and Institutions, St Joseph's church, British Embassy Paris files
HW 12/278 (107342), decrypt of intercepted diplomatic communications, 1–31 July 1942
HW 12/300/12 (decrypt 131938), Government code and cypher school, diplomatic section and predecessors, decryption of intercepted diplomatic communications (BJ series), May 1944
HW 12/300/20, Government code and cypher school, diplomatic section and predecessors, decryption of intercepted diplomatic communications (BJ series), May 1944
HW 12/302/7 (decrypt 133385), Government code and cypher school, diplomatic section and predecessors, decryption of intercepted diplomatic communications (BJ series), July 1944
HW 12/303/4, Government code and cypher school, decrypt of intercepted diplomatic communications, 1–31 August 1944
HW 12/304/8 (Ireland 136384, 136134), Government code and cypher school,

diplomatic section and predecessors, decryption of intercepted diplomatic communications (BJ series), September 1944

KV2/303, Guy Vissault de Coëtlogon (also KV2/301)

KV2/423, Susan Hilton, Security Service personal file (pf series), statement to British interrogators, 1 July 1945

KV2/769, Kurt Haller (incl. statements by John P. O'Reilly and Frank Stringer)

KV2/1292, Frank Ryan

KV2/1313, Beckett report (original reference PF 601.715) contained in Security Service report on Gabrielle Cecile (Jeannine) Martinez Picabia

KV2/2739, Charles Murphy

KV2/6347 and KV2/6349, Desmond Patrick Nolan

KV4/8, report on the operations of Camp 020 and Camp 020–R (B1E) in connection with the interrogation of enemy agents during the Second World War (Joseph Lenihan)

KV4/14, 'A Digest of Ham – Volume Two'

KV4/14 and KV4/60920, Joseph Lenihan

KV4/190, Guy Liddell diary, Security Service Policy (Pol F series)

SPG KV23314/1298, Brian Desmond Barker, www.cometeline.org/ficheD370.html, www.evasioncomete.org/fbarkerbd.html

SPG 1665, Clarence Howard Witheridge, www.cometeline.org/fiche230.html

WO 208/3308, escape reports for Bill McGrath and Oliver James

WO 208/3322/95, Davidson, Robert and Starling, T P., Prisoners of War Section. Escape/Evasion Reports: Code MI9/SPG: 2345

WO 339/1448, Count O'Kelly de Gallagh war service record

WO 361/1849, Prisoners of War, Germany: Ilag VIII, Tost; Ilag VIIIZ, Kreuzberg; Ilag Lebebau; Ilag Biberach

University of Ulster, Coleraine, Co. Londonderry

Francis Stuart diaries

UNITED STATES OF AMERICA
National Archives and Records Administration (NARA), Washington DC

Record Group 498: Records of Headquarters, European Theater of Operations, United States Army (World War II); Escape and Evasion Reports 1942–1945 (MIS-X), https://catalog.archives.gov/id/305270

E&E 16, John W. Spence, https://catalog.archives.gov/id/5554658

E&E 31, Iva Lee Fegette and William A. Whitman, https://catalog.archives.gov/id/5554673

E&E 47 Arthur B. Cox (reference to Robert Armstrong), https://catalog.archives.gov/id/5554687

E&E 103, N. Allen Robinson, https://catalog.archives.gov/id/5554743

E&E 355, Sidney Casden, https://catalog.archives.gov/id/5554995

Records of Headquarters, European Theater of Operations, United States Army (Record Group 498), Case files relating to French citizens proposed for assisting American Airmen, compiled 1945–1947
ARC Identifier 5682722/MLR Number UD 193
Box 912: Robert Armstrong
Box 919: Elisabeth Barbier
Box 935: Jean and Lucienne Bodin
Box 935: Natacha Boeg
Box 949: Frank Bulfield
Box 1065: Pierre and Marie-Thérèse Labadie
Box 1097@290, 55/30/5: Miss Janie McCarthy
Box 1115@290, 55/31/1: Fr Kenneth Monaghan

GERMANY
International Tracing Service (ITS), Bad Arolsen
www.its-arolsen.org/en/archives/
Camp registration cards and list of possessions for following individuals: Cecil Atkinson; Mary Ellen Cummins; Agnes Flanagan; William O'Connor; Patrick Sweeney; Robert Vernon
Neuzugänge vom 19 January 1944, List of new arrivals at Buchenwald from various locations, Doc. 5267739#1

Politisches Archiv des Auswärtigen Amt, Berlin
R 101.083, Reichssicherheitshauptamt-Inland, Charles Bewley, 'Der irische Ministerium für Auswärtige Angelegenheiten', memo to Reich foreign ministry, 11 October 1940, with an accompanying handwritten note, dated 15 October 1940, Martin Luther of Abteilung Deutschland at the Auswärtiges Amt
R 2342–2345, Deutsche Botschaft Paris, Foreigners interned in France and interventions in their favour, Militärarchiv, Freiburg

BELGIUM
Files for Agnès Margaret Flanagan
SPF Sécurité Sociale – DG Victimes de Guerre, Service Archives et Documentation:
SVG–d019003, dossier personnel
SVG–PPE 24681/2178, dossier statut de prisonnier politique étranger
SVG–RC 777073/41551, dossier de résistant civil
Ministère de la Défense – Sous-section 'Notariat', 1140 Evere, Commission d'Appel d'Agréation des Prisonniers Politiques et Ayant Droit – Dossier Agnès Flanagan

SECONDARY SOURCES

BOOKS

Adam, Peter, *Eileen Grey, Architect, Designer: A Biography* (Thames & Hudson, 2000)

Adams, Bernard, *Denis Johnston: A Life* (The Lilliput Press, 2002)

Auda, Grégory, *Les Belles Années du Milieu* (Editions Michalon, 2013)

Audiat, Pierre, *Paris pendant la Guerre* (Hachette, 1946)

Aziz, Philippe, *Le Livre Noir de la Trahison: Histoires de la Gestapo en France* (Editions Ramsay, 1984)

Beevor, Anthony, *Paris after the Liberation 1944–1949* (Penguin Books, 2007)

Belleret, Robert, *Piaf: Un mythe français* (Fayard, 2013)

Berlière, Jean-Marc and François Le Goarant de Tromelin, *Liaisons Dangereuses: Miliciens, Truands, Résistants, Paris 1944* (Perrin, 2013)

Bewley, Charles, *Memoirs of a Wild Goose* (The Lilliput Press, 1989)

Bleicher, Hugo, *Colonel Henri's Story* (William Kimber & Co., 1962)

Bodson, Herman, *Downed Allied Airmen and Evasion of Capture: The Role of Local Resistance Networks in World War Two* (MacFarland & Co., 2005)

Boiry, Philippe and Gaëtan de Salvatore, *Paris Auteuil sous les Bombes, Septembre 1943* (L'Harmattan, 2000)

Bourget, Pierre, *Histoires Secrètes de l'Occupation de Paris* (Hachette, 1970)

Bowker, Gordon, *James Joyce – A Biography* (Weidenfeld & Nicolson, 2011)

Briscoe, Robert, *For the Life of Me* (Longmans, 1958)

Burrin, Philippe, *La France à l'Heure Allemande, 1940–1944* (Editions du Seuil, 1995)

Cointet, Jean-Paul, *Paris 40–44* (Perrin, 2001)

Constant, Caroline, *Eileen Grey* (Phaidon, 2000)

Couprie, Alain, *Et Paris devint Allemand: Comment les Parisiens le Vécurent (9–14 Juin 1940)* (Le Cherche Midi, 2015)

Cronin, Seán, *Frank Ryan: The Search for the Republic* (Repsol Publishing, 1980)

Crowe, Catriona, Ronan Fanning, Michael Kennedy, Dermot Keogh and Eunan Halpin (eds), *Documents on Irish Foreign Policy, vol. VI (1939–1941)* (Royal Irish Academy, 2008)

Crowe, Catriona, Ronan Fanning, Michael Kennedy, Dermot Keogh and Eunan Halpin (eds), *Documents on Irish Foreign Policy, vol. VII (1941–1945)* (Royal Irish Academy, 2010)

Desprairies, Cécile, *Ville Lumière, Années Noires, les Lieux du Paris de la Collaboration* (Denoël, 2008)

Desprairies, Cécile, *Paris dans la Collaboration* (Seuil, 2009)

Dictionary of Irish Biography (University of Cambridge Press, 2010)

Dumont de Montroy, Jacques, *Mes Voyages en Angleterre et en Irlande de 1947 à 1993* (Jacques Dumont de Montroy, 2006)

Eder, Cyril, *Les Comtesses de la Gestapo* (Editions Grasset & Fasquelle, 2006)

Eisner, Peter, *The Freedom Line* (Harper Collins, 2004)

Elborn, Geoffrey, *Francis Stuart: A Life* (Raven Arts Press, 1990)

Ellmann, Richard (ed.), *Selected Letters of James Joyce* (Faber & Faber, 1975)

Ellmann, Richard, *James Joyce* (Oxford University Press, 1983)

Faligot, Roger, *Paris, Nid d'Espions: les Services de l'Ombre dans la Ville Lumière* (Parigramme, 2009)

Fehsenfeld, Martha Dow and Lois More Overbeck (eds), *The Letters of Samuel Beckett, vol. 1, 1929–1940* (Cambridge University Press, 2009)

Fehsenfeld, Martha Dow, George Craig, Dan Gunn and Lois More Overbeck (eds), *The Letters of Samuel Beckett, vol. 2, 1941–1956* (Cambridge University Press, 2011)

Foot, Michael R. and J. M. Langley, *MI9 Escape & Evasion, 1935–1945* (Biteback Publishing, 2011)

Forde, Frank, *The Long Watch* (Gill & Macmillan, 1981)

Frei, Bruno, *Die Männer von Vernet: Ein Tatsachenbericht* (Deutscher Militärverlag, 1961)

Genet-Rouffiac, Nathalie and David Murphy (eds), *Franco-Irish Military Connections, 1590–1945* (Four Courts Press, 2009)

Glass, Charles, *Americans in Paris: Life & Death under Nazi Occupation* (Harper Press, 2009)

Guggenheim, Peggy, *Out of this Century: Confessions of an Art Addict* (Universe Books, 1979)

Gulbenkian, Nubar, *Pantaraxia: An Autobiography* (Hutchinson, 1965)

Hastings, Max, *The Secret War: Spies, Codes and Guerillas* (William Collins, 2015)

Hilton, Susan, *Eine Irin erlebt England und den Seekrieg* (Falken Verlag, 1942)

Hull, Mark, *Irish Secrets: German Espionage in Wartime Ireland, 1939–1945* (Irish Academic Press, 2003)

Hull, Mark, 'Perdition's Guests: Irish in Germany during World War II', in Claire O'Reilly and Victoria O'Regan (eds), *Ireland and the Irish in Germany – Reception and Perception* (Nomos Verlag, 2014)

Husser, Beate, Jean-Pierre Besse and Françoise Leclere-Rosenzweig, *Frontstalag 122, Compiègne-Royallieu, un Camp d'Internement Allemand dans l'Oise, 1943–1944* (Archives départementales de l'Oise, 2008)

Kennedy, Michael and Joseph Morrison Skelly (eds), *Irish Foreign Policy, 1919–1966: From Independence to Internationalism* (Four Courts Press, 2000)

Keogh, Dermot, *Ireland & Europe: A Diplomatic & Political History, 1919–1989* (Hibernian University Press, 1989)

Keogh, Dermot, *Jews in Twentieth-Century Ireland: Refugees, Anti-Semitism and the Holocaust* (Cork University Press, 1998)

Keogh, Niall, *Con Cremin, Ireland's Wartime Diplomat* (Mercier Press, 2006)

Kiely, Kevin, *Francis Stuart, Artist and Outcast* (The Liffey Press, 2007)

Klarsfeld, Serge, *Vichy–Auschwitz: Le rôle de Vichy dans la solution finale de la question juive en France, 1942* (Fayard, 1983)

Knowlson, James, *Damned to Fame: The Life of Samuel Beckett* (Bloomsbury, 1996)

Koestler, Arthur, *The Scum of the Earth* (Eland Publishing, 2012 ebook edition)

Lacroix-Riz, Annie, *Industriels et Banquiers sous l'Occupation: La Collaboration économique avec le Reich et Vichy* (Armand Colin, 1999)

Le Boterf, Hervé, *La Vie Parisienne sous l'Occupation* (Editions France-Empire, 1974)

Lee, Rowland V., 'Adventures of a Film Director' (unpublished manuscript, copyright American Film Institute, 1970)

Lodwick, John, *Gulbenkian: An Interpretation of Calouste Sarkis Gulbenkian*, (Heinemann, 1958)

Lormier, Dominique, *Le Gestapo et les Français* (Pygmalion, 2013)

Maddox, Brenda, *Nora: A Biography of Nora Joyce* (Houghton Mifflin, 1988)

McMahon, Paul, *British Spies and Irish Rebels, 1916–1945* (Irish Academic Press, 2005)

Mémorial de 'L'Alliance' (Association Amicale 'Alliance', 1954)

Miannay, Patrice, *Dictionnaire des Agents Doubles dans la Résistance* (Le Cherche Midi, 2005)

Murphy, Brian P., *John Chartres: Mystery Man of the Treaty* (Irish Academic Press, 1995)

Murphy, Seán, *Letting the Side Down: British Traitors of the Second World War* (Sutton Publishing, 2003)

Ní Mheara, Róisín, *Recollections* (Xlibris, 2015 ebook edition)

Noël, Lucie, *James Joyce and Paul Léon: The Story of a Friendship* (The Gotham Book Mart, 1950)

Nolan, Aengus, *Joseph Walshe: Irish Foreign Policy, 1922–1946* (Mercier Press, 2008)

O'Brien, Eoin, *The Beckett Country* (The Black Cat Press, 1986)

O'Donoghue, David, *Hitler's Irish Voices* (Beyond the Pale Publications, 1998)

O'Halpin, Eunan, *Spying on Ireland: British Intelligence and Irish Neutrality during the Second World War* (Oxford University Press, 2008)

O'Kelly, Donal, *My Brother Jack* (Donal O'Kelly, 1968)

O'Reilly, Terence, *Hitler's Irishmen* (Mercier Press, 2008)

Ottis, Sherri Greene, *Silent Heroes: Downed Airmen and the French Underground* (University Press of Kentucky, 2001)

Paxton, Robert, *Vichy France: Old Guard and New Order, 1940–1944* (Columbia University Press, 2001)

Perry, George, *Bluebell: The Authorised Biography of Margaret Kelly, Founder of the Legendary Bluebell Girls* (Pavilion, 1985)

Peschanski, Denis, *La France des Camps: L'Internment, 1938–1945* (Gallimard, 2002)

Rajsfus, Maurice, *La Police de Vichy: Les forces de l'ordre françaises au service de la Gestapo 1940–1944* (Le Cherche Midi, 1995)

Roth, Andreas, *Mr Bewley in Berlin: Aspects of the Career of an Irish Diplomat, 1933–1939* (Four Courts Press, 2000)

Saunders, Frances Stoner, *The Woman Who Shot Mussolini.* (Faber & Faber, 2010)

Shearer, Stephen Michael, *Gloria Swanson: The Ultimate Star* (Thomas Dunne Books, 2013)

Shloss, Carol Loeb, *Lucia Joyce: To Dance in the Wake* (Bloomsbury, 2004)

Stephan, Enno, *Spies in Ireland* (Four Square Books, 1965)

Stradling, Robert A., *The Irish and the Spanish Civil War 1936–1939* (Manchester University Press, 1999)

Stuart, Francis, *States of Mind: Selected Short Prose, 1936–1983* (Raven Arts Press, 1984)

Stuart, Francis, *Black List, Section H* (The Lilliput Press, 1995)

Stuart, Madeleine, *Manna in the Morning: A Memoir, 1940–1958* (Raven Arts Press, 1984)

Sweet, Matthew, *Shepperton Babylon: The Lost Worlds of British Cinema* (Faber & Faber, 2005)

Tartière, Dorothy, *The House near Paris: An American Woman's Story of Traffic in Patriots* (Simon & Schuster, 1946)

Thoraval, Anne, *Paris, les Lieux de la Résistance* (Parigramme, 2007)

Turner, Frédéric, *Les Oubliés de 39–45, la Rafle des Britanniques* (JAFT, 2010)

Walter, Gérard, *Histoires Secrètes de l'Occupation de Paris* (2 volumes) (Hachette, 1971)

Weber, Ronald, *The Lisbon Route: Entry and Escape in Nazi Europe* (Ivan R. Dee, 2011)

ARTICLES

1944 – Débarquements, Résistances, Libérations, Le Monde hors-série (May–July 2014)

'A Cork Nun's Extraordinary Life at War', *Irish Examiner*, 4 August 2014

'A Passionist in Occupied France', *Pembrokeshire Guardian*, 20 May 1969

'An Irish Club in Paris', *Irish Independent*, 6 October 1956

'Catholics Give Party to 500 German Children', *Catholic Herald*, 31 December 1948

'Cork Woman Receives First Irish Honour for Saving Jewish Victim of the Holocaust', *The Irish Times*, 2 April 2015

'Echoes from East Kerry' (contains reminiscence of Janie McCarthy shortly after her death), *The Kerryman*, 2 January 1965

'Fifty Years in the Front Line', *The Sunday Times* magazine, 23 August 1981

'Fr Monaghan Appointment to Paris', *Catholic Herald,* 18 November 1938

'Hat, Ribbons & Refugees' (accessed January 2014) and 'The Ettie Steinberg Story' (accessed May 2014), Holocaust Education Trust Ireland, hetireland. org/index.php?page= ireland_hats

'I call you today from Dublin', William Hickey column, *Daily Express*, 5 August 1965

'In Paris the Nuns Can Give a Good Cup of Irish Tea', *The Universe*, July 1969

Ina Foley obituary, *The Irish Times*, 28 April 1997

'Irish Heroes of the French Resistance', *The Sunday Business Post*, 22 July 2001

'Irish Historical Mysteries: The Trade in Joyce Manuscripts', homepage.eircom. net/~seanjmurphy/irhismys/joyce.htm

'James Joyce Chose a British Passport', Letters page, *Financial Times*, 15 May 2014

'Janie McCarthy, French Patriot from Kerry' (obituary), *The Irish Times*, 2 January 1965

Keogh, Dermot, 'La neutralité irlandaise, la Shoah et la Seconde Guerre Mondiale' part of 'Les neutres européens face au Génocide', in *Révue d'Histoire de la Shoah*, n. 203, October 2015

'Lenihan's Uncle Revealed as a Cranky Spy for Nazis and MI5', *Irish Independent*, 25 July 2008

'Lord Ashbourne obituary', *Catholic Herald*, 30 January 1942

'Mary Elmes, 1908–2002', Toulouse Quakers Weblog, https://toulousequakers.wordpress.com/2012/04/28/mary-elmes-1908-2002/

'McCarthy, Miss Janie', *The Kerryman*, Golden Jubilee supplement, 11 December 1954

'Mémoires de Guerre, 1936–1939–1945, premier volet, Le camp de Gurs', Archives départementales des Pyrénées-Atlantiques, 2010

'No Love Letters in Joyce's Secret Trunk', *Irish Independent*, 16 December 1991

'Paris Honours Irish Who Fought, Spied and Died for France', *The Irish Times*, 6 October 2014

'Playboy Who Set Europe Talking', unknown British newspaper report, dated 1 January 1946, Gloria Swanson papers held at the University of Texas, Austin

'Poor Servants of the Mother of God, Paris 1890–1990', *Community Link* (1967)

'Problem Offered by French Camps', *The New York Times*, 27 April 1941

'Raised to the Priesthood: He Lived under Death Sentence in Russia', *Donegal News*, 19 January 1929

'Remember – *Luimneach*', maritimeinstituteofireland.wordpress.com/history-2/remember/kenneth-king-paintings/luimneach/

'Report on Skirmishes on VE Day, Including Breaking of Window at Jammet's', *The Irish Times*, 9 May 1945

'Retire? Gloria Swanson wouldn't think of it!', *Motion Picture*, May–June 1933

'Senior Irish Diplomat Dies' (Count O'Kelly obituary), *The Irish Times*, 4 January 1968

'Serge Philipson – an Appreciation', *The Irish Times*, 22 October 1988

'Social & Personal', *The Irish Times*, 2 June 1945

'Talented Killarney Lady', *The Cork Examiner*, 11 February 1920

'The Hidden Life of Miss Bluebell', *The New York Times*, 26 December 2004

'The Incredible Life of William Coman', *History Ireland*, vol. 23, no. 3, May/June 2015

'The Man that Gloria Married', *Photoplay Magazine*, February 1932

'The Remarkable Life of Miss Bluebell', *The Irish Times*, 11 October 2000

Thomas, P. D., 'A Catholic Father Operated as British Contact in Paris in WWII', *OSS Society Newsletter,* Summer/Fall 2007

'Time Now to Salute Ireland's Uncelebrated Resistance Heroes', *The Irish Times*, 11 November 2010

Travers, Fr Patrick, 'Some Experiences during the War Years: The Irish College in Paris 1939–1945', republished in *Colloque,* the quarterly review of the Irish Vincentians (no. 18, autumn 1988)

'U–46 and the "Luimneach", 1940', Drogheda Port Company, www.droghedaport.ie/cms/publish/article_953.shtml

'Worst Paid Diplomat', *Irish Independent*, 5 January 1968

'Yeats: papers confirm bones sent back to Sligo were not poet's', *The Irish Times*, 18 July 2015

TV AND RADIO BROADCASTS

'Diplomat's Diary Reveals Joyce's Attachment to Ireland', *RTÉ News*, 13 January 2016, www.rte.ie/news/special-reports/2016/0112/759567-james-joyce/

'Flight to Freedom', broadcast on BBC Northern Ireland, 21 June 2005

'In the Shadow of Death' (the Mary Cummins story), RTÉ 1 radio, January 1993, available on Doc On One, www.rte.ie/radio1/doconone/2010/1209/646590-radio-documentary-shadow-of-death-countess-mary-de-galway-mary-cummins-belgian-resistance/

'Passeports pour Vittel', first broadcast on France 3 Télévision, 2007

WEBSITES

Anti-foreigner decrees in France: pages.livresdeguerre.net/pages/sujet.php?id=docddp&su=103&np=308

Escape lines in France: www.conscript-heroes.com

Fondation de la France Libre: www.france-libre.net

French escape lines and crash sites of individual Allied aeroplanes: francecrashes 39-45.net/evasion.php

French franc-euro converter (allowing for purchasing power parity): www.insee.fr/fr/information/2417794

French helper database: https://wwii-netherlands-escape-lines.com

Histoires de Français libres ordinaries: francaislibres.net

Interactive list of French internment camps: www.apra.asso.fr/Camps/En/Accueil-Camps.html

Le camp de concentration du Vernet d'Ariège, 1939–1944: www.campduvernet.eu

List des convois: www.memorial-compiegne.fr/iso_album/14._convoi_du_17_janvier_1944.pdf

Mémoires et Espoirs de la Résistance: www.memoresist.org

Mémorial de l'internement et de la déportation, Camp de Royallieu: www.memorial-compiegne.fr

Persecution of Jews in France, 1940–1944: www.ajpn.org. (This site also contains extensive material on many other aspects of life in France during the Occupation. For example, an excellent account of the internment camp at Vittel can be found at: www.ajpn.org/internement-camp-de-vittel-215.html)

RAF crew member stories (notably that of Oliver James): www.rafcommands.com

Scoop!: www.scoop-database.com

The Comet Escape Line: www.evasioncomete.org

The story of the Shelburn escape network: evasionaviateurs.free.fr/index.php

INDEX